# Lifetime Reading List

Institute of Reading Development, Inc.

# Introduction

This booklist reflects our belief that reading is one of the most wonderful experiences available to us. There is something magical about how a set of marks on a page can become such a source of pleasure and delight, how they can transport us to new worlds and guide us along new paths of knowledge and discovery. The many persons who have had a role in creating this booklist have all found books to be a deeply pleasurable and meaningful part of their lives. This booklist is our way of sharing our enthusiasm and excitement about reading with you.

Prior to the modern age, reading was the province of a very few—typically that of the clergy, the scholar, or the wealthy. Only in the last one to two hundred years have people from all walks of life had access to education and books. To this day, people in many parts of the world lack the freedom to read. We are fortunate indeed to have the ability and freedom to experience, in the solitude of our hearts and minds, the wonderful pleasure of reading.

Reading allows us to transcend our limitations. It opens up new worlds of thought and feeling and gives us a sense of the richness and diversity of human experience. Reading can give us insight into what makes life meaningful, and it can help to shape our most deeply held values. Reading can also provide us with the pleasure that comes from learning about the world and how it works, often helping us to see things we never noticed before.

One of the richest reading experiences is when a book presents a new way of thinking about the world and we find ourselves responding in a thoughtful, critical way. We feel as if we're in a conversation with the author, weighing the author's ideas against our own views and considering what to accept or reject.

One of the most unsettling reading experiences can also be one of the most rewarding. Once in a while we find that the book we are reading is actually reading us—telling us things about ourselves that we have always intuited deep down inside but have never really thought about. The reward comes if we accept the challenge to reflect upon our lives and come to terms with our flaws and shortcomings.

All of these reading experiences have a great deal of value. But underlying every single one of them is the simple pleasure we get when we find ourselves lost in a good book. That's the source of reading's power, the experience of being absorbed in a good book and imaginatively participating in the world the author has created.

It is our intention that this booklist serve as a resource and guide, no matter what your interests as a reader may be. The great comic Groucho Marx once said, "Outside a dog, a book is man's best friend. Inside a dog, it's too dark to read." We are confident that you will find many best friends waiting to be discovered here.

There are more than 1,000 books listed and briefly described in this booklist, more or less evenly divided into two distinct parts. Part One, *Contemporary Fiction and Nonfiction*, is comprised of contemporary books from 20 different subject areas. Part Two, *The Humanities: History, Biography, and the Classics*, is comprised of some of the greatest works of Western and World literature, as well as a selection of compelling histories and biographies. Our goal was to choose the finest books that we could find for each section—books that are engaging, accessible, and well-written.

## Part One
*Contemporary Fiction and Nonfiction*

Part One is divided into two sections: "Contemporary Fiction" and "Contemporary Nonfiction." We first annotate in "Contemporary Fiction" more than 100 of the finest contemporary novels. We go on to annotate many enjoyable, engaging books in several additional genres: science fiction and fantasy, historical fiction, and mystery. With their absorbing stories and intriguing characters, you will find yourself lost in these books from the very beginning.

In the mood for some poetry, or perhaps a short story? You will also find here lists of wonderfully engaging poetry anthologies and short story anthologies, ones that will appeal to the newcomer and experienced reader alike. You will also find in this section a list entitled "Introduction to the Classics," representing some of the most compelling and accessible of the classics from Part Two. If you're new to the classics, this is a good list to try.

We experience a different kind of pleasure in reading good nonfiction, the pleasure of learning and the satisfaction of curiosity. In "Contemporary Nonfiction," we annotate almost 250 books from a variety of subject areas, including, for example, travel and adventure, the arts, games and sports, and memoir. These books have a unique power to inspire, challenge, and entertain—sometimes all at once! The "Introduction to History" list in this section includes some of the most engaging and accessible works of history from Part Two.

## Part Two
*The Humanities: History, Biography, and the Classics*

One of the most exquisite pleasures available to readers is the experience of reading the classics. Great literature communicates a unique vision of life in a compelling and extraordinary way. The classics make their impact on us by challenging, inspiring, and ennobling us in ways that we can't always articulate but can always sense.

Part Two represents our efforts to identify these works for you, as well as interesting, well-written works of history and biography. Our list of classics in Part Two is introductory, not comprehensive. The books we have chosen require little prior knowledge of the region or period in which they were written, and little prior experience reading the classics.

Part Two is divided into two sections: "Western History and Literature," and "World History and Literature." The first of these, "Western History and Literature," is organized chronologically by period and region; for example, there are sections on Greece, and Rome, and the Middle Ages. "World History and Literature" is organized by civilization or region, for example China and Latin America. The sections are organized so that you can focus on history or literature, or read both together for the mutual illumination they provide.

Before you begin selecting books to read, we recommend that you read the Table of Contents, as well as the introductions and a few annotations in each section. This will give you a clear sense of what is on offer and will help you make your decision about where to begin. You may also find useful the Guide to Reading the Annotations (p. 351). Happy reading!

# Contents

## Part One
## Contemporary Fiction and Nonfiction

## Part Two
## The Humanities: History, Biography, and the Classics

# Part One
# Contemporary Fiction and Nonfiction

# Introduction to Part One
# Contemporary Fiction and Nonfiction

Part One of this booklist contains compelling works of contemporary fiction, including novels, short stories, and poetry, and engaging works of contemporary nonfiction on a wide range of topics. The Contemporary Fiction list contains both literary fiction and gripping page-turners in genres such as Science Fiction and Mystery. On the Contemporary Nonfiction list you'll find books, essays, and journals that will inform and entertain you. The Nonfiction list is divided into 13 sections, ranging from Travel and Adventure, Science, and Business, to Memoir, Psychology, and Philosophy and Religion.

In addition, the Fiction list includes an Introduction to the Classics section, and the Nonfiction list includes an Introduction to History section. These sections comprise short, representative selections of some of the best literature and history books to be found in Part Two of the booklist.

The books in Part One reflect the experiences of the 20th and early 21st Centuries: the people, places, ideas, movements, and discoveries that made the world what it is today. At the heart of this momentous era is the experience of World War and Cold War, the struggle for equality, economic transformation, and technological progress. The novelist's vision, the expert's analysis, and the journalist's description all capture facets of contemporary experience in their own way. The books in Part One are clearly written, accessible, and engaging; we believe they represent the best of contemporary fiction and nonfiction.

There are several ways to use Part One:

1. To find books of personal interest: just look through the list and choose individual books of interest, whether novels or books on sports or business. You could spend years just trying books from different genres and different sections.

2. To get a good introduction to contemporary literature or one of the genres of fiction, or to one of the areas of nonfiction. Perhaps you've always been curious about astrophysics, human origins, psychology, or philosophy. Or maybe you love a good mystery or would like to try some poetry. Choose a section that interests you and read the books that are particularly appealing. When you've satisfied your curiosity in one area, try another.

3. To get an introduction to the classics and/or to history: read books that interest you on the Introduction to the Classics or Introduction to History lists. Then use the books on these lists as links to Part Two of the booklist, where you will find a wide selection of literary classics and works on history and biography.

This is your booklist: you choose how to use it. There are enough books here for many years of enjoyable reading.

# Contemporary Fiction

The following seven sections of the booklist include books that will draw you in with their wit, wisdom, and depth of feeling. What gives these books their power? Good fiction is a portal to a world of discovery, revealing human nature and the infinite variety of human experience. The novels, short stories, and poetry on this list offer multiple avenues for exploring the human spirit and contemporary social reality. The more popular works of fiction, including fantasy, sci-fi, and mysteries, offer great entertainment. These books transport you to other worlds and other times by engaging your imagination, sometimes providing an adrenaline rush in the bargain. Whether you read fiction for self-understanding, knowledge of the world, or fun, or for all of these reasons, reading fiction is immensely rewarding.

Part One of this booklist offers excellent examples of the main types of contemporary fiction. The Fiction list is divided into seven sections: Novels, Fantasy and Science Fiction, Mystery, Historical Fiction, Short Stories, Poetry, and an Introduction to the Classics. The first six sections include literature that is contemporary in tone and written from the second half of the 20th Century to the present. The seventh section includes literary classics written over a wide span of time. Here is what to look for:

1. **Novels:** more than 100 of the best contemporary novels, some realistic, some stylistically cutting-edge. Every book on the list opens a window onto the contemporary world.

2. **Fantasy and Science Fiction:** nearly 50 fantasy and sci-fi adventures. These books mingle elements of escapist fantasy and social commentary, and offer great entertainment value.

3. **Mystery:** fiction's brain-teasers, including 50-plus titles from page-turners to complex mystery novels.

4. **Historical Fiction:** nearly 50 books that take you back in time. In their representations of historical figures, events, and eras, these books provide a fascinating view of the past.

5. **Short Stories:** an invitation to read great fiction in one sitting. Read stories from the 18 single-author collections on the list, or sample well-crafted masterpieces from two short story anthologies.

6. **Poetry:** eight anthologies of great poems from a wide variety of traditions.

7. **Introduction to the Classics:** fifteen of the best works of literature from Part Two of the booklist. Readers who want to embark on an exploration of literary classics can use this list to read some of the greatest works of Western Literature. If you like what you read here, continue on by reading the great literature listed in Part Two of the booklist.

# 1. Novels

Readers of contemporary novels immerse themselves in the best of literature from the West and around the globe. The authors of these contemporary novels explore modern-day characters and current reality and ideas.

Novels of the second half of the 20th Century and the early 21st Century are notable for their great diversity of form and expression. Contemporary novels may be written in the first or third person, or they may be written from multiple points of view. The novels on this list are coming-of-age stories, novels of manners and morals, satirical works, tales of love and family, novels about time and memory, and novels of contemporary realism. This list features over 100 books by acclaimed authors. The books on this list range from English-language novels to novels translated from the French, German, Italian, Portuguese, Russian, Norwegian, Czech, Japanese, and Hebrew.

Use the book descriptions to find novels of interest. Each of the hundred-odd authors listed has written additional works of fiction, nonfiction, or both. If you find an author you like, look for more novels or additional writing by that author.

❖       ❖       ❖

Ali, Monica. *Brick Lane*
Scribner, 2008 (2003), 448 pages.

An apparent stillborn, a Pakistani girl is left to her fate. But soon Nazneen is immersed in the life of a Muslim household and its crises involving her disaffected mother and sister. When she enters an arranged marriage and moves to London, she remains the calm at the center of the storm. Gradually, as immigrant experience changes her, she questions her fatalism. Facing the decision of her life, Nazneen discovers her true place in the world.

Allende, Isabel. *The House of the Spirits*
Dial Press, 2005 (1982), 448 pages.

The political murder of Severo del Valle's beautiful daughter Rosa saddens her sister Clara and devastates Rosa's suitor, Esteban Trueba. Allende's saga of the Trueba family begins when Esteban returns ten years later to the del Valles and, as Clara foresaw, asks to marry her. This story of a Latin American family from the post-colonial era to a 1970s military dictatorship weaves character and destiny together with politics and magic.

Anaya, Rudolfo. *Bless Me, Ultima*
Grand Central Publishing, 1999 (1972), 304 pages.

As a child, Antonio is torn between fulfilling his father's unrealized dream of being a cowboy, and his mother's dream that he become a priest. Then Ultima comes to stay with his family, and Antonio learns his true destiny. Antonio's neighbors accuse Ultima of being a witch, but when she teaches him that good is stronger than evil, Antonio recognizes Ultima's goodness and prepares to protect her, come what may.

Auster, Paul. *The New York Trilogy*
Green Integer, 2007 (1985), 586 pages.

The three interlocking novellas that make up this work are mysteries of a most unusual sort. They read like the literary equivalent of film noir where the intrigue is not so much about solving clues as it is about confronting the slipperiness of identity and reality. While this makes for an unsettling reading experience at times, the reader looking for something a little different will not be disappointed.

Bellow, Saul. *Seize the Day*
Penguin Classics, 2003 (1956), 144 pages.

Bellow's tightly wound tale takes place during one day on which the main character confronts his demons. Wilhelm, a middle-aged man who has left his job, wife, and children, has come to a dark place in the middle of life's road. Hoping for a reprieve, he angles for a loan from his elderly father and chases windfall profits. Bellow's masterful study invites us to laugh at Wilhelm's folly as we experience his painful course of self-knowledge.

Berg, Elizabeth. *Never Change*
Washington Square Press, 2002 (2001), 240 pages.

Myra's world is turned upside down when Chip, her high school crush, is suddenly back in her life, this time as a cancer patient. A visiting nurse, Myra cares for a circle of patients whose lives she deeply enriches. To succeed at nursing, Myra leads a regulated life. At first, her head-over-heels involvement with the adult Chip upsets her emotional balance. Then the resurfacing of the past leads Myra to a deeper appreciation of her life.

Berry, Wendell. *Jayber Crow*
Counterpoint, 2001 (2000), 384 pages.

The fiction of Wendell Berry is one of the lesser known treasures of American literature. Berry's numerous novels and short stories all center around the fictional community of Port William, a farming community in rural Kentucky. *Jayber Crow* is an ideal introduction to this world as Jayber Crow, a bachelor barber and longstanding member of the community, reflects back upon the sorrows and joys of his life in the community.

Bradbury, Ray. *Dandelion Wine*
William Morrow, 1998 (1946), 288 pages.

This nostalgic novel evokes the small-town America that dwells in collective memory. Bradbury describes the childhood of 12-year-old Douglas Spaulding of Green Town, Illinois, for whom gathering dandelions for his grandfather's wine is a magical event. So lyrical is Bradbury that you can taste his dandelion wine. Green Town bursts with summer joys. When a stalker casts a shadow, it only makes the summer more golden.

Bulgakov, Mikhail. *Heart of a Dog*
Translated by Michael Glenny. Harvill Press, 1999 (1968), 128 pages.

It's a dog's life, and in 1920s Moscow that means stealing scraps and getting scalded by an angry cook. A stray, Sharik has his pride, and he gets suspicious when a professor takes him home and heals him. The professor turns out to be a Russian Frankenstein, making the dog human. And what a human! Sharik becomes a corrupt Soviet official. Bulgakov uses outrageous humor to skewer the Russian bureaucracy and human iniquity.

Byatt, A. S. *The Virgin in the Garden*
Vintage, 1992 (1978), 432 pages.

Frederica's life is enriched by her close family: mother Winifred, tough-minded father Bill, beautiful sister Stephanie, and elusive brother Marcus. As she prepares for her exams, Frederica's attention is divided between family affections and the wider world. Cast as Elizabeth I in a play celebrating the coronation of Elizabeth II, she develops significant ties to other young adults and a new sense of herself. The novels *Still Life* and *Babel Tower* continue Byatt's story of Frederica and her family.

Capote, Truman. *Breakfast at Tiffany's*
Vintage, 1993 (1958), 192 pages.

Holly Golightly is a free spirit living in 1950s New York. When she's not playing guitar, partying, or paying unannounced visits to the story's narrator, Holly can be found making prison visits to mobster Sally Tomato. Life isn't all fun, and when Holly gets the "mean reds," she visits Tiffany's. Capote's novel abounds with quirky characters, improbable twists, and insight into the waywardness of the human heart.

Chabon, Michael. *The Amazing Adventures of Kavalier and Clay*
Random House, 2000, 656 pages.

Jewish artist Kavalier escapes from Europe to New York in 1939 and teams up with his enterprising cousin, Sammy Clay. Together, they create dynamic comic books with themes geared to the menace of war and featuring The Escapist, a Houdini-like character who rescues the persecuted. While Kavalier sometimes finds art a substitute for fighting, at other times he sees The Escapist as an impossible hero waging a war that can never be won.

Coelho, Paulo. *The Alchemist*
Translated by Alan R. Clarke. HarperCollins, 1988, 167 pages.

Santiago, a Spanish shepherd, dreams of a trip to Egypt in search of treasure. On the advice of a wise man, he sells his sheep and travels to Africa, only to be robbed in the streets of Tangier. Realizing his dream, Santiago eventually journeys to Egypt and meets an alchemist who provides a key to his destiny. In this fable Coelho offers insights about life's journey.

Cunningham, Michael. *The Hours*
Picador, 2002 (1998), 240 pages.

In this well-crafted novel, alternating chapters titled "Mrs. Dalloway," "Mrs. Woolf," and "Mrs. Brown" trace the stories of three women separated by time and place but joined by deeper affinities. Clarissa Vaughn plans a party in 1990s New York; Virginia Woolf writes a novel in 1920s London; and Laura Brown struggles as a housewife in 1950s suburban Los Angeles. Transcending time, the three stories come together at the end.

Dean, Debra. *The Madonnas of Leningrad*
Harper Perennial, 2006 (1989), 227 pages.

A survivor of the siege of Leningrad, Marina once possessed a rich storehouse of memories. As a tour guide, she knew the paintings of the Hermitage so well she could describe them even after they were removed for safekeeping. Settled in America now, Marina struggles to attend to daily life as she is drawn by distant memories of Russia. This story celebrates the power of memory while charting the poignancy of its loss.

Dillard, Annie. *The Maytrees*
HarperCollins, 2007, 224 pages.

Annie Dillard, known for her lyrical observations of nature in *Pilgrim at Tinker Creek*, here turns her talent to depicting the lives of the Maytrees, a couple whose apparently quiet existence on 1950s Cape Cod is belied by the sometimes disorderly drama of their lives. The Maytrees' quiet lives tell the story of a love touched by harmony, devotion, absence and loss, and finally, compassion.

Divakaruni, Chitra Banerjee. *The Mistress of Spices*
Anchor, 1998 (1997), 352 pages.

When Tilo becomes an immortal Mistress, she vows to sacrifice personal desires for the sake of the power to heal. After setting up shop in Oakland, Tilo takes her customers' concerns to heart, daring to transform their lives with her remedies. But Tilo is changing too, and her love for the Lonely American tempts her to leave her old woman's body. Tilo's story combines the texture of contemporary reality with the resonance of myth.

Doctorow, E. L. *Ragtime*
Random House, 2007 (1975), 336 pages.

In this groundbreaking novel, E. L. Doctorow redefines historical fiction as a wholly original product of the writer's imagination. The historical characters and events in *Ragtime* belong to an invented past that is more realistic than real. The novel's fictional protagonist, black ragtime musician Coalhouse Walker, Jr.—who raises an armed rebellion while seeking reparation for his damaged Model T—is a fully credible character, though an historical impossibility.

Doig, Ivan. *The Whistling Season*
Harvest Books, 2007 (2006), 352 pages.

This patiently told but lovely story is set against the backdrop of the Montana landscape in the early 1900s. Paul Million, the story's narrator, recalls the fateful autumn of his 13th year when his widowed father hired a housekeeper, sight unseen, to help care for his three sons. She brings along her quirky, bookish brother, Morris. When the local schoolteacher suddenly departs, Morris takes over teaching with surprising and inspiring results.

Dorris, Michael. *A Yellow Raft in Blue Water*
Picador, 2003 (1987), 384 pages.

This generational saga begins with the story of Ray, a 15-year-old Indian girl who returns with mother Christine to a Montana reservation. When Christine takes off, Ray moves in with Aunt Ida. No sooner is Ray introduced to Father Tom's reservation youth group than events send her off on her own. Dorris weaves together the three stories so that Ray's story gains depth and meaning as you read Christine's story and, finally, Ida's story.

Doyle, Roddy. *Paddy Clarke Ha Ha Ha*
Penguin, 1995 (1993), 288 pages.

Rollicking talk from the mean streets of Dublin conveys childhood's adventures as well as its hardships in this tale told by 10-year-old Paddy Clarke. But don't be deceived by the book's childish language into thinking this is a simple tale. Because the events of Paddy's story are arranged as though in a child's mind, readers must solve the riddle of their order. Paddy's story of maturity born of conflict is comically, painfully real.

Eggers, Dave. *A Heartbreaking Work of Staggering Genius*
Vintage, 2001 (2000), 496 pages.

When Dave Eggers' parents died of cancer within five months of each other, 22-year-old Dave was left to care for his younger brother, Toph. In this vivid narration of these experiences, Eggers wonderfully captures his struggle to balance self-discovery with self-sacrifice.

Enger, Leif. *Peace Like a River*
Atlantic Monthly Press, 2002 (2001), 320 pages.

In this tale of family tragedy and redemption, Reuben recounts the remarkable events of his 11th year, telling us to "Make of it what you will." When Reuben's big brother Davy commits a crime and flees his Minnesota home, Reuben, his sister Swede, and their father set off in pursuit of him, as does the law. Reuben's father is no ordinary man, and the family's trip to retrieve Davy becomes a spiritual quest with a surprising outcome.

Foer, Jonathan Safran. *Extremely Loud and Incredibly Close*
Mariner Books, 2006 (2005), 368 pages.

When the father of a precocious nine-year-old is killed in the attack on the World Trade Center, the boy's obsessive need to understand his father causes him to try matching a key of his father's to a deposit box that could be anywhere in the city. Gradually obsession yields to insight as the people he meets help Oskar to understand his loss. Foer uses innovative techniques to interweave Oskar's tale with that of Oskar's grandparents.

Ford, Richard. *Independence Day*
Vintage, 1996, 464 pages.

In this Pulitzer Prize-winning novel, Frank Bascombe, a sportswriter-turned-real estate agent, narrates a long Fourth of July weekend spent with a troubled teenage son and a head full of ruminations on life's little conundrums. One intriguing aspect of the novel is how Frank uses the language of real estate to comment in surprisingly apt ways upon the complexities of modern existence and the possibilities and limitations of the American Dream.

Franzen, Jonathan. *The Corrections*
Picador, 2002 (2001), 576 pages.

This sharply observed novel takes a wry look at the state of modern life by focusing upon the Lambert family as they prepare to spend Christmas weekend together. Alfred and Enid and their three adult children each possess their share of dysfunctions, but rarely do we look down upon them. Rather, their personal tribulations and oftentimes frustrated desire for meaning and connection can make them at times seem heroic—beaten down but never giving up.

Frayn, Michael. *Headlong*
Picador, 2000 (1999), 352 pages.

Less than admirable motives animate philosophy professor Martin Clay in his headlong rush into a scheme to defraud his country neighbor of a painting that could be a long-lost art treasure. Clay's machinations and delusions of grandeur are akin to the human folly satirized in paintings by Bruegel, the artist Clay thinks made the painting he craves. As Clay pursues his scheme, he creates a comedy of suspense, reversals, and comeuppance.

Frazier, Charles. *Cold Mountain*
Grove Press, 2006 (1997), 464 pages.

Frazier's novel of displacement in the American South tells the Civil War story of Confederate soldier Inman and his beloved Ada. Following recovery in a Virginia hospital from battle wounds, Inman travels west to Cold Mountain and Ada, guided by his vision of a life of harmony with nature. Frazier counterpoints Ada's stewardship of the land with Inman's painful odyssey, balancing themes of disillusionment and hope.

Gaines, Ernest J. *A Lesson Before Dying*
Serpent's Tail, 2001 (1993), 256 pages.

Demoralized by racism in 1940s Louisiana, college-educated Grant is reluctant to take up the cause of Jefferson, a simple African American condemned to die after being found at the scene of a shootout. At the core of Gaines' novel is his exploration of the men's characters as Grant visits Jefferson in jail to persuade him of his importance to the black community. Gaines strikes a fine balance between exposing the harsh realities of the Jim Crow South and suggesting the capacity for redemption in his troubled characters.

Galvin, James. *The Meadow*
Owl Books, 1993 (1992), 240 pages.

Galvin's novel of the West tells the story of a hundred years in the life of a meadow on the Colorado-Wyoming border. The author tells how the meadow becomes home to generations of ranchers, using brief scenes to recount their struggles to survive. The ranchers' names are on the deed, but "if you want to know who owns it even more, just look out the window in a blizzard. That's the landlord's face looking in."

Gardner, John. *Grendel*
Vintage, 1999 (1989), 192 pages.

Grendel, who epitomizes evil in the Anglo-Saxon epic poem, *Beowulf*, is given a more sympathetic treatment in this surprising tale. Gardner imagines Grendel as a victim of the warriorly Danish civilization that encroaches ever further into his domain. When Grendel's friendly overtures are met with violent rebuffs, we begin to understand why he would resort to violence in turn.

Giono, Jean. *The Horseman on the Roof*
Translated by Jonathan Griffin. North Point Press, 1996 (1951), 430 pages.

Giono's adventure novel begins when young Colonel Angelo Pardi flees his native Italy for the south of France. Arriving in the midst of an epidemic, Pardi searches for his foster brother, flees conspirators, and defies the French army while protecting a Frenchwoman searching for her husband. The description of the 1832 cholera epidemic forms the backdrop for this tale of passion in conflict with a sense of honor that survives chaos.

Glass, Julia. *Three Junes*
Anchor, 2003 (2002), 368 pages.

This well-crafted novel spins a tale around two generations of a Scottish-American family, focusing on events occurring in three Junes during 1989–99. Part I describes the lives of the McLeod parents, while Parts II and III unravel the impact of the parents' lives on their adult children. Though the characters' aspirations and romantic designs prove elusive, their lives also prove fulfilling in ordinary and unexpected ways.

Goldberg, Myla. *Bee Season*
Anchor, 2001 (2000), 288 pages.

The four members of the Naumann family each seek the spirit amidst the demands of family life. While mother Miriam creates her own "Perfectimundo" and brother Aron chants prayers, father Saul transmits the heritage of Jewish mysticism to daughter Eliza. Eliza becomes radiant with confidence after her first national spelling bee, but when her father's ambition for her drives the family apart, she must make a difficult choice.

Gordimer, Nadine. *The Pickup*
Penguin, 2002 (2001), 288 pages.

Following a chance encounter, a privileged young woman begins a romance with an Arab man who has illegally immigrated to South Africa. The improbable romance is followed by an even more improbable marriage, and when Abdu is deported, Julie returns with him to his home in the desert. Gordimer's novel is a study in cultural contrasts and a fine delineation of a relationship between two people from different worlds.

Greene, Graham. *Monsignor Quixote*
Penguin Classics, 2008 (1982), 224 pages.

When the priest Quixote is suddenly made a Monsignor, his bishop tells him he must leave his small parish in Spain. Teaming up with the local mayor, Sancho Zancas, Quixote leaves the province of La Mancha in his old car, "Rosinante." Quixote and Sancho travel the country, conquering windmills and debating politics and religion. You'll enjoy the author's humor in this whimsical spin-off of the literary classic *Don Quixote*.

Harris, Joanne. *Chocolat*
Penguin, 2000 (1999), 320 pages.

Harris's sensory details will entice you to marvel at the confections of Vianne Rocher while admiring the feats of self-denial needed by the enemies of her village chocolate shop. The power of Vianne's chocolates—something between art and magic—causes trouble during Lent. Suspected of witchcraft, Vianne boldly befriends gypsies and town loners, and plans an Easter festival. Who will win the contest of abstinence versus indulgence?

Haruf, Kent. *Plainsong*
Vintage, 2000, 301 pages.

This simply told but affecting story, set against the stark landscape of Holt, Colorado, presents a humane and thoughtful portrait of intersecting lives where kindness and compassion finally trump cruelty and despair. Centering the novel are two rough-around-the-edges bachelors who in their old age take in a young unwed mother, and a schoolteacher who raises his two young sons by himself after they are abandoned by their mother.

Hellenga, Robert. *The Fall of a Sparrow*
Scribner, 1999, 464 pages.

Life will never be the same for the Woodhulls: on August 15,1980, their daughter Cookie is among those killed by a terrorist bomb in an Italian railway station. Seven years later, Cookie's mother has become a nun, her sisters are grown, and father Woody struggles to break free of his past even as he prepares to attend the trial of the terrorists. Hellenga compassionately describes the slow process of recovery.

Herriot, James. *All Creatures Great and Small*
St. Martin's Paperbacks, 1998 (1972), 448 pages.

In this autobiographical novel, James Herriot shares stories from his time as a veterinarian in rural England. By turns humorous, sad, and heartwarming, these stories are all united by the great humanity of Herriot, whose love for animals is matched by the colorful cast of characters he comes to know.

Hersey, John. *A Bell for Adano*
Vintage, 1988 (1944), 288 pages.

After American forces take over a small Italian town during World War II, Major Joppolo is given the task of not only meeting the physical needs of the town's beleaguered citizens but of winning over their hearts and minds as well. At the center of the novel is Joppolo's attempt to replace the town's historic bell that had been stolen by the Germans. You'll enjoy this novel as much for its humor as for its gentle treatment of a town that may have lost its prized bell but hasn't lost its heart.

Hosseini, Khaled. *The Kite Runner*
Riverhead Books, 2003, 371 pages.

"There is a way to be good again," says Rahim Khan in a phone call from Pakistan, and on the other end of the line, Amir, now living in San Francisco, listens, and sets off on a journey to Taliban-occupied Afghanistan. In heeding the call to do good, Amir must journey into his past, reliving his boyhood friendship with Hassan and the events surrounding his betrayal of his friend. Hosseini's novel is a masterpiece of storytelling.

Irving, John. *A Prayer for Owen Meany*
Modern Library, 2002 (1989), 627 pages.

Irving's comic story, related by Owen Meany's friend Johnny, is full of pranks, antics, and outrageous mishaps. A dwarf, Owen Meany is a larger-than-life presence in staid New England, where his actions have an elusive meaning and dramatic consequences. Whether he's playing baseball, performing in a pageant, or welcoming Vietnamese orphans at the airport, Owen Meany profoundly affects the lives of those around him.

Ishiguro, Kazuo. *The Remains of the Day*
Vintage, 1990 (1989), 256 pages.

Ishiguro flays the British class system in his portrait of Stevens the butler, who is closely identified with his former master Lord Darlington and the glories of Darlington Hall. When Stevens takes an unaccustomed holiday, his ambivalence about his employer emerges, for Lord Darlington's insidious political beliefs have sealed the fate of two young women in his service. Ishiguro's controlled narrative gradually exposes a soul ruled by bad faith and lies.

Jhabvala, Ruth Prawer. *The Householder*
W. W. Norton, 2001 (1960), 192 pages.

Ready or not, Prem, of Dehli, enters a new stage of life and becomes a householder. How easy life was before he had to cope with his assertive bride and the demands of his mother, his landlord, and his boss! Tempted by a swami's lifestyle and by the spirituality of his European friends, Prem knows deep down that he must first embrace life as a husband and father. Jhabvala's comic tale is full of empathy for her ludicrous characters.

Japrisot, Sébastien. *A Very Long Engagement*
Translated by Linda Coverdale. Picador, 2004 (1991), 336 pages.

This tale of love and devotion begins in a snowy no-man's-land between enemy lines, where, in 1917, five soldiers have been left as punishment for self-mutilation. Sensing that her fiancé was among them, Mathilde Donnay sets out to discover the truth about his fate. Crippled since childhood, Mathilde is resourceful and relentlessly persistent. The impetus behind Mathilde's quest is matched by Japrisot's evocation of hope against hope.

Kingsolver, Barbara. *The Poisonwood Bible*
Harper Perennial Modern Classics, 2006 (1998), 576 pages.

Kingsolver's novel, set in the Congo, is narrated from five different points of view. Told by his wife Orleanna and their four daughters, the story of Baptist minister Nathan Price exposes the clash between his mission and the realities of indigenous culture. As the family's story unfolds amidst political upheaval, Orleanna and her daughters change and adapt, while the character of Nathan Price remains static.

Klima, Ivan. *Waiting for the Dark, Waiting for the Light*
Translated by Paul Wilson. Grove Press, 2006 (1993), 240 pages.

The end of Soviet control means freedom for the Czechs in 1989, but what of those who abandoned their dreams to serve the communist state? Klima contrasts the fates of Pavel, a successful filmmaker who compromised his principles and so lost the great love of his life, and of Peter, who refused to serve a repressive regime and won love. The author's dark lyricism aptly evokes the advent of freedom in an unfree nation.

Kundera, Milan. *The Unbearable Lightness of Being*
Translated by Michael Henry Heim. HarperCollins, 2004 (1984), 320 pages.

Tereza is moved by Tomás' tender love, but hurt by his affairs with other women. When Russia invades Prague in 1968, she discovers a new passion: photographing Czech protesters in the presence of Russian tanks. After the Soviet takeover, Tereza gives up photography and Tomás is forced to choose between his honor and his job as a surgeon. Kundera explores human nature, body and soul, in this tale of love in a demoralized nation.

Lahiri, Jhumpa. *The Namesake*
Harper Perennial, 2004 (2003), 291 pages.

Gogol Ganguli knows that his name is linked to his father's love of Russian literature, but as a first-generation South Asian American, he is too preoccupied by the challenge of assimilation to think much about it. After struggling with his parents' expectations and with tentative love relationships, the young man solves the riddle of his identity when he makes a discovery about his name and takes a trip to Calcutta.

Lawson, Mary. *Crow Lake*
Dial Press, 2002, 320 pages.

In this poignant novel, set in a farming community in northern Ontario, the four Morrison children find their lives dramatically altered when their parents die in a car crash. The story is narrated by Kate, who, many years and another tragedy later, returns home for a special event. The visit becomes an opportunity for Kate to reflect upon how her older brothers, Luke and Matt, who were 19 and 17 at the time of the accident, sacrificed their dreams in order to care for Kate and her younger sister.

Lessing, Doris. *The Memoirs of a Survivor*
Vintage, 1988 (1974), 224 pages.

While watching "it"—scenes of a disintegrating society—a city woman has unnerving "personal" experiences. The woman's ability to survive catastrophe is supported by her detached observations and her compassion for 12-year-old Emily, a child placed in her care. Perhaps most crucially, the woman survives due to her uncanny ability to see scenes from her life and Emily's as she gazes behind a wall into past, present, and future.

Lévy, Justine. *The Rendezvous*
Translated by Lydia Davis. Scribner, 1999 (1995), 144 pages.

The narrator's voice in this evocative novel set in a Paris café is alternately anxious and reflective—anxious when she thinks she's been stood up, and reflective when recalling the past. Mama is back, but Louise's elusive Mama is not like other mothers, and the 18-year-old girl doesn't even know if she'll show. Waiting for Mama, Louise ponders her love for a disappointing parent whose failings she willingly accepts.

Lively, Penelope. *Judgment Day*
Grove Press, 2003 (1980), 288 pages.

Clare Paling is young, intelligent, assertive—and restless. Recently arrived in an English village with a historically significant church, she becomes involved in preservation efforts in spite of her discomfort with faith. Initially detached in her perspective on the villagers, Clare becomes a concerned witness as she ponders the fate of a troubled boy and the threat posed by local vandals to the church and its place in the community.

Lodge, David. *Nice Work*
Penguin, 1993 (1988), 288 pages.

David Lodge's town-and-gown satire is based on the premise of an "Industry Year" public relations scheme requiring foursquare businessman Victor Wilcox to shadow radical feminist Robyn Penrose as she goes about her university teaching job, just as she is to shadow him while he runs his factory. Lodge, a master at creating social types, uses this improbable scheme to create humor, conflict, and eventual insight on the part of his unwilling protagonists as their alien worlds collide.

Makine, Andreï. *Once Upon the River Love*
Translated by Geoffrey Strachan. Penguin, 1999 (1994), 224 pages.

Three boys growing up by the river Amur, deep in the forsaken wilds of Siberia, are inspired by a film at the town cinema to explore the nature of life and love. Makine's lyrical, earthy tale, narrated by the adult Mitya, depicts young men driven to test themselves through love, writing, and adventure. As Mitya and friends Utkin and Samurai pursue boyhood dreams, their diverging paths take them from their small village in Siberia to the locations around the globe that shape their destinies.

Malone, Michael. *Handling Sin*
Sourcebook Landmark, 2002 (1983), 640 pages.

Michael Malone's sprawling romance is classic picaresque, with an adventuring hero and his sidekick on an episodic journey through an American South rife with fascinating characters. On the Ides of March, Raleigh Whittier Hayes finds that his father has escaped from the local asylum, leaving him a mysterious list of seven daunting tasks. Raleigh and pal Mingo set off on a mission to rescue Raleigh's father, encountering mobsters, drug runners, Klansmen, and other surprising characters along the way.

Malouf, David. *An Imaginary Life*
Vintage, 1996 (1978), 160 pages.

Roman Emperor Augustus sent the poet Ovid into exile in a village on the Black Sea. Malouf uses the few known facts of Ovid's life to tell this largely fictional story of the poet's exile. Ovid learns a barbaric language, joins a hunt, and adopts a wild child. But the villagers fear the child and suspect Ovid of wizardry. Ovid struggles to keep peace and protect the boy, but finds that he is limited by his own status as an outsider.

Maraini, Dacia. *Voices*
Translated by Dick Kitto and Elspeth Spottiswood. Serpent's Tail, 1996 (1994), 257 pages.

What starts as a fast-paced thriller becomes a labyrinthine journey when the novel's heroine, Michaela Canova, decides to use her investigative skills to research the murder of a young woman who lived in her apartment building in Rome. As a radio journalist, Michaela is especially sensitive to the nuances of voices, and it is the voices she hears and records that offer clues to understanding the young woman's character and fate.

Martel, Yann. *Life of Pi*
Harvest Books, 2004 (2001), 420 pages.

In this fable the author sets his hero, 16-year-old Pi, adrift on the ocean in a lifeboat holding a hyena, an orangutan, a zebra, and a tiger. Soon the battle for survival comes down to Pi and the tiger, and Pi must use his wits during 227 days at sea. Yann Martel prompts the reader to question the nature of reality when Pi's rescuers doubt his survival story, and the boy must invent a second version of his months at sea.

Mason, Daniel. *A Far Country*
Random House, 2007, 268 pages.

The setting of Daniel Mason's novel is an unnamed land where thousands migrate from the parched countryside to live marginal lives in the city. Among the migrants is 14-year-old Isabel, a clairvoyant in search of her brother. Mason's generic depiction of the conflict between the social class that owns the city and the class of transitory workers is fleshed out by credible details. Isabel's dreamy, stalwart character is entrancing.

McCarthy, Cormac. *The Road*
Vintage, 2008 (2006), 304 pages.

Cormac McCarthy, known for his haunting, poetic evocations of the West, outdoes himself in this dark, brooding masterpiece. Set in an undetermined future in an America that has been devastated by an unnamed catastrophe, a father and his young son struggle to survive as they make their way across the barren, blackened landscape. For all of its darkness, however, the novel is infused with a meditation on the resiliency of the human spirit and on the inextinguishable force of love.

McDermott, Alice. *Charming Billy*
Dial Press, 1999 (1998), 256 pages.

When Billy's Irish-American family gathers at his funeral, they grieve, celebrate the stories of his life, and ponder the alcohol abuse caused by the tragic death of Eva, Billy's first love. The storytelling about Billy results in the emergence of family secrets, prompting the daughter of Billy's best friend to journey to Ireland to solve the riddle of Billy's lost love. Alice McDermott's family saga explores the nature of truth and the consequences of lying, even with the best intentions.

McEwan, Ian. *Atonement*
Anchor, 2007 (2001), 296 pages.

Ian McEwan, known for his multilayered novels of hard won self-knowledge, creates a narrative with a smooth surface around the character of Briony, a girl living a privileged life in 1930s England. Briony's imagination grants her control as a playwright and causes havoc when she misinterprets an encounter between her sister and the son of a servant. McEwan plumbs the depths of Briony's character in this study of guilt and reparation.

McMurtry, Larry. *The Last Picture Show*
Simon & Schuster, 1999 (1966), 288 pages.

Larry McMurtry's *The Last Picture Show*, set in 1950s Thalia, Texas, is the bittersweet coming-of-age story of Duane Moore, his best friend Sonny, and his girlfriend Jacy. Populated by a cast of typical small-town types, McMurtry's novel chronicles the growing pains of three teenagers on the path to maturity. In addition to McMurtry's wry humor, this novel is perhaps best known for its depiction of small-town America, as embodied by Sam the Lion, owner of the town's only diner, pool hall, and movie theater.

Messud, Claire. *The Emperor's Children*
Vintage, 2007 (2006), 496 pages.

Claire Messud's lively novel bristles with conversation and intrigue. From the outset the author plots the development of unlikely ties between characters who are so realistic they make each coincidence seem plausible. Messud's New Yorkers hurtle towards the climax of individual crises that will end or dissipate on September 11, 2001. The grouping of chapters according to the six months before September creates a tension between Messud's leisurely narrative and the reader's anticipation of impending catastrophe.

Mitchell, David. *Black Swan Green*
Random House, 2007 (2006), 304 pages.

*Black Swan Green* is a coming-of-age novel meant for adults as much as for teens. Set in a small town in contemporary England, the story is narrated by Jason Taylor, a 13-year-old who is challenged both by a stuttering problem and by parents who are on the brink of divorce. Jason never wallows in self-pity, however, but finds ways to embrace life in all its complex glory. While each chapter reads like a short story, taken as whole the novel is a moving meditation on the trials and tribulations of growing up.

Morrison, Toni. *Beloved*
Vintage, 2004 (1987), 352 pages.

Toni Morrison's Pulitzer Prize-winning novel is based on the life of slave Margaret Garner. Morrison's novel examines with an imaginative, mythical resonance the lives of the descendants of slaves. To a home in Ohio of the 1870s, now deserted by all family save Sethe and daughter Denver, comes "Beloved," who appears to be the ghost of the daughter Sethe killed. Morrison describes the haunting of Sethe by a seemingly irredeemable past as Beloved all but consumes Sethe's life force. Beloved comes from the past, but whose past?

Murakami, Haruki. *After Dark*
Translated by Jay Rubin. Vintage, 2008 (2007), 256 pages.

It's after dark in Tokyo's entertainment district as we zoom in on a 19-year-old coffee-drinking student whose presence here is anomalous. Mari is keeping an all-night vigil for sister Eri, at home in the suburbs and lost in a deep, months-long sleep. As the story shifts between Mari's eventful night and a surreal evocation of Eri—her soul siphoned off into a TV in an empty room—Murakami weaves a web of meaningful interactions between his seemingly solitary characters.

Murdoch, Iris. *The Sea, the Sea*
Penguin, 2001 (1978), 528 pages.

The sea, with its ruminative ebb and flow and occasional churning, is the backdrop for Murdoch's novel of late love. Adrift after retirement, London's lion of the theater, Charles Arrowby, starts a journal as a prelude to writing a memoir in his hermitage by the sea. But Arrowby's life is far from over—by coincidence, he has moved next door to his first love, whose marriage he now sets out to undo. Beset by poltergeists and a sea monster, Arrowby glimpses release from obsession in the wisdom of his Buddhist cousin.

Narayan, R. K. *The Guide*
Penguin Classics, 2006 (1958), 224 pages.

Just out of prison, Raju finds a new career when local peasants mistake him for a priest. Though at first he impersonates a holy man to get food and shelter, Raju gradually grows into the role of spiritual adviser. Narayan's deft and humorous narrative interweaves Raju's adventures as a holy man with flashbacks in which he reflects upon childhood, his career as a tour guide, and the events that led to his imprisonment.

Naipaul, V. S. *A Bend in the River*
Vintage, 1989 (1979), 288 pages.

Set in an unnamed African state, V. S. Naipaul's novel illustrates the country's transition from tribal culture to modernity, primarily through the consciousness of Salim, an African merchant of Indian descent. Salim treks to the country's interior to begin a new life, but encounters social turmoil in the town by a bend in the river. Alongside the development of Salim's consciousness, Naipaul presents a wry parody of African politics as seen in the Big Man and his army, whose power is rapidly replacing that of the tribes.

Norman, Howard. *The Bird Artist*
Picador, 1995 (1994), 289 pages.

This stark tale of love and violence is set against the backdrop of a windswept lighthouse on Witless Bay, Newfoundland. Fabian Vas, a bird artist, tells with disconcerting detachment the story of how and why he murdered the village lighthouse keeper. After hearing Fabian's confession, readers are invited to ponder the responsibility of other characters for the tragedy as well as the community's share in Fabian's crime.

Oates, Joyce Carol. *Black Water*
Plume, 1993 (1992), 160 pages.

*Black Water* may be read as a cautionary tale, a political allegory, or a thriller. Oates' story is written from the perspective of Kelly Kelleher, a young woman whose brief liaison with a famous senator ends in her death. This fast-paced novel, divided into 32 brief chapters, explores through flashbacks the motives that led to the death. The character of Kelly Kelleher is explored in depth, while that of the Senator is left vague, reversing media coverage of the 1969 Chappaquiddick incident on which the novel is based.

O'Brien, Tim. *The Things They Carried*
Broadway Books, 1998 (1990), 260 pages.

Tim O'Brien and his soldier buddies use words to distance themselves from the realities of war, but they also use stories to tell war's truths. This nonfiction novel features O'Brien as narrator and protagonist, and a supporting cast of characters with the names of soldiers he knew in Vietnam. The stories told by O'Brien, Kiley, and Sanders may not be factually true, yet they are true-to-life evocations of war and the bond between soldiers.

Öe, Kenzaburo. *A Personal Matter*
Translated by John Nathan. Grove Press, 1994 (1969), 165 pages.

"My son was wounded on a dark and lonely battlefield that I have never seen," thinks Bird. Twenty-seven, married, and a teacher at a cram-school, Bird, as immature as his nickname, reacts to the birth of his firstborn with a mix of compassion and revulsion. Numbing himself with alcohol and sex, Bird delays making a decision about the fate of his brain-damaged son. Öe's gut-wrenching, suspenseful novel takes readers on a wild, bumpy ride as Bird evades, rationalizes, and finally faces the crisis of fatherhood.

Ondaatje, Michael. *The English Patient*
Vintage, 1995 (1992), 320 pages.

Though the Second World War is over, an American nurse tends a lone patient in an abandoned Italian villa. Is the patient English, as he says, or is he an Hungarian who spied for the Germans? Ondaatje uses the nurse's love for her patient as a frame for the slowly unfolding story of the geologist whose plane crashed in the desert, bringing him to the nurse's care. At the heart of the English patient's story is his love of the desert—where the rules of civilization can be suspended with sometimes dangerous consequences.

Oz, Amos. *The Same Sea*
Translated by Nicholas de Lange. Harcourt, 1999, 201 pages.

This novel about an Israeli family recovering from loss is a story, a series of poems, and a meditation on isolation and commonality. Each short chapter reflects the feeling-state of a character, moving the plot imperceptibly forward. The author's inventive style is simply articulated. The reader's experience is like the experience of the story's characters: fragmentary yet ultimately connected by awareness of the whole—the same sea.

Patchett, Ann. *Bel Canto*
Harper Perennial, 2005 (2001), 352 pages.

When a bungled kidnapping disrupts a party at a South American mansion, the ensuing melee results in the guerillas taking the entire party hostage. The main events of Patchett's novel take place in the fragile, artificial world created by terrorism, in which hostages bond with each other and with their captors. Lacking a common language, rebels and hostages find meaning in the music practice of a captive singer. Patchett lets the reader decide whether or not art can provide meaning in a world beset by violence.

Paton, Alan. *Cry, the Beloved Country*
Vintage, 2002 (1948), 256 pages.

Paton's tale of South Africa begins with a hymn to the Umzimkulu Valley, now emptied of young people seeking work in the city. When the Zulu pastor Kumalo travels to Johannesburg to find his son, he learns that the temptations of city life have placed the young man in harm's way. Soon Kumalo's life intersects with that of Jarvis, his white neighbor. Now two fathers must share an understanding of the fate that binds their sons.

Pelevin, Victor. *Omon Ra*
Translated by Andrew Bromfield. New Directions, 1998 (1994), 153 pages.

Omon wants to break free—from rule-bound society and even from earth's gravity—and hopes to become a Soviet cosmonaut. Following a brief stint at the Air Force Academy, Omon is recruited by the KGB to complete a top-secret, one-way mission to the moon. Pelevin's surreal, sometimes macabre novel delivers a pointed satire of the Soviet space program along with mystical hints regarding the spiritual odyssey of Omon Ra.

Petterson, Per. *Out Stealing Horses*
Translated by Anne Born. Picador, 2005 (2003), 238 pages.

Trond Sander always longed for solitude. A widower, he moves to a remote cabin where an encounter with a childhood neighbor prompts him to revisit the past. The author's spare, lyrical style captures the vitality of Trond's rural childhood and the quiet he sets as a bulwark against his adolescent turmoil. Once he's secure in his chosen life, Trond is finally able to tell his story of friendship and adventure, of sexual awakening, and of his complex bond with his father.

Rand, Ayn. *Atlas Shrugged*
Plume, 1999 (1957), 1,200 pages.

"Who is John Galt?" That is the mystery posed at the beginning of Ayn Rand's epic meditation on human freedom. Although some 1,200 pages in length, the story is so captivating and well-told that the length quickly ceases to be an issue. Centering the novel is the story of a handful of persons who refuse to let their dreams of success be thwarted. And although their lives seem to be ruled by selfishness and self-interest, we care deeply about them because of how they come to stand for the relentless drive of the human spirit.

Robbins, Tom. *Jitterbug Perfume*
Bantam, 1990 (1984), 352 pages.

Tom Robbins' *Jitterbug Perfume* is a heady brew of a saga drawn from myth, folklore, and the imagined lives of eccentric, contemporary characters. Robbins traces the genesis of a mythical elixir from the forests of ancient Bohemia to the modern-day world, where perfumers in Seattle, New Orleans, and Paris covet the elixir and plot to possess it. Readers will prize the humor and the exuberant energy of this lighthearted romp through imagined times and exotic places.

Robinson, Marilynne. *Gilead*
Picador, 2005 (2004), 256 pages.

The narrator of this lovely, meditative novel is Rev. John Ames, an aging pastor who, nearing his death, reflects upon the joys and sorrows of his life. Although themes of forgiveness, grace, sin, and redemption are interwoven throughout the story, even readers who aren't Christian will appreciate the wisdom, compassion, and yes—even humor that shine through the story.

Roth, Philip. *American Pastoral*
Vintage, 1998 (1997), 432 pages.
In this novel, Roth evokes the conflicting values and experiences of Greatest Generation success story Swede Levov and his daughter Merry, a true believer whose zeal morphs from political to religious fanaticism. Golden boy Swede Levov, a former star athlete married to a former Miss New Jersey, is the American dream incarnate, until, of course, he spots the blight at the heart of the idyll: a daughter inexplicably turned terrorist. Roth brilliantly depicts the American dream and its fragility.

Roy, Arundhati. *The God of Small Things*
Random House, 2008 (1997), 352 pages.

Set in Kerala, India, during the social upheavals of the 1960s, Roy's novel interweaves the story of fraternal twins Estha and Rahel with that of their mother Ammu and untouchable family friend Velutha. Roy's characters are irreparably affected by the clash between communism and the caste system. Her theme of conflicted love is tinged with sadness, but her vibrant characters and enchanting descriptions infuse the novel with zest.

Rushdie, Salman. *Midnight's Children*
Random House, 2006 (1981), 560 pages.

On midnight of August 15, 1947, as India gains independence from Britain, a midwife changes the name tags of two babies, giving a poor Hindu child to a wealthy Muslim family, and vice versa. Rushdie uses the changeling motif to trace the destinies of the sons of Muslims and Hindus in this intricately crafted 30-year panorama of Indian history.

Salzman, Mark. *The Soloist*
Vintage, 1995 (1994), 304 pages.

Renne, a 36-year-old music teacher, finds his life transformed when he takes on a promising student and becomes a juror in the trial of a man accused of murdering his Zen master. Salzman explores the themes of perfectionism and self-transcendence through the story of Renne, a former child prodigy now unable to perform, and the story of Philip Weber, a disturbed young man whose literal interpretation of a Zen koan led him to kill. Once defined by his musicality, Renne comes into his own as a teacher and a juror.

Saramago, José. *Blindness*
Translated by Giovanni Pontiero. Harvest Books, 2008 (1995), 352 pages.

Saramago's fable of a country beset by an epidemic of blindness exhibits the evils of the modern age: social chaos, misguided government, and the loss of individual rights. At the heart of this fable is the story of the doctor's wife, who feigns blindness in order to accompany her husband into quarantine. Amidst the degradation of quarantine, she emerges as a natural leader who generates social cohesion through her gift for survival.

Schlink, Bernhard. *The Reader*
Translated by Carol Brown Janeway. Vintage, 1999 (1995), 224 pages.

Michael looks back on his youth in Berlin, where he fell in love with a streetcar worker named Hanna. Hanna's secretive nature concealed a dark side, and Michael wonders if hindsight has destroyed his memory of their love. Apparently happy, especially when Michael read to her, Hanna abruptly disappeared. Years later, at a war crimes trial, Michael recognizes Hanna in the dock. The author examines the souls of Michael, Hanna, and Germany itself in his tale of the second post-war generation confronting the past.

Senna, Danzy. *Caucasia*
Riverhead Books, 2003 (1998), 413 pages.

Bi-racial Birdie knows how to be a chameleon: living in 1970s New Hampshire with her white mother, she adapts to white culture and passes for white. But Birdie cannot discover who she truly is apart from her black father and darker-skinned sister who have decamped to Brazil. To find her sister and reconnect with the missing part of herself, Birdie leaves quiet New Hampshire for a world of unsettling difference and ambiguity.

Seth, Vikram. *An Equal Music*
Vintage, 2000 (1999), 400 pages.

Seth's novel introduces the reader to the intense, collaborative world of classical music performance via the character of Michael, a violinist who shares his passion for music and romance with a concert pianist named Julia. Though Michael's weaknesses are apparent, his love of music, and Julia, bring out his inner strength. The novel becomes plot-driven when Michael discovers a secret that could ruin Julia's career, and acts to protect her.

Shields, Carol. *The Stone Diaries*
Vintage Canada, 2008 (1993), 400 pages.

The diaries of Daisy Stone Goodwill and related documents reveal a life by turns conventional and self-defining in this fictionalized autobiography of a 20th-Century woman. Though Daisy's youthful independence is submerged for several years in marriage and motherhood, she re-emerges as a person in her own right later in life, and is able to view herself, and much of the century, with retrospective understanding.

Smith, Zadie. *On Beauty*
Penguin, 2005, 446 pages.

Zadie Smith's tribute to E. M. Forster adapts the storyline of Forster's *Howard's End* to the multi-ethnic, politically correct American university world of the 1990s. In Smith's tale, the fates of two families are forever changed when the West Indian Kipps move to a town inhabited by the mixed-race Belseys. While the brilliantly drawn characters of the fathers and their teenage children enliven the tale, the relationship between the two mothers drives the plot.

Tan, Amy. *The Joy Luck Club*
Penguin, 2006 (1989), 288 pages.

When Suyuan Woo, the deceased founder of the Joy Luck Club, is replaced at the Mahjong table by daughter Jing-mei, the stories of four Chinese-American women and their daughters begin. Tan combines Jing-mei's tales of her mother and herself with stories of past and present told by the other mothers and daughters in this rich tapestry of women's lives.

Thomas, D. M. *The White Hotel*
Penguin, 1993 (1981), 288 pages.

This startling novel presents the story of Lisa Erdman, a fictitious opera singer, through an assemblage of documents: a poem, a story, a case history, a traditional narrative, and a description of the massacre at Babi Yar that blends fiction and fact. The character of Lisa, first introduced as a patient of Sigmund Freud, becomes a template for the suffering and turmoil of 20th-Century history. The separate documents comprising the novel are shaped into a unified story reflecting Thomas's theme of the individual's relation to history.

Toibin, Colm. *The Master*
Scribner, 2005 (2004), 338 pages.

This intelligently imagined novel recounts the life of writer Henry James. Toibin's fictionalized biography covers the five years during which James mastered his craft, from his 1895 failure as a playwright to the years when he achieved literary success and a balance between his life and his work. Based on historically accurate and invented scenes, the novel includes flashbacks to James' early life. Toibin's research and inventiveness contribute equally to this portrait of a master writer.

Toole, John Kennedy. *A Confederacy of Dunces*
Penguin Classics, 2000 (1980), 352 pages.

A true genius? "You may know him by this sign, that the dunces are all in a confederacy against him." So wrote Jonathan Swift, whose mordant wit inspired this tale of comic hero Ignatius Reilly and the eccentric characters that surround him. Set in New Orleans, Toole's novel recounts the adventures of the scholarly slacker Ignatius Reilly as he pursues ideas and employment. Toole's keen ear for American speech enlivens the tale, as do his vividly drawn secondary characters.

Tyler, Anne. *The Accidental Tourist*
Ballantine, 2000 (1985), 352 pages.

Macon Leary, author of a travel guidebook series called *Accidental Tourist*, hates travel and has become habituated to a quiet life at home with his siblings. All this changes when larger-than-life Muriel bursts on the scene, prompting Macon to shake things up. Anne Tyler's affection for her characters— from the conventionally stuffy to the vulnerably eccentric—allows her to realize their destinies in a credible way.

Wolff, Tobias. *Old School*
Vintage, 2004 (2003), 208 pages.

Set at an East Coast boarding school, this novel tells of a scholarship boy and the impact on him of campus visits by famous authors. Wolff's narrator, who has been disingenuously concealing his lower middle-class family background, starts to question how much of his identity he should sacrifice to become a writer. Still, he'd do almost anything to impress the final guest author: Hemingway. This story of a boy's struggle to be a writer charts his process of self-discovery in a surprising way.

Yalom, Irvin D. *When Nietzsche Wept*
HarperCollins, 1993 (1992), 320 pages.

Psychiatrist Irvin Yalom takes two historical figures, pioneer psychoanalyst Joseph Breuer and philosopher Friedrich Nietzsche, and stages a fictional encounter between them. In Yalom's tale, Breuer treats Nietzsche with the new "talking cure" on the pretext that Nietzsche is treating him as well. Soon the tables are turned for real, and Nietzsche's therapy for migraines becomes Breuer's treatment for obsessional neurosis. Yalom brings his characters, their ideas, and their milieu—19th-Century Vienna—vividly to life.

Yamashita, Karen Tei. *Through the Arc of the Rain Forest*
Coffee House Press, 1990, 192 pages.

Deep in the heart of the Amazon Rain Forest lies a bedrock of—plastic. The discovery of this substance leads to media hype, business ventures, and mystical healing: globalization on a grand scale. Yamashita treats global themes in a magical-realist style, interweaving the fates of a three-armed entrepreneur, a Japanese Brazilian whose forehead sprouts a satellite, a native healer, and more in her story of human cohabitation with planet Earth.

Yehoshua, A. B.  *Mr. Mani*
Translated by Hillel Halkin.  Harvest Books, 1993 (1992), 384 pages.

Each chapter in this book is like a little drama in which a character delivers a monologue to a silent but active listener.  The one-sided conversations feature stories about six generations of the Mani family, tracing the transmission from father to son of the will to survive along with guilt over a "sin" committed by patriarch Avraham Mani.  Yehoshua uses the images of birth, snow, imprisonment, and mirrors to suggest aspects of the Manis' spiritual struggle on their journey from Eastern Europe and Greece to Jerusalem.

Zusak, Markus.  *The Book Thief*
Knopf, 2007 (2006), 576 pages.

Appearing on the scene when Liesel's brother dies, Death narrates the story of Liesel, a German child who goes to live with a foster family in wartime Munich.  As Zusak's omniscient narrator tells us, Liesel is a book thief—one who reads and shares books as a way of surviving the hardships and horrors of war.  In this daring book, the author takes a clear-eyed view of harsh realities while creating vivid characters.

# 2. Fantasy and Science Fiction

For the sci-fi reader who likes to envision the future and the fantasy reader who enjoys legend and magic, these 49 books offer entertainment and insight into possible worlds, potential technologies, and imaginary realms of experience.

The fantasy writers on this list include Marion Zimmer Bradley, whose novel *The Mists of Avalon* retells the Arthurian legend, and William Goldman, whose novel *The Princess Bride* combines adventure, romance, and humor. Science fiction writers explore outer space, time travel, and the impact of technology in sci-fi classics like Isaac Asimov's *Foundation*, Arthur C. Clarke's *2001: A Space Odyssey*, and Philip K. Dick's *Do Androids Dream of Electric Sheep?*

Use the book descriptions to find fantasy or science fiction books of interest. Sub-genres like military sci-fi and alternative history are indicated in the descriptions. Several listed authors have written series, and virtually all have written numerous books. If you find an author you like, look for more fantasy or science fiction by that author.

❖　　　　　❖　　　　　❖

Adams, Douglas. *The Hitchhiker's Guide to the Galaxy*
Del Rey, 1995 (1976), 320 pages.

Join Arthur Dent, earthling, and Ford Prefect, alien researcher for *The Hitchhiker's Guide to the Galaxy*, in an intergalactic journey. Ejected into space, they're rescued by a spaceship powered by the Infinite Improbability Drive (and what are the chances of that?). Will they visit Magrathea? Will Earth be rebuilt? Will mice run Earth? The computer Deep Thought knows, but it may take a few million years to calculate the answer.

Asimov, Isaac. *Foundation*
Spectra, 2004 (1951), 256 pages.

When Hari Seldon predicts that Trantor, city of forty billion, will lie in ruins in three centuries, he's met with dismay. Then he predicts the decline and fall of the Galactic Empire. Soon Seldon and 100,000 of the best human minds are exiled to Terminus—a planet on the edge of the Galaxy. Now they face a series of daunting challenges to shorten the interregnum between the decline of the Galactic Empire and its Renaissance. *Foundation* is the first volume in a seven-volume series that won the Hugo Nebula award for "Best All-Time Series" in 1966.

Asimov, Isaac. *I, Robot*
Spectra, 2008 (1950), 256 pages.

Asimov's stories introduce robots and their humans. Meet Robbie, a metallic nursemaid, whose child Gloria overrides his dismissal. Meet robots that befuddle field-testers Powell and Donovan: QT-1 ("Cutie"), who founds a robot-centered religion, and DV-5 ("Dave"), who gets amnesia when unsupervised. Meet Dr. Calvin, robot psychologist, and mind-reader RB-34 ("Herbie"), whose positronic brain receives mixed signals from humans.

Atwood, Margaret. *The Handmaid's Tale*
Anchor, 1998 (1985), 320 pages.

A handmaid in the Republic of Gilead (formerly the United States), Offred is heavily monitored, forbidden to read, and encouraged to get pregnant—or else. Whether a paranoid feminist fantasy or a darkly prescient satire, this story of the drastic change in women's status in a brave new world with a declining birth rate will give you chills.

Balzac, Honoré de. *The Wild Ass's Skin*
Translated by Herbert J. Hunt. Penguin Classics, 1977 (1831), 288 pages.

When Raphael stumbles into an old curiosity shop, he is attracted to a magical piece of animal hide. Ignoring the shopkeeper's advice, he buys the skin and uses it to gain his desires. Balzac's fable of the skin that shrinks with every wish it grants depicts the conflict between desire and longevity: as the skin dwindles, so does its owner's life.

Bradbury, Ray. *Fahrenheit 451*
Simon & Schuster, 2003 (1953), 208 pages.

This prophetic novel depicts a future in which human life is structured by television. Books, which might entice people to imagine a richer existence, are banned. Enter Guy Montag, a fireman whose job is to burn confiscated books. When Montag starts to question his world and ponder the power of books, he runs afoul of the authorities, propelling him into an odyssey of survival and discovery.

Bradley, Marion Zimmer. *The Mists of Avalon*
Del Rey, 2000 (1982), 912 pages.

*The Mists of Avalon* is an extensive retelling of the Arthurian legend from the point of view of the female characters. Morgaine (Morgan Le Fay) and Gwenhwyfar (Guinevere) play major roles in the story, giving Arthur Excalibur and struggling for power. By the same token, Guinevere is chiefly to blame for the demise of Camelot in this feminist retelling.

Bujold, Lois McMaster. *Cordelia's Honor* (*Shards of Honor* and *Barrayar*)
Baen, 1999 (1986), 608 pages.

Marooned on a newly discovered planet, captain Cordelia Naismith meets Aral Vorkosigan, "the Butcher of Komarr." Realizing that his evil reputation is unearned, Cordelia helps him avoid a mutiny but becomes an outcast on her own planet. When Cordelia marries Vorkosigan and bears him a child, she is forced out of retirement after the infant becomes a target of high-tech assassins in a dynastic civil war.

Butler, Octavia E. *Kindred*
Beacon Press, 2004 (1979), 287 pages.

A child is drowning, and Dana intervenes to save his life. It all makes sense—except that this is a child of the antebellum South, and Dana lives in Los Angeles in 1976. Though the child Rufus is the white son of a plantation owner, and Dana is African American, she will travel back in time on several occasions to rescue him. Butler's artful blend of fantasy and history combines suspense with an accurate picture of the nation's past.

Calvino, Italo. *Fantastic Tales: Visionary and Everyday*
Vintage, 1998 (1997), 608 pages.

Italo Calvino edited this collection of 26 fantastic stories from the 19th Century, including classic tales by E. T. A. Hoffman, Sir Walter Scott, Balzac, Gogol, Dickens, Turgenev, de Maupassant, and, of course, Poe. This anthology provides a history of 19th-Century fantastic literature and a magical mystery tour of the thrills of the horror genre, with its vampires, ghosts, and other macabre manifestations of the dark side of the soul.

Card, Orson Scott. *Ender's Game*
Starscape, 2002 (1985), 336 pages.

Child prodigy Ender goes to Battle School and becomes a leader. He passes tests in the Battle Room, moves on to Officer's School, and then to Commander's School on the asteroid Eros. Trained by Rackham, the only man to defeat the alien enemy in battle, Ender becomes fleet commander and plays Rackham on the school's simulator. Ender plays a high-stakes game to save Earth from the aliens—a game that almost seems real.

Clarke, Arthur C. *2001: A Space Odyssey*
Roc, 2000 (1968), 320 pages.

Clarke's novel takes you on a trip to Saturn's enigmatic moon. On board the spaceship *Discovery* are astronauts Bowman and Poole and Hal 9000, the ship's central nervous system. When Hal's miscue sends Poole floating off into space, Bowman must decide about Hal's future on board the *Discovery*. Written in 1964, *2001: A Space Odyssey* reveals a world of human potential and predicts developments in modern science.

Clarke, Susanna. *Jonathan Strange & Mr. Norrell*
Tor Books, 2006 (2004), 1,024 pages.

Set in a disenchanted world that resembles England of the 1800s, Susanna Clarke's first novel tells of Mr. Norrell, a wealthy recluse determined to reclaim the magical potency of England's legendary magicians. When his alter ego, rival magician Jonathan Strange, appears on the scene, a struggle over the uses and abuses of magic ensues. Readers of this commodious novel will be rewarded by humor, thrills, and a fully imagined universe.

Cook, Robin. *Coma*
Signet, 2002 (1977), 400 pages.

Twenty-three-year-old medical student Susan Wheeler turns sleuth when two patients at Boston Memorial Hospital mysteriously go into comas after their operations. Wheeler's life is in danger when she disguises herself as a nurse and goes undercover to investigate the link between the high incidence of comas at her hospital and an organ transplant "factory." This book was voted the number one thriller of 1977 by the *New York Times*.

Crichton, Michael. *The Andromeda Strain*
Avon, 2003 (1969), 368 pages.

The tightly-wound plot of Michael Crichton's techno-thriller revolves around the efforts of the U.S. government's Wildfire team to analyze and neutralize a toxic microorganism from outer space—the Andromeda strain. After the microbe all but wipes out the town of Piedmont, Arizona, scientists engage in a race against time to save the planet.

Dick, Philip K. *Do Androids Dream of Electric Sheep?*
Del Rey, 1996 (1968), 256 pages.

Philip K. Dick's post-apocalyptic thriller is set on an Earth damaged by nuclear war, where androids escaped from off-world colonies try to avoid termination by blending in with the human population. Enter Rick Deckard, bounty hunter, in pursuit of six androids slated for termination. But how to distinguish an android from a human? Even the Voight Kampff empathy test leaves wide open the question of what it means to be human.

Donohue, Keith. *The Stolen Child*
Anchor, 2007 (2006), 336 pages.

This absorbing debut novel tells the story of Henry Day, kidnapped by hobgoblins at age seven, and exchanged for an imposter who replaces him in his small-town American family. Donohue's fairy tale for adults explores issues of love and loss as it switches back and forth between the stories of the two Henrys. This double story of a divided life imaginatively delineates the identities of the changeling and the adopted human.

Doyle, Sir Arthur Conan. *The Lost World*
Modern Library, 2002 (1912), 272 pages.

Malone, a young journalist, visits Professor Challenger to investigate his claim to have seen prehistoric animals in the Amazon rain forest. Is Challenger a fraud, or a Columbus of science who has found a lost world? Soon Malone joins a second, dangerous expedition to verify Challenger's claim. This fast-paced, humorous novel is full of surprising twists worthy of the master of classic detective fiction.

Gaiman, Neil. *Anansi Boys*
Harper Torch, 2006 (2005), 416 pages.

Fat Charlie Nancy just wants his old life back—the life that was stolen when his brother Spider got him fired from his London agency job and romanced his fiancée. But returning to normalcy may be easier said than done since Charlie and Spider are sons of Anansi, the trickster god. Neil Gaiman's storytelling abounds with wit, adventure, and magic.

Gibson, William. *Pattern Recognition*
Berkley, 2005 (2003), 384 pages.

Freelance market-researcher Cayce Pollard accepts an unusual job—tracking the creator of video footage that has become an Internet cult—in the hope of solving the riddle of her ex-CIA father's disappearance. But is what she finds in the course of her globetrotting a true conspiracy, or a case of faulty pattern recognition? Gibson's intricately plotted novel examines the impact of technology on consciousness in this tale of a "cool hunter."

Goldman, William. *The Princess Bride: S. Morgenstern's Classic Tale of True Love and High Adventure*
Harcourt, 2007 (1973), 464 pages.

Readers will enjoy the "Good Parts" version of *The Princess Bride*, abridged by William Goldman. The author promises: "Fencing. Fighting. Torture. Poison. True Love. Hate. Revenge. Giants"—and more. He delivers on his promise with this humorous tale of Buttercup and her true love Westley who use wit, courage, and a little help from their friends to thwart the deadly designs of the wicked Prince Humperdinck.

Haldeman, Joe. *The Forever War*
St. Martin's Griffin, 2009 (1974), 304 pages.

William Mandella has an IQ above 150, so he gets drafted to fight in humanity's interstellar war against the Taureans. Because of time dilation, he ages slowly in space, complicating his reintegration into society when he returns to Earth. Haldeman's novel, which depicts war as meaningless, has been viewed as a response to *Starship Troopers*.

Heinlein, Robert A. *Starship Troopers*
Ace Books, 1987 (1959), 272 pages.

Against his father's advice, Johnnie Rico joins up with the Terran military in peacetime and trains as a soldier with the Mobile Infantry. As Johnnie undergoes battleship space drops and fights Bugs in an intergalactic war, he gives a realistic account of boot camp, military hierarchy and discipline, and officers' training. Once the Terran Federation declares war, Johnnie discovers his mission as a fighter.

Helprin, Mark.  *The Winter's Tale*
Harvest Books, 2005 (1983), 768 pages.

Immigrant Peter Lake lives in an alternative-universe New York, a late 19th-Century city besieged by arctic winters.  Forced to commit a robbery, Peter meets a visionary young girl who will change his life.  The dream-like sequences of this novel of events and ideas lead Peter and his white horse into a cloud wall and back again to rescue a world in peril.

Herbert, Frank.  *Dune: Dune Chronicles, Book I*
Ace Trade, 2005 (1965), 544 pages.

Paul Atreides arrives on Arrakis expecting to see his father made king, but the Harkonnen refuse to turn over the reins of power.  Betrayed, young Atreides flees to Arrakis' desert, where he meets the planet's native Fremen.  There he trains the Fremen to fight the Harkonnen and undergoes mystical experiences and tests of will.  Herbert's masterpiece of science fiction is an exploration of character, destiny, and the potential of the human mind.  There are numerous sequels.

James, Henry.  *The Turn of the Screw*
Prestwick House, 2006 (1898), 142 pages.

This famous story begins when a young woman takes a job as governess to two children on condition that she never contact her employer.  Initially timid, she gains confidence after meeting the angelic Flora and Flora's brother, Miles.  Things get creepy when the governess sees the ghosts of her deceased predecessor and the valet—ghosts no one else can see.  Are the ghosts real?  Can the governess protect the children from ghostly harm?

Jordan, Robert.  *The Eye of the World* (*The Wheel of Time, Book I*)
Tor Fantasy, 1990, 832 pages.

Rand and his pals are forced to flee the sleepy village of Edmond's Field when an attack by the Trollocs endangers Rand's kith and kin.  Guided by the mysterious Moiraine, the companions journey across a fantasy landscape inhabited by creatures of good and evil.  Author Jordan has acknowledged his debt to J. R. R. Tolkien in this story of Rand's encounter with the Dark One.

King, Stephen.  *The Gunslinger* (*The Dark Tower, Book I*)
Plume, 2003 (1982), 264 pages.

Inspired by Robert Browning's poem, "Childe Roland to the Dark Tower Came," Stephen King's story begins with Roland of Gilead, the Last Gunslinger, in pursuit of the Man in Black, who is fleeing across a surreal desert.  Though Roland shares part of his quest with dead man Jake Chambers, he must ultimately face his journey into good and evil alone.  *The Gunslinger* is the first volume in the *Dark Tower* series.

Koontz, Dean. *Watchers*
Berkley, 2003 (1987), 496 pages.

While hunting in the woods, Delta Force soldier Travis Cornell meets Einstein, a dog with human intelligence who is being pursued by a hybrid creature called The Outsider and a mafia hit man. Attempting to save Einstein, the product of a government experiment, Travis finds that he and girlfriend Nora must flee too. Koontz's novel mingles a somber worldview with the hope that individuals can reclaim their freedom.

Laski, Marghanita. *The Victorian Chaise-Longue*
Persephone Books, 1999 (1953), 99 pages.

Charming Melanie, recovering from illness, persuades her doctor to let her sit up in the drawing room. There her daybed transports her to 1864, where she is Millie, a young woman dying in strange circumstances. Melanie struggles to understand her new world, the people around her, and the person she has become. But time is running out. Can she find the key to exit Millie's deathly world and re-enter her own, with its promise of life?

Le Guin, Ursula K. *The Left Hand of Darkness*
Ace, 2000 (1969), 320 pages.

In Le Guin's tale of a human envoy's interstellar journey to the alien planet Winter, Genly Ai makes contact with Winter's inhabitants to persuade them to join the galactic coalition. Though baffled by Winter's androgynous inhabitants, Genly forms a bond with Winter's leader Estraven—a bond that is tested by cross-cultural and political crises.

Lem, Stanislaw. *Solaris*
Harvest Books, 2002 (1961), 204 pages.

When Kris Kelvin arrives at a space station orbiting the planet Solaris, his plan to find out whether the planet is an intelligent life form is both confirmed and disrupted. Kelvin's encounter with a likeness of his long-dead lover disturbs his rational thinking, leading him to recognize in Solaris a massive brain that incarnates memories. Lem uses this encounter between man and super-mind to inquire into what it means to be human.

Lethem, Jonathan. *As She Climbed Across the Table*
Vintage, 1998 (1997), 224 pages.

Philip Engstrand's study of academic environments doesn't prepare him for what he finds in the physics lab at Beauchamp U: Lack, a black hole that selectively swallows objects. Alice Coombs, a physicist and Philip's love, becomes as obsessed with Lack as Philip is with Alice. Lethem's sci-fi satire leads to a merry chase through the dim land of Lack.

Martin, George R. R. *A Game of Thrones* (*A Song of Ice and Fire, Book I*)
Spectra, 2002 (1996), 704 pages.

Set in the fabled Winterfell, a land now subject to the vagaries of climate change, George R. R. Martin's novel spins several subplots around the central contest between two Winterfell families for the Iron Throne. Sorcerers and soldiers as well as lords and ladies play the game of thrones in this tale of intrigue, romance, and adventure.

McDevitt, Jack. *Seeker*
Ace, 2006 (2005), 384 pages.

When a mysterious woman bearing a 9,000-year-old relic contacts space-archeologists Alex Benedict and Chase Kolpath, the partners trace the antique cup to the spaceship Seeker. Further research reveals that the Seeker may have succeeded in establishing a free world: a colony called Margolia. Can Alex and Chase locate Margolia?

Miller, Walter. *A Canticle for Leibowitz*
Eos, 2006 (1960), 352 pages.

Miller's post-apocalyptic novel begins with the discovery of the sacred relics of Saint Leibowitz by a monk keeping vigil in the Utah desert. The relics—including the blueprint of a fallout shelter and a shopping list—point to Leibowitz's existence before the Flame Deluge. Leibowitz, a nuclear scientist turned monk, is a potent symbol of man's perpetual folly in this darkly ironic classic of science fiction.

Niffenegger, Audrey. *The Time Traveler's Wife*
Harvest Books, 2004 (2003), 560 pages.

This novel about the risks of loving features librarian Henry DeTamble, who tries to live a normal life with a steady job, love, and a family. But he's challenged by a rare genetic disorder that makes him time-travel unpredictably. His wife Clare knows that their love is fated, having met him on one of his journeys into her past, but like Henry she's unable to control his movements in time, and can't save him from the risks inherent in his condition.

Niven, Larry. *Ringworld*
Del Rey, 1985 (1970), 362 pages.

It's 2855, and 200-year-old earthling Louis Wu is bored after a couple of lifetimes of adventure. Suddenly he's invited by alien Nessus to join a secret interplanetary mission. Its object: to investigate Ringworld, an artificial, populated world encircling a distant star. The team must land on Ringworld, explore, and find out how to get back into space.

Piercy, Marge. *He, She and It*
Fawcett, 1993 (1991), 448 pages.

When Shira returns to her 21st-Century native Jewish village of Tikva, she is recruited to help create Yod, a cyborg. While listening to her grandmother's tale of the golem of Prague—an artificial being created to protect the historic Jewish ghetto—Shira endeavors to reconcile her feelings for Yod with the knowledge that Yod is not human.

Priest, Christopher. *The Prestige*
Tor Books, 2006 (1995), 368 pages.

Christopher Priest's genre-bending novel is equal parts sci-fi, historical fiction, and fictitious memoir. Written in the form of diaries kept by the protagonists, *The Prestige* builds suspense around the obsessive rivalry of two stage magicians in turn-of-the-century London—a rivalry that spurs two careers and brings tragedy in its wake.

Russell, Mary. *The Sparrow*
Ballantine, 1996, 448 pages.

*The Sparrow* tells the story of Emilio Sandoz, a charismatic Taino linguist and Jesuit priest who assembles a team to investigate a distant planet. This harrowing account of first contact with an alien civilization offers flashbacks describing the mission, alongside a contemporary (2060) postmortem. The novel is rich in social anthropology, character development, and plot twists.

Sagan, Carl. *Contact*
Pocket, 1997 (1985), 448 pages.

It's 1999, and the New Mexico night has a thousand eyes—an array of radio telescopes for Project Argus, the government search for extra-terrestrial intelligence. When scientist Ellie Arroway detects transmissions emanating from an intelligent civilization in deep space, she must convince her colleagues to help her investigate, and then convince humankind to believe what she finds.

Scott, Melissa. *Trouble and Her Friends*
Tor Books, 1994, 384 pages.

The government has closed off the computer nets of cyberspace, except for the free-wheeling virtual world, Seahaven. Now gone corporate, former netwalker Trouble finds someone is using her identity in Seahaven for criminal hacking. To restore her reputation, Trouble must enter Seahaven and expose her double, courting danger on the electronic frontier and beyond while rebuilding ties with netwalker friends and former partner Cerise.

Stephenson, Neal. *Snow Crash*
Bantam, 2000 (1992), 438 pages.

Real world Hiro delivers CosaNostra pizza; in the virtual world he's a warrior. When Hiro's hacker pal, Da5id, blacks out after trying the virtual drug Snow Crash, Hiro vows to solve the mystery. Hiro's real-world self and his avatar intertwine as the world's fate meshes with the fate of the Internet. Who's behind the metavirus Snow Crash, and how is Snow Crash tied to a mobster's plot against America? Hiro risks his life to find out.

Tepper, Sheri S. *Beauty*
Spectra, 1992 (1991), 496 pages.

Sheri S. Tepper's retelling of the Sleeping Beauty fairy tale turns out to be a vast reshaping of the tale as fantasy, social criticism, and time-travel. The fairy tale, told in the form of a journal, begins with a wicked aunt's curse that launches 16-year-old Beauty on a journey to the parallel world of Faery and into the dystopian future.

Tolkien, J. R. R. *The Fellowship of the Ring (The Lord of the Rings, Part I)*
Houghton Mifflin, 2002 (1954), 400 pages.

In the first novel of Tolkien's trilogy, Frodo is faced with a huge task when Gandalf reveals the dark side of Frodo's ring. The One Ring must be taken to Mordor and destroyed before the evil Sauron can claim it. Tolkien renders the epic journey of Frodo and his companions with a rare mix of archetypal fantasy and psychological realism, so that readers experience the frustrations, fears, and hopes of Frodo's journey as their own. *The Lord of the Rings* is widely considered to be the best fantasy series ever written.

Van Vogt, A. E. *The Voyage of the Space Beagle*
Manor Books, 1976 (1950), 192 pages.

When the Space Beagle's crew takes an alien on board, little do they know the danger it poses. Coeurl the cat feeds on id creatures (like humans) and could potentially destroy the crew. But Coeurl is nothing compared to Ixtl, the deep-space monster with a superior mind. Grosvenor, youngest member of the crew and expert in mind-control, knows how to deal with Coeurl and Ixtl, but will those in authority allow him to carry out his plans?

Verne, Jules. *Journey to the Center of the Earth*
Sterling, 2007 (1864), 256 pages.

Professor Lidenbrock's nephew hesitates to reveal that he's cracked the code giving directions to the center of the earth. For once the professor knows the directions, he and his nephew are mountain climbing in Iceland, descending into earth through the crater of a volcano, and traveling beneath earth's surface through caverns and across subterranean waters. Join the professor and his nephew for the journey of a lifetime.

Wells, H. G. *The Invisible Man*
Penguin Classics, 2005 (1897), 208 pages.

A stranger staggers into the Coach and Horses, his face wrapped in bandages, and becomes the talk of the town. Are the bandages a villain's disguise? Soon there's talk of mysteries like flying furniture and empty sleeves, and the folks of Iping suspect the stranger is an invisible man. Readers will enjoy this fast-paced thriller-chiller about a scientist's dream to possess a special kind of power, and the consequences of that dream.

# 3. Mystery

Everyone loves a good mystery. Whether you read mysteries for the mental challenge or for the thrill of the chase, you'll find rewarding reading here. These 51 books by acclaimed mystery writers are page-turners of recognized quality.

The mystery books on this list encompass all tastes, ranging from detective fiction featuring police inspectors, private eyes, and amateur sleuths to spy thrillers and mystery novels. Mystery novels like Zafón's *The Shadow of the Wind* are stories in which an investigation becomes a personal quest. Mystery novels are written in a more literary style than hardboiled detective fiction or spy thrillers.

Use the book descriptions to find mysteries of interest. Descriptions indicate mysteries with historical settings and thrillers featuring popular sleuths: Inspector Morse, PI Philip Marlowe, and Agatha Christie's Hercule Poirot are all on this list. Many of the 51 authors listed have written series. If you find an author you like, look for the author's other mysteries.

❖     ❖     ❖

Akunin, Boris. *The Winter Queen*
Translated by Andrew Bromfield. Random House, 2004 (1998), 264 pages.

No sooner does a crazed student shoot himself in Czarist Moscow's public gardens than Erast Fandorin is put on the case. Young Fandorin's superior officer is sure the boy will never make it as a detective, but Fandorin's deductive logic and street smarts lead him to the heart of an international conspiracy linked to the suicide. This is the first of nine volumes of Akunin's Inspector Fandorin historical mystery series.

Atkinson, Kate. *Case Histories*
Black Swan, 2008 (2004), 416 pages.

Kate Atkinson's fifth novel begins as a crime novel with PI Jackson Brodie investigating three cold cases involving the disappearance of a child, a brutal killing, and a reunion between a killer's sibling and a crime witness. This same novel has been described as a comedy of manners, a blend of tragedy and comedy, and a family saga. Atkinson is that rare writer who is able to combine suspense with a deft exploration of love and loss.

Buchan, John. *The Thirty-Nine Steps*
Penguin, 2008 (1915), 140 pages.

In London to amuse himself after making his fortune in South Africa, Richard Hannay is bored—till a stranger shows up on his doorstep with a little black book. When the stranger is murdered, Hannay must flee. Using a series of disguises, he travels to a remote corner of Scotland, eluding both police and agents of the Black Stone. Can Hannay decode the black book and clear his name? This fast-paced tale is a classic mystery.

Butor, Michel. *Passing Time*
River Run Press, 1980 (1957), 288 pages.

Jacques Revel, the diarist-narrator of Butor's mystery novel, wanders the labyrinthine paths of Bleston, an industrial city in England. A temporary resident of the city, Revel tries to solve a fratricide foreshadowed by the depiction of Cain in the stained glass of Bleston's Old Cathedral. The attempted murder of a local novelist, author of *The Murder of Bleston*, entices Revel to risk his safety and sanity to solve the crime.

Camilleri, Andrea. *The Shape of Water*
Translated by Stephen Sartarelli. Penguin, 2005 (1994), 240 pages.

In the first mystery in this popular series, Inspector Montalbano is determined to investigate a death that appears to result from natural causes, only to have his superiors pressure him to close the case. As Montalbano probes the death of an honest politician in a small town in Sicily, the characters he investigates gradually reveal their motives and complexities.

Carr, Caleb. *The Alienist*
Random House, 2006 (1994), 512 pages.

Street-smart reporter John Moore and police secretary Sara Howard team up with Professor Laszlo Kreizler—a psychologist or "alienist"—to solve a murder in 1890s New York. This fast-paced novel shows the investigating team breaking new ground in criminology by using the professor's suspect discipline to compile a psychological profile of the killer.

Chandler, Raymond. *The Big Sleep*
Vintage, 1988 (1929), 234 pages.

When the Depression put an end to his career as an oil magnate, Raymond Chandler became the premier writer of hard-boiled crime fiction in America. In *The Big Sleep,* Private Investigator Philip Marlowe unravels a complex web of intrigue when millionaire General Sternwood asks his help in protecting the Sternwood family name. *The Big Sleep* has inspired movies of the same name that epitomize the film noir genre.

Christie, Agatha. *Murder on the Orient Express*
Berkley, 2004 (1934), 336 pages.

The murder of Mr. Ratchett—fugitive kidnapper of three-year-old Daisy Armstrong—would have been the perfect crime but for the fact that detective Hercule Poirot was on the train when it took place. After probing clues and passengers, Poirot assembles 12 suspects to announce two alternative explanations of the crime. The preferred solution to the murder on the Orient Express is then passed on to the local police.

Collins, Wilkie. *The Moonstone*
Modern Library, 2001 (1868), 528 pages.

Called "the first and greatest of English detective novels" by T. S. Eliot, *The Moonstone* tells of a huge diamond stolen from an Indian shrine, bequeathed to heiress Rachel Verinder, and stolen again. Sergeant Cuff of Scotland Yard uses his powers of deduction to scrutinize the suspects, including three Hindus, Rachel's cousin, and her suitor. Told in a series of enticing narratives, *The Moonstone* is a page-turner steeped in atmosphere.

Deighton, Len. *Game, Set, and Match (Trilogy)*
Knopf, 1989 (1983, 1984, 1985), 857 pages.

Master of suspense Len Deighton sets his three-volume spy thriller in Cold War Berlin, Mexico City, and London. In *Berlin Game* British spy Bernie Samson goes behind the Iron Curtain to rescue an agent; in *Mexico Set* he must entice a disaffected KGB agent to defect; in *London Match*, Samson tests the motives of recent KGB defector Erich Stennis, and tries to root out a mole from among his own colleagues in London.

DeMille, Nelson. *The Charm School*
Grand Central Publishing, 1999 (1988), 816 pages.

The Kremlin has a big secret: a course in how to pass as an American taught by POWs from the Vietnam War at a "Charm School" for Soviet agents. When an American tourist in Russia stumbles upon a rumor about the Charm School—and after trying to contact the Moscow embassy, suffers an appalling death—it's up to two American attachés and the chief of the CIA's Moscow station to uncover the truth.

Dexter, Colin. *The Wench is Dead*
Fawcett, 1999 (1989), 290 pages.

Confined to a hospital bed with a bleeding ulcer, Inspector Morse decides to entertain himself by reading about an unsolved crime: *Murder at the Oxford Canal.* Morse becomes convinced that the men hanged for the 1859 murder were innocent, and with the help of his more mobile assistant, Inspector Lewis, he sets out to discover the real culprit.

Dickens, Charles. *The Mystery of Edwin Drood*
Penguin Classics, 2002 (1870), 432 pages.

*The Mystery of Edwin Drood* is a mystery twice over: Edwin Drood disappears in the course of the story, and Drood's ultimate fate is unknown because Dickens' novel remains unfinished. Nevertheless, Dickens' unsurpassed character portrayals and the hints in his careful plotting may enable you to guess who murdered Edwin Drood.

Doyle, Sir Arthur Conan. *The Mysterious Adventures of Sherlock Holmes*
Puffin, 1996 (1891–92), 246 pages.

This collection of Sherlock Holmes mysteries is an ideal introduction to Sir Arthur Conan Doyle's most famous literary creation. The mysteries collected here are particularly interesting for the way they dramatize the origin and development of the various myths that we associate with the character of Holmes. After reading this delightful story collection, you'll want to read through the rest of Doyle's Sherlock Holmes stories.

Du Maurier, Daphne. *Rebecca*
Avon Books, 1997 (1938), 416 pages.

After the narrator marries Maxim de Winter—whose first wife, Rebecca, has died—the couple settles at Manderley, an estate haunted by Rebecca's lingering presence. Insecure in her new role, Mrs. de Winter begins to doubt her husband's love. There are many surprising twists in this novel, in which the second Mrs. de Winter must learn about the life and death of Rebecca before she understands the mystery of her husband's heart.

Dürrenmatt, Friedrich. *The Inspector Barlach Mysteries: The Judge and His Hangman* and *Suspicion*
Mysterious Press, 1992 (1954), 224 pages.

In the first mystery, an ailing Inspector Barlach plots to bring his opposite number to justice. Can Inspector Barlach catch his nemesis despite illness, and despite the fact that he is preoccupied with guiding the ambitious Officer Chanz through an investigation of the death of a fellow policeman? Perhaps, for Chanz and Barlach's superior officer are only pawns in his game. In the second mystery, Barlach schemes against a war criminal posing as a physician at a private Zürich clinic.

Falkner, J. Meade. *Moonfleet*
Puffin Classics, 1994 (1898), 288 pages.

Like everyone else in the town of Moonfleet, John Trenchard knows about Blackbeard, the ghost who haunts the churchyard searching for lost treasure. Now the innkeeper's son has been killed, and strange sounds are coming from under the church. Could these events be linked to Blackbeard? John will find out all too soon.

Fleming, Ian. *Casino Royale*
Penguin, 2002 (1953), 192 pages.

Ian Fleming drew upon his experience as a Moscow correspondent and member of British Naval Intelligence to craft 14 spy novels featuring the incomparable James Bond. In Fleming's first spy novel, 007 pursues a French agent of the U.S.S.R. amidst the high-stakes world of gambling, with plenty of time for romantic dalliance along the way.

Forsyth, Frederick. *The Odessa File*
Bantam Books, 1983 (1972), 369 pages.

In 1963, Peter Miller, a young German reporter, gains possession of a file with initials denoting an international Nazi organization whose members are former SS men. Miller sets about infiltrating the organization and tries to discover the whereabouts of the "Butcher of Riga," a former concentration camp commander. Frederick Forsyth's pulse-pounding novel inspired a film that led to the exposure of the real-life "Butcher of Riga."

Francis, Dick. *Under Orders*
Berkley, 2007 (2006), 384 pages.

Death at the races is not uncommon, but when three jockeys die on Gold Cup Day—one of them from a bullet wound—PI Sid Halley is called in to investigate. A retired jockey himself, Halley is also asked by the government to assess the consequences of the legalization of Internet gambling. In spite of death threats, Halley is unflinching in his exploration of the linkage between crime at the races and gambling.

Giménez-Bartlett, Alicia. *Prime Time Suspect*
Translated by Nicholas Caistor. Europa Editions, 2000, 299 pages.

Barcelona police inspector Petra Delicado and her partner, Fermin Garzon, discover that their murder case involving an unsavory journalist overlaps with other suspicious deaths, including that of a highly placed government official. Giménez-Bartlett's well-drawn characters make this second novel in the Petra Delicado series a literary *tour de force*.

Grady, James. *Six Days of the Condor*
No Exit, 2008 (1974), 256 pages.

Ronald Malcolm has a quiet job analyzing the plots of spy novels, but as an employee of the CIA he finds himself in the crosshairs of a sinister plot. When armed men destroy his work section and kill his colleagues, Malcolm—code name "Condor"—seeks the agency's protection, only to find that a rogue group has been controlling his section for its own purposes. Adrift in a world of danger, Condor risks his life to uncover the truth.

Greene, Graham. *The Third Man*
Penguin, 1999 (1949), 160 pages.

Rollo Martins tells the Vienna literary society the title of his next novel: *The Third Man*. In Vienna for the funeral of friend Harry Lime, Martins has been investigating the circumstances of Lime's death. Why are there conflicting versions of Lime's accident? Who was the third man spotted at the scene? Was Harry Lime murdered? Was he involved in one of the rackets in post-war Vienna? Martins is determined to find out.

Hammett, Dashiell. *The Maltese Falcon*
Orion, 2005 (1930), 224 pages.

When Private Eye Sam Spade's partner is murdered at a stakeout, Spade is drawn into the investigation of a crime involving three adventurers vying for the priceless golden statuette of a falcon. In the course of the investigation, Spade is powerfully attracted to a beautiful redhead who seeks his help, but he plays his cards close to his chest as he works out the complicated solution to the theft of the Maltese falcon.

Harris, Joanne. *Gentlemen and Players*
Harper Perennial, 2006, 448 pages.

When sinister deeds occur at St. Oswald's School for Boys, loyal teacher Roy Straitley is determined to find out who is behind the attacks on the school. This mystery novel is narrated by Straitley and by an anonymous character, and its plot is designed as a chess match between Straightley and his foe. A fully-realized setting and complex characters add richness and depth to this novel of suspense.

Harris, Robert. *Enigma*
Ballantine Books, 1996 (1995), 384 pages.

Tom Jericho is at work on a top-secret government project at Bletchley Park in England. While he works to break Enigma, the Nazi's code, his girlfriend Claire goes missing. Then Jericho finds stolen intercepts in her room and suspects her of spying. This thriller about the race to decode Enigma dramatizes the impact on individual lives of war, secrecy, and the rumored massacre of thousands of Polish army officers by the Soviets.

Hillerman, Tony. *A Thief of Time*
Harper Torch, 1990 (1988), 352 pages.

Tony Hillerman's mystery adventure features worldly-wise Lt. Joe Leaphorn and his younger, more spiritually-inclined assistant, Sgt. Jim Chee, of the Navajo Tribal Police. Leaphorn and Chee investigate the disappearance of a Southwestern anthropologist suspected of being a pot hunter, i.e., a thief of Native-American artifacts.

Hilton, James. *Lost Horizon*
Harper Perennial, 2004 (1933), 256 pages.

In 1931, a plane carrying three Englishmen and a woman missionary crashes on the China-Tibet border. The four survive, having landed at the center of a mystery. Who are their hosts at the nearby Buddhist monastery? Are the survivors guests or prisoners? Will they ever meet the High Lama? And who is Lo Tsien, the gifted Chinese girl? Hilton's tale of Shangri-La is a modern fable of man's desire to surpass human limitations.

Holton, Hugh. *The Devil's Shadow*
Forge Books, 2002 (2001), 384 pages.

Chicago police detective Hugh Holton's eighth police procedural features Chief of Detectives Larry Cole in pursuit of master thief Julianna Saint and Mafia don Jake Romano. When a writer investigating the Mafia takes a dive from a Chicago skyscraper, Cole and his team set out to solve two interrelated crimes. Holton's intricately plotted novel is based on his experience as an African-American career cop.

Hope, Anthony. *The Prisoner of Zenda*
Borgo Press, 2002 (1894), 212 pages.

Red-headed, straight-nosed Englishman Rudolph Rassendyll bears a striking resemblance to the king of Ruritania. On a visit to Ruritania, Rudolph finds himself caught up in a plot to impersonate the king. Will Rudolph succumb to the temptation to replace the king, or will he devote his spirit and derring-do to the cause of putting the rightful king on the throne? Readers will enjoy the humor, fast pace, and romance of this tale.

Household, Geoffrey. *Rogue Male*
NYRB Classics, 2007 (1959), 224 pages.

Told in the form of a diary, *Rogue Male* is the story of a hunter who becomes hunted, and is in imminent danger of being run to ground by his pursuers. When a professional big game hunter is captured and tortured while attempting to break into a Central European dictator's compound, his escape is followed by his relief upon reaching his homeland. But the pursuit continues, and the hunter must go into the wild to survive.

James, P. D. *An Unsuitable Job for a Woman*
Touchstone, 2001 (1972), 256 pages.

Cordelia Gray finds herself in charge when her boss dies and leaves her Pryde's Detective Agency. Private Investigator Gray's first solo case involves the suspicious death of young Cambridge student Mark Callender. Callender's family proves to be a nest of vipers, and Gray learns about the dark side of human nature while solving the crime.

Kaminsky, Stuart M. *A Fine Red Rain*
Scribner, 2000 (1987), 224 pages.

In this mystery in the Inspector Rostnikov series, Rostnikov seeks to investigate the deaths of two of three performers in a high-wire act and to protect the surviving aerialist. Set in the Soviet Union of the 1980s, *A Fine Red Rain* interweaves this suspenseful story with a subplot involving black market machinations in Russia's crumbling empire.

King, Laurie R.  *The Beekeeper's Apprentice*
Picador, 2007 (1994), 495 pages.

When a chance meeting between a retired detective and a girl becomes a meeting of the minds, the detective decides to tutor her in criminal investigation.  Soon Sherlock Holmes and Mary Russell are solving cases of espionage and kidnapping.  But someone is trying to destroy the new partnership, and the detectives' biggest challenge will be to capture the mastermind who has planted bombs targeting Russell, Holmes, and Watson.

Le Carré, John.  *The Spy Who Came in from the Cold*
Walker and Company, 2005 (1963), 256 pages.

Graham Greene called Le Carré's book "the finest spy story ever written."  In this Cold War classic, British agent Alec Leamus is sent into East Germany to frame Hans-Dieter Mundt, an agent of the East German secret police.  When a power struggle within East Germany's espionage unit pits Mundt against Fiedler, his second in command, the ensuing trial of Mundt, Fiedler, and Leamus reveals the twists of an intricate plot.

Lehane, Dennis.  *Mystic River*
HarperCollins, 2003 (2001), 416 pages.

Dennis Lehane's sixth crime novel, set in a blue-collar Boston neighborhood, probes the psychology of three childhood friends grown to adulthood, grown apart, and reunited when the daughter of one of them is found murdered.  Sean Devine, a homicide cop, investigates the murder of his friend's daughter, and the possible involvement of the third friend, whose childhood wounds have forced him to lead a complicated double life.

Malone, Michael.  *Uncivil Seasons*
Sourcebooks Landmark, 2001 (1983), 368 pages.

Michael Malone's Southern voice imbues this comedy-of-manners mystery with an edgy charm.  When blue-blood policeman Justin Saville of Hillston, North Carolina, is deputed to investigate the death of his uncle's wife, his genteel relatives expect him to charge the obvious suspect.  Justin may belong to Hillston's founding family, but he's more interested in carrying out a thorough investigation than in protecting the family name.

McCall Smith, Alexander.  *The No. 1 Ladies' Detective Agency*
Anchor, 2009, 272 pages.

McCall Smith's mystery stories sparkle with wit in this novel about Mma Ramotswe and her maverick business: Botswana's No. 1 Ladies' Detective Agency.  Precious Ramotswe exposes a fraudulent father, evaluates a worker's injury claim, and solves the riddle of a Jekyll-and-Hyde doctor in this tale of an independent woman in a traditional society.

Mortimer, John. *Rumpole and the Penge Bungalow Murders*
Penguin, 2004, 215 pages.

This prequel to the famed Horace Rumpole series provides the background to the oft-mentioned Penge Bungalow affair—Rumpole's first case, in which he defended Simon, the son of a murdered Second World War hero. While defending a burglar and courting future wife Hilda, barrister Rumpole stumbles on a clue that is key to Simon's defense.

Mosley, Walter. *Devil in a Blue Dress*
Washington Square Press, 2002 (1990), 272 pages.

This first novel in the Easy Rawlins series features a black PI in pursuit of a woman involved in a political scandal in 1940s Los Angeles. Written in the hard-boiled tradition of Chandler and Hammet, Mosley's novel explores the dark side of Southern California through the eyes of a decent World War II veteran with a tenuous hold on his place in society.

Pears, Iain. *An Instance of the Fingerpost*
Berkley Books, 1998, 735 pages.

Iain Pears' well-researched mystery combines fictional characters with historical characters such as John Locke and Christopher Wren in this tale of murder in 17th-Century England. The murder of an Oxford don and the trial of the accused are told from the point of view of four characters: an Italian physician, a student, a mathematician, and an historian. Readers will enjoy evaluating the narratives for reliability and accuracy.

Pérez-Reverte, Arturo. *The Club Dumas*
Translated by Sonia Soto. Harvest Books, 2006 (1996), 368 pages.

Those who enjoyed *The Three Musketeers* will especially enjoy this mystery, in which a rare book expert, hired to authenticate a long lost chapter of Dumas' adventure story, encounters characters from the pages of the book, devil worshippers, and more. Book sleuth Lucas Corso risks life and limb on assignments from two very different clients.

Perry, Anne. *No Graves as Yet*
Ballantine, 2005 (2003), 384 pages.

The assassination of Archduke Ferdinand overlaps with a personal tragedy for Captain Joseph Reavley, whose parents are killed on the same day. Personal tragedy soon leads to international intrigue when Reavley learns that his father possessed a document that could threaten Europe's future. In *No Graves As Yet*, the first book in Anne Perry's late Victorian series, Reavley traces a series of unlikely events during the build-up to World War I.

Peters, Ellis. *A Morbid Taste for Bones*
Mysterious Press, 1994 (1977), 208 pages.

Brother Cadfael sets off on an expedition to a Welsh village to dig up the bones of Saint Winifred and bring them back to his monastery in England. Cadfael is skeptical of the plan, especially when the villagers resist parting with their saint. When the village leader is murdered, suspicion falls on a suitor of the victim's daughter, but is it possible that the monks are implicated? Cadfael sets a trap to catch the killer.

Rendell, Ruth. *From Doon with Death*
Ballantine Books, 2007 (1964), 240 pages.

In this novel, the first in her Inspector Wexford series, Ruth Rendell probes the psychological motivations of her characters. Police Inspector Wexford is initially baffled by the violent murder of respectable Margaret Parsons—until he discovers that her books bear passionate inscriptions from someone named "Doon." Ruth Rendell explores one woman's double life and the duplicity of the community that surrounds her.

Sayers, Dorothy L. *Gaudy Night*
HarperTorch, 1995 (1935), 512 pages.

Renowned scholar and mystery writer Dorothy Sayers sets *Gaudy Night* at an Oxford women's college where Harriet Vane is attending her reunion. In this early feminist mystery novel, Harriet probes a series of bizarre pranks at the college, women's roles in academia, and her own ambivalence towards marriage. Harriet's preoccupations move closer to resolution when her partner, Lord Peter Wimsey, arrives on the scene.

Simenon, Georges. *The Bar on the Seine*
Translated by David Watson. Penguin, 2006 (1932), 160 pages.

The prolific Georges Simenon wrote over 100 Inspector Maigret mysteries. In *The Bar on the Seine*, a tip from a condemned man prompts Maigret to investigate a murder. Maigret sniffs out clues in a suburban bar amidst a diverse cast of characters. Then the gears start to turn, and Maigret is hot on the killer's trail as the story proceeds to its inevitable close.

Smith, Martin Cruz. *Gorky Park*
Ballantine Books, 2007 (1981), 384 pages.

Martin Cruz Smith's crime novel, set in Brezhnev-era Russia and featuring Chief Inspector Arkady Renko of the Moscow police, is notable for its tightly-wound plot, intriguing characters, and accurate portrayal of Soviet society. While investigating a triple murder in a Moscow amusement park, Inspector Renko must outwit the KGB, the FBI, and the New York City Police to get at the truth.

Tey, Josephine. *The Daughter of Time*
Touchstone, 1995 (1951), 208 pages.

British school children all learn that wicked King Richard murdered his nephews. So too believes Inspector Alan Grant, until a forced bed rest gives him time to pursue an inquiry. Captivated by a portrait of Richard III, Grant uses his powers of deduction to prove him innocent. Tey's well-researched detective story has become a resource for historians.

Todd, Charles. *Wings of Fire*
St. Martin's Paperbacks, 1999 (1998), 320 pages.

Charles Todd is the pen name of mother-and-son writing team Caroline and Charles Todd. In the Todds' *Wings of Fire*, Scotland Yard detective Ian Rutledge rushes to Cornwall to investigate three deaths, including the apparent suicide of poet Olivia Manning. In solving the crime, Rutledge struggles to keep his logic intact in spite of his emotional involvement with Manning and her poetry.

Zafón, Carlos Ruiz. *The Shadow of the Wind*
Translated by Lucia Graves. Penguin, 2001, 487 pages.

It's 1945 in Barcelona, Spain, when Daniel visits the Cemetery of Forgotten Books with his father, and is entrusted with the care and preservation of a rare novel by contemporary author Julian Carax: *The Shadow of the Wind*. As Daniel grows up in a country under dictatorship, he braves state terror in his quest to locate Carax and his missing works, and endeavors to solve the mystery of the author's persecution and disappearance.

# 4. Historical Fiction

Arm chair travelers, history buffs, and connoisseurs of exotica all love historical fiction.  The historical novel keeps readers turning page after page while giving a meaningful shape to history.  The 48 books on this list recreate history in diverse ways.

Several books on this list tell stories of real or legendary figures in the form of fictional biographies.  In other books, the central character has a front-row seat on history by virtue of a key relationship, or even a trade: in *Girl with a Pearl Earring*, the painter Vermeer is seen through the eyes of his servant, and in *People of the Book*, a rare book expert uncovers the past through her craft.  Some historical fiction profiles a man or woman of an era, as does Yasushi Inoue's *Shirobamba*.  Other books, like the Civil War novel *March,* offer a panorama of a major event.  Finally, books like Pat Barker's *Regeneration* highlight specific historical issues.

Use the descriptions to find books that interest you.  If you are intrigued by a time period, you'll find books set in Ancient Rome, World War Two, medieval England, and numerous other fascinating times and places.  You'll find books by acclaimed contemporary writers like Roddy Doyle, and character-driven books like *The Conformist*.  When you find an author you like, look for other books by that author.

❖        ❖        ❖

Allende, Isabel. *Zorro*
HarperCollins, 2005, 390 pages.

Born to a hidalgo father and an Indian mother, Diego grows up in Alta, California as a privileged child with roots in Indian culture.  When he and friend Bernardo undergo initiation, Diego receives the name Zorro and Bernardo regains speech.  Later, in Spain, Zorro fights injustice with Bernardo at his side.  Allende's  Zorro tale ends with Diego's return to California to reclaim his family estate and seek justice for the oppressed.

Barker, Pat. *Regeneration*
Plume, 1993 (1991), 256 pages.

This first novel in a World War I trilogy tells the real life story of poet Siegfried Sassoon, a decorated soldier who is diagnosed with shell shock as a consequence of his opposition to the war.  Sent to Edinburgh's Craiglockhart War Hospital for treatment, Sassoon influences army psychiatrist W. H. R. Rivers and other soldiers being treated, including poet Wilfred Owen, in this suspenseful story of war and madness.

Bradshaw, Gillian. *The Sand-Reckoner*
Forge Books, 2001 (2000), 320 pages.

When King Hieron of Syracuse sees a seven-ton ship pulled by a pair of hands and the power of one mind, he knows the man he has hired is invaluable. But once Archimedes finishes building catapults, will he move on to the court of Ptolemy? As Hieron schemes to retain Archimedes, the scholar looks for a way to support his family, serve the city-state, and marry the girl he loves—all while pursuing mathematics, his true vocation.

Brooks, Geraldine. *People of the Book*
Viking, 2008, 384 pages.

When Hanna Heath is hired to conserve a rare Hebrew manuscript, her research takes her back in time from 1940s Sarajevo to 1480s Seville. Using artifacts like an insect's wing found in the book, Heath traces the harrowing journey of the Sarajevo Haggadah from Spain to Bosnia. The author brings to life the people who cherished and preserved the Haggadah while telling the contemporary story of Hanna and Muslim librarian Karaman.

Cather, Willa. *Death Comes for the Archbishop*
Virago, 2006 (1927), 256 pages.

Cather's narrative account of the attempt by Bishop Jean Marie Latour and Father Joseph Vaillant to establish a Catholic diocese in the New Mexico Territory is an amalgam of legend, history, and lyrical description. The author relates the quiet determination of the priests amidst the machinations of Spanish-Mexican clerics and the abiding influence of Hopi and Navajo religion, while paying tribute to the beauty of the American Southwest.

Chevalier, Tracy. *Girl with a Pearl Earring*
Plume, 2001 (1999), 240 pages.

The title of this novel refers to a famous painting by the great 17th-Century Dutch painter, Jan Vermeer. This compelling novel invites us to imagine the story behind the painting of this masterwork by dramatizing the relationship between Vermeer and his servant, Griet (the girl in the painting), an artistically sensitive young woman whose quiet but thoughtful presence offsets the chaotic atmosphere of the Vermeer household.

Costain, Thomas B. *The Silver Chalice*
Loyola Press, 2006 (1952), 820 pages.

Inspired by the archeological discovery of a 1st-Century silver chalice in Antioch, Costain's *The Silver Chalice* brings to life 1st-Century biblical and historical figures in this story of the crafting of a silver chalice to hold the Holy Grail. Basil, a silversmith, is commissioned by the apostle Luke to create the chalice. Basil travels to Jerusalem, Greece, and Rome, meets the apostles, and braves persecution in order to fulfill his task.

De Bernières, Louis. *Corelli's Mandolin*
Vintage, 1995 (1994), 448 pages.

To the Greek island of Cephallonia, where the ancient gods once appeared to men and the local saint still intervenes in their lives, come Captain Correlli and the invading Italian army. Louis de Bernières' novel of World War II examines the themes of love, loyalty, and betrayal, and dramatizes the clash between history and the island's timeless beauty.

De Moor, Margriet. *Duke of Egypt*
Translated by Paul Vincent. Arcade Publishing, 2003 (1996), 256 pages.

Every spring, Joseph leaves his wife Lucie on their horse farm in Holland to rejoin his wandering family. Every autumn, he returns with stories of his people. This tale of the improbable marriage between a Dutchwoman and a gypsy frames De Moor's account of the persecution of the gypsies in the Netherlands, from their 18th-Century expulsion and gradual return through the 1944 roundup that was followed by extermination, resistance, and survival.

Doctorow, E. L. *The March*
Random House, 2006 (2005), 384 pages.

In 1864, General Sherman burned Atlanta and marched his army through Georgia to the sea. The historical march is dramatized by the story's characters: a freed slave, a Union surgeon, two rebel soldiers, and a Southern woman who becomes a regimental nurse. The author depicts Sherman's army as a microcosm of civilization, complete with engineers, a commissary, a hospital, cooks, musicians, carpenters, servants, and guns.

Douglas, Lloyd C. *The Robe*
Mariner Books, 1999 (1942), 528 pages.

Sent to command a garrison in Palestine, Tribune Gallio stands guard at the crucifixion of Jesus. After winning Jesus' robe in a bet, Gallio becomes despondent. Helped by his slave Demetrius and by Christians from Cana to Capernaum, Gallio learns of Jesus' unique mission. In Rome, Gallio must choose between his country and his faith. This novel vividly recreates the world of the Jews and early Christians in Roman Palestine.

Doyle, Roddy. *A Star Called Henry*
Penguin, 2004 (1999), 402 pages.

Born in a small room in the slums, Henry Smart witnesses tumultuous change in Ireland in the 20th Century. A typical child who lives out his boyhood on the mean streets of Dublin, Henry becomes a larger-than-life hero through his participation in Ireland's formative crises. As a soldier in the Irish Rebellion, Henry becomes part of history.

Eco, Umberto. *Baudolino*
Translated by William Weaver. Harvest Books, 2003 (2000), 544 pages.

As a peasant adopted by Emperor Frederick Barbarossa, Baudolino is exceptionally well placed to move among all levels of society and to engage in the big events of his time, from the historical sack of Constantinople to the fantastic quest in search of priest-king Prester John. Eco brilliantly captures the history and the imagination of medieval Europe.

Follett, Ken. *The Pillars of the Earth*
NAL Trade, 2002 (1989), 976 pages.

This story of the building of one of the greatest medieval Gothic cathedrals is set in the fictional town of Knightsbridge, England, and traces the fortunes of two generations of a stonemason's family. Woven into the fabric of the novel are fictional leaders of church and state, descriptions based on the author's passion for architecture, and accurately depicted historical events like the battle of Lincoln and the murder of Thomas Becket.

Frayn, Michael. *Spies*
Picador, 2002, 272 pages.

This wonderfully imagined novel of boyhood adventure is deeply imbued with the atmosphere of wartime London of the 1940s. When Stephen's friend Keith confides his suspicion that his mother is a spy, the boys decide to spy on her. The gap between childhood games and grown-up double-dealing narrows as the boys ply their spycraft.

Gaudé, Laurent. *The House of Scorta*
Translated by Stephen Sartarelli and Sophie Hawkes. MacAdam/Cage, 2007 (2005), 289 pages.

Laurent Gaudé's prize-winning novel is the story of a family. The Scorta genealogy begins with a passionate, benighted coupling in Southern Italy that produces the thief Rocco Scorta. When Rocco disinherits his own three children, Carmela, Giuseppe, and Domenico must decide between emigrating to America or finding a way to shake off the stigma of being a Scorta and make it in their native land.

Graves, Robert. *I, Claudius*
Vintage, 1989 (1934), 468 pages.

This tale of Rome's Imperial family is a fictional autobiography by future Emperor Claudius. While the royals vie for power, Claudius is camouflaged by his status as a self-effacing royal historian. Writing for posterity, Claudius tells all, describing Emperors Augustus, Tiberius, and Caligula, and powerful Empress Livia. As the Empire declines and the memory of the Republic fades, Claudius reveals his family's role in history.

Grenville, Kate. *The Secret River*
Canongate, 2006 (2005), 349 pages.

William Thornhill, a Thames waterman, is caught stealing and sentenced to death. Reprieved by the efforts of wife Sal, he is exiled to New South Wales, in present-day Australia. There he labors to build a life for his family, farming and transporting goods up and down the Hawkesbury River. But with the Aboriginals nearby, he never feels the land is his own. "Take a little, give a little," advises a neighbor. But can he and Sal coexist with the Aboriginals?

Guterson, David. *Snow Falling on Cedars*
Vintage, 1995, 480 pages.

In 1954, Japanese American Kabuo Miyamoto of San Piedro Island is being tried for the murder of a local fisherman. Reporting on the trial is Ishmael Chambers, a white man who grew up on the island and fell in love with a Japanese girl who became the defendant's wife. Soon Chambers begins to question not only Miyamoto's prosecution, but the wider injustice of incarcerating Japanese Americans during World War II.

Harris, Joanne. *Five Quarters of the Orange*
Harper Perennial, 2007 (2001), 336 pages.

Joanne Harris tells the story of a misunderstood childhood in German-occupied France retrospectively from an adult's point of view. Framboise Simon tries to make sense of her memories by returning to the village where her mother was blamed for a local tragedy. Impressed by the way her grandfather's tales differed from official accounts of the Occupation, Harris has written an intentionally subjective account of this historical era.

Harris, Robert. *Imperium: A Novel of Ancient Rome*
Pocket, 2007 (2006), 320 pages.

Cicero is a "new man" who attained the supreme *imperium*, or power, of the Roman consulship at the age of 42. Unlike consuls who belonged to the aristocracy, possessed a fortune, or headed an army, Cicero achieved power by his skill as a public speaker in the Roman Senate, and as an advocate in the courtroom. Cicero's story is narrated by his secretary Tiro, who invented shorthand to record Cicero's great speeches.

Holthe, Tess Uriza. *When the Elephants Dance*
Penguin, 2003 (2002), 384 pages.

"When the elephants dance, the chickens must be careful," says 13-year-old Alejandro Karangulan as his family huddles in their cellar. Outside, the elephants—the Americans and the Japanese—are fighting over the Philippines. In a dark cellar, the Karangulan family and their friends tell magical tales to stoke their courage. Holthe's World War II novel features three remarkable storytellers with ties to the magic of the islands.

Inoue, Yasushi. *Shirobamba: A Childhood in Old Japan*
Translated by Jean Oda Moy. Peter Owen Publishers, 1992 (1962), 200 pages.

Kosaku lives in the country while his parents live in the city. Granny Onui of the Lower House cares for him, while Cousin Sakiko of the Upper House sees to his education. Though Kosaku's elite family expects him to study hard and be first in his class, traditional games and seasonal festivals tie him to the Japanese country folk, and to the rhythms of the land. Will Kosaku decide to join his parents in the city, or remain in the country?

Kantor, MacKinlay. *Andersonville*
Plume, 1993 (1955), 768 pages.

MacKinlay Kantor's Pulitzer Prize-winning novel about the War Between the States chronicles the lives of inmates of the Andersonville prison, in which tens of thousands of Northern soldiers were incarcerated. This meticulously researched novel profiles the camp commandant, Union soldiers, the camp doctor, a plantation owner, and scores of other characters from the North and South.

Kundera, Milan. *Ignorance*
Translated by Linda Asher. Harper Perennial, 2003 (2000), 208 pages.

In 1968, Irena flees Prague in the wake of the Russian invasion. In October 1969, after seeing Prague draped in red Soviet flags, Joseph decides to leave the country. Twenty years later, former acquaintances Irena and Joseph return to the Czech Republic where they meet again, only to find themselves estranged from their country and from one another.

Lagerkvist, Par. *Barabbas*
Vintage, 1989 (1950), 160 pages.

The author's gift for describing sacred history from both a realistic and a supernatural perspective illuminates a story meaningful to skeptics and believers alike. Lagerkvist imagines the life of Barabbas, the thief in the New Testament who was pardoned instead of Jesus. Doubtful of the holiness of Jesus, Barabbas travels to Golgotha and Rome in an attempt to understand the meaning of Jesus' life.

Laski, Marghanita. *Little Boy Lost*
Persephone Books, 2001 (1949), 220 pages.

This tenderhearted story of a man's search for his lost son is agonizingly suspenseful. Separated from his pregnant wife in wartime, Hilary Wainwright traces his five-year-old son to an orphanage in post-war France, then struggles with indecision regarding his duty to the child. Crushed by the death of his wife at the hands of the Gestapo, Hilary is torn between the lure of a life of self-gratification and the hard struggle to love again.

Liss, David. *The Coffee Trader*
Random House, 2003, 400 pages.

It's 1659, and Miguel Lienzo has lost a fortune on Amsterdam's commodities exchange. A member of Amsterdam's Portuguese Jewish community, Lienzo walks a thin line between the ways of the commodities exchange and the strict rules of the Jewish ghetto council. In order to gain financial redemption along with his newly-won religious freedom, Lienzo plots to corner the market in a new commodity: coffee. This gripping, intricately plotted novel recreates an era.

Mackay, Shena. *The Orchard on Fire*
Harvest Books, 1997 (1995), 224 pages.

It's 1953: around the world it's the year of the ascent of Everest, of the execution of the Rosenbergs, and of Stalin's death. In England, it's the Coronation year of Elizabeth II. When April's family moves to Stonebridge, national events mix with her and her parents' personal fortunes in unexpected ways in this chronicle of a year in the life of a young girl.

Manning, Olivia. *The Levant Trilogy* (*Fortunes of War*)
Phoenix, 2003 (1960), 570 pages.

Olivia Manning's *Levant Trilogy* follows the fortunes of British subjects Guy and Harriet Pringle, who have arrived in Egypt as refugees from the Second World War. As in Manning's *Balkan Trilogy*, lecturer Guy promotes British culture and learning while his wife Harriet struggles to develop an independent identity. A subplot brings Harriet close to the Desert War through soldier Simon Boulderstone, deepening her understanding of war.

Mason, Daniel. *The Piano Tuner*
Vintage, 2002, 312 pages.

Daniel Mason's novel of adventure, set during the Burmese colonial wars of the 1880s, pits idealistic British Surgeon-Major Carroll, who wants peace with the Shan tribesmen, against his fellow officers, who want war. Into this scene of British occupation comes Edward Drake, a piano tuner sent by the British government to repair Carroll's piano. Drake travels into the heart of the jungle, bearing witness to Carroll's quest.

Moravia, Alberto. *The Conformist*
Translated by Tami Calliope. Zoland Books, 1999 (1951), 375 pages.

This novel of prewar Italy of the 1940s centers upon psychologically repressed minor official Marcello Clerici. Marcello's desire for a normal life is transformed by fascism into a brand of conformity that stifles empathy and ethics. Asked by the fascist government to spy on his former professor, Marcello agrees, initiating an unexpected cascade of violent events.

Nemirovsky, Irene. *Suite Française*
Translated by Sandra Smith. Vintage, 2007 (2004), 448 pages.

Nemirovsky, who wrote *Suite Française* during Germany's occupation of France in the 1940s, completed Parts 1 and 2 of what she intended to be a five-part novel. In Part 1, "Storm in June," Parisians flee the city on the eve of the invasion. Part 2, "Dolce," describes the survival strategies of the inhabitants of an occupied village: fraternization, collaboration, and resistance. Nemirovsky views history with irony and insight.

O'Brian, Patrick. *Master and Commander*
W. W. Norton, 2003 (1970), 412 pages.

This first volume in the Jack Aubrey and Stephen Maturin series tells the tale of Captain Aubrey of the British Navy during the Napoleonic Wars. With the assistance of his friend Maturin, ship's surgeon and secret intelligence agent, Aubrey engages in a series of thrilling sea battles aboard HMS *Sophie*. O'Brian's action-packed novel is notable for the richness of detail with which the author depicts the ship, the crew, and life at sea.

Pears, Iain. *The Dream of Scipio*
Riverhead Trade, 2003 (2002), 416 pages.

This multi-layered story of three turning points in Western civilization explores complex moral choices. In the 300s AD, a bishop chooses between friendship and the preservation of Rome; in the 1350s, poet Olivier de Noyen chooses between loyalty and love; in the 1940s, scholar Julien Barneuve chooses between friendship and saving lives. Behind these conflicts is the spiritual quest described in a manuscript by Cicero called *The Dream of Scipio*.

Piercy, Marge. *Gone to Soldiers*
Fawcett, 1988 (1987), 800 pages.

Piercy's epic novel of the Second World War encompasses the stories of ten key characters whose lives play out on the home front and in battle. Piercy's vivid characters include war correspondent Louise, OSS agent Oscar, code-breaker Daniel, and Women's Air Force Service Pilot Bernice, providing both male and female perspectives on the war.

Pressfield, Steven. *Gates of Fire: An Epic Novel of the Battle of Thermopylae*
Bantam, 2005 (1998), 400 pages.

During the ancient Greeks' war with Persia, 300 Spartans held a mountain pass in northern Greece against what modern scholars estimate to have been an army of at least 100,000 Persian warriors. Steven Pressfield's thrilling account of the famous Battle of Thermopylae in 480 BC is told by Xeones, the sole survivor of the Spartan warriors ordered to delay King Xerxes' invading army for as long as possible.

Remarque, Erich Maria. *All Quiet on the Western Front*
Ballantine Books, 1987 (1929), 304 pages.

Erich Maria Remarque's famous anti-war novel, written from the perspective of German soldier
Paul Bäumer, tells the story of the men who fought in the First World War and were either killed or
injured physically or psychologically. Paul and his classmates enthusiastically enlist, but are subject to
dehumanizing conditions in the trenches.

Saramago, José. *Baltasar and Blimunda*
Translated by Giovanni Pontiero. Harvest Books, 1998 (1982), 360 pages.

In Portugal of the early 1700s, land of wars and the Inquisition, Padre Lourenço enlists the aid of
a one-handed war veteran and a clairvoyant. In the war of King Dom João, Baltasar lost his hand,
and in the War of the Holy Inquisition, Blimunda lost her mother, yet when their losses bring them
together, the love of Baltasar and Blimunda for one another fires their devotion to Padre Lourenço, the
"Flying Man," who plans to build a flying machine.

Saylor, Steven. *Roman Blood: A Novel of Ancient Rome*
St. Martin's Minotaur, 2000 (1991), 416 pages.

Summoned to the house of Cicero, Gordianus the Finder is asked to investigate a purported case
of patricide. Gordianus' investigation plunges him into a labyrinth of lies and double-talk as he
interviews arrogant noblemen, clever slaves, and regular citizens in his pursuit of the truth about the
death of Sextus Roscius. Saylor's novel offers a vivid depiction of Rome in 80 BC, and a dynamic
portrait of a young lawyer named Cicero who was destined to become the greatest Roman orator,
philosopher, and legislator of all time.

Scott, Paul. *The Jewel in the Crown (The Raj Quartet, Book I)*
University of Chicago Press, 1998 (1966), 462 pages.

Paul Scott's novel of the British in India begins in 1942, just as Gandhi warns the British to "quit
India." The author uses the incident of a violent crime against a British woman to examine stresses and
strains in the edifice of British rule. Written in the form of interviews and reports assembled by the
narrator, *The Jewel in the Crown* is notable for its suspenseful plot and complex characters, and for its
questioning of British power.

See, Lisa. *Snow Flower and the Secret Fan*
Random House, 2006 (2005), 288 pages.

Lisa See weaves a story of women's lives around *nu shu*, a language invented by women in 19th–
Century China for communicating with one another. Snow Flower and Lily, paired in childhood
as *laotongs* or "old sames," seal their intimate friendship by trading messages on a fan. Reflecting on
their marriages and the social turmoil around them, they remain "old sames" until a misunderstanding
disrupts their lifelong friendship.

Shaara, Michael. *The Killer Angels*
Random House, 2004 (1974), 608 pages.

Michael Shaara's character-driven novel of the Battle of Gettysburg is told from the point of view of Confederate Generals Lee, Longstreet, and Armistead, and Union General Buford and Colonel Chamberlain. This well-researched work of historical fiction is notable for the way in which the author portrays the key historical figures' thoughts, as well as the decisive action and "fog-of-battle" confusion of the soldiers fighting the war.

Tsukiyama, Gail. *Women of the Silk*
St. Martin's Griffin, 1993 (1991), 288 pages.

The women of the silk of the title were silk workers in 1920s China, many of whom were girls as young as eight when delivered to the factories by their parents. Tsukiyama's well-researched novel tells the story of Pei, a child whose seeming abandonment by her parents is eased when she bonds with the sisterhood of silk workers. The author offers fascinating details of the lives of these women in a period of social upheaval in China.

Uris, Leon. *Exodus*
Wings, 2000 (1958), 640 pages.

This story of the birth of the modern state of Israel begins with a ship carrying Jewish orphans from the devastation of World War II, and a British blockade preventing its entry into Palestine. A children's hunger strike on board ship is a public relations coup and the British open the gates to the Jews. Life is more than challenging for the pioneers, who learn farming along with self-defense. *Exodus* is a masterpiece of historical fiction.

Van der Post, Laurens. *A Story Like the Wind*
Harvest Books, 1978 (1972), 384 pages.

This coming-of-age novel, written by the chronicler of Africa's Stone Age Kalahari Bushmen, tells of 13-year-old François, raised by European parents and by a bushman woman and Matebele tribesmen, and torn between his European and his African roots. This story of a young boy's friendship with the Bushmen is richly informed by the author's knowledge of the Kalahari desert and its indigenous people.

Wouk, Herman. *The Caine Mutiny: A Novel of World War II*
Back Bay Books, 1992 (1951), 560 pages.

Playboy Willie Keith is unlikely to succeed in the navy, especially after he runs afoul of his first commanding officer on board the minesweeper *Caine*. As officer of the deck, Keith tries to get along with the next captain. But he soon begins to doubt Captain Queeg's ability to lead. When the ship founders in a typhoon, Queeg behaves erratically and Keith relieves him of duty. The novel concludes with Keith's trial for mutiny.

Yourcenar, Marguerite. *Memoirs of Hadrian*
Translated by Grace Frick. Farrar, Straus and Giroux, 2005 (1951), 408 pages.

This fictionalized autobiography of the Roman Emperor Hadrian, written as a valedictory letter to his putative successor, Marcus Aurelius, recounts Hadrian's accomplishments, his hopes for Rome, and his mixed record of establishing tolerance. Yourcenar's novel recaptures 2nd-Century Rome through meticulous research and insight into the character of Hadrian, whose memoir gives coherent shape to the events of his life.

# 5. Short Stories

For those who enjoy reading a work of fiction in one sitting, the short story is the genre of choice. Short stories, with their tight plotting, realism, and frequent surprise endings, yield their rewards in a brief space of time. The 20 books on this list, including two anthologies and 18 collections by individual authors, represent the best in contemporary short story writing.

Use the book descriptions to find short stories of interest. If you find a short story writer you like, look for other short stories or longer works by that author.

## Anthologies

Kenison, Katrina and John Updike, Editors. *The Best American Short Stories of the Century* Houghton Mifflin, 2000, 864 pages.

This collection of 55 stories, culled from editions of *The Best American Short Stories* from 1915 to 1999, includes masters of the short story like Eudora Welty, Faulkner, Hemingway, and Flannery O'Connor, as well as works by lesser-known writers. The stories in this volume, chosen for their realism, lyrical beauty, and significance, reflect American experiences such as immigration, and rural, urban, and suburban living.

Wolff, Tobias, Editor. *The Vintage Book of Contemporary American Short Stories* Vintage, 1994, 576 pages.

Tobias Wolff chose this collection of 33 stories, written in the 1980s and early '90s, for their adherence to the hallmarks of American short story writing: realism and an effective use of narrative voice. This selection includes classic stories by writers Ann Beattie, Raymond Carver, and Andre Dubus, as well as contributions by well-known authors such as Tim O'Brien, Jamaica Kincaid, Joyce Carol Oates, and Amy Tan.

## Short Story Collections

Adams, Alice. *After You've Gone* Random House, 1990 (1986), 224 pages.

Best known for her beautifully wrought stories about middle class American women coping, often on their own, with the challenges of modern life, Alice Adams has written 14 stories in which the traditional themes of love and loss are treated with a cool detachment. Comprised of an accumulation of ordinary details and occasional lyric imagery, Adams' realism brings to life her typical characters and their familiar world.

Beattie, Ann. *Follies: New Stories*
Scribner, 2006 (2005), 320 pages.

Ann Beattie, minimalist chronicler of youth adrift in the 1970s and '80s, captures the same generation in its wayward maturity in nine short stories. Crafted in her trademark spare language, Beattie's stories crystallize moments in the lives of her upscale characters coping with aging parents, struggling children, and tenuous relationships. This collection includes the novella "Flechette Follies," in which a CIA agent goes on a risky mission.

Bennett, Alan. *The Clothes They Stood Up In* and *The Lady in the Van*
Random House, 2002 (1994), 240 pages.

When the Ransomes are divested of all—literally all—of their possessions by a mysterious burglar, the staid couple has the opportunity to start over. Alan Bennett's sympathetic study of a midlife marriage is paired with the comic tale of an acquisitive homeless woman. These contemporary stories, with their irony, character development, and plot twists, stimulate us to reflect on human nature and the meaning of possessions.

Calvino, Italo. *Marcovaldo, or The Seasons in the City*
Harvest Books, 1983 (1963), 128 pages.

Flashes of genius ripple through stories sequenced cyclically according to the seasons and unified by their subject: Marcovaldo, a lowly Italian worker whose rare imagination brings him delight, disapproval, and insight. The tone of these stories is ambiguous, combining equal parts of humor and poignancy. Only Marcovaldo can see a harvest in the city streets, use clotheslines to trap pigeons, and become a human snowman.

Canin, Ethan. *The Palace Thief: Stories*
Random House, 2006 (1994), 224 pages.

In this collection, chosen as one of the best books of 1994 by *Publisher's Weekly*, the author probes intergenerational conflict and the competition and empathy intrinsic to family relationships. Self-awareness comes to a boy struggling to understand his gifted brother, to an accountant tempted by the magic of baseball, to the son of a clueless but well-meaning father, and to an idealistic teacher.

Carver, Raymond. *Where I'm Calling From*
Vintage, 1989, 544 pages.

In this collection of 37 stories, including seven appearing for the first time and the award-winning "Where I'm Calling From," Raymond Carver's blue-collar Americans seek happiness and hope amidst the debris of lost opportunities. Carver's stories of job loss, broken marriages and relationships, and alcohol addiction and recovery feature surprisingly resilient characters vividly portrayed in his terse, graceful style.

Cheever, John. *The Stories of John Cheever*
Vintage, 2000 (1978), 704 pages.

This comprehensive collection by short story writer John Cheever, chronicler of the mores and morals of America's "greatest generation," contains 61 stories, including his masterpieces "The Enormous Radio," "Good-bye, My Brother," and "The Swimmer." Cheever's simple prose gives an elegant formality to these tales of water and light, hard work and failure, and love and loss.

Desai, Anita. *Games at Twilight and Other Stories*
Penguin, 1990 (1978), 144 pages.

Eleven short stories by the author of *Fire on the Mountain* explore the inner lives of children, women, and men, and ordinary people and artists. This collection of stories set in India includes a tale about the magic and the hidden disappointments of childhood, the story of a homesick American who seeks out the hippies of the Indian hills, and the tale of an artist who creates pictures of creatures seen only in his mind's eye.

Maclean, Norman. *A River Runs Through It and Other Stories*
University of Chicago Press, 2001 (1976), 239 pages.

These stories by a retired professor who first wrote fiction at age 70 reflect the author's deep love of nature grounded in his youthful days logging the woods of the western Rockies. The title novella, "A River Runs Through It," is widely recognized as an American classic. The author ponders the limits of human responsibility in this autobiographical tale of foursquare Norman and his gifted, bedeviled brother.

Munro, Alice. *Something I've Been Meaning to Tell You*
Vintage, 2004 (1974), 256 pages.

Canadian Alice Munro is known for short stories set in Huron County, Ontario, focusing on coming-of-age and mature relationships. The degree to which Munro's characters are molded and limited by their small-town environment can be seen in the title story, in which the sudden reappearance of a woman's childhood sweetheart after several years transforms the relationship of the woman and her sister.

Nevai, Lucia. *Normal*
Algonquin Books, 1997, 217 pages.

Normalcy is a touchstone for these stories, but what is normal? Is it Howie and Glenda's chaotic, loving family, or the family of their strict, Afro-Caribbean social worker, "Monsieur Allé?" Nevai poses a similar question in "Thanksgiving with Dorrie and Heck." In "The Talking Woman," a mid-level manager on a raft trip shrinks from contact with a fellow passenger, only to find himself marked by their commonality.

Packer, ZZ. *Drinking Coffee Elsewhere*
Riverhead Trade, 2004 (2003), 288 pages.

With a few sentences ZZ Packer reels you in, involving you in the rude awakenings of her young characters. Their coming of age is a coming to awareness of racism, a social inequality that mediates experience. Packer's African-American characters awaken to reality in moments painful, funny, self-censoring, or full of brash honesty. Her settings, from the Ivy League to the Million Man March, lend tangibility to her vision.

Pritchett, V. S. *A Careless Widow and Other Stories*
Random House, 1989, 172 pages.

V. S. Pritchett, best known for his memoirs and short stories, has written over 40 books. In *A Careless Widow*, he offers six stories in which characters reflect on their lives. In "A Careless Widow," a hairdresser goes on holiday only to meet his talkative neighbor. In "Cocky Olly," the narrator looks back on her childhood friendship with a troubled boy. In "The Image Trade," a photographer captures a writer's image for posterity.

Proulx, Annie. *Fine Just the Way It Is*
Scribner, 2008, 240 pages.

Annie Proulx's crisp prose style and skilled storytelling illuminate these tales of the people of Wyoming from the pioneer days to the Iraq War. The winner of two O. Henry Prizes, Proulx is known for her vivid representation of life in the American West. Proulx is both empathetic and detached in her descriptions of cowboys, ranchers, rodeo riders, and homesteaders whose hardscrabble lives tell the tale of survival in a harsh land.

Sillitoe, Alan. *The Loneliness of the Long-Distance Runner*
Plume, 1993 (1959), 176 pages.

The narrator of the title piece in this book of stories tells a breathtaking tale of survival against the odds. Born into poverty, he has the skill to excel as a runner and the grit to win the big race. While running the race of his life, he comes to see winning in the light of his father's courage and the plight of his working-class peers. This famous story, like the other stories in this volume, brings 1950s Nottingham vividly to life.

Taylor, Peter. *The Old Forest and Other Stories*
Picador, 1995, 368 pages.

The dense texture of Peter Taylor's intimate stories creates the sensation of a world both strange and familiar. The world of these stories, that of the American South, is familiar in its modernity, but retains the strangeness of lingering patrician codes. In "The Old Forest," a young man uncovers a complex social system while searching for a working girl who has mysteriously disappeared. This volume contains 14 gripping stories.

Updike, John. *The Music School*
Knopf, 1966, 272 pages.

John Updike, chronicler of 20th Century middle-class America, conveys the intensity of small, bright moments in these stories of ordinary people experiencing subtle epiphanies. Updike evokes the autumn colors of a weekend football game, the quiet transformation in a couple who donate blood, and the crisis of a man whose child blossoms through music while he craves renewal in the act of taking the Eucharist.

Wolff, Tobias. *The Night in Question*
Vintage, 1997, 224 pages.

In his third short story collection, Tobias Wolff presents 15 well-crafted stories, many of them centered upon a male protagonist in his late teens or early twenties whose awakening allows him to rediscover human connections. Wolff's tales also uncover the slippery nature of truth: in "Mortals," a mistaken obituary has consequences, as does a mistaken death report in "The Other Miller." These tales offer suspense and surprises.

# 6. Poetry

The pleasure of reading poetry has everything to do with its relationship to song. A good poem is one that sings to the truth of human experience—to the nature of our desires, fears, memories, and dreams—in a language that is rich, moving, and endlessly surprising. The anthologies listed here represent many different kinds of poems from a variety of traditions. Choose an anthology that interests you and read away.

## Anthologies

Hass, Robert. *Now and Then: The Poet's Choice Columns, 1997–2000*
Counterpoint, 2008, 320 pages.

During his stint as Poet Laureate of the United States, Robert Hass instituted the Poet's Choice column for the *Washington Post Book World*. The purpose of this weekly column was to introduce readers to the experience of reading great poetry by commenting upon one poem per week. This book includes the pieces Hass wrote for the column between 1997 and 2000. True to Hass's vision for the column, these pieces, written in an accessible and engaging style, offer a rich engagement with poetry for readers and non-readers of poetry alike.

Hass, Robert, Editor. *Essential Haiku*
Ecco, 1995, 329 pages.

This wonderful anthology brings together selections from four Japanese masters of Haiku. The traditional Japanese verse form of Haiku holds a place of honor in the poetic tradition because of its ability to capture in three short lines an entire experience. A typical Haiku poem will sketch some aspect of the natural world in a striking way and will provide some simple comment upon this observation. The effect is to transform our awareness of the natural world and of ourselves.

McClatchy, J. D., Editor. *The Vintage Book of Contemporary American Poetry*
Vintage, 2003, 656 pages.

This anthology brings together a selection of poems written by many of the greatest American poets from the mid-20th Century to the present. Readers who are new to poetry will find this to be a wonderful introduction both to the experience of reading poetry and to the richness and variety of contemporary American poetry.

McClatchy, J. D., Editor. *The Vintage Book of Contemporary World Poetry*
Vintage, 1996, 688 pages.

This anthology includes a representative selection of poems from some of the finest poets writing in the world today. These poems are culled from a broad range of national literatures, including those of Europe, Asia, Africa, the Middle East, and Latin America. While the interested reader will find here an extraordinary diversity of styles and subjects, what these poems have in common are their ability to transcend differences of language and culture in speaking to our shared human condition.

Milosz, Czeslaw, Editor.  *A Book of Luminous Things: An International Anthology of Poetry*
Harvest Books, 1998, 344 pages.

This rich anthology of poetry includes some 300 poems from a broad range of poets writing across the ages.  The poems were selected for their vitality and accessibility, and are usefully categorized by theme (e.g. "Nature," "Travel," "The Moment").  Czeslaw Milosz, a masterful poet in his own right, also comments briefly on many of the poems, helping the reader to further access their meaning and depth.

Pinsky, Robert and Maggie Dietz, Editors.  *An Invitation to Poetry: A New Favorite Poem Project Anthology*
W. W. Norton, 2006 (2004), 308 pages.

This intriguing anthology consists of well-known poems that are introduced by persons coming from a variety of occupations, none of whom are specialists in poetry.  What these persons share, however, is a love of poetry and an interest in sharing this love with others.  The book is accompanied by a delightful DVD that includes videos of many of these persons introducing and reading their chosen poems.  The project is proof positive that poetry is not for an elite audience of readers but for anyone interested in the pleasures of this most ancient verse form.

Ferguson, Margaret, Jon Stallworthy, and Mary Jo Salter, Editors.  *The Norton Anthology of Poetry*
W. W. Norton, Shorter 5th edition, 2005, 1,424 pages.

This substantial poetry anthology includes representative poems by the finest poets in the Western literary tradition, from the Middle Ages to the present.  See the poetry list in Part Two for recommendations and guidance in reading through this anthology.

Rexroth, Kenneth, Translator.  *One Hundred Poems from the Chinese*
New Directions, 1971, 150 pages.

This classic collection of poetry is far more than an introduction to ancient Chinese poetry.  Because of the beauty and accessibility of these poems, it may serve more generally as an introduction to the exquisite pleasures of poetry.  Take, for example, the concluding lines of "Visiting Tsan, Abbot of Ta-Yun": "Tomorrow in the sunlight / I shall walk in the manured fields, / and weep for the yellow dust of the dead."

# 7. Introduction to the Classics

The books listed here represent some of the greatest works in the Western literary tradition. They are also among the most accessible, making them an ideal place to begin for the reader who is new to the classics.

There are a number of good reasons for readings the classics. One reason is because of the unique power they have to inspire, challenge, and transform us due to the compelling stories they tell and their vibrant, original use of language. A second reason is because of the prominence they have in our culture. Our language and role models, our way of thinking about ourselves and the meaning of human existence, our sense of the past and of future possibility—all have been in important ways shaped by the classics. Even a modest familiarity with the classics helps us understand and connect to the culture in which we live. But perhaps the best reason for reading the classics is the sheer delight they give us. They are *fun* to read.

After reading one or several of the works listed here, you will find many equally wonderful works in Part Two of the Booklist.

❖        ❖        ❖

Homer. *The Odyssey* (c. 8th Century BC)
Translated by Stanley Lombardo. Hackett, 2000, 414 pages.

While Homer's epic poem, the *Iliad*, chronicles the events of the Trojan War, this companion piece chronicles the Greek hero Odysseus's efforts to get back home after the Greeks have finally defeated the Trojans. The poem shifts back and forth between Odysseus's various misadventures at sea and the chaos that rules at home as Odysseus's wife and son faithfully wait for his return. Readers new to Greek literature will readily appreciate the brilliant tapestry of scene, incident, character, and language that are the hallmarks of this remarkable work.

Sophocles. *Antigone* (c. 442 BC)
In *The Three Theban Plays*. Translated by Robert Fagles. Penguin Classics, 2000, 430 pages.

The Greek playwright Sophocles (496–406 BC) wrote tragedies notable for their penetrating insight into the complex interplay of fate and choice in determining human action. *Antigone*, one of Sophocles' most intense and thoughtful plays, is at one level about one woman's refusal to compromise her moral integrity and sense of religious duty, even to the point of death. A deeper reading of the play suggests that Antigone's actions are also driven by a sense of despair over the misfortunes that have dogged her family line, including the tragic fate of her father, Oedipus.

Virgil. *The Aeneid* (29–19 BC)
Translated by Robert Fagles. Penguin Classics, 2008, 384 pages.

This epic poem, written nearly 800 years after Homer wrote the *Iliad* and the *Odyssey*, continues Homer's narration of the Trojan War and its aftermath by telling the story of the founding of Roman civilization. The poem chronicles the attempts of the Trojan hero, Aeneas, to found a new city (what is to become Rome) after the destruction of Troy. Like Homer's poems, Virgil's epic is rich in character, language, and incident. It is also deeply symbolic, as Virgil intended for it to be a testament to the glory of Roman civilization.

Ovid. *Tales From Ovid* (c. 8 AD)
Translated by Ted Hughes. Farrar, Straus and Giroux, 1999, 272 pages.

The *Metamorphoses*, written by the Roman poet Ovid (43 BC–17/18 AD), is one of the most popular and influential works of classical literature due to Ovid's highly inventive take on popular Greek myths. His reworkings are chiefly notable for their unorthodox treatment of heroes and gods—a treatment that reflects the skeptical attitude of Roman civilization toward the Greek pantheon. Ted Hughes, a renowned poet in his own right, brings to life some of the most compelling of these myths in this vibrant translation.

Heaney, Seamus, Translator. *Beowulf* (c. 8th–11th Century AD)
W. W. Norton, 2001, 215 pages.

This epic poem, written sometime between the 8th and 11th Centuries AD, is one of the lasting expressions of Anglo-Saxon culture at a time when it was being slowly transformed by Christianity. Set in Scandinavia, although written in England, the poem chronicles the magnificent actions of the great hero Beowulf as he battles a series of evil monsters, including the hellish monster Grendel and Grendel's vicious mother. This translation, by Nobel Prize-winning poet Seamus Heaney, is accessible and absorbing.

Chaucer, Geoffrey. *The Canterbury Tales* (1380–1400)
Translated by Burton Raffel. Modern Library, 2008, 672 pages.

*The Canterbury Tales* is one of the great literary accomplishments of the Middle Ages. The many tales that make up this masterwork are by turns comic, serious, irreverent, and pious, and are uniformly delightful to read. The frame for the tales is provided in the Prologue, where we read how a diverse group of men and women preparing to set off on a pilgrimage decide to relieve the tedium of the journey by holding a contest to see who can tell the best tale. Read especially "The Prologue," "The Knight's Tale," "The Man of Law's Tale," "The Nun's Priest's Tale," "The Pardoner's Tale," "The Clerk's Tale," "The Franklin's Tale," and "The Second Nun's Tale."

Shakespeare, William. *A Midsummer Night's Dream* (1595)
Folger Shakespeare Library. Washington Square Press, 2004, 256 pages.

This comedy serves as an excellent introduction to Shakespearean drama. The play is a delightful stew of comedy, fantasy, and romance, with just the right pinch of dramatic tension thrown in for good measure. At the center of the plot is a mysterious drug that causes the person who unwittingly takes it to fall in love with the first person he or she sees. Needless to say, desire turns topsy-turvy while true-love waits in the wings.

Shakespeare, William. *Henry IV, Part 1* (1597)
Folger Shakespeare Library. Washington Square Press, 1994, 336 pages.

If you are new to Shakespeare, this history play will serve as an ideal introduction. It is among Shakespeare's most popular for a reason: it is a compelling character study filled with humor and drama and driven by Shakespeare's remarkable use of language. The play tells the story of an errant Prince who wiles away his youth in the company of a colorful cast of misfits that includes the grand comic figure of Falstaff. But when rebellion threatens to topple the English crown, Henry is given an opportunity to redeem his bad name.

Marlowe, Christopher. *Dr. Faustus* (1604)
Broadview Press, 2007, 320 pages.

Marlowe's play about the brilliant Dr. Faustus who sells his soul to the devil is one of the highlights of Renaissance drama. Although the legend of Faust was well known throughout Europe, Marlowe invested it with dramatic tension, wit, insight, and macabre humor as Faust frivols away his powers on ephemeral goods. The play takes on a rich complexity, however, when Faust, despite his eventual misery and despair, resists repenting of his hellish bargain. The play's ambiguous ending makes us wonder, even so, if salvation is still his for the taking.

Austen, Jane. *Pride and Prejudice* (1813)
Penguin Classics, 2002, 480 pages.

Artfully constructed and masterfully written, *Pride and Prejudice* is generally regarded as Austen's greatest novel. Level-headed Elizabeth Bennett observes the follies of her four sisters with a mixture of pity and chagrin, increasingly convinced that romance is not for her. Certainly there is no chance of falling in love with the handsome but disdainful Mr. Darcy. But how well do we ever know ourselves, much less others? This engaging and ultimately quite moving novel argues, not very well!

Dickens, Charles. *David Copperfield* (1849–50)
Penguin Classics, 2004, 1,024 pages.

Readers new to Dickens will find *David Copperfield* to be an excellent introduction. In what is considered to be Dickens' most autobiographical novel, David Copperfield narrates the story of his own life from birth into adulthood. It is a bumpy road indeed as David confronts the flaws in the world around him and in his own character. Dickens' trademark weave of wry humor and deep pathos is fully on display here, as is his remarkable use of language.

Dostoevsky, Fyodor. *Crime and Punishment* (1866)
Translated by Richard Pevear and Larissa Volokhonsky. Vintage, 1993, 592 pages.

Dostoevsky's penetrating novel is one of the marvels of 19th-Century literature. The brilliant university student, Raskolnikov, is driven by poverty and philosophical idealism to commit a heinous crime. When the sly detective, Porfiry Petrovich, takes over the investigation, a psychological game of cat and mouse ensues, one that promises either destruction or redemption for Raskolnikov. Notable for its complex engagement with philosophical ideas and its deeply compassionate vision of human existence, this novel is not one to be missed.

Orwell, George. *Nineteen Eighty-Four* (1949)
Plume, 2003, 368 pages.

Orwell's masterpiece of dystopian literature imagines a world in which the government controls every facet of social and political life, from its language and history to the behavior and thoughts of its citizens. Enter Winston Smith, an ordinary citizen whose work rewriting historical documents for the ruling party leads him to question its authority. When an intense, prohibited relationship with a beautiful co-worker seals his disenchantment with the party, Winston attempts to discover whether there is any hope of avoiding the lethal gaze of Big Brother.

Malamud, Bernard. *The Assistant* (1957)
Farrar, Straus and Giroux, 2003, 264 pages.

As this thoughtful and challenging novel opens, Morris Bober, a Jewish immigrant and small store owner, is down on his luck. Salvation comes in the unlikely form of Frank Alpine, an enigmatic drifter who helps to revive Morris' struggling business. Complications ensue, however, when Frank becomes infatuated with Morris' beautiful daughter, Helen. A novel of tremendous spiritual depth and human insight, *The Assistant* is one of the masterpieces of 20th-Century American literature.

O'Connor, Flannery. *The Complete Stories* (1971)
Farrar, Straus and Giroux, 1971, 555 pages.

Flannery O'Connor is one of the most original and visionary writers in American literature. Her work powerfully provokes the reader into considering the place and purpose of faith in the modern world, often through her characters' transformative experience of violence. All 31 of O'Connor's short stories collected here demonstrate her extraordinary use of language in crafting characters who are shocked out of their everyday existence into a profound engagement with meaning and truth. Read especially "A Good Man Is Hard To Find," "The Displaced Person," "Everything That Rises Must Converge," and "Revelation."

# Contemporary Nonfiction

Do you enjoy expanding your knowledge of the real world?  Nonfiction is informative writing that describes and interprets reality.  If you have an appetite for learning – if you enjoy books that pique your curiosity and broaden your horizons – you'll find compelling reading on the nonfiction list.  This part of the booklist includes books, essays, and journals.  Some of the sections are particularly exciting and expose you to new and fascinating experiences and ideas, like the sections on Travel and Adventure, the Arts, Games and Sports, and Science.  Others offer a penetrating look at human experience and social interaction, like Psychology, Philosophy and Religion, Politics, and Social Commentary.  In all these sections, the books are lively, accessible, and exceptionally well-written.

This part of the booklist offers a rich selection of contemporary nonfiction, as well as a starter list of history books.  The Nonfiction list is divided into the following 13 sections:

1. **Travel and Adventure:**  Travel and the exploration of the natural world.

2. **Psychology:**  Clinical Psychology, Psychiatry, and Neuroscience.

3. **Business, Economics, and Personal Finance:**  Business management, the economy, and money-management.

4. **Politics, Government, and International Relations:**  U.S. politics, government institutions, and foreign policy.

5. **Social Commentary:**  Commentary on American society and global trends from a wide array of political perspectives.

6. **The Arts:**  Music and the visual arts.

7. **Games and Sports:**  American sports, poker, chess, and fishing.

8. **Memoir:**  Lives of eminent people, witnesses of history, and self-reflective individuals.

9. **Philosophy and Religion:**  Books of reasoned inquiry and books on the experience of faith.

10. **Science:**  Physical Science and Life Science.

11. **Essays:**  Short prose writings on a range of topics.

12. **Introduction to History:**  We've chosen 11 of the best history books from Part Two of the booklist to create a history starter list.  History is a fascinating record of humanity's past.  The history books on this list are particularly accessible, well-written introductions to the ancient, medieval, and modern eras.  If these books interest you, continue on by reading history books from Part Two of the booklist.

13. **Journals:**  Magazines on politics, current events, culture, science, social science, and technology.

There are a few different ways you can use this list:

1. Find books of personal interest.  The nonfiction list contains almost 250 books carefully selected for interest, accessibility, and clarity of writing.  Just read through the annotations, find a book of personal interest, and read.  Then find another book of interest.

2. Find a section of interest. Choose a section of the booklist that looks interesting, and read a number of books in that section.

3. Sometimes when using the first approach, you'll find you want to pursue a topic in greater depth after you've been introduced to it. In that case, go from the first approach to the second. And after you've satisfied your curiosity on a particular topic, you may decide to read about another topic, or you may decide to go back to the first approach.

# 1. Travel and Adventure

Travel and adventure books make for exciting reading. Travel writers brave culture shock and physical danger so that readers can enjoy authentic tales from far-off lands. Listed here are 20 books telling of unprecedented journeys, transformative experiences, and dramatic encounters with nature. These writers share their enthusiasm and knowledge about foreign cultures and the natural world.

❖     ❖     ❖

Berendt, John. *The City of Falling Angels*
Penguin, 2005, 414 pages.

In early 1996, Archimede Seguso saw the Venice opera house burn from the window of his Venetian glassworks. While experts debate its cause, an American journalist links the fire to stories of Venice's movers and shakers. Debunking official posturing and claims of civic virtue, Berendt exposes the rivalries and political clashes revealed by the fire.

Fredston, Jill A. *Snowstruck: In the Grip of Avalanches*
Harcourt, 2005, 362 pages.

Jill Fredston was 24 and held a degree in polar studies when she was named director of the Alaska Avalanche Forecast Center. The problem? She knew nothing about avalanches. A quick study, she learned from the experts. Decades later, she recounts tales of predicting avalanches, teaching potential victims, and directing rescue efforts.

Goldhill, Simon. *Jerusalem: City of Longing*
Belknap Press, 2008, 368 pages.

Even cynic Mark Twain wrote longingly of Jerusalem's Church of the Holy Sepulchre. With monuments sacred to three world faiths, Jerusalem is a city of longing as well as a place of strife. Author Simon Goldhill describes Jerusalem's Christian, Jewish, and Muslim holy sites, the Old City, and Jerusalem's recent historical development.

Gopnik, Adam. *Paris to the Moon*
Random House, 2001 (2000), 368 pages.

This collection of 23 essays grew from American journalist Gopnik's five-year sojourn in Paris with his wife and son. Gopnik finds humor in Parisian society while praising the city as the epitome of commonplace civilization. A keen observer of the French, Gopnik ultimately learns about being American by comparing French and American ways.

Iyer, Pico. *The Lady and the Monk: Four Seasons in Kyoto*
Vintage, 1992 (1991), 352 pages.

Pico Iyer goes to Kyoto, Japan to study Zen Buddhism. He finds the former imperial capital to be a center of both Buddhist tradition and Japan's female arts. Soon Iyer's developing friendship with housewife Sachiko forms a counterpoint to his life in a Kyoto monastery. Ultimately, he sees Japan as much through Sachiko's eyes as through the eyes of a monk.

Kapuscinski, Ryszard. *The Shadow of the Sun*
Vintage, 2002 (2001), 325 pages.

These essays covering Africa from 1957 to the 1990s combine vivid accounts of daily life with an in-depth understanding of Africa's post-colonial history. Based on four decades of reporting in Africa, Kapuscinski's essays describe the euphoria of independence, interethnic wars, the rise of the warlords, and Africa's uneasy relationship with Europe.

Krakauer, Jon. *Into Thin Air: A Personal Account of the Mt. Everest Disaster*
Anchor Books, 1999 (1997), 368 pages.

Through a fog of conflicting emotions, mountaineer Krakauer tries to make sense of the Everest disaster in which four of his five teammates perished after reaching the top. The resulting post mortem of the1996 expedition offers a dispassionate analysis of mistakes that doomed the climb, while paying tribute to the courageous spirit of the climbers.

Leigh Fermor, Patrick, and Jan Morris. *A Time of Gifts: On Foot to Constantinople: From the Hook of Holland to the Middle Danube*
NYRB Classics, 2005 (1977), 344 pages.

In 1933, a young man made an extraordinary journey on foot from Holland to Constantinople. In *A Time of Gifts*, Leigh Fermor travels as far as Hungary through a Europe that will be forever changed by war. Amidst the rise of National Socialism in Germany, he encounters intriguing strangers and depends on kind hosts along the way.

Levenstein, Harvey. *A Seductive Journey: American Tourists in France from Jefferson to the Jazz Age*
The University of Chicago Press, 1998, 378 pages.

Americans have visited France for different reasons at different times in their national history. Levenstein's fascinating account of American tourists in France describes the American people who traveled to France in each succeeding generation, why they went abroad, what they found when they arrived, and how the experience changed them.

Matthiessen, Peter. *Snow Leopard*
Penguin Classics, 2008 (1978), 368 pages.

Considered to be a classic of nature writing, Matthiessen writes about his journey into the heart of the Himalayas in search of the elusive snow leopard. The drama of this search is complemented by wonderful passages describing the beauty of the landscape. The journey also becomes a rich spiritual odyssey as Matthiessen, a practicing Zen Buddhist, ponders questions of human existence and the mysteries of the created world.

Mayes, Frances. *Under the Tuscan Sun*
Broadway Books, 2003 (1996), 336 pages.

Mayes is a poet, professor, gourmet cook, and food and travel writer. In this memoir she tells the story of her buying and restoring an abandoned villa in Tuscany, where she found new life after a painful divorce, and of returning to live there part of every year with her new husband. The story beautifully depicts the life, culture, and countryside of rural Italy for an American audience. For those enamored with Italian cuisine, the narrative includes a number of the author's recipes.

Mayle, Peter. *A Year in Provence*
Vintage, 1991 (1989), 207 pages.

After years of vacationing in the South of France, the Mayles take the plunge and move to rural Provence. Peter Mayle's month-by-month journal of their first year recounts the British couple's delight in French cuisine, their frustrations with French bureaucracy, and their gradual acquaintance with the neighbors and townspeople who define Provence.

Mehta, Suketu. *Maximum City: Bombay Lost and Found*
Vintage, 2005, 560 pages.

Bombay, the planet's most populous city, has been marked by a cataclysmic event: the Muslim-Hindu riots and bombings of 1993. Mehta describes the impact of the riots on this city of power and pleasure, tracing Hindu-Muslim tensions, police treatment of Muslims, and the growth of Hindu and Muslim gangs in the Bombay underworld.

Meier, Andrew. *Black Earth: A Journey Through Russia After the Fall*
W. W. Norton, 2005 (2003), 516 pages.

From 1996 to 2001, Meier covered Russia and the former Soviet states for *Time* magazine. In *Black Earth*, he travels the country, describing the people and politics of post-Soviet Russia in metro areas and outlying regions. His first-hand experience allows him to predict whether Russia will achieve democratic reform or succumb to tyranny.

Milton, Giles. *Nathaniel's Nutmeg: Or, the True and Incredible Adventures of the Spice Trader Who Changed the Course of History*
Penguin, 2000 (1999), 400 pages.

In 1616, Nathaniel Courthope sailed from England to Run, the most valuable of the Spice Islands, where he confronted the Dutch navy. The ensuing four-year conflict between the British and the Dutch East India Company over Run's nutmeg crop forced hardship upon Nathaniel and his crew as they fought to defend the most dangerous of the Banda Islands.

Pamuk, Orhan. *Istanbul: Memories and the City*
Translated from the Turkish by Maureen Freely. Vintage, 2004 (2003), 384 pages.

In *Istanbul*, Nobel Prize winner Pamuk describes a city of historical significance as he experienced it from childhood on. Istanbul may evoke the melancholy of lost empire, but its river, the Bosphorus, sings of pleasure and happiness. Pamuk's account of family life in Istanbul is accompanied by historical vignettes and humorous advice on city living.

Parks, Tim. *Italian Neighbors*
Grove, 2003 (1992), 280 pages.

Many an Englishman has sought an alternative lifestyle in the lands of the Mediterranean, and Tim Parks is no exception. *Italian Neighbors* is Parks' account of ten years of living in a condominium in Verona with his Italian wife. A keen observer of Italian idiosyncrasies and foibles, Parks gradually becomes enmeshed in the communal life of Verona.

Powell, Dilys. *An Affair of the Heart*
Penguin, 1957, 304 pages.

From 1931 to 1936, Dilys Powell spent part of each year in Greece, where she attended excavations with her archeologist husband. In *An Affair of the Heart*, she describes three visits to Greece following her husband's death. Her visits in 1945, 1953, and 1954 encompass the post-war occupation, the civil war, and the beginning of national recovery.

Stevenson, Helen. *Instructions for Visitors: Life and Love in a French Town*
Washington Square Press, 2002 (2000), 256 pages.

Helen Stevenson's story of life in a small town in southwestern France begins as a guide for visitors to the village and morphs into an intimate portrait of village life. The author delivers lyrical descriptions of the natural surroundings, witty character sketches of the villagers, and a suspenseful story about her affair with a local Frenchman.

Theroux, Paul. *Dark Star Safari: Overland from Cairo to Capetown*
Mariner, 2004 (2003), 496 pages.

Fabled traveler Theroux embarks on a unique safari, crossing the African continent from Egypt to South Africa by train, bus, truck, and canoe. Forty years ago, Theroux served with the Peace Corps in Malawi. He now returns to see what has changed. Theroux's journey reveals a fascinating continent whose diverse nations face many challenges.

# 2. Psychology

Psychology, literally "the study of the soul," is the science of mind and behavior. Listed here are 17 psychology books by authors with expertise in fields as diverse as clinical psychology, psychiatry, and neuroscience. These books offer enlightening explorations of human emotion, cognition, and behavior.

❖     ❖     ❖

Apter, Terri E. *You Don't Really Know Me: Why Mothers and Daughters Fight and How Both Can Win*
W. W. Norton, 2005 (2004), 280 pages.

Why do mothers and their teenage daughters fight? Psychologist Terri Apter examines the roots of mother-teenage daughter conflict and offers guidelines for conflict resolution. Apter's typology of mother-daughter arguments is illuminated by her understanding of teen identity issues and how these are expressed through conflict.

Ariely, Dan. *Predictably Irrational: The Hidden Forces that Shape Our Decisions*
HarperCollins, 2008, 304 pages.

Dan Ariely, professor of Behavioral Economics, has a mission: he wants you to rethink the way you make decisions. Ariely demonstrates the irrational factors that cause people to miss the mark when evaluating choices, and he shows how to overcome the irrational biases that complicate decision-making.

Bettleheim, Bruno. *The Uses of Enchantment: The Meaning and Importance of Fairy Tales*
Vintage, 1977 (1975), 323 pages.

Children's therapist Bruno Bettleheim shows how fairy tales help children understand life's meaning in developmentally appropriate ways. With his deft interpretations of fairy tales from "Hansel and Gretel" to "Snow White," Bettleheim encourages parents to read stories to their children that mirror the children's emotional lives.

Fromm, Erich. *The Art of Loving*
Harper Perennial, 2006, 176 pages.

In this brief but deeply insightful text, Fromm argues that love is not an emotion or a sentiment, but rather an artful form of action that involves courage, self-knowledge, responsibility, and maturity. In an age of ephemeral pop psychology, Fromm also reminds the reader that love, like anything truly worth having, requires nothing less than the commitment of the whole self and persuades the reader of the crucial value of this effort.

Goleman, Daniel. *Emotional Intelligence: Why it Can Matter More Than IQ*
Bantam, 2005 (1996), 384 pages.

While most people equate intelligence with IQ, Goleman persuasively argues in this influential book that success and happiness depend even more upon "emotional intelligence." Goleman defines emotional intelligence as, among other things, the ability to cooperate with others, to demonstrate empathy and care, and to exercise self-discipline. Providing scientific evidence as well as practical insight, you won't think of the "smarts" in the same way after reading this.

Maslow, Abraham. *Toward a Psychology of Being*
Wiley, 1998 (1968), 320 pages.

Maslow is most well-known for visualizing the hierarchy of human needs as a pyramid with self-actualization at the top. In *Toward a Psychology of Being*, his most influential work, he elaborates in clear, concise, and eloquent language upon this hierarchy, arguing that human beings are driven by their very nature to achieve happiness and fulfillment. Written as much for the general reader as for the specialist, this is a thoughtful and inspiring work.

May, Rollo. *Love and Will*
W. W. Norton, 2007 (1969), 352 pages.

In describing modern man's experience, May explores love as sex drive, relationship, and care, and traces manifestations of will from Victorian "will power," to permissiveness, to the integration of will with love. May shows how man can move beyond being controlled by impersonal drives to self-understanding and the experience of the transpersonal.

Montagu, Ashley. *On Being Human*
Hawthorne Books, 1966 (1950), 128 pages.

Montagu was a renowned 20th-Century anthropologist, humanist, and social critic who was among the first to question the validity of race as a biological concept. A prolific author of over 50 books, he sought to integrate and popularize the findings of the human sciences in order to contribute to the betterment of human society. In his later years he focused on the significance of human love as the key ingredient. This brief work captures his essential humanistic ideas.

Morris, Desmond. *The Naked Ape: A Zoologist's Study of the Human Animal*
Delta, 1999 (1967), 256 pages.

The author, a zoologist and ethologist, became known world-wide when this controversial book was first published. It is an unabashed look at the animal nature of the human species. Morris points out our similarity with primates and argues that human behavior largely evolved to meet the challenges of prehistoric hunter-gatherers. This book, which opened the field of evolutionary anthropology, is a thought-provoking reminder that humans are part of the animal kingdom.

Piaget, Jean. *The Psychology of the Child*
Basic Books, 2000 (1962), 192 pages.

Today, Jean Piaget's theory of the stages in a child's cognitive development is basic to the field of psychology. In this synthesis of his key ideas, Piaget explains how a child's perceptions, emotions, language, and thinking change from infancy through adolescence. This book offers a comprehensive introduction to the work of Piaget.

Ramachandran, V. S. and Sandra Blakeslee. *Phantoms in the Brain: Probing the Mysteries of the Human Mind*
Harper Perennial, 1999, 352 pages.

This provocative and entertaining book by one of the world's foremost brain researchers explains the advances made in neurology in the last 30 years. It is based on the author's clinical work with patients possessing strange neurological disorders (such as amputees feeling their phantom limbs). Like a detective, he explores the mysteries of the human mind and sheds light on the very nature of consciousness and the self. The very readable text is aided by helpful illustrations.

Rogers, Carl. *On Becoming a Person: A Therapist's View of Psychotherapy*
Mariner Books, 1995 (1961), 448 pages.

After having spent 30 years developing his humanistic vision of the human person, Rogers finally wrote its quintessential expression. The result, *On Becoming a Person*, is as fresh and inspiring today as when it was first written. Central to Rogers' vision of the human person is his belief that happiness is best achieved through immersing oneself completely and courageously in life, and by allowing oneself to fully develop according to one's unique talents and abilities.

Sacks, Oliver. *The Man Who Mistook his Wife for a Hat*
Touchstone, 1998 (1970), 256 pages.

Neurologist Oliver Sacks presents case histories with a difference, telling as much about his patients' lives as about their diseases. Focusing on the personhood of the patient, he vividly brings to life the ways in which ill people inhabit the world, illuminating everything from their idiosyncratic behavior to episodes of visionary experience.

Tannen, Deborah. *You Just Don't Understand: Women and Men in Conversation*
Harper, 2001 (1990), 352 pages.

Linguist Deborah Tannen uses the analysis of everyday speech patterns to explore psychological differences between women and men. Whether or not you agree with her conclusions about the differences between men's and women's speaking styles, you will find her sample conversations fascinating and her interpretations thought-provoking.

Winnicott, D. W.  *The Child, the Family, and the Outside World*
Perseus, 1992 (1957), 256 pages.

A child psychiatrist talks in plain English about child development, normalcy, creativity, and play. Winnicott's rare gift for describing natural adaptation by parent and child and their mutual learning puts him firmly in the parent's, and child's, corner.  Rather than advice, Winnicott offers a sensitive, intelligent appreciation of childhood and family life.

Yalom, Irvin D.  *Momma and the Meaning of Life: Tales of Psychotherapy*
Harper Perennial, 2000 (1999), 272 pages.

A psychiatrist sees his deceased mother in a dream in which he's a child facing his fears who waves and asks, "How'd I do, Momma?"  Wondering why as an adult he is still asking that question, he writes this tribute to his mother, who couldn't read.  In his therapy sessions with patients, Yalom explores key familial relationships and the meaning of life.

# 3. Business, Economics, and Personal Finance

The word "economics" derives from a Greek word meaning "household management." Whether you want to know about business management, learn about the economy, or put your own financial house in order, these books will inform you. The 25 books listed here include eight business books, 12 economics books, and five books on personal finance, all of them readable.

## Business

Bing, Stanley. *Rome, Inc.: The Rise and Fall of the First Multinational Corporation*
W. W. Norton, 2007 (2006), 224 pages.

*Fortune* columnist Stanley Bing presents Roman history as a template for modern corporate culture. The author's extended analogy between Rome and the business world is satire with the purpose of instruction. Bing analyzes Rome's success in the light of Roman leadership styles and corporate culture, offering practical lessons from history.

Buchholz, Todd. *New Ideas from Dead CEOs: Lasting Lessons from the Corner Office*
Collins, 2007, 320 pages.

Former Harvard teacher, hedge fund manager, and Broadway producer Buchholz offers lessons from innovative CEOs in this companion to *New Ideas from Dead Economists*. Buchholz profiles A. P. Giannini of Bank of America, Estee Lauder, Walt Disney, and others in this entertaining and informative book of exemplary lives in business.

Collins, Jim. *Good to Great: Why Some Companies Make the Leap . . . and Others Don't*
Collins Business, 2001, 300 pages.

Jim Collins put his management think tank to work researching over a thousand companies in search of a few that made the leap from good to great. The various good to great companies featured have in common a culture of sustained discipline based on purposeful leadership and a unique product or service.

Drucker, Peter. *The Effective Executive: The Definitive Guide to Getting the Right Things Done*
Collins Business, 2006 (1967), 208 pages.

Consultant Peter Drucker offers business leaders five steps to more effective management. Using examples from history and from the corporate world, Drucker illuminates five key skill sets of business managers: time management, awareness of what each employee contributes, mobilizing strengths, prioritizing, and decision-making.

Leavitt, Harold J. and Homa Bahrami. *Managerial Psychology: Managing Behavior in Organizations*
University of Chicago Press, 1989 (1958), 364 pages.

Now in its fifth edition, *Managerial Psychology* examines business psychology from the point of view of the individual, two-person relationships, and small groups, and explores leadership issues, whole organizations, and relationships between organizations. This edition includes a new section highlighting managerial skills.

Novak, Michael. *Business as a Calling: Work and the Examined Life*
Free Press, 1996, 256 pages.

This book explores business not just as a career but also as a vocation from a religious point of view. The author is a distinguished Catholic theologian, journalist, and diplomat, who is a strong advocate of "enlightened capitalism." He shows how business enterprises promote the common good through the virtues of cooperation, courage, creativity, honesty, industry, innovation, and practicality. Written in the spirit of vocational counseling, the book is inspiring and instructive.

Peter, Laurence J. and Raymond Hull. *The Peter Principle: Why Things Always Go Wrong*
Collins Business, 2009 (1969), 208 pages.

Educator Laurence Peter became famous on publication of *The Peter Principle*, in which he argues that in hierarchical organizations, "every employee rises to his level of incompetence." This groundbreaking study in organizational behavior examines human competence and incompetence in a humorous, insightful way.

Seidman, Dov. *How: Why How We Do Anything Means Everything…in Business (and in Life)*
Wiley, 2007, 352 pages.

How we do it matters as much as what we do, argues the author of this book on business ethics. Dov Seidman, CEO of business advisory firm LRN, shows businesses how to shape an ethical culture and outperform competitors in the marketplace. Seidman identifies five keys: how we know, behave, relate, and recognize and pursue goals.

## Economics

Bonner, William and Addison Wiggin. *Financial Reckoning Day: Surviving the Soft Depression of the 21st Century*
Wiley, 2004 (2003), 306 pages.

*Financial Reckoning Day* ponders history's lesson that saving leads to prosperity while excess spending leads to collapse, and looks at the handwriting on the wall for the U.S. economy. Contrarian Bonner explains how high-borrowing consumerism leveraged the U.S. economy and what to expect from the "soft, slow depression" in the decade ahead.

Collier, Paul. *The Bottom Billion: Why the Poorest Countries are Failing and What Can Be Done About It*
Oxford University Press, 2008 (2007), 224 pages.

Why do impoverished countries fail to develop economically, despite international aid? It is because of the various traps they fall into (e.g., civil war, overdependence on natural resources, bad governance). The author analyzes these traps and advocates focusing economic assistance on those 50+ countries on the bottom, where the need is greatest. This illuminating book offers practical policies for fighting poverty in an era of international conflict and globalization.

Friedman, David D. *Hidden Order: The Economics of Everyday Life*
Collins Business, 1997 (1996), 352 pages.

David Friedman's accessible primer avoids statistics and jargon, using everyday examples to guide the reader through micro and macroeconomics. Starting from the premise that rationality best predicts behavior, Friedman uses economics to explain traffic and muggings as well as such standard topics as stocks, subsidies, and trade.

Friedman, Milton and Rose. *Free to Choose: A Personal Statement*
Harvest Books, 1990 (1980), 360 pages.

A monetarist and supporter of the free-market, Friedman was a celebrated Nobel laureate and leading 20th-Century economist. This popular restatement of his policy views, written with his wife, explains how freedom and prosperity are eroded by federal social programs and interventionist government regulations. This is a classic statement of laissez-faire economics and the workings of free-market capitalism.

Galbraith, John Kenneth. *The Essential Galbraith*
Mariner Books, 2001, 400 pages.

One of the leading economists of the 20th Century, Galbraith was a prolific author who wrote bestsellers in the 1950s and 1960s. His progressive, Keynesian approach to economics greatly influenced the "war on poverty" in the Kennedy and Johnson administrations. This anthology contains selections from his most important works and includes new introductions that place his writings in their historical context.

Gilder, George. *Wealth and Poverty*
ICS Press, 1993 (1980), 320 pages.

A strong critic of New Deal liberalism and government welfare programs, Gilder made a strong practical and moral case for what became known as supply-side economics during the early Reagan administration. In this bestseller he argued that only unfettered entrepreneurship can overcome poverty and increase economic prosperity. This reprint edition includes a new introduction by the author.

Greenspan, Alan. *The Age of Turbulence: Adventures in a New World*
Penguin, 2008 (2007), 576 pages.

From the vantage point of his 18 years as chairman of the Federal Reserve, Greenspan looks at challenges posed by the new global economy. His book includes chapters on his service as Fed chairman under four presidents and on topics in economics. He is uniquely able to offer economic analysis, a first-hand account of presidential politics, and intriguing predictions about the future.

Krugman, Paul. *The Conscience of a Liberal*
W. W. Norton, 2007, 352 pages.

The author, a professor of economics at Princeton, won the 2009 Nobel Prize in Economics for his analysis of trade patterns. Readers of Krugman's column in the *New York Times* will recognize his central thesis concerning income inequality. Krugman argues that the recent rise in income inequality threatens American prosperity.

Mackay, Charles. *Extraordinary Popular Delusions and the Madness of Crowds*
Dover, 2003 (1841), 112 pages.

In this wry study of economic behavior, Charles Mackay surveys classic instances of collective folly. Before the housing bubble and the dot-com bubble, similar patterns of irrational investing appeared in the tulipomania that swept Europe in 1624, in John Law's Mississippi scheme of 1719-1720, and in the South Sea Bubble of the early 1700s.

Soros, George. *The New Paradigm for the Financial Markets: The Credit Crash of 2008 and What it Means*
Public Affairs, 2008, 238 pages.

Storied investor George Soros argues that an understanding of supply and demand offers only a rudimentary knowledge of what drives financial markets. According to Soros' new paradigm, the biases of individuals engaged in market activity can change the fundamentals of the economy, sometimes leading to disequilibrium. In his analysis of the current financial crisis, Soros addresses the recession, price bubbles, and challenges to the dominance of U.S. economic power.

Wheelan, Charles. *Naked Economics: Undressing the Dismal Science*
W. W. Norton, 2003, 260 pages.

This absorbing, witty, and clearly written book introduces basic economic principles to people with little knowledge of economics. The author explains the nuts and bolts of the global free market system without depending on inscrutable concepts, diagrams, equations, or any math. This accessible book makes the "dismal science" fun and interesting, and thus is a good place to begin to understand the "big picture" as well as the everyday economic issues that affect us all.

Yunus, Muhammad.  *Banker to the Poor: Micro-Lending and the Battle Against World Poverty*
Public Affairs, 2003, 296 pages.

In 1976, Nobel Peace Prize winner Muhammad Yunus applied the concept of micro-lending—making small loans to the poor—by founding Bangladesh's Grameen Bank, today a $2.5 billion enterprise.  In *Banker to the Poor*, Yunus describes how he improved imports and exports in Bangladesh by loaning to bamboo furniture-makers whose profits previously went to moneylenders.

## Personal Finance

Bogle, John C.  *Common Sense on Mutual Funds: New Imperatives for the Intelligent Investor*
Wiley, 2000 (1999), 496 pages.

John C. Bogle, founder and CEO of Vanguard, the world's largest no-load mutual fund group, offers a primer on understanding the capital markets along with sound advice on investing.  In addition, Bogle cautions: "Buyer, beware!" in his examination of the conflict of interest between buyer and seller in today's investment management industry.

Gibson, Roger C.  *Asset Allocation: Balancing Financial Risk*
McGraw-Hill, 2008 (1990), 317 pages.

Now in its fourth edition, Gibson's guide to portfolio management helps the investor design a portfolio that sustains its performance in bull and bear markets.  Gibson explains how and why asset allocation works, highlighting risk assessment, psychological barriers to wise investing, the dangers of market timing, and multiple-asset-class investing.

Kiyosaki, Robert T. and Sharon L. Lechter.  *Rich Dad, Poor Dad: What the Rich Teach Their Kids About Money—That the Poor and Middle Class Do Not!*
Business Plus, 2000 (1997), 207 pages.

Richard Kiyosaki's *Rich Dad, Poor Dad* is not so much a guide to the specifics of investing as an inspirational account of two "dads," and their contrasting views on life and work.  Kiyosaki advises investors to achieve financial literacy and autonomy by, for example, learning how to form corporations.  Kiyosaki's book abounds with life lessons.

Malkiel, Burton G.  *A Random Walk Down Wall Street: The Time-Tested Strategy for Successful Investing*
W. W. Norton, 2007 (1973), 416 pages.

Now in its seventh printing, Burton Malkiel's classic on the stock market has been updated to include 21st-Century investment topics such as Roth IRAs and equity REITs.  Since the market eventually corrects bubbles, Malkiel critiques investment strategies that aim to outperform the market, advocating investment in a broad range of index funds.

Orman, Suze.  *Women & Money: Owning the Power to Control Your Destiny*
Spiegel & Grau, 2007, 272 pages.

Suze Orman promotes financial literacy in this commonsense tutorial on everything from balancing a checkbook to managing investments and long-term financial planning.  While her narrative is geared to women seeking financial independence, her comprehensive advice is equally relevant to men who would like to maximize their earnings through investment.

# 4. Politics, Government, and International Relations

"Politics" comes from the Greek word "polis," meaning the city or the state. These books on politics and government offer a penetrating examination of the U.S. presidency, the courts, the military, and intelligence and foreign policy conundrums from the Cold War to the present. Listed here are 13 readable books covering topics from political theory to the nuts-and-bolts workings of democracy.

❖　　　　❖　　　　❖

Bernstein, Carl and Bob Woodward. *All the President's Men*
Pocket, 2005 (1974), 480 pages.

President Nixon's resignation was the ultimate act in a chain of events that included media coverage linking the President's re-election campaign to the burglary of the Democratic National Committee headquarters. *Washington Post* reporters Woodward and Bernstein recount the Watergate break-in, the cover-up, and the ensuing scandal.

Bowden, Mark. *Black Hawk Down: A Story of Modern War*
Signet, 2001 (1999), 496 pages.

Mark Bowden's heart-thumping nonfiction novel—a blow-by-blow account of the 1993 Battle of Mogadishu—is a modern war classic. Bowden uses interviews, army reports, and radio transcripts to recreate the raid into an African city where U.S. soldiers were surrounded by armed Somali militia and fought in close combat to achieve their mission.

Burnett, D. Graham. *Trying Leviathan: The Nineteenth-Century New York Court Case That Put the Whale on Trial and Challenged the Order of Nature*
Princeton University Press, 2007, 304 pages.

Is whale oil fish oil? Is a whale a fish? Historian Graham Burnett shows how the 1818 case of Maurice v. Judd hinged on the answers to these questions. Burnett offers insight into 19th-Century science in his analysis of the trial that pitted Linnaeus' 1758 classification system against popular understanding of taxonomy based on Genesis.

Crile, George. *Charlie Wilson's War: The Extraordinary Story of How the Wildest Man in Congress and a Rogue CIA Agent Changed the History of Our Times*
Grove Press, 2007 (2003), 560 pages.

Before 9/11, the U.S. spent billions arming and training Afghan tribesmen in their war against the Soviet Union. *Charlie Wilson's War* tells how a Texas congressman and a CIA agent masterminded the biggest secret war in history. Author Crile describes the CIA's victory in Afghanistan and the unintended consequences of waging a secret war.

Diamond, Larry. *The Spirit of Democracy: The Struggle to Build Free Societies Throughout the World*
Times Books, 2008, 464 pages.

Larry Diamond is bullish on democracy. Compared to 1974, when a quarter of all nations were democracies, today three-fifths of the world's states are democratic. Diamond gives the end of the Cold War partial credit for the trend, but argues the greater significance of the commitment of citizens in establishing democracies worldwide.

Huntington, Samuel P. *The Clash of Civilizations and the Remaking of World Order*
Simon & Schuster, 1998 (1996), 368 pages.

In this challenging but incisive work, the author presents a provocative analysis of the international political scene after the fall of communism. Focusing not on states or superpowers but on a few major cultures as the primary players, he argues that post-Cold War conflicts will be driven by resurgent religious faith and cultural identity more than ideology. Considered a prescient book after 9/11, it proclaimed the challenge of Islam to the West before it was popular.

Kagan, Robert. *The Return of History and the End of Dreams*
Knopf, 2008, 128 pages.

This is a sobering essay on the looming international conflicts that America will face in the years ahead. Hopes for a peaceful international order at the end of the Cold War have been dashed. A growing China, a resurgent Russia, a restless India, a turbulent Middle East, and a competitive Europe all make for global strife in a world of limited resources. With his vast knowledge of geopolitics, Kagan weighs in on the trouble ahead and how America should meet the challenge.

Lewis, Anthony. *Gideon's Trumpet*
Vintage, 1989 (1964), 288 pages.

In 1962, Florida prisoner Clarence Gideon wrote to the U.S. Supreme Court claiming that the Constitution entitled him to legal representation at trial. In describing his case, Lewis points to the uniqueness of the Supreme Court, an institution that decides social questions like whether the state must hire a lawyer for a poor man accused of a felony.

Lucas, Edward. *The New Cold War: Putin's Russia and the Threat to the West*
Macmillan, 2008, 272 pages.

As Moscow bureau chief for *The Economist*, Lucas witnessed Putin's rise to power after the fall of the Iron Curtain. Here Lucas describes the sweep of Putin's power and Russia's threat to the West in the form of energy dominance, "pipeline politics," and aggressive intentions towards its Eastern European neighbors.

Meyer, Sir Christopher.  *DC Confidential: The Controversial Memoirs of Britain's Ambassador to the U.S. at the Time of 9/11 and the Iraq War*
Phoenix, 2006 (2005), 344 pages.

In these recollections, Sir Christopher Meyer, Britain's ambassador to Washington from 1997 to 2003 and a supporter of the Iraq War, indicts the Blair administration for its neglect of Foreign Office warnings that Washington's plans for the invasion and administration of Iraq were defective.

Murray, Craig.  *Dirty Diplomacy: The Rough-and-Tumble Adventures of a Scotch-Drinking, Skirt-Chasing, Dictator-Busting and Thoroughly Unrepentant Ambassador Stuck on the Frontline of the War Against Terror*
Scribner, 2007 (2006), 384 pages.

Made British Ambassador to Uzbekistan at 43, Craig Murray saw his brilliant career threatened by his opposition to the Uzbek government's treatment of political dissidents.  Recognizing that U.S.-U.K. alliances with such countries compromised the War on Terror, Murray became a champion of human rights in Central Asia.

Toobin, Jeffrey.  *The Nine: Inside the Secret World of the Supreme Court*
Anchor, 2008 (2007), 480 pages.

Jeffrey Toobin, senior legal analyst for CNN, describes conflict and consensus inside the Supreme Court from the Reagan administration to the present day.  In spite of a preponderance of conservative judicial appointments during this time, Toobin sees the Court trending towards the middle as swing votes and judicial intuition trump ideology.

Waters, T. J.  *Class 11: My Story Inside the CIA's First Post-9/11 Spy Class*
Plume, 2007 (2006), 320 pages.

Waters tells the inside story of the training of Class 11: the first class to enter the CIA after the September 11 attacks.  Volunteers to this diverse class learn about tradecraft, the workings of the agency, and the threat posed by Al-Qaeda.  Waters, an older, non-military recruit, describes the impact of secrecy on marriage and family life.

# 5. Social Commentary

Classic studies like David Riesman's *The Lonely Crowd,* as well as more recent essays like Allan Bloom's *The Closing of the American Mind,* are cultural milestones in our understanding of what it means to be American. Listed here are 32 shrewd, insightful books by writers from right, left, and center on American and global social trends.

❖　　　❖　　　❖

Baldwin, James. *The Fire Next Time*
Holt, Rinehart and Winston, 2000 (1963), 167 pages.

Baldwin, who is best known for his fiction, published this influential essay in 1963 on race relations in the United States. Baldwin provocatively argues here that oppression by one group of another inevitably results in chaos and murder, and criticizes both Christianity and the Nation of Islam for offering deceptively easy solutions to complex problems. Baldwin also manages to sound hopeful throughout, trusting that thoughtful discourse will win out where violence has not.

Berry, Wendell. *The Unsettling of America: Culture & Agriculture*
Sierra Club Books, 1986 (1977), 234 pages.

Wendell Berry, writer, teacher, and farmer, describes how agribusiness has affected the national character by removing farming from families. Thus, agribusiness has created a crisis in values as well as an ecological crisis. To save the environment, Americans must change the way we live and work, and return to family values.

Bloom, Allan. *The Closing of the American Mind*
Simon & Schuster, 1998 (1987), 400 pages.

Political philosopher Allan Bloom argues in this engagingly written polemic that the purpose of a liberal arts education is to learn how to recognize and respond to the good. Bloom finds that this idea has been betrayed, however, through the incursion of relativism and political correctness into higher education. Readers of all political persuasions will appreciate Bloom's thoughtful evaluation of what constitutes a true education.

Buckley, William F. *God and Man at Yale: The Superstitions of Academic Freedom*
Regnery, 1977 (1951), 240 pages.

As a young man, William F. Buckley was vigorously attacked by the Establishment for the claims he made in *God and Man at Yale:* that teaching at Yale undermined students' religious faith and the values of the free market, and that alumni should exercise control over teaching. Although the 1950s elite derided Buckley's book, his critique of secular liberalism launched his career as a leader of the American conservative movement.

Diamond, Jared. *Guns, Germs, and Steel: The Fates of Human Societies*
W. W. Norton, 2005 (2003), 512 pages.

This celebrated Pulitzer Prize winner is a history of cultural progress covering 13,000 years since the last ice age. The author attempts to explain why Eurasian civilizations prospered and became technologically developed while others did not. He argues that favorable environmental factors helped pre-historic Eurasian cultures develop farming, which led to food surpluses, population growth, specialized labor, ruling classes, and eventually the rise of empires.

D'Souza, Dinesh. *What's So Great About America*
Penguin, 2003 (2002), 240 pages.

Public policy expert D'Souza assesses the nature of the threat of Islamic terrorism to the U.S. and parries criticism of America by European and American intellectuals. In his defense of the American ideal, D'Souza argues that America is unique in allowing its citizens to "write the script of their own lives," and justifies his patriotism.

Ehrenreich, Barbara. *Nickel and Dimed: On (Not) Getting By in America*
Metropolitan Books, 2001, 224 pages.

In 1998, writer Ehrenreich reinvented herself as an unskilled homemaker re-entering the workforce, took a series of jobs that paid poverty-level wages, and took notes. Ehrenreich's experiences as a waitress, maid, cleaning woman, nurse's aide, and clerk taught her about the virtues of America's low-paid workers and the challenges they face.

Friedman, Thomas L. *The World is Flat 3.0: A Brief History of the Twenty-first Century*
Picador, 2007 (2005), 672 pages.

Friedman's analysis of globalization in the 21st Century posits a level playing field where all can freely compete. He lists ten "flatteners" of the global playing field, including the Web and open-sourcing. Internet innovations, the outsourcing of the service sector, and the off-shoring of manufacturing, which have all created new economic opportunities.

Gladwell, Malcolm. *The Tipping Point*
Back Bay Books, 2002, 304 pages.

Why did Paul Revere succeed in rallying colonial troops, while rider William Dawes failed to rouse the militia on his circuit? Why did crime rates in New York plunge in the 1990s? How do fads catch fire? Gladwell answers such questions in his biography of an idea, offering insight for understanding trends and their impact on society.

Heath, Chip and Dan Heath.  *Made to Stick: Why Some Ideas Survive and Others Die*
Random House, 2008 (2007), 323 pages.

In *Made to Stick,* the Heath brothers explain what enables ideas in business, education, and public policy to survive and thrive.  Using examples from across the career spectrum, the Heaths highlight the elements of effective communication.  This exceptionally well-organized book provides guidance and concrete suggestions for making ideas stick.

Howell, Joseph T.  *Hard Living on Clay Street: Portraits of Blue Collar Families*
Waveland Press, 1990, 405 pages.

Joseph Howell conducted a study of blue-collar families by moving into a working-class neighborhood in Washington, D.C. and getting to know the Shacklefords and the Mosebys.  Howell's portrait of the Shacklefords as a "hard living" family facing multiple challenges, and the Mosebys as a more stable family "caught in between," shows the two faces of blue-collar life on Clay Street.

Jacoby, Susan.  *The Age of American Unreason*
Pantheon, 2008, 356 pages.

In the early chapters, the author covers the history of American anti-intellectualism from colonial days to the present.  The rest of the book analyzes the cultural factors that contribute to the rise of "junk thought" and the decline of middlebrow American culture.  The work is essentially a jeremiad against the loss of reason and the "dumbing down" of a populace prone to social and political apathy as well as the manipulations of the mass media and fundamentalist religion.

Jenkins, Henry.  *Convergence Culture: Where Old and New Media Collide*
New York University Press, 2008 (2006), 336 pages.

Jenkins, director of MIT's Comparative Media Studies program, focuses on the vast changes occurring in our time due to the complex interaction of old and new media.  Arguing that the convergence of different media is a cultural as well as a technological phenomenon, he foresees a world in which grassroots access to diverse technologies will allow people to have more influence on the media.  Jenkins explains how consumer savvy makes technology and media professionals more responsive, and shows how savvy entrepreneurs can use diverse media to promote their interests.

Lasch, Christopher.  *The Culture of Narcissism: American Life in an Age of Diminishing Expectations*
W. W. Norton, 1991 (1979), 302 pages.

Christopher Lasch draws on the psychological definition of narcissism in his analysis of the American character: 20th-Century Americans have lost their work ethic and become sundered from vital modes of social cohesion.  In consequence of their isolation from family and community, says Lasch, Americans have become self-absorbed and shallow.

Lee, Jennifer. *The Fortune Cookie Chronicles: Adventures in the World of Chinese Food*
Twelve, 2008, 320 pages.

New York Times reporter Lee visited six continents, 23 countries, and 42 states in search of stories linking food culture, immigration, and identity. Writing as an American-born Chinese, Lee explores Chinese food as a global phenomenon and a hallmark of American culture, from Chinese restaurants to the stories of the immigrants who established them.

Lessig, Lawrence. *Free Culture: The Nature and Future of Creativity*
Penguin, 2005 (2004), 368 pages.

Lawrence Lessig, law professor and founder of the Stanford Center for the Internet and Society, offers a provocative critique of our current laws regulating intellectual property. Lessig argues that the complex regulation of Internet technology at the behest of big media has led to the shrinkage of ideas in the public domain. Lessig discusses the way copyright laws affect the availability of software, peer-to-peer file sharing, and more.

MacCannell, Dean. *The Tourist: A New Theory of the Leisure Class*
University of California Press, 1999, 272 pages.

Dean MacCannell surveys contemporary tourism—part sightseeing, part pilgrimage—in all of its contradictory aspects. Taking the tourist as the prototype of modern man, MacCannell explores the ways in which international tourism has become linked to the expansion of modernity. In this anthropology of tourism, the author shows modern travelers in search of their roots via ever more "authentic" experiences of pre-modern and exotic foreign cultures.

Masters, Alexander. *Stuart: A Life Backwards*
Delta, 2007, 320 pages.

This story of a life is told in reverse, starting from the present in which Stuart, a homeless man, awaits trial, and moving backwards through hardships, poor decisions, and traumas to the time when Stuart was a gregarious 13-year-old. Stuart's friendship with author Alexander Masters, an advocate for the homeless, is chronicled in this unusual biography. Masters explores Stuart's life as commentary on contemporary society.

McPhee, John. *The Control of Nature*
Farrar, Straus and Giroux, 1990 (1989), 272 pages.

Pulitzer Prize-winning author McPhee describes places around the globe where man is pitted in a battle against nature. McPhee visited the largest river swamp in America to witness the battle for river control between the U.S. Army Corps of Engineers and nature. McPhee reports on the crumbling hillsides of Los Angeles, an Icelandic island leaking lava, and more, detailing the challenges and strategies relevant to the control of nature.

Mills, C. Wright. *The Power Elite*
Oxford University Press, 2000 (1956), 448 pages.

American sociologist C. Wright Mills coined the term "power elite" in his 1956 book examining how small groups in America exerted a disproportionately large amount of influence. Mills follows his region-by-region survey of American elites with an analysis of the interlocking structures of military, corporate, and political power. Alan Wolfe's afterword to this new edition looks at which of Mills' predictions have come true.

Mortenson, Greg and David Oliver Relin. *Three Cups of Tea: One Man's Mission to Promote Peace… One School at a Time*
Penguin, 2007 (2006), 368 pages.

Alone and disoriented after his heroic assault on the world's highest mountain got derailed, Greg Mortenson was taken in by local villagers. In gratitude, Mortenson undertook the equally heroic effort of funding and building a school for the village. *Three Cups of Tea* is a fascinating account of the extensive cross-cultural networking, negotiations, and collaboration that preceded the realization of the villagers' dream.

Needleman, Jacob. *The American Soul: Rediscovering the Wisdom of the Founders*
Tarcher, 2003 (2002), 400 pages.

This is an historical and philosophical meditation on the spiritual meaning of America and its legacy. The author recovers the wisdom of America's founding documents and iconic figures (chiefly Washington and Jefferson) while interjecting his own experiences and beliefs about the ideals of American democracy as well as its flaws. Accordingly, he addresses America's two most grievous sins, slavery and the destruction of Native Americans. A richly provocative work.

Pollan, Michael. *In Defense of Food: An Eater's Manifesto*
Penguin, 2008, 256 pages.

The take-away from Michael Pollan's book on food is on the cover: "Eat food. Not too much. Mostly plants." Pollan arrives at these crisp conclusions by analyzing the impact of nutritional science on American eating patterns. This book on eating to reclaim health covers the evolution of the Western diet, its legacy, and advice on healthy eating.

Postman, Neil. *Amusing Ourselves to Death: Public Discourse in the Age of Show Business*
Penguin, 2005 (1985), 208 pages.

Postman takes an incisive look here at the way electronic media shapes our perceptions of reality. Between George Orwell's vision of a totalitarian society ruled over by Big Brother in *Nineteen Eighty-Four* and Aldous Huxley's vision of a society numbed by media saturation in *Brave New World*, Postman claims that Huxley's vision has turned out to be the more prescient. We have become, he eloquently argues, a society ruled by the pleasures of the ephemeral image.

Riesman, David. *The Lonely Crowd: A Study of the Changing American Character*
Yale University Press, 2001 (1950), 392 pages.

This classic study of the American character traces American culture from its traditional roots to the modern day. Noting the waning of cohesive social forces, Riesman describes Americans since World War II who have lost their inner-directed values of work and family and become other-directed conformists influenced by peer groups and popular culture.

Schlosser, Eric. *Fast Food Nation*
Harper Perennial, 2005 (2001), 416 pages.

In 1999, investigative journalist Eric Schlosser wrote an exposé of America's fast-food industry for *Rolling Stone* magazine. That article evolved into his bestselling book, *Fast Food Nation*. Here Schlosser examines the health and safety aspects of the industry, as well as its impact on America's landscape and economy and upon the global economy.

Schwartz, Barry. *The Paradox of Choice: Why More is Less*
Harper Perennial, 2005 (2004), 265 pages.

Professor Barry Schwartz makes a compelling case that the success of the marketplace presents Americans with an overwhelming number of choices. Americans can attain greater satisfaction in life by becoming "satisficers" (people who make quick, decisive choices), Schwartz argues, and offers his readers tips on streamlining decision-making.

Soyinka, Wole. *Climate of Fear: The Quest for Dignity in a Dehumanized World*
Random House, 2005 (2004), 176 pages.

Nobel Prize winner Soyinka describes a climate of fear in which small groups of violent fanatics have leveraged their influence over global affairs, from the 1989 bombing of a UTA passenger plane over Niger to the present. Soyinka urges the world community to oppose terrorism and other violations of human rights and human dignity.

Surowiecki, James. *The Wisdom of Crowds*
Anchor Books, 2005 (2004), 306 pages.

Business writer Surowiecki demonstrates the virtues of collective decision-making with fascinating contemporary and historical examples of the wisdom of crowds. Covering such topics as committees, companies, markets, and democracy, the author shows the application of research on crowds to the way we organize our work and our lives.

Terkel, Studs. *Working: People Talk About What They Do All Day and How They Feel About What They Do*
New Press, 1997 (1974), 640 pages.

Pulitzer Prize-winning author Studs Terkel uses the method of oral history to examine the working lives of Americans in the latter part of the 20th Century. Gleaning testimony from hundreds of interviews, Terkel assembles a composite portrait of working America. Americans from all walks of life discuss topics such as the challenge and meaning of work, workplace relationships, and upward mobility.

Weaver, Richard M. *Ideas Have Consequences*
University of Chicago Press, 1984 (1948), 198 pages.

Weaver traces the decline of the West to the deleterious effects of nominalism: the belief that there are no absolute truths. The consequences of this idea can be seen in a variety of social ills visited upon an easily manipulated populace. The author proposes remediation through the values of piety, justice, communication, and private property.

Winchester, Simon. *Krakatoa: The Day the World Exploded: August 27, 1883*
Harper Perennial, 2005 (2003), 424 pages.

New York Times bestselling author Winchester uses his skills as a geologist and historian to describe the 1883 eruption of Krakatoa's volcano and its impact on nature and politics. In addition to its devastating toll in human lives, the explosion affected the demise of Dutch colonialism in Indonesia, provided a laboratory for studying plate tectonics, and gave rise to a wave of anti-Western Muslim fundamentalism in the region.

# 6. The Arts

Reading about the arts will introduce you to new ideas and enrich your understanding of human creativity. Listed here are eight books on music and 11 books on visual art, including movies and architecture. Whether you enjoy listening to rock, Elvis, or opera, or want to learn about Gaudi or Frank Lloyd Wright, these books on the arts will inform and entertain.

❖     ❖     ❖

Azerrad, Michael. *Our Band Could Be Your Life: Scenes from the American Indie Underground 1981–1991*
Back Bay Books, 2002 (2001), 528 pages.

With the popularity of alternative music in the 1990s and the success of such bands as Pearl Jam and Nirvana, connoisseurs of musical history will be intrigued by Azerrad's study of the unsung heroes who made this story possible. As it turns out, amidst the radio-friendly commercial fare of the 1980s, a vibrant music scene was happening just below the radar—one driven by a willingness to experiment and an anti-commercial sensibility.

Bassegoda Nonell, Juan. *Antonio Gaudi: Master Architect*
Abbeville Press, 2001 (2000), 285 pages

Antonio Gaudi (1852–1926) was one of the best known architects of the 20th Century. His daring modernist style continues to influence architects and designers. This is essentially a picture book, but the text discusses in some depth his life and work. It includes 200 color photos of his designs and innovative buildings, found mostly in his native Catalonia, as well as a chronology of his work. The book comes in both a portable pocket-size and a large, hardcover edition.

Berger, John. *Ways of Seeing*
Penguin, 1990 (1972), 176 pages.

This book, groundbreaking when first published, is used today as a fine arts textbook. *Ways of Seeing* consists of seven essays that can be read in any order. The author's unifying theme is that art is best understood in its historical context. Berger analyzes art in the age of mechanical reproduction, the nude, oil painting, and art and advertising.

Clark, Kenneth. *The Nude: A Study in Ideal Form*
Princeton University Press, 1972 (1956), 458 pages.

Kenneth Clark's classic study describes the evolution of the nude in Western sculpture and painting from antiquity to modernity. The nude, an art form invented by the 5th-Century Greeks, embodies an ideal vision of human nature. The nude is unique in its representation of human beauty, power, energy, ecstasy, humility, and suffering.

Conrad, Peter. *A Song of Love and Death: The Meaning of Opera*
Graywolf Press, 1996 (1987), 406 pages.

This book on the meaning of opera focuses on opera's psychological meaning and its emotional impact on the audience. Organized into sections on opera as ritual, opera repertory, and performances, Conrad's book describes some of opera's key figures, the history of the art form, and contemporary interpretations and opera house design.

Dolnick, Edward. *The Rescue Artist: A True Story of Art, Thieves, and the Hunt for a Missing Masterpiece*
Harper Perennial, 2006 (2005), 270 pages.

This is the story of Scotland Yard's Anglo-American art detective Charley Hill who was hired by the Norwegian police to track down Edvard Munch's famous painting, *The Scream*, when it was stolen from Norway's National Gallery in 1994. It's a rollicking adventure story that takes the reader into the art underworld. Though the successful outcome is known, the author keeps the reader in suspense in this fast-paced, real-life whodunit. Includes a brief biography of Munch.

Ebert, Roger. *The Great Movies*
Broadway, 2003 (2002), 544 pages.

The celebrated syndicated film critic offers 100 brief essays on great movies, each a gem of populist, critical appreciation. Ebert's selection represents a wide range of genres, periods, and nationalities. His reviews often include interesting background information on the making of the movie. Stills from each film enhance the text. This is a great guide for film lovers by a true cinephile. Ebert's follow-up collection, *The Great Movies II*, was published in 2006.

Ferris, William. *Blues from the Delta: An Illustrated Documentary on the Music and Musicians of the Mississippi Delta*
Da Capo Press, 1988 (1978), 250 pages.

Mississippi-born Ferris uses documentary text and photos to trace the development of the blues in America from its Delta roots to blues greats B. B. King and Muddy Waters. Ferris describes the evolution of the blues from post-Civil War guitar music, African-American work songs, and blues proverbs into the sophisticated musical genre it is today.

Guralnick, Peter. *Last Train to Memphis: The Rise of Elvis Presley*
Back Bay Books, 1995 (1994), 576 pages.

"Elvis lives" in the pages of Guralnick's exhaustive, two-volume biography. Based on hundreds of interviews and nearly a decade of research, this first volume covers Presley's early years, focusing on his rise to stardom. It ends when he was drafted into the army at the age of 24. This objective, scholarly portrait of the "king" of rock and roll will inform both fans and critics alike. Guralnick's second volume, *Careless Love: The Unmaking of Elvis Presley*, was published in 1999.

Hadju, David. *Positively 4th Street: The Lives and Times of Joan Baez, Bob Dylan, Mimi Baez Fariña and Richard Fariña*
North Point Press, 2001 (2002), 336 pages.

David Hadju tells the story of how the young Bob Dylan made his way into the heart of the Greenwich Village folk scene in the early 1960s and rapidly won over its leading lights. It is in Hadju's hands a quintessential American story of personality, ambition, and raw talent. It's also a multifaceted story of love, friendship, and loss as Hadju also writes of the small group of friends who surrounded Dylan during his critical years.

Hughes, Robert. *The Shock of the New: The Hundred-Year History of Modern Art, Its Rise, Its Dazzling Achievement, Its Fall*
McGraw-Hill, 2nd ed., 1990 (1980), 448 pages.

The Australian art critic provides a comprehensive history of 20th-Century art based on the BBC Time-Life television series that covered the history of modern art since the Impressionists. Hughes chronicles the development of painting, sculpture, and architecture from the rise of cubism to the end of avant-garde. This incisive, witty, and readable text has become a classic. The revised edition covers the 1980s and includes 275 illustrations.

MacDonald, Ian. *Revolution in the Head: The Beatles' Records and the Sixties*
Chicago Review Press, 3rd ed., 2007 (1994), 544 pages.

Popular music critic MacDonald wrote the definitive commentary on the Beatles' entire canon. He provides a critical, song-by-song analysis of all 241 tracks in the order they were recorded. An introductory essay on the 1960s places the Fab Four in their musical, social, and cultural context. For the die-hard fan, this is the ultimate Beatles' Bible. For those seeking a better appreciation of their music, it is an indispensible guide.

Malraux, André. *The Voices of Silence*
Translated by Stuart Gilbert. Doubleday, 1978 (1953), 661 pages.

André Malraux debunks the study of art in the context of historical eras, offering instead a conceptual framework focused on the art book as a pan-cultural museum without walls, and art itself as a decodable language. Malraux's comprehensive and imaginative study includes commentary on hundreds of great works of art.

Marcus, Greil. *Mystery Train: Images of America in Rock 'n' Roll*
Plume, 5th ed., 2008 (1975), 432 pages.

More than 30 years after it was first published, this book remains one of the finest studies of American rock and roll and its impact on pop culture. Marcus focuses on six key artists. After an initial assessment of early pioneers Harmonica Frank and Robert Johnson, he examines The Band, Sly Stone, Randy Newman, and Elvis Presley. Some might lament the absence of Chuck Berry, Bob Dylan, and Brian Wilson, but the chapter on Elvis, entitled "Presliad," is a classic.

Ondaatje, Michael. *The Conversations: Walter Murch and the Art of Film Editing*
Knopf, 2004 (2002), 368 pages.

Few people appreciate the craft of filmmaking behind the scenes. Next to screenwriting, the most important craft is film editing. Through a series of personal conversations, novelist Ondaatje investigates the work and career of Walter Murch, one of Hollywood's great film editors of the last 40 years. Readers learn just how artful and intricate the editing process is from a master. For serious film buffs and would-be filmmakers, this is a must read.

Richardson, John. *The Sorcerer's Apprentice: Picasso, Provence, and Douglas Cooper*
University of Chicago Press, 2001 (1999), 328 pages.

The famed biographer of Picasso wrote this vivid memoir of his long encounter with the acerbic art collector and critic Douglas Cooper. In the 1950s, the two lived together for ten years in a Provence chateau entertaining a circle of friends that included Jean Cocteau, W. H. Auden, Tennessee Williams, Pablo Picasso, and other famous artists of the period. Their stormy relationship was held together by a shared, passionate love of art. Splendidly illustrated.

Rivera, Diego (with Gladys March). *My Art, My Life*
Dover, 1992 (1960), 224 pages.

Mexican muralist Diego Rivera reflects on his life and art, including encounters with world political leaders and his marriages to artists Lupe Marin and Frida Kahlo. Journalist Gladys March recorded Rivera's thoughts from 1944 until his death in 1957. The result: a larger-than-life portrait of the artist who revolutionized modern painting.

Smith, Kathryn. *Frank Lloyd Wright: America's Master Architect*
Abbeville Press, 1998 (1992), 285 pages.

This is an ideal introduction to America's most celebrated architect. Smith provides a concise overview of Wright's long life (1867–1959) and brilliant career. His numerous achievements (buildings, houses, furniture, and decorative arts) are captured in over 200 photographs and drawings. The book concludes with a view of Wright's prized Asian art collection. Both a portable pocket-size and a large, hardcover edition are available.

Vickers, Hugh. *Great Operatic Disasters*
St. Martin's Griffin, 1985 (1979), 108 pages.

Opera buff Vickers pokes fun at the grandeur of opera in his account of great on-stage disasters, from the occasion of diva Callas unexpectedly bouncing on a trampoline to the mobbing of the stage by the animals in a production of *Aida*. Vickers' humorous tales provide plenty of entertainment along with lessons on the complexity of staging opera.

# 7. Sports and Games

Sports fans who appreciate the game for its own sake, and readers fascinated by the way in which sports hold up a mirror to American society, will enjoy the 11 books listed here. Mainstream sports like football, basketball, and baseball are covered, as are the competitive worlds of poker and chess and the quiet world of angling.

❖          ❖          ❖

Bissinger, H. G. *Friday Night Lights: A Town, a Team, and a Dream*
Da Capo Press, 2003 (1990), 371 pages.

Pulitzer Prize-winning journalist Bissinger went to Odessa, Texas, in 1988 to witness a year in the life of the town's champion high-school football team. In Odessa he found a town where the residents' self-esteem derived from the success of their football team. The author profiles coaches, players, and fans in a so-so year for the team and the town.

Feinstein, John. *The Last Amateurs: Playing for Glory and Honor in Division I College Basketball*
Back Bay Books, 2001 (2000), 480 pages.

John Feinstein's book chronicles the 1999–2000 basketball season of the Patriot League, consisting at the time of seven teams: Bucknell, Army, Navy, Lehigh, Lafayette, Holy Cross, and Colgate. Feinstein's account focuses on the efforts of scholar-athletes (the last amateurs) to balance sportsmanship and athletics with academic excellence.

Frazier, Ian. *The Fish's Eye: Essays About Angling and the Outdoors*
Picador, 2003 (2002), 176 pages.

Frazier is an accomplished essayist with a storyteller's instincts. This book collects 17 essays about fishing that he wrote for *The New Yorker* over a period of 20 years. Even non-fishers will enjoy reading about Frazier's diverse and variably satisfying experiences chasing after the big one.

Halberstam, David. *Summer of '49*
Harper Perennial, 2006 (1989), 384 pages.

Journalist David Halberstam gives a riveting account of the pennant battle between the New York Yankees and the Boston Red Sox. Baseball, in a lull during World War II, had come roaring back by 1949, as seen in the intense rivalry of the two teams spearheaded by the Sox's best hitter, Ted Williams, and the Yankees' best player of all time, Joe DiMaggio.

Hallman, J. C. *The Chess Artist: Genius, Obsession, and the World's Oldest Game*
St. Martin's Griffin, 2004 (2003), 352 pages.

Writer J. C. Hallman and chessmaster Glenn Umstead go on a surreal tour of the chess world, taking in Manhattan's Washington Square Park, the giant electronic room of the Internet Chess Club, and a mini-town called Chess City in Kalmykia, a Russian province ruled by a chess prodigy. Hallman explores chess as passion, eccentricity, and obsession.

Holden, Anthony. *Big Deal: One Year as a Professional Poker Player*
Simon & Schuster, 2007 (1990), 416 pages.

Before TV poker and today's vast tournament fields, poker was an intimate culture for aficionados. Enter journalist Anthony Holden, who spent 1989 as a professional player. Stacking his chips against the likes of Johnny Chan, Holden played the circuit from Las Vegas to Marrakech. Holden's book describes poker strategy, psychology, and history.

Lewis, Michael. *Moneyball: The Art of Winning an Unfair Game*
W. W. Norton, 2004 (2003), 320 pages.

Oakland A's Manager Billy Beane defied conventional wisdom. In 2002, instead of paying big bucks for big-name talent, Beane put together a winning team by hiring affordable young and veteran players. Baseball stats guided Beane's negotiations for a team of high on-base percentage hitters and pitchers who got lots of ground outs.

MacCambridge, Michael. *America's Game: The Epic Story of How Pro Football Captured a Nation*
Anchor, 2005 (2004), 608 pages.

In his history of football from before World War II to the present, MacCambridge explains how professional football became America's game. At the center of his in-depth account of football players, coaches, and owners, MacCambridge's portrait of NFL Commissioner Pete Rozelle demonstrates how Rozelle's tenure assured the cultural primacy of football.

Maraniss, David. *Clemente: The Passion and Grace of Baseball's Last Hero*
Simon & Schuster, 2007 (2006), 416 pages.

Clemente, for 18 years the star outfielder of the Pittsburgh Pirates, was one of major league baseball's greatest players. He was also that rare athlete who rose above sports to help others in need, as symbolized by his tragic death in a plane crash in 1972 while on a humanitarian mission to Nicaragua. Maraniss brings to life the man behind the bat and glove to reveal a genuine hero who in many ways was the Jackie Robinson of Latino baseball players.

Robinson, Jackie (with Alfred Duckett). *I Never Had It Made: An Autobiography of Jackie Robinson*
Harper Perennial, 2003 (1972), 320 pages.

In 1947 Jackie Robinson broke the color barrier in major league baseball. In this candid memoir, originally published the year of his death, he recalls his struggles to become the first black man to play in the major leagues, and what it was like to live in the public frenzy that surrounded him. He also recounts his life after baseball working as a civil rights activist. This is an enlightening self-portrait (as told to Alfred Duckett) of one of America's great sports heroes.

Shenk, David. *The Immortal Game: A History of Chess, or How 32 Carved Pieces on a Board Illuminated Our Understanding of War, Art, Science, and the Human Brain*
Anchor, 2007 (2006), 327 pages.

This is an entertaining history of chess from its origins in Persia 1500 years ago to the present. But it is so much more, as Shenk sees chess as a metaphor for life, war, and the human mind. Interspersed throughout is a play-by-play account of the "immortal game" played in 1851 between Adolf Anderssen and Lionel Kieseritzky, which has been studied by chess students ever since. It's aimed at novice players who wish to know more about this very old, popular game.

# 8. Memoir

Memoirs provide a fascinating glimpse into the lives of people who tell their stories to make sense of the world, to illuminate an important event, or to explore their own development. The 30 books listed here reveal the inner lives of key literary and artistic figures, historically important individuals, and writers who use memoir to discover the meaning of life experiences.

❖      ❖      ❖

Addams, Jane. *Twenty Years at Hull-House: With Autobiographical Notes*
University of Michigan Press, 2009 (1910), 522 pages.

A daughter of privilege, Jane Addams spearheaded the settlement house movement in Chicago from 1889–1909, becoming America's most prominent social worker. In *Twenty Years at Hull House*, Addams describes her early life, her vocation, and the settlement house that became the central community focus for generations of American immigrants.

Albom, Mitch. *Tuesdays with Morrie: An Old Man, a Young Man, and Life's Greatest Lesson*
Broadway, 2002 (1997), 192 pages.

This is the touching story about the author's relationship with his beloved college professor, Morrie Schwartz. Sixteen years after graduation, the career-driven sports columnist reconnected with his mentor who was dying from Lou Gehrig's disease. Their rekindled relationship became a final "class" on the right way to live. This best-selling memoir of all time imparts a profound wisdom about life, love, and death that is clear and profound.

Angelou, Maya. *I Know Why the Caged Bird Sings*
Bantam, 1983 (1969), 304 pages.

Angelou recounts the joys and sorrows of her childhood in this classic memoir. The narrative begins when Maya, age three, and her older brother are left in the care of their maternal grandmother in Arkansas after their parents' divorce. Annie Henderson proves to be a positive influence in Maya's life as she navigates through the deeply embedded racism of the South and later struggles to overcome a terrible act of violence while staying with her mother in Missouri.

Armstrong, Lance (with Sally Jenkins). *It's Not About the Bike: My Journey Back to Life*
Berkley Books, 2001, 304 pages.

This is the inspirational story of the world famous cyclist and his fight against testicular cancer, which nearly killed him. Armstrong shares the triumphs and tragedies of his long, horrific ordeal and his remarkable recovery. Some of what Armstrong recounts is about the bike, but it's mostly a gripping, personal story of a courageous soul and his fight for life. This autobiography ends with Armstrong's first Tour de France victory. He went on to win six more.

Auster, Paul. *The Invention of Solitude*
Penguin, 2007 (1982), 192 pages.

In the first part of this intriguing two-part memoir, Auster writes of his father, an enigmatic man who lived his life behind an impregnable wall of solitude and whose death sends the author on a fascinating journey of discovery. In the second part, the author writes of his own experiences as a father and the chance happenings that compel him to evaluate the reliability of memory, meaning, and truth.

Bauby, Jean-Dominique. *The Diving Bell and the Butterfly: A Memoir of Life in Death*
Vintage, 2007 (1997), 144 pages.

Try to imagine writing a book when all you can do is blink one eyelid. That is the amazing achievement of the French journalist Jean-Dominique Bauby after he suffered a rare stroke at the age of 43. This very affecting memoir, about life trapped inside the "diving bell" of his paralyzed body, is a lasting testament to the human will to live even if only in one's mind that "takes flight like a butterfly." Bauby died just three days after his book was published in France.

Brown, Christy. *My Left Foot*
Collins Educational, 1998 (1954), 184 pages.

Born disabled, Christy Brown was misdiagnosed as an imbecile by doctors who advised his parents to institutionalize him. In *My Left Foot*, Brown tells of his upbringing in a caring family and of how he struggled to communicate his intelligence and creativity. His remarkable story begins with learning to write and ends with Brown becoming an author.

Didion, Joan. *The Year of Magical Thinking*
Vintage, 2007, 240 pages.

Joan Didion won the National Book Award for this courageous memoir. Didion writes of a year in which she experiences the loss of her husband and the near-loss of her daughter, who is stricken by a mysterious illness. Didion doesn't look for easy answers or simple consolations in reflecting upon this difficult period. Rather, she comes to understand the complex texture of grief and the ability of human beings to persevere in the face of great sorrow and loss.

Dylan, Bob. *Chronicles: Volume I*
Simon & Schuster, 2004, 304 pages.

Even those who have come to expect the unexpected from this protean master of disguises were surprised at the publication of this memoir in 2004. An even greater surprise for some may have been how good it is. Written in an idiom that is literate, hip, and compulsively readable, Dylan's reflections on one of the most varied careers in the history of popular music provide incomparable insight into the development of his musical sensibility.

Frank, Anne. *The Diary of a Young Girl*
Bantam, 1993 (1967), 304 pages.

Anne Frank was 11 years old in 1940 when her family went into hiding from the Nazis. She began her diary two years later on her 13th birthday and continued writing in it until her family was finally discovered and sent to Auschwitz. The diary is an extraordinary document of one girl's coming-of-age in the most dire circumstances imaginable. It is all the more extraordinary for the vibrant, thoughtful voice that sounds from its pages.

Gage, Nicholas. *Eleni*
Ballantine Books, 1996 (1983), 480 pages.

In 1948, Greek peasant Eleni Gatzoyiannis planned her children's escape from their would-be abductors, the Communist guerillas, and was executed for the deed. Eleni's son Nicholas Gage grew up with the mission of discovering the truth about her death. Returning to Greece as an investigative reporter, Gage uncovers the facts of Eleni's story.

Gardiner, Muriel. *Code Name "Mary": Memoirs of an American Woman in the Austrian Underground*
Yale University Press, 1987 (1983), 200 pages.

Muriel Gardiner, an American medical student in 1930s Vienna, made the fight against fascism her cause. A key member of the anti-Nazi underground, Gardiner risked her life as a smuggler of passports, courier of needed funds, and lifeline to people escaping Austria. *Code Name "Mary"* is the memoir of a distinguished educator and psychoanalyst.

Gilbert, Elizabeth. *Eat, Pray, Love*
Penguin, 2007 (2006), 352 pages.

This is a soul-searching travelogue by a young woman who seeks new life after her painful divorce. She recounts her year-long trip to Rome, India, and Bali, where she respectively pursues the pleasures of food, spirituality, and "balance." Her journey ends with a new love affair. This memoir is an odyssey of self-discovery written with intelligence and self-deprecating humor.

Goodwin, Doris Kearns. *Wait Till Next Year: A Memoir*
Simon & Schuster, 1998 (1997), 272 pages.

In this engaging memoir, Goodwin, a Pulitzer Prize-winning historian, writes of her childhood growing up on Long Island in the 1950s. At the heart of the memoir is Kearns's love of baseball, a love instilled in her by her father when she was six. No less important is the love of books that was instilled in her by her mother. The memoir provides a rich sense of a particular place and time in American life.

Hammarskjöld, Dag. *Markings*
Vintage, 2006 (1963), 256 pages.

This inspiring collection of diary reflections and poems by the Swedish diplomat and second Secretary-General of the UN was published after his tragic death in an airplane crash in 1961. Hammarskjöld was known as a great statesman and peacemaker who devoted his life to public service. These personal meditations reveal the rich inner life of a public man. A foreword by W. H. Auden puts this spiritual classic in the context of Hammarskjöld's life.

Hampl, Patricia. *I Could Tell You Stories: Sojourns in the Land of Memory*
W. W. Norton, 2008 (1990), 242 pages.

This collection of essays is comprised of personal recollections and literary reflections on the nature of memory and memoir. The author examines her own landscape of memory and her writing life through the autobiographical writings of St. Augustine, Walt Whitman, Sylvia Plath, Anne Frank, Edith Stein, and Czeslaw Milosz. Throughout we are invited into a world where memory and fiction intersect to provoke a higher emotional truth beyond the realm of facts.

Hillesum, Etty. *An Interrupted Life: The Diaries, 1941–1943*
Holt, 1996 (1984), 384 pages.

Hillesum was a young, Dutch Jewish thinker and mystic who died at Auschwitz at the age of 29. Her diaries and letters describe life under Nazi rule in Amsterdam during the German occupation of the Netherlands. They include her most intimate thoughts about the horror and struggles all around her, and reveal an unconquerable spirit that rose above hatred and despair to proclaim a clear love of God and humanity. As a Holocaust memoir, this is a very inspiring work.

Keller, Helen. *The Story of My Life: The Restored Classic*
W. W. Norton, 2003 (1903), 352 pages.

Helen Keller (1880–1968) is a revered figure in American history. Struck deaf and blind at 19 months from scarlet fever, she triumphed over her handicaps by learning to speak, read, and write. She went on to receive a college education and became a writer and activist. Written in her college years, Keller's autobiography details her early life, especially her experiences with her teacher Anne Sullivan. This centennial edition was restored to include excised material.

Koppel, Lily. *The Red Leather Diary: Reclaiming a Life Through the Pages of a Lost Journal*
HarperCollins, 2009 (2008), 352 pages.

As an ambitious, artistic teenager, Florence Wolfson recorded her life every day for five years from 1929 to 1934. When Lily Koppel discovered Wolfson's long-forgotten diary in a dumpster on the Upper West Side of Manhattan in 2003, she set out to find its author. Koppel's tale, which paints a vivid picture of 1930s New York, is the story of a young, headstrong dreamer and how Koppel found her diary and later the 90-year-old author herself living in Florida.

Kovaly, Heda Margolius. *Under a Cruel Star: A Life in Prague, 1941–1968*
Holmes & Meier, 1997 (1985), 192 pages.

The author was a Czech Jew who suffered under two brutal regimes, Nazism and Communism, while living in Prague in the mid-20th Century. Her chilling memoir begins in 1941 when her family was taken away to the Lodz Ghetto. After surviving Auschwitz, she returns to Prague only to live under Stalinist oppression until the Soviet invasion of Czechoslovakia in 1968 compelled her to emigrate to the United States. This is a heart-rending story of human resilience.

Lamott, Anne. *Operating Instructions: A Journal of My Son's First Year*
Anchor, 2005 (1993), 272 pages.

Rarely does the mother of an infant accurately record detailed impressions and considered thoughts of her child's first year of life. Anne Lamott does this and more, describing baby Sam's early development and how the community of family, friends, and church molds their relationship. This stirring memoir of a new life reads like a novel.

Levi, Primo. *Survival in Auschwitz*
Classic House Books, 2008 (1947), 170 pages.

Levi, who was deported to the Auschwitz concentration camp in 1943, survived to become one of the most penetrating chroniclers of the Holocaust and the system of concentration camps. Rather than play upon a preconditioned set of responses to the Holocaust and concentration camps, Levi documents instead the complex humanity of the prisoners who were thrust into a dehumanized and disorienting world. A profoundly courageous and humane work.

Lewis, C. S. *Surprised by Joy: The Shape of My Early Life*
Harcourt, rev. ed., 1995 (1955), 240 pages.

In this autobiography the popular fiction writer, literary critic, and Christian apologist recounts his spiritual journey during his early years. Lewis's story centers on his search for "joy" and how that led him on a meandering path from faith to devout atheism and back to faith. It's primarily an intellectual journey as Lewis's conversion was formed by the world of books and ideas. In many ways this unabashedly honest work is a modern-day Augustine's *Confessions*.

Lindbergh, Anne Morrow. *Gift from the Sea*
Pantheon, 1991 (1955), 144 pages.

While on vacation on Captiva Island off the Gulf coast of Florida, Lindbergh wrote these lyrical meditations on her life and the lives of American women in general, taking her inspiration from the shells on the beach. In mid-life she ruminates on love and marriage, youth and age, and peace and contentment, imparting a soulfulness and wisdom that is timeless. This slim book, written as a prose poem, beautifully captures the sensibilities of the female psyche.

McBride, James.  *The Color of Water: A Black Man's Tribute to His White Mother*
Riverhead Books, 2006 (1996), 352 pages.

McBride was raised in the public housing projects of New York City as one of 12 children.  He wrote this inspiring memoir in honor of his remarkable mother.  Born in Poland to Orthodox Jews and raised in the South, she fled to Harlem, found a home in the black church, married a black minister, converted to Christianity, and then raised 12 children, seeing all of them through college.  This is a powerful meditation on love, race, religion, and the search for identity.

McCourt, Frank.  *Angela's Ashes*
Simon & Schuster, 1999 (1997), 368 pages.

McCourt's sad, haunting story of his impoverished boyhood is told with humor and compassion from the point of view of a child.  Born in Brooklyn during the Depression, McCourt's family moved back to Ireland when he was only four.  Life in Limerick is worse, as his often unemployed, alcoholic father squanders in bars whatever money he makes.  This Pulitzer Prize-winning tale of a desperate childhood is a testament to the resiliency of youth.

Merton, Thomas.  *The Seven Storey Mountain*
Harvest Books, 1999 (1948), 496 pages.

Thomas Merton began writing his autobiography while living as a Trappist monk at Gethsemane Abbey in Kentucky.  The result is this moving and inspirational work in which Merton writes of his life as a spiritual journey in which, through much pain and suffering, he progressively comes to understand his fundamental purpose in life—to glorify God through living a life of solitude and prayer.

Sedaris, David.  *Me Talk Pretty One Day*
Back Bay Books, 2001 (2000), 272 pages.

Humorist Sedaris offers up his fourth collection of side-splitting stories, only these are about his own twisted life and the people who inhabit it.  His 27 autobiographical tales range from his childhood in North Carolina to his early adulthood in New York to his more recent years living in France.  Sedaris's hyperbolic imagination and wry, self-deprecating humor will leave you either laughing out loud or scoffing at the absurdity of his warped and quirky world, or both.

Sheff, David.  *Beautiful Boy: A Father's Journey Through His Son's Addiction*
Mariner Books, 2009 (2008), 336 pages.

Journalist Sheff's charming son Nic had everything going for him at age 17, until he began experimenting with drugs and alcohol.  It was the beginning of a decade-long, downward spiral into drug abuse and addiction to crystal meth.  Sheff's brutally honest chronicle of his son's harrowing addiction and recovery is a painful but hopeful story.  Nic Sheff wrote his own memoir about his addiction entitled *Tweak: Growing Up on Methamphetamines* (Atheneum, 2009).

Trout, Nick. *Tell Me Where It Hurts: A Day of Humor, Healing, and Hope in My Life as an Animal Surgeon*
Broadway Books, 2008, 304 pages.

This book could have been titled *A Day in the Life of a Veterinarian*, for Trout condenses 25 years as a vet surgeon into one long, very busy day at an animal hospital. His funny and sad anecdotes about pets (mostly dogs) and their owners will make the reader laugh and cry. Along the way he describes the advances made in veterinary science and tackles the difficult ethical issues people face in caring for their animals. A great read for pet lovers and would-be veterinarians.

# 9. Philosophy and Religion

Philosophy, which means "love of wisdom," seeks to know the truth of things based on reason, while religion is rooted in experiences of faith. Listed here are nine philosophy and nine religion books, all interesting and accessible works that inform our search for truth and meaning in our lives.

## Philosophy

De Botton, Alain. *The Consolations of Philosophy*
Vintage, 2001 (2000), 272 pages.

In this original attempt to popularize philosophy, the author seeks to console the reader through everyday problems by presenting the thought of a particular philosopher that speaks to a specific difficulty: Socrates on unpopularity, Epicurus on money, Seneca on frustration, Montaigne on inadequacy, Schopenhauer on love, and Nietzsche on hardship. This engaging romp through the thought of six philosophers makes philosophy enjoyable and relevant.

Frankl, Victor. *Man's Search for Meaning*
Beacon Press, 2006 (1946), 165 pages.

Frankl, a Viennese psychiatrist and Holocaust survivor, wrote this memoir based on Nietzsche's saying that "He who has a *why* to live can bear almost any *how*." In the first part Frankl recounts the torments he and his fellow inmates suffered at Auschwitz, Dachau, and other Nazi death camps. The second part spells out his theory of logotherapy that holds that our primary drive is not pleasure but the discovery and pursuit of meaning. It's a riveting story of spiritual survival.

Gaarder, Jostein. *Sophie's World: A Novel About the History of Philosophy*
Farrar, Straus and Giroux, 2007 (1996), 544 pages.

The author is a Norwegian high school teacher who recounts the history of philosophy from Socrates to Sartre through the character of a 14-year-old girl who engages in a complex correspondence with a strange mentor. Her philosophical journey is made all the more forceful at the end when the reader discovers the unreliable narration and metafictional character of the novel. It's a long, unraveling story but a fun and intriguing way to learn the basics of philosophy.

Gray, J. Glenn. *The Warriors: Reflections on Men in Battle*
Bison Books, 1998 (1959), 242 pages.

This is a philosophical meditation on warfare and its effects on the soldiers who fight. Gray's Ph.D. in philosophy was conferred on the same day his draft notice arrived in May, 1941. Serving as an intelligence officer on numerous fronts in World War II, he recorded his experiences and reflections in journals and letters. Fourteen years later he wrote this remarkable analysis of love, death, fear, guilt, human nature, and the enduring appeal of battle.

Kolakowski, Leszek. *Why is There Something Rather Than Nothing?: 23 Questions from Great Philosophers*
Basic Books, 2007, 240 pages.

Written by an eminent Polish philosopher, this is a tour through the history of thought that makes comprehensible the essential ideas of 23 important philosophers from Socrates to Husserl. In short, interpretative essays the author addresses a philosophical question relevant to each thinker. This introductory survey will provoke further reading and reflection on the perennial questions.

Kreeft, Peter. *Philosophy 101 by Socrates: An Introduction to Philosophy via Plato's Apology*
Ignatius Press, 2002, 100 pages.

This is an excellent beginner's guide to philosophy, written mostly for college freshmen but enjoyable and informative for anyone. Kreeft draws on three of Plato's dialogues (*Apology*, *Euthyphro*, and *Phaedo*, but mostly *Apology*) and their central character, Socrates, the father of Western philosophy, to illuminate the method and manner of philosophical inquiry. The author's Christian perspective is made clear when he presents parallels between Socrates and Jesus.

Needleman, Jacob. *The Heart of Philosophy*
Tarcher, 2003 (1982), 256 pages.

The heart of philosophy is not formal arguments or technical concepts but rather the personal quest for truth, reality, and the right way to live. Needleman shows us how philosophy, as the quest for ultimate meaning, can engage us all. Along the way he discusses the ideas of several major thinkers, including Pythagoras, Socrates, Plato, Descartes, Kant, and Wittgenstein, and he weaves in his own experiences as a teacher of philosophy to illuminate the love of wisdom.

Phillips, Christopher. *Six Questions of Socrates: A Modern-Day Journey of Discovery through World Philosophy*
W. W. Norton, 2005 (2004), 334 pages.

In this second in a trilogy of books that introduce philosophy to a lay audience, Phillips travels the world, challenging ordinary people from many different backgrounds with Socratic questions such as: What is virtue? What is justice? What is piety? He weaves together his unscripted conversations with the texts of Plato, Aristotle, and other thinkers both Eastern and Western. The product is a philosophical travelogue that illuminates the Socratic method of inquiry.

Solomon, Robert C. and Kathleen M. Higgins. *A Short History of Philosophy*
Oxford University Press, 1996, 329 pages.

This book is exactly what it purports to be—a short history of philosophy. Unlike other such surveys, however, Solomon and Higgins excel at covering the history of Eastern and Western philosophy in a succinct and engaging way. One comes away with not only a knowledge of the central figures and schools in the history of philosophy but also with a rich sense of the abiding significance and value of the philosophical endeavor.

# Religion

Bowker, John, Editor. *Cambridge Illustrated History of Religions*
Cambridge University Press, 2002, 336 pages.

This is a comprehensive survey of world religions from pre-history to the present. Every major religion is covered in depth by an expert in the field and is supported by lavish illustrations. Even aboriginal religions, as well as the religions of ancient Greece, Rome, Egypt, Persia, and Mesopotamia are included. New religious movements are briefly discussed. The text includes both a graphic and a detailed chronology for each religion and an extensive bibliography.

De Lange, Nicholas. *Introduction to Judaism*
Cambridge University Press, 2000, 269 pages.

The volume in Cambridge University Press's *Introduction to Religion* series provides a solid foundation for the study of contemporary Judaism in all its richness and variety. Jewish history is discussed along with Jewish rituals and practices, the family and community, Jewish theology, and issues that Judaism must confront today. Useful as a reference work, this book contains illustrative tables and maps, a comprehensive glossary, chronology, bibliography, and index.

Lewis, C. S. *Mere Christianity*
Harper, 2001 (1943), 256 pp.

The essays collected here originated as radio lectures delivered during World War II when Europe was on the brink of collapse, and then published separately in three books. Lewis, a Christian apologist, addresses the central beliefs of Christianity common to all Christians, explicating their traditional wisdom against the detractors of the age. Many have declared this work the most important and accessible defense of Christianity of the 20th Century.

Naipaul, V. S. *Beyond Belief: Excursions Among the Converted Peoples*
Vintage, 1999 (1998), 432 pages.

"This is a book about people," claims Naipaul of his survey of the non-Arab Islamic countries he visited in 1979 and again in 1995. Naipaul's wide-ranging conversations with individuals from Indonesia, Iran, Pakistan, and Malaysia inform this account of the devotion, doubts, and tribulations of people in four nations that have converted to Islam over the past 1,400 years.

Neihardt, John. *Black Elk Speaks: Being the Life Story of a Holy Man of the Oglala Sioux*
Bison Books, 2004 (1932), 320 pages.

This is the story of Nicholas Black Elk (1863–1950), the Lakota holy man, and his people during the last part of the 19th Century when the Lakota way of life was extinguished. It is based on a series of conversations he had with John Neihardt in 1930. Black Elk speaks of his early life (he was present at the battles of Little Big Horn and Wounded Knee) and his spiritual visions. This religious classic depicts the great mystery of life from a Native American perspective.

Novak, Philip, Editor. *The World's Wisdom: Sacred Texts of the World's Religions*
Harper One, 1995 (1994), 448 pages.

This is the companion to Huston Smith's *The World's Religions*, assembling in one volume selections of key texts from the world's religious traditions. The selections are chosen according to their inspirational power and instructional value, and are organized to mirror Smith's chapters, thus covering eight religious traditions. As a very useful resource for studying the world's religions, this anthology of sacred texts amounts to something like a world Bible.

Smith, Huston. *The World's Religions: Our Great Wisdom Traditions*
Harper & Row, 1991 (1958), 399 pages.

Long considered the best and most accessible introduction to the world's religions, this revised edition of Smith's classic beautifully conveys the spirit of each religion while explaining its origins, teachings, and beliefs. The religions covered are Hinduism, Buddhism, Confucianism, Taoism, Islam, Judaism, Christianity, and Primal Religions. Smith attends to the mainline tradition of each religion, casting it in its best light with sympathetic respect.

Spink, Kathryn. *Mother Teresa: A Complete Authorized Biography*
Harper One, 1998, 336 pages.

This is a full account of the life of the Albanian Catholic nun Agnes Bojaxhiu, known to the world as Mother Teresa. This revered woman dedicated her life to serving the poorest of the poor in the slums of India. This sympathetic biography covers her entire life, from her childhood in the Balkans, to her founding the Missionaries of Charity in 1950, to her being awarded the Nobel Peace Prize in 1979, to her death in 1997. It is an inspiring story of a modern-day saint.

Stark, Rodney. *Discovering God: The Origins of the Great Religions and the Evolution of Belief*
Harper One, 2008 (2007), 496 pages.

A sociologist of religion, Stark provides a sweeping survey of the origins of the world's faiths. He traces the rise of religious belief from Stone Age spirituality through the world's major religions. This is not just another work in comparative religion. Stark's Judeo-Christian point of view and comparative judgments are bound to be controversial, but this compelling study is hard to ignore, especially in light of recent books promoting the "delusional" theory of religion.

# 10. Science

For readers who want to satisfy their curiosity about how the world works, these 20 books on science will fascinate and inform with their accounts of cutting-edge discoveries and their current depictions of the physical world. These books cover topics from current research in astronomy to evolution, animal behavior, and medicine.

❖          ❖          ❖

Bryson, Bill. *A Short History of Nearly Everything*
Broadway, 2004 (2003), 560 pages.

In this intellectual odyssey, presented as a biography of the universe, Bryson covers the history of science from the 18th to the 20th Century. It's a fascinating story of scientists and their discoveries in various fields: cosmology, geology, chemistry, paleontology, biology, astronomy, and physics. Infused with humor and an anecdotal style, this instructive and entertaining book includes a wealth of scientific knowledge that is made clear and comprehensible for lay readers.

## Physical Sciences

Ferris, Timothy. *The Whole Shebang: A State of the Universe(s) Report*
Simon & Schuster, 2008 (1997), 400 pages.

Ferris, a journalist and science writer, has written a number of popular books on astronomy. Here he gives a lucid summary of current research in physics and astronomy in order to explain how scientists envision the universe as a whole based on the Big Bang theory of origins. It's a splendid introduction to the field for a general audience seeking an explanation of contemporary cosmology. Not only science buffs will take delight in the awesomeness of the subject.

Hawking, Stephen and Leonard Mlodinow. *A Briefer History of Time*
Bantam, 2008 (2005), 176 pages.

When Hawking's *A Brief History of Time* was published in 1988, it quickly became an "unread bestseller" because many found its concepts difficult to grasp. This abridged, simplified version makes the range of subjects in cosmology (big bang, black holes, superstring theory, etc.) more accessible. It has now been updated to address new developments. Some might prefer *The Illustrated A Brief History of Time*, an expanded and updated version published in 1996.

Sacks, Oliver. *Uncle Tungsten*
Vintage, 2002, 352 pages.

The title refers to the author's Uncle Dave, a chemist who owned a business making incandescent light bulbs from tungsten filament. Sacks wrote this memoir about his childhood to explain his early interest in chemistry, his refuge while growing up in wartime England. His story depicts the formation of a young enquiring mind in troubled times. Seamlessly woven into Sacks' luminous stories of his youth is a very readable account of the history and science of chemistry.

Singh, Simon. *Big Bang: The Origin of the Universe*
Harper Perennial, 2005 (2004), 560 pages.

This is one of the best introductions to the world of astronomy and cosmology. The first chapter tells the history of cosmology from the early Greeks up to 1900. The rest of the book chronicles 20th-Century developments and the Big Bang model of the universe. Along the way we learn of the many brilliant scientists who shaped our view of the cosmos. Each chapter of this entertaining guide ends with handwritten "notebook" sketches summarizing the main points.

Swimme, Brian and Thomas Berry. *The Universe Story*
Harper One, 1994 (1992), 320 pages.

The authors, a cosmologist and cultural historian, provide a comprehensive story of the universe by uniting scientific cosmology with a mythological vision. From the "primordial fireball" to the emergence of humans, they describe the awesome forces and processes in each step of evolution, ultimately seeking to explain the role of humanity in the unfolding story of earth and the cosmos. The tale they tell is a rapturous journey through time, a tale that puts it all together from an integral perspective.

Strathern, Paul. *Mendeleyev's Dream: The Quest for the Elements*
Berkley Trade, 2002, 329 pages.

This is an enlightening book about the history of chemistry. The bulk of the book covers the history of the science from the ancient Greeks to the mid-19th Century. This history culminates in the story of the Russian scientist Dmitri Mendeleyev (introduced in the prologue) who in 1869 discovered the periodic table that he first conceived in a dream. It's a witty and engaging work of popular science. Unfortunately, the periodic table itself is not included.

Zukav, Gary. *The Dancing Wu Li Masters: An Overview of the New Physics*
Harper One, 2001 (1979), 416 pages.

The "new physics" is the science of quantum mechanics and relativity, here presented without the rigor of logical precision. Gary Zukav takes insights from a conference of Eastern and Western physicists to explain the new physics, using descriptive prose, anecdotes, and metaphors. Zukav promotes scientific literacy in this book for laymen.

## Life Sciences

Behe, Michael. *Darwin's Black Box: The Biochemical Challenge to Evolution*
Free Press, 2006 (1996), 352 pages.

Though Darwin's theory of natural selection is widely accepted today as the foundation of biology, there are dissenting voices. Behe, a widely known challenger of Darwinism, is a biochemist who advances the argument from design based on the "irreducible complexity" of biological systems. As this work lays out Intelligent Design from within biology, it amounts to a scientific argument for the existence of God.

De Waal, Frans. *Our Inner Ape: A Leading Primatologist Explains Why We Are Who We Are*
Riverhead Trade, 2006, 304 pages.

De Waal is a recognized biologist and ethologist whose studies on primate behavior cast light on human behavior. In this enjoyable book he draws upon his work with chimpanzees and bonobos, two ape species with vastly different traits, to explore four realms of human behavior: power, sex, violence, and kindness. He argues that humans are "bipolar apes" because we are as much like chimps as like bonobos—competitive and aggressive, but also caring and peaceable.

Gawande, Atul. *Complications: A Surgeon's Notes on an Imperfect Science*
Picador, 2003, 288 pages.

This wonderfully thought-provoking work examines the complex decision-making processes that surgeons undergo in their practice. Gawande illustrates his points by drawing upon numerous cases from his long career as a surgeon, many of which are intriguing medical dramas that will have you on the edge of your seat. Readers will be comforted by the efforts doctors make to learn from their mistakes and by their desire to do whatever they can to save lives.

Groopman, Jerome. *How Doctors Think*
Mariner Books, 2008, 336 pages.

Dr. Groopman, who has written numerous articles for the New Yorker addressing various aspects of the practice of medicine, writes in this book about the complex ways of seeing and thinking that influence how doctors diagnose patients. While most of the time doctors are correct in their diagnoses, Groopman focuses upon those instances where errors in judgment, in many instances resulting from unconscious biases, influence a doctor's diagnosis.

Goodall, Jane. *Through a Window: 30 Years Observing the Gombe Chimpanzees*
Mariner Books, 2000 (1990), 272 pages.

This is the follow-up to Goodall's classic, *In the Shadow of Man*, bringing up to date her observations of chimpanzees in the wild of Gombe National Park in Tanzania over a period of 30 years. Written in the form of a memoir, it's an engrossing account that often draws parallels between animal and human behavior. Goodall's research revolutionized the field of primate ethology. This is her best, most accessible work, and includes numerous photos.

Leakey, Richard and Roger Lewin. *The Origin of Humankind*
Basic Books, 2006 (1996), 190 pages.

The accomplished paleoanthropologist (and son of the famous Louis Leakey) wrote this condensed survey of human origins, focusing on the key events that highlight the evolution of hominids. In the last three chapters, the author explores the evolution of art, language, and consciousness, seeking to explain what makes humans human. It doesn't include the most recent findings, but for those seeking an overview of human origins, it's an excellent place to start.

Lorenz, Konrad Z. *King Solomon's Ring: New Light on Animal Ways*
Plume, 1997 (1952), 272 pages.

Konrad Lorenz's shrewdly told tales of animal life are so lighthearted you might not know that you are learning about imprinting, releaser mechanisms, and combat and display from a pioneer of animal behavior. Committed to observing animals that can move freely in a simulated environment, Lorenz creates true scenes of animal life.

Mayr, Ernst. *What Evolution Is*
Basic Books, 2002, 336 pages.

Mayr was one of the leading evolutionary biologists of the 20th Century. In this work, published shortly before he died at the age of 100, he offers an introductory survey of evolutionary theory that is authoritative but suitable for anyone seeking to learn about the history of the science and the current debates and latest theories. He addresses the central questions raised by Darwinism and its critics. Included are a helpful glossary and an appendix that answers FAQs on evolution.

Miller, Kenneth R. *Finding Darwin's God: A Scientist's Search for Common Ground Between God and Evolution*
Harper Perennial, 2007 (1999), 368 pages.

Miller is a biologist who firmly believes in evolution. He also believes in God. This book seeks to reconcile the two seemingly opposing viewpoints. Miller gives warrant to neither the skeptical evolutionists who find in Darwinian theory no room for religious belief, nor the defenders of Intelligent Design who believe in a supernatural intervention in nature. Instead, he finds a middle ground that attempts to do justice to both science and faith on their own terms.

Pollan, Michael. *The Botany of Desire: A Plant's-Eye View of the World*
Random House, 2002 (2001), 304 pages.

Pollan's insightful, accessible, and wonderfully engaging style is fully on display in this original and thought-provoking study. Pollan's purpose here is to discuss some of the ways in which plants and human beings have come to depend upon each other by focusing upon the natural history of four plants—apples, potatoes, tulips, and cannabis. You won't look at plant life in quite the same way after reading this book.

Thomas, Lewis. *The Lives of a Cell: Notes of a Biology Watcher*
Penguin, 1978 (1973), 160 pages.

In this collection of essays originally published in *The New England Journal of Medicine*, a physician writes about the organized intelligence of organic life. Lewis Thomas uses his knowledge of cellular biology, the human genome, and diverse animal species to ponder the meaning of life and death from the point of view of the organism.

Wade, Nicholas. *Before the Dawn: Recovering the Lost History of Our Ancestors*
Penguin, 2007 (2006), 320 pages.

Scientists are now using DNA research to understand human evolution and the dispersal of *homo sapiens* around the world. The author of this book, a veteran science journalist, draws upon these recent discoveries in genetics to tell the story of how the human ancestral line emerged from northeast Africa about 50,000 years ago and continues to evolve today. This is a cutting-edge report that will enlighten those interested in human origins.

# 11. Essays

The word "essay" comes from a French word meaning "to try." An essay is a short piece of writing in which an author tries out his or her ideas about an important topic. The nine books of essays listed here include commentary on language and society, nature writing, literary criticism, observations of daily life, and personal reflections.

❖     ❖     ❖

Baker, Russell. *The Good Times*
Signet, 1992 (1989), 412 pages.

Russell Baker's mother often told him to "Make something of yourself!" In this sequel to his memoir, *Growing Up*, Baker tells how he did just that. Starting out as a police reporter, Baker eventually won a Pulitzer Prize for his *New York Times* "Observer" column. Each chapter in this book is as humorous and pithy as his acclaimed column.

Bryson, Bill. *Made in America*
Harper Perennial, 1996 (1994), 432 pages.

Bill Bryson views American English with the eyes of a foreigner, his 20 years' residence in England having given him a double perspective on the English language. In *Made in America,* Bryson explains how American speech came to be what it is. Bryson traces the development of American speech from the *Mayflower* to modern advertising.

Didion, Joan. *We Tell Ourselves Stories in Order to Live*
Everyman's Library, 2006, 1,160 pages.

Didion, one of the most accomplished essayists of our age, writes in an elegant, incisive language on a variety of subjects ranging from politics to the arts to matters of cultural import. All of her writing is informed by an interest in exploring the various stories we tell ourselves, both as individuals and as a society, about how and what we are, and the complex ways in which these stories are shaped and transformed.

Dillard, Annie. *Pilgrim at Tinker Creek*
Harper Perennial Modern Classics, 2007 (1974), 304 pages.

Annie Dillard sees Tinker Creek, with its wondrous creatures and surrounding woods, as a microcosm of the world. Like any naturalist with a notebook, she records her observations to focus her attention. Dillard even captures evanescent experiences that border on the mystical, yet her writing is always lively and grounded in a love of nature.

Kingsolver, Barbara. *Small Wonder: Essays*
Harper Perennial, 2005 (2002), 288 pages.

Novelist Barbara Kingsolver offers 23 essays written or rewritten in the shadow of the September 11, 2001 attacks on the U.S. Kingsolver's topics range from the overtly political to the more general, including essays on the Grand Canyon, gardening, and "What is a Story?" Kingsolver is by turns humorous, didactic, and persuasive.

Leopold, Aldo. *A Sand County Almanac, with Essays on Conservation*
Oxford University Press, 2001 (1949), 194 pages.

When this classic of nature writing by renowned conservationist Leopold (1887–1948) was first published, it became a landmark in the American conservation movement. The first part is the almanac itself, which traces the seasonal changes in nature in his native Wisconsin. The second part includes an essay on the wild marshland and Leopold's thoughts on developing a land ethic. This illustrated edition includes 80 photos taken on Leopold's former Wisconsin farm.

Mamet, David. *Writing in Restaurants*
Penguin, 1987 (1986), 176 pages.

American playwright, screenwriter, and director David Mamet discusses contemporary America and the theater in 30 trenchant and entertaining vignettes. In addition to his essays on theater and related topics, such as acting, radio drama, and the Academy Awards, Mamet opines on the vanishing American pool hall, poker, and more.

Oates, Joyce Carol and Robert Atwan. *The Best American Essays of the Century*
Houghton Mifflin, 2000, 596 pages.

From Mark Twain to Saul Bellow, Oates collects 55 essays by America's best-known and a few lesser-known writers from the 20th Century. General themes include the problems of race, science and nature, social change, and the vast range of American identity. Arranged chronologically, these essays give the reader a good sense of where America has been over the course of the past century. The volume is beautifully introduced by both Oates and Atwan.

O'Connor, Flannery. *Mystery and Manners: Occasional Prose*
Farrar, Straus and Giroux, 1990 (1961), 256 pages.

Although best known for her original and provocative short stories that typically dramatize the possibility of faith in a modern, secular society, O'Connor was also a gifted essayist. In the essays collected here, O'Connor reflects upon the nature of her art, the relationship of her art to her faith, and the responsibilities of writers. She also makes occasional and delightful forays into such idiosyncratic topics as her love of peacocks.

# 12. Introduction to History

*Historia* is a Greek word that means "inquiry." History is the story of the past that investigates the record of human events over time. Listed here are 11 books that can get you excited about history– ancient, medieval, and modern. They are interesting, accessible, well-written, and relatively brief. There are many more to choose from in Part Two of this booklist.

❖    ❖    ❖

Cahill, Thomas. *How the Irish Saved Civilization: The Untold Story of Ireland's Heroic Role from the Fall of Rome to the Rise of Medieval Europe*
Anchor, 1996 (1995), 256 pages.

Cahill's popular book on the medieval Irish is the inaugural work in a seven-volume series entitled *The Hinges of History*. This delightful history of the "Dark Ages" tells how the monks and scribes in the land of St. Patrick, untouched by the barbarian invasions on the European continent, preserved the great texts of Greek and Roman antiquity. The work is an homage to the Irish character and the role these Irish scholars played in preserving our civilization.

Craig, Albert M. *The Heritage of Japanese Civilization*
Prentice Hall, 2003, 173 pages.

This brief survey of Japan's history covers its rich heritage from its origins to today. The work highlights the five major eras of Japan's history but also addresses social, economic, and cultural developments that cut across these distinct periods. A number of translations of passages from Japanese literature are included alongside the narrative. Written as a text for students, the five chapters are supplemented by an ample number of review questions, maps, photos, and graphs.

Ellis, Joseph J. *Founding Brothers: The Revolutionary Generation*
Vintage, 2002 (2000), 304 pages.

This collection of stories of seven founding fathers—Franklin, Washington, Jefferson, Adams, Hamilton, Burr, and Madison—tells how they confronted overwhelming challenges in the post-revolutionary period when the success of our nation was still in doubt. Written by a renowned Pulitzer Prize-winning historian, these six stories—from the Hamilton-Burr duel to Jefferson and Adams's famous correspondence—combine a lively and elegant style with deft interpretation.

Fritze, Ronald H. *New Worlds: The Great Voyages of Discovery 1400–1600*
Praeger, 2003 (2002), 285 pages.

This beautifully illustrated book narrates the important period in Western history when the European world and worldview were transformed. Beginning with a portrait of medieval Europe, the work focuses on the great voyages of discovery by Columbus, da Gama, Cabot, Magellan, etc., which led to the huge expansion of trade and the rise of colonial empires. New research brings to life this critical period that gave birth to the modern world.

Hamilton, Edith. *The Greek Way*
W. W. Norton, 1994 (1930), 212 pages.

This is not so much a history but an inspiring account of the achievements of the Greeks: their religion, politics, art, philosophy, science, and literature. Aimed at an audience unfamiliar with Greek history and culture, Hamilton preserves the legacy of the Greeks in a work that is a joy to read. This work is one of the best introductions to the Greeks and their contribution to Western civilization.

Howarth, David. *1066: The Year of the Conquest*
Penguin, 1981 (1977), 208 pages.

The focus of this story is just one year—the watershed year in European history when England was conquered by the Normans. The book opens up the entire world of the Middle Ages and describes some of its more significant characters, particularly Duke William "The Conqueror" and King Harold. Told from the viewpoint of a common Englishman, this engaging story explains the background of the conquest and culminates in the final battle at Hastings.

Pagden, Anthony. *Peoples and Empires: A Short History of European Migration, Exploration, and Conquest from Greece to the Present*
Random House (Modern Library Chronicles), 2003 (2001), 256 pages.

This is the story of the great European Empires—Greek, Roman, Spanish, French, and British— their colonies and culture, and their impact on people. The historical range is sweeping and the theme of conquest is universal. An expert on the history of human migrations, the author gives a compact but lively account of the rise and fall of empires and the forced migrations of people that result. Included are a chronology and an annotated list of important historical figures.

Pipes, Richard. *Communism: A History*
Random House (Modern Library Chronicles), 2003, 192 pages.

A scholar of Russian history, Pipes tells the story of the rise and fall of Communism and its catastrophic impact on the modern world. The work is essentially a history of the Soviet Union from the October Revolution to its collapse seven decades later, though the spread of Communism to other countries is discussed as well. The author's concise account of Soviet ideology and atrocities is a stark and grim story.

Wills, Garry. *Lincoln at Gettysburg: The Words That Remade America*
Simon & Schuster, 2006 (1993), 320 pages.

This Pulitzer Prize-winning work analyzes the most famous speech in American history in its political and historical context. Wills details the heavy influence of the early Greeks (particularly Pericles) and the 19th-Century Transcendentalists on this brief literary masterpiece. Originally panned by newspaper reviewers, Lincoln's 272 immortal words have never before been submitted to such a provocative and illuminating study.

Wood, Gordon. *The American Revolution: A History*
Random House (Modern Library Chronicles), 2003 (2000), 224 pages.

This is a concise and lucid account of the events and circumstances surrounding our nation's birth. Written by a premier Pulitzer Prize-winning historian, this engaging story of the Revolution addresses the great themes of liberty, power, and rights. It's a great synthesis that doesn't argue for any new interpretation but reflects the scholarship of the last 30 years. Included are four maps and a chronology of events.

Zoch, Paul A. *Ancient Rome: An Introductory History*
University of Oklahoma, 2000 (1998), 300 pages.

This is an introductory history of ancient Rome for the general reader, covering the period from Rome's mythical origins to the reign of Marcus Aurelius. The focus is political and military history but is weighted toward early Rome and the Republic. Though the imperial period is condensed, this straightforward, informative overview brings to life the most important figures and episodes in Rome's history, as well as their moral and political lessons.

# 13. Journals and Magazines

Journal reading is one of the best ways to keep current and to gain new information about a field of interest.  Listed here are 16 well-known journals on politics, literature, culture, science, social science, and technology.  Read any of these journals as an introduction to a subject area or to update your knowledge.

## Business and Finance

*Business Week.*  Publisher: McGraw-Hill; First issue: 1929; Circulation: 986,000/week.

A weekly business magazine with up-to-date information and breaking news.  Its articles focus on business, management, finance, economics, technology, and occasionally other topics.  The magazine's focus is more American than global and more corporate than personal.  Its target audience is business managers and business students.  *Business Week's* annual ranking of MBA programs in American business schools is considered authoritative.

*The Economist.*  Publisher: The Economist Group (UK); First issue: 1843; Circulation: 1.3 million/week (616,000/week in US).

A prestigious, weekly news and international affairs magazine written in an engaging and readable style.  Its editorial stance is classical liberal, favoring free markets and globalization with minimum government intervention.  *The Economist* is a British publication with a global emphasis.  It targets educated readers, keeping them on top of world events, economic trends, and political developments.  There are no book or movie reviews, and almost no pop culture.

*Forbes.*  Publisher: Forbes Media; First issue: 1917; Circulation: 900,000/biweekly.

A biweekly business magazine known for its annual list of richest Americans (Forbes 400).  The motto of *Forbes* is "The Capitalist Tool."  It targets top corporate management and investors, profiles successful companies and individuals, and offers financial and business analysis.  Its website, Forbes.com, advertises itself as the "Home Page for the World's Business Leaders" and claims to be the most widely visited business website.

*Harvard Business Review.*  Publisher: Harvard Business Publishing; First issue: 1922; Circulation: 246,000/month.

*Harvard Business Review,* published monthly by Harvard Business Publishing, is one of the top authorities on leadership, management, and the sources of success in the global economy.  Its focus is on helping managers become better leaders, as well as on decision-making, entrepreneurship in the modern world, and how to use technology to help your business succeed.  Most issues also include profiles of innovative and inspiring leaders and corporations.

# Political

*The American Spectator.*  Publisher: American Spectator Foundation; First issue: 1967; Circulation: 50,000/month.

A monthly, conservative journal of public opinion covering news and politics.  It features investigative reporting, informed analysis, and comprehensive book reviews.  The magazine gained prominence in the 1990s for its reporting on political scandals and its attacks on President Clinton.  *The American Spectator* features conservative writers such as George Will, Ben Stein, Patrick Buchanan, Thomas Sowell, and P. J. O'Rourke.

*Commentary.*  Publisher: Commentary, Inc.; First issue: 1945; Circulation: 27,000/month.

Founded by the American Jewish Committee, *Commentary* is an American monthly magazine covering politics, international affairs, Judaism, and social, cultural, and literary issues.  It bills itself as "America's premier monthly magazine of opinion."  It began as a liberal, anti-Communist voice, but since the 1970s it has become the flagship for neoconservatism.  Each issue includes reviews of books on various topics.

*The Nation.*  Publisher: The Nation Company, L.P.; First issue: 1865; Circulation 174,000/week.

A weekly periodical devoted to politics and culture.  It bills itself as "the flagship of the left" and remains proudly independent of political parties and corporate interests.  It champions civil liberties, human rights, and economic justice.  *The Nation*, founded by abolitionists at the end of the Civil War, is the oldest, continuously published weekly in the U.S.

*National Review.*  Publisher: Jack Fowler; First issue 1955; Circulation 162,091/biweekly.

A biweekly, conservative magazine founded by William F. Buckley.  It bills itself as "America's most widely read and influential magazine and web site for Republican/conservative views, commentary, and opinion."  Considered the voice of the American Conservative movement for the last half-century, many of its writers are affiliated with conservative think tanks like the Heritage Foundation and the American Enterprise Institute.

*The New Republic.*  Publisher: CanWest Global Communications; First issue: 1914; Circulation: 60,000/biweekly.

*The New Republic* is a center-left, biweekly magazine of politics, international affairs, and the arts.  The magazine generally supports liberal social and economic politics, while taking a hawkish view on foreign policy.  It offers reportage and analysis of the news in an engaging, argumentative style.  The second half of each issue is devoted to criticism of books, theater, film, music, and art.

## Literary and Cultural

*The Atlantic.*  Publisher: Atlantic Media Company; First issue: 1857; Circulation: 400,000/issue.

Originally a monthly (and known as *The Atlantic Monthly*), the magazine is now issued ten times a year.  *The Atlantic* publishes articles in politics, foreign affairs, economics, cultural trends, arts, and the humanities.  It also contains letters to the editor, poetry, and sections on travel, food, and book reviews.  Since 2005 it no longer publishes fiction except for a newsstand-only annual fiction issue edited by C. Michael Curtis.

*Harper's Magazine.*  Publisher: HarperCollins; First issue: 1850; Circulation: 220,000/month.

A monthly, general-interest magazine covering politics, culture, finance, science, literature, and the arts.  It offers substantive essays on current issues, as well as short fiction and book reviews.  *Harper's* is an American institution, being the second-oldest, continuously published magazine (after *Scientific American*) in the U.S.  It includes some popular features such as "Harper's Index," a list of statistical facts arranged for ironic and thoughtful effect.

*The New Criterion.*  Publisher: Foundation for Cultural Review; First issue: 1982; Circulation 6,500/month.

A monthly, literary journal (10 issues annually) that publishes artistic and cultural criticism with regular sections on poetry, theater, art, music, the media, and books.  As a defender of Western civilization and high culture, *The New Criterion* bills itself as being "in the forefront both of championing what is best and most humanely vital in our cultural inheritance and in exposing what is mendacious, corrosive, and spurious."

*The New Yorker.*  Publisher: Advance Publications; First issue: 1925; Circulation: 1 million/issue.

A cultural and literary magazine that publishes 47 issues per year.  It includes reportage, commentary, criticism, essays, fiction, film, satire, and poetry.  *The New Yorker* has established itself as the leading forum for serious journalism and fiction.  It is particularly known for its covers and cartoons, as well as its urban, liberal, New Yorker's view of the world.  With 48 national magazine awards, *The New Yorker* is the most honored magazine in publishing history.

## Science and Social Science

*Nature.* Publisher: Nature Publishing Group, U.K.; First issue: 1869; Circulation 65,000/week.

A premier, British scientific journal published weekly. *Nature* is one of the few science journals that publishes peer-reviewed, original research in a wide range of scientific fields. Though the primary target audience is scientists, many of the research articles are made accessible to the general public. *Nature* estimates its readership is about ten times its circulation.

*Psychology Today.* Publisher: Sussex Publishers Network; First issue: 1967; Circulation: 300,000/bimonthly.

A bimonthly magazine that publishes articles related to psychology for the mass market. Often based on psychological surveys, its articles focus chiefly on popular issues like love, sex, relationships, health, happiness, depression, mind-body connection, and related areas. *Psychology Today* features a regular education column and advice column, and its web site offers valuable resources in the areas of health and therapy.

*Scientific American.* Publisher: Scientific American, Inc.; First issue: 1845; Circulation 645,000/month.

A monthly, popular science magazine. It is the oldest, continuously published magazine in the U.S. *Scientific American* is not a peer-reviewed science journal like *Nature*, but a forum where scientific theories and discoveries are explained to a general audience. Aimed at educated readers interested in the latest advances in the physical sciences, the magazine has broadened its appeal by offering articles on the social sciences as well.

## Computers and Technology

*Wired Magazine.* Publisher: Condé Nast Publications; First issue: 1993; Circulation: 706,000/month.

A monthly magazine that reports on how technology affects culture, based on the founder's belief that technology can change the world. It targets a tech-savvy audience familiar with computers and the Internet. It has published some agenda-setting articles by pioneers in the high-tech industry. Its full-color pages employ experimental design and arresting photography. *Wired* has been lauded for its originality and vision, and impact on culture.

# Part Two
# The Humanities: History, Biography, and the Classics

# Introduction to Part Two
# The Humanities: History, Biography, and the Classics

The humanities section of this booklist includes many of the greatest works our human heritage has to offer. Found here are essential works that represent the major civilizations in world history. The humanities list is divided into two parts: Western History and Literature, and World History and Literature. Each part contains history books and biographies, followed by the classics. Our selection of classics is introductory, not comprehensive. Like the history and biography books, they were chosen for their interest level and accessibility. Taken as a whole, this humanities list is a record of human experience that helps us remember our past, live fully in our present, and envision our future.

The classics foster an ideal: an open mind and soul engaged in a study of the accumulated knowledge, truth, and wisdom that a civilization has to offer. We study the classics in order to develop our full humanity, for these books illuminate what is essentially human in us. They guide our intellectual, moral, and spiritual formation by exposing us to the true, the good, and the beautiful, as well as to the dark side of human nature. They help us pursue a life of excellence by expanding our horizons and attuning us to what is highest in human experience. Great books help us answer the timeless questions: What does it mean to be human? What is the right way to live?

Since the dawn of civilization, people just like us have lived, worked, loved, and struggled. Do I struggle to find worthwhile work that pays enough to support me or my family? Am I having a hard time finding meaning in my life, or a meaningful path through it? And what about love, is it reflected in my relationships? The classics are classics because they have lasted, and they have lasted because they speak clearly to us of the struggles we face every day. They encourage us to strive for meaning and value in life, and help us recognize these things when we find them.

History books and biographies provide historical context for the classics, and are fun and rewarding to read in their own right. By narrating the sweep of human events, they capture the unfolding drama of the human story. By revealing the infinite variety of human character, they provide an array of lives and deeds for us to either emulate or condemn. Together, they capture the grand pageant of human existence. If it weren't for histories and biographies, we would have no idea what is true about human nature, since these genres tell us the truth about what people have really done. These works illuminate the patterns of human events in time, and thus offer an endless source of insight into our own lives and time. They give us a fascinating account of what has actually transpired in the past, which is often stranger and more entertaining than fiction.

There are several ways to use this list:

1. To read books of personal interest. Just look through the list and find individual works of interest, whether history, biography, or literature. Simply choose a title and read. You could productively keep with this approach for years. If you follow this path, you may become especially interested in one of the periods or places you read about. If that happens, this approach could naturally morph into the second or third approach described below.

2. To get an education in the history and literature of the West. The West is our civilization, and it is alive. It is valuable to know the sweep and spirit of this long tradition, as it has formed our consciousness today. Indeed, Western history and literature provide the framework for our contemporary culture. The truth, wisdom, and beauty inherent in this tradition are the sources of our civilization's hope.

   There are a couple of approaches you could use to get an education in the history and literature of the West. One approach would be to read the history and/or literature of a particular period or place, like Ancient Greece or the United States. If you like this approach, you could follow it with other periods or regions that interest you. Another, very ambitious approach would be to read chronologically through each major period in Western history from antiquity to the present. No matter what your approach, read as much or as little of the history and/or literature in each period as your interests dictate.

3. To learn about a major world civilization like China or India. This booklist includes many histories and classic works of literature from important world cultures. Reading these works can add to our knowledge of the world and enrich our lives. For example, the ancient traditions of India and China—found in the Hindu, Buddhist, Daoist, and Confucian texts on the list—offer tremendous resources for our intellectual, moral, and spiritual development. Other cultures and regions of the world represented on the list have their own unique traditions that are just as valuable.

   To educate yourself in a particular civilization, read its history and/or literature. Choose a civilization based on your own personal interest or heritage and read a selection of books from that section. If you find that approach enriching, you could do the same for another region or civilization that sparks your interest.

This is your booklist. You determine how you want to use it. There are enough good books on this list to keep you reading for many years and through many changes of circumstance and purpose.

A note on the selected titles: The literature books are established classics. These works are readily available because they remain in print. Most of the history books and biographies were published in the last 25 years or so and are also readily available.

# Western History and Literature

Western History and Literature is divided into five major sections. The first section is comprised of general surveys of Western history covering antiquity to the present. The heart of the list follows and is organized into three main sections: Antiquity, the Middle Ages and the Early Modern Period, and the Modern Period. Each of these three main sections is divided into subsections, which are arranged chronologically by sub-period or by region. Each of these subsections in turn is organized by genre: history first, biography second, and literature third. The final section, Specialized Histories, includes works that cross historical periods, such as art history and military history.

In most of these subsections, the list of history books begins with broad surveys of an historical period, listed under History: Survey. These are followed by history books that are more focused and that offer the author's perspective on events, listed under History. Also included here are biographies, autobiographies, and memoirs, listed under Biography. For many people, these are a particularly interesting way to learn history.

The classics from the ancient, medieval, and early modern periods, as well as great works of modern literature, are listed in each section under Literature. For those new to the literature of Greece, Rome, the Middle Ages, and the Early Modern Period, we list reading guides at the beginning of these literature sections under Literature: Reading Guide. The list of modern literature is comprised principally of novels and plays, but there is also a selection of short stories and poetry. All together, the titles in these sections represent an introduction to the Western canon—the greatest works of literature in the Western tradition. Reading these texts can have a profound impact on us. They reveal the drama of human existence, and encourage us to live lives of meaning and value.

# I. Surveys of Western History

Alcock, Antony. *A Short History of Europe: From the Greeks and Romans to the Present Day*
Palgrave Macmillan, 2nd ed., 2002 (1998), 344 pages.

In this substantive but condensed work, the sweep of European history is covered in its political, economic, social, and cultural aspects from the Greek city states to the end of the 20th Century. The engaging narrative highlights the three key pillars of European civilization: Greek political thought, Roman law, and the Christian religion. It ends with a discussion of Europe's increasing political and cultural integration. The revised edition brings the material up to date.

Blainey, Geoffrey. *A Very Short History of the World*
Penguin, rev. ed., 2007 (2004), 496 pages.

This abridged account of the author's *A Short History of the World* makes his sketch of human history even more accessible. Beginning when humans first left Africa to settle the globe, this lucid and entertaining account traces the course of human progress around the world. The author favors technical, economic, and geographic factors at the expense of political developments, but this allows the reader to get a feel for how daily life has changed over the millennia.

Davis, James C. *The Human Story: Our History from the Stone Age to Today*
HarperCollins, 2004, 466 pages.

A work that covers 4000+ years of world history under 450 pages is bound to be sketchy, but this splendid tour of the human story brings together the major developments in a very readable volume. It covers Eastern and Western history (though mostly Western). Written in an engaging, light-hearted fashion free of academic jargon, this survey makes a great introduction to world history or a fine review for those who slept through high school history classes.

Dunn, John. *Democracy: A History*
Atlantic Monthly Press, 2005, 246 pages.

Dunn is a British political theorist who presents here a general history of democracy and its basic conditions, principles, and challenges. He begins with the first appearance of democracy in ancient Greece, and covers the liberal rights tradition, the rise of the American republic, the French Revolution, and the recent resurgence of democracy in Eastern Europe. He explains why democracy is such a compelling idea and how it has evolved and triumphed in the modern world.

Pagden, Anthony. *Peoples and Empires: A Short History of European Migration, Exploration, and Conquest from Greece to the Present*
Random House (Modern Library Chronicles), 2003 (2001), 256 pages.

This is the story of the great European Empires—Greek, Roman, Spanish, French, and British—their colonies and culture, and their impact on people. The historical range is sweeping and the theme of conquest is universal. An expert on the history of human migrations, the author gives a compact but lively account of the rise and fall of empires and the forced migrations of people that result. Included are a chronology and an annotated list of important historical figures.

# II. Antiquity

Antiquity is divided into five sections: Surveys, The Ancient Middle East, Greece, Rome, and the Judeo-Christian Period. The first section, Surveys, contains two overviews of ancient history. The other four sections are organized in general chronological order. Each of these is subdivided into history, biography, and literature.

Western civilization rests on three pillars: Jerusalem, Athens, and Rome. From Jerusalem derives our spiritual ideals and moral values; from Athens our rationality, science, sense of beauty, and understanding of virtue; from Rome our understanding of how justice can be achieved through law and government. All the works of literature of this period, particularly the literature of ancient Greece and Rome, are the classics. Traditionally, the classics were the principal study of the humanities, for they contain, it was held, "the best of what has been thought and said in the world." These primary texts from classical antiquity provide the animating vision that underlies Western culture. Their depth of wisdom and achievement in beauty are the source of their immense influence and authority.

Familiarity with this ancient literature is valuable not only for one's intellectual, moral, and spiritual development, but also for understanding later works of Western literature that stand downstream from the classics. A knowledge of ancient mythology is also useful for understanding Western culture, which is particularly full of references to Greek myths and legends. Finally, the Bible—the Hebrew Bible (the Old Testament to Christians) and the New Testament (Christian)—is an absolute prerequisite for understanding Western civilization, particularly its moral and spiritual development. Along with the literature, the history books and biographies listed here are accessible and inviting works. The ancient lives and events they narrate provide us real insight into the truth of human nature. They all have the power to stir us.

There are a number of ways you could use this list. You could just find individual books of interest, whether history, biography, or literature. If this gets you excited about a particular period, you could then read as much of its history and literature as you find interesting. Or, you could decide in advance to educate yourself in a particular period. For example, you might choose ancient Greece or ancient Rome and read a selection of books from that section. If you like that approach, you could do the same for another period. If you are very interested in the foundations of Western civilization, you could read chronologically through this entire section, period by period. This is your list; you decide how you want to use it.

## A. Surveys

Bauer, Susan Wise. *The History of the Ancient World: From the Earliest Accounts to the Fall of Rome*
W. W. Norton, 2007, 868 pages.

In this first of a projected four-volume series on the history of the world, the author presents a political history of the major ancient civilizations: Mesopotamia, Egypt, Greece, Rome, India, and China. This comprehensive but fast-paced tour is organized in the form of discrete essays that recount the parallel development of each part of the ancient world. Generously illustrated with pictures, maps, and 85 timelines, this rich tapestry is a great place to begin a study of antiquity.

Hollister, C. Warren and Guy Rogers. *Roots of the Western Tradition: A Short History of the Ancient World*
McGraw-Hill, 8th ed., 2007, 304 pages.

Written for students, this brief survey covers the histories of the Near East, Greece, and Rome from about 3000 BC to 500 AD. The author highlights the connections between the Near Eastern cultures and Greco-Roman civilization, as well as historians' varying interpretations. This is a good introduction that provides a guide for further study. The eighth edition has been updated to include the latest scholarship and new timelines.

# B. The Ancient Middle East

The Ancient Near East encompassed the civilizations of Southwest Asia between the Mediterranean and Iran. This included Mesopotamia (Iraq), the Levant (Syria, Israel, Lebanon, and Jordan), and Asia Minor (Turkey). If you add Egypt, the Arabian Peninsula, and Iran, then this larger region is what is today called the Middle East.

The ancient civilizations of Mesopotamia and Egypt are the oldest in human history. By the middle of the 6th millennium BC, early agricultural settlements had sprung up in the Tigris-Euphrates River Valley as well as along the Nile. In the 18th Century BC, the cities of the whole Mesopotamian region were conquered by the king of Babylon, Hammurabi, and incorporated into the Old Babylonian Empire. Thereafter, various empires ruled Mesopotamia until 539 BC, when the whole region was conquered by Persia (Iran) under Cyrus the Great. In ancient Egypt, King Menes founded the First Dynasty around 3100 BC. Over the next three millennia, Egypt's history unfolded in a series of three stable periods: the Old Kingdom, the Middle Kingdom, and the New Kingdom. Eventually, at the end of its last Kingdom, Egypt was conquered by Cyrus's son and also absorbed into the Persian Empire.

Many ancient myths and religions emerged from this region of the world. The civilizations of Egypt, Mesopotamia, and ancient Persia (Iran) had a major influence on the Hebrew Bible, as well as on Greek philosophy and culture. As a result, their legacy still lives on in the Judeo-Christian tradition of the West.

The annotated works that follow are organized by genre: first history, then literature. The history books include an historical survey of the Ancient Near East, a history of Mesopotamia, and a history of ancient Egypt. The literature includes three important texts to emerge from Mesopotamia. Of these, most readers will find *The Epic of Gilgamesh* to be of greatest interest. The most critical writings to emerge from the Ancient Near East are the Hebrew scriptures. These texts lie at the origin of the Judeo-Christian tradition and form the Old Testament of the Christian Bible. These sacred writings are must reading because they contain the timeless principles and spiritual insights that underlie the entire Western tradition.

## HISTORY: SURVEY

Van De Mieroop, Marc. *A History of the Ancient Near East, ca. 3000–323 BC*
Blackwell, 2nd ed., 2006 (2004), 341 pages.

This is a clear and concise survey of the history of Sumeria, Babylonia, Assyria, Persia, and the Hittite Empire. The author addresses political, social, and cultural developments from the appearance of Mesopotamian city states to Alexander's conquest of Persia. Also discussed are key texts, such as the Bible and *The Epic of Gilgamesh*. Well illustrated with photos and useful maps, this updated edition incorporates the latest scholarship and expands the guides to further reading.

## HISTORY

Ascalone, Enrico. *Mesopotamia: Assyrians, Sumerians, Babylonians*
University of California Press, 2007, 368 pages.

This beautifully illustrated guide to the three ancient civilizations of Mesopotamia is packed with information about the people, politics, art, religion, and key places of the region. The author is an archeologist who examines the surviving artifacts to paint a vivid picture of the Mesopotamian way of life. Scholarly but accessible, this volume includes color photos, detailed maps, and sidebars that make it an enjoyable companion for the armchair traveler and archeologist.

Silverman, David P., Editor. *Ancient Egypt*
Oxford University Press, 2003 (1997), 256 pages.

A team of scholars contributed to this splendid overview of Ancient Egypt, which includes the latest theories and discoveries. From the lives of the pharaohs to the mystery of hieroglyphics, all aspects of Egyptian life are covered in 15 chapters. The topics include history, geography, culture, economy, archeology, religion, myths, art, architecture, and language. The lavishly illustrated book contains over 200 color photographs, maps, and charts, along with a glossary.

## LITERATURE

**Saunders, N. K.,** Translator. *The Epic of Gilgamesh* (22nd Century BC and later)
Penguin Epics, 2006 (1960), 80 pages.

*The Epic of Gilgamesh* predates the Homeric poems by at least 1,000 years. The separate poems that make up the epic were recorded by the second millennium BC. Gilgamesh, king of Uruk in Mesopotamia, is literature's first hero, and his search for immortality is literature's first quest. In addition to stories of the adventures of Gilgamesh and his friend, Enkidu, the Gilgamesh cycle includes the Story of the Deluge.

**Dalley, Stephanie,** Translator. *Myths from Mesopotamia: Creation, the Flood, Gilgamesh, and Others* (18th Century BC and later)
Oxford World's Classics, 2008, 368 pages.

The *Enuma Elish* is a Babylonian creation myth that dates from about the 18th Century BC. It tells the story of how Marduk defeated Tiamat and thus became the supreme god over all Mesopotamian gods. The oldest and greatest literary composition from the ancient Near East is the fragmentary *Epic of Gilgamesh*, which tells the story of the king's heroic quest for fame and immortality, here provided in a verse translation. This Oxford edition also includes other Mesopotamian myths along with helpful study aids.

**King, L. W.,** Translator.  *The Code of Hammurabi* (c. 1790 BC)
Forgotten Books, 2007, 81 pages.

Created by the sixth Babylonian king, Hammurabi (ruled c. 1796–1760 BC), this is one of the earliest sets of laws that survive.  The Code is basically a list of crimes and their draconian punishments.  Excavated in 1901, the 282 laws were carved in cuneiform on an eight-foot high basalt stone monument for all to see, so no one could plead ignorance of the law.  This edition contains an explanatory introduction from the Eleventh Edition of the Encyclopedia Britannica (1910–1911).

**The Hebrew Bible,** or *Tanakh* (c. 10th–3rd Centuries BC)

The Hebrew Bible (for Christians, the Old Testament) is the religious literature of the Jewish people.  This collection of 39 books was written almost entirely in Hebrew from the 11th to the 2nd Centuries BC.  Traditionally it consists of the Law, Prophets, and Writings.  The richness of this religious literature is unparalleled, and none has exerted a greater influence on Western Civilization.  A study edition is recommended, such as *The New Oxford Annotated Bible* (NRSV).

**Armour, Robert A.**  *Gods and Myths of Ancient Egypt*
American University in Cairo Press, 2nd ed., 2001 (1986), 207 pages.

Egyptian mythology has a treasure of marvelous tales that entertain and inspire.  This collection includes stories of the sun god Ra, the adventures of Osiris and Isis, the battle of Horus and his uncle Seth, the Book of Thoth, and the famous Tale of Two Brothers.  Armour's retelling of these classic tales includes an illuminating overview and commentary.  The revised edition has updated appendices and bibliography, over 50 new photographs, and drawings that depict the gods and goddesses.

# C. Greece

Ancient Greek civilization began with the Minoans and Mycenaeans. The Minoans were a bronze-age people who flourished on the island of Crete from roughly 2700 to 1500 BC. They were followed by the Mycenaeans, who dominated mainland Greece from about 1500 to 1200 BC. Both groups established high civilizations that developed writing, art, commerce, and a complex social structure. Mycenaean civilization collapsed around 1200 BC, probably due to an invasion by barbarian tribes, inaugurating four hundred years of the Greek Dark Ages.

After the Dark Ages, the history of ancient Greece can be divided into three periods:

The Archaic Age (c. 800–500 BC), the period that saw the rise of the Greek city-states.

The Classical Age (c. 500–323 BC), the period when Greek civilization reached its peak and produced its greatest works in politics, philosophy, art, architecture, history, and literature.

The Hellenistic Age (323–146 BC), the period that began with the death of Alexander the Great and ended with the Roman conquest of Greece.

The literature of ancient Greece includes historical and philosophical writings as well as poetry and plays. Greek literature first emerged during the Archaic Age, often referred to as the Homeric Age due to the centrality of Homer's great epic poems. These poems tell of epic heroes Achilles (*The Iliad*) and Odysseus (*The Odyssey*), whose stories are part of the myth cycle of the Trojan War. Homer's works symbolize the operation of divine presence in human affairs. His tales evoke the forces of order and disorder in the human soul and society, as well as the interplay between divine and human reality.

Greek civilization reached its acme during the Classical Age, which gave birth to Western history, philosophy, and drama. Prior to this time, the Greeks understood their civilization through the reenactment and retelling of myths that were transmitted from generation to generation. In the Classical Age, Greek philosophers began a rigorous investigation into the truth of these myths, not to debunk them, but to inquire into the reality they symbolized. These philosophers discovered reason as the unique human faculty that apprehends the truth of things. At the same time, Greek historians inaugurated a new understanding of the past based on the interpretation of evidence from primary sources, giving us historical records of events such as the Persian Wars and the Peloponnesian War.

At the center of Greek cultural development was the city-state of Athens, whose democratic institutions flourished in the Classical Age. The flowering of Athenian theater gave birth to both tragedy and comedy. For Greek audiences, tragedy was something like a group religious experience. By witnessing a play that dealt with a conflict in contemporary society or in Greek prehistory or in the world of Greek myths, Greek citizens imaginatively participated in a just or moral resolution of the conflict. Comedies, on the other hand, offered them a humorous questioning of contemporary Greek society. The greatness of Greek drama cannot be overstated. The works of the Greek tragedians are still considered some of the best plays ever written.

The books listed under History: Survey, History, Biography, and Literature: Reading Guide provide a substantive overview of ancient Greece. These books tell the fascinating story of a very modern civilization that started almost 5,000 years ago and reached its peak almost 2,500 years ago. They are also excellent introductions to Greek literature, philosophy, and historical writing, as they provide a valuable context for understanding the primary texts that follow.

### HISTORY: SURVEY

Cartledge, Paul, Editor. *Cambridge Illustrated History of Ancient Greece*
Cambridge University Press, 2002, 400 pages.

The cultural history of ancient Greece is rendered visually luminous in this richly illustrated portrait for the general reader. The chapters, written by experts in their fields, are arranged topically and cover every aspect of Greek civilization, including Greek wars, social structure, myths, religion, art, science, lifestyle, and politics. The enormous legacy of the Greeks is splendidly told in this visual *tour de force*, which can be read by both beginner and classicist alike.

Martin, Thomas R. *Ancient Greece: From Prehistoric to Hellenistic Times*
Yale University Press, 2000 (1996), 254 pages.

The course of Greek civilization is made accessible and engaging in this compact but comprehensive introduction. The author integrates social, cultural, political, and military history in a way that brings alive the people and times of ancient Hellas. The major focus is on the rise and development of the Greek city-state, which culminates in the Golden Age of Athens. Illustrations and timelines supplement this very readable overview for the general reader.

### HISTORY

Hanson, Victor Davis. *The Wars of the Ancient Greeks*
HarperCollins, 2006 (2002), 240 pages.

Hanson, a renowned historian of ancient Greece, explains the nature of Greek warfare and its impact on world history. He traces the evolution of Greek fighting from the Mycenaean age to the Macedonian period, explaining how warfare was an integral part of Greek society. Emphasis is given to describing hoplite culture, tactics, and technology, but not naval warfare. This is a highly readable work enriched by photographs, battle maps, and other illustrations.

Perrottet, Tony. *The Naked Olympics: The True Story of the Ancient Games*
Random House, 2004, 240 pages.

In this entertaining work, the author provides a fascinating look at the ancient Greeks by focusing on their sports. The Olympics were an essential part of Hellenic culture and Perrottet examines every feature of the games and the athletes in all their glory (and brutality). Filled with interesting anecdotes, the book includes illustrations (mostly of original vase paintings), a timeline, and an appendix detailing the quadrennial Olympic Program, which occurred over five raucous days.

**BIOGRAPHY**

Kagan, Donald. *Pericles of Athens and the Birth of Democracy* (c. 495–429 BC)
Free Press, 1998 (1991), 287 pages.

Kagan is the foremost authority on the Golden Age of Athens and the Peloponnesian War. In this biography of Pericles, which is also an illuminating account of the birth of democracy in ancient Greece, he brings to life the great Athenian general and statesman against the background of turbulent times in the Greek 5th Century. Writing for a general audience, Kagan enriches his discussion by drawing numerous parallels with modern history.

Renault, Mary. *The Nature of Alexander the Great* (356–323 BC)
Penguin, 2001 (1975), 240 pages.

There are dozens of biographies of Alexander the Great. This is arguably the best. Renault, who is known for her historical fiction, presents a compelling character study of the towering figure of ancient Greece who conquered much of the known world by the age of 30. Her passionate reconstruction of the charismatic leader and most successful military commander of all time is an unforgettable story that reads like a novel.

**LITERATURE: READING GUIDE**

Cahill, Thomas. *Sailing the Wine-Dark Sea: Why the Greeks Matter*
Random House, 2004, 304 pages.

This fourth volume in Cahill's *Hinges of History* series is not a history of the Greeks but an exploration of the major contributions they made to Western civilization. In each chapter, Cahill examines a particular social role that portrays an essential contribution, such as the warrior, the poet, the politician, and the philosopher. While lengthy quotations substitute for any new interpretations or insights, Cahill provides an interesting and accessible overview of the Greek legacy.

Guthrie, W. K. C. *The Greek Philosophers: From Thales to Aristotle*
Harper, 1975 (1950), 168 pages.

Though written over 50 years ago, this remains the best short introduction to Greek philosophy. The work sketches the progression of philosophical ideas from the Presocratics and the Sophists to Socrates, Plato, and Aristotle, focusing especially on cosmology, theology, the nature of the soul, ethics, and politics. This lucid and concise survey will give those new to Greek philosophy a basic understanding of these great thinkers as well as insight into the ancient Greek world.

Hamilton, Edith. *The Greek Way*
W. W. Norton, 1994 (1930), 212 pages.

This is not so much a history but an inspiring account of the achievements of the Greeks: their religion, politics, art, philosophy, science, and literature. Aimed at an audience unfamiliar with Greek history and culture, Hamilton preserves the legacy of the Greeks in a work that is a joy to read. This work is one of the best introductions to the Greeks and their contribution to Western civilization.

LITERATURE

**Schwab, Gustav.** *Gods and Heroes of Ancient Greece*
Pantheon, 2001 (1946), 768 pages.

Schwab retells the central Greek myths as a continuous narrative, allowing the reader to grasp familiar story cycles such as those of Jason and the Argonauts and heroes Herakles and Theseus in their entirety. Because such myth cycles—well known to audiences in ancient Greece—form the basis for the poetic and dramatic masterpieces of antiquity, it is useful, as well as enjoyable, for the modern reader to become acquainted with these tales by following a sequence of story arcs from beginning to end.

**Homer** (c. 8th Century BC). Homer is the Greek epic poet known in ancient times as the author of the *Iliad* and the *Odyssey*. Because some scholars have found evidence that the Homeric poems derive from more than one source, multiple authorship of the poems has been suggested. However, recent scholarship confirms the authorship of "one Homer." The source material for the epics, including myths and stories about Troy, originated between the 12th and the 9th Centuries BC.

*The Iliad* (c. 8th Century BC)
Translated by Stanley Lombardo. Hackett, 1997, 516 pages.

Homer's great epic war poem is remarkable for its story, characters, and theme, and for the detailed realization of its historical setting. The *Iliad*'s theme is the anger of Achilles—the Greeks' best warrior—over his dishonoring by Agamemnon, leader of the Greek army at the siege of Troy. The psychology of Homer's characters is realistically rendered, especially in the case of Achilles, the first tragic hero in Western literature.

*The Odyssey* (c. 8th Century BC)
Translated by Stanley Lombardo. Hackett, 2000, 414 pages.

While Homer's epic poem, the *Iliad*, chronicles the events of the Trojan War, this companion piece chronicles the Greek hero Odysseus's efforts to get back home after the Greeks have finally defeated the Trojans. The poem shifts back and forth between Odysseus's various misadventures at sea and the chaos that rules at home as Odysseus's wife and son faithfully wait for his return. Readers new to Greek literature will readily appreciate the brilliant tapestry of scene, incident, character, and language that are the hallmarks of this remarkable work.

**Hesiod** (c. 8th Century BC). Hesiod was a Greek poet who likely composed his works in the late 8th Century BC. A Boeotian farmer, Hesiod's work represents the epic tradition of mainland Greece, which focused on moral maxims, technical aspects of daily life, and religion.

*Works and Days* and *Theogony* (c. late 8th Century BC)
Translated by Stanley Lombardo. Hackett, 1993, 128 pages.

*Works and Days.* The four parts of this 828-line poem are unified by Hesiod's moral purpose: to demonstrate how best to live in a world beset by strife. To that end, Hesiod explains the origin of evil, exhorts his audience to work and shows how work defeats want, offers precepts for domestic life, and provides a farmer's almanac. Woven into the narrative are the myths of Prometheus and Pandora and an account of the Five Ages of the World.

**Hesiod (cont.)**

*Theogony.* This narrative of the Greek gods' family tree tells how the gods came into being, and how conflicts among them climaxed in a battle leading to the permanent divine pantheon and the rule of Zeus. The many divine genealogies included in the poem are part of the poet's overall design: to show the origin of the gods and the universe. Hesiod's poem provides the most complete surviving continuous narrative on the genesis of the Greek gods.

**Aesop** (c. 620–560 BC). Aesop, renowned as a storyteller, was said by Herodotus to have been a slave who lived in Greece during the reign of Amasis of Egypt, in the mid-6th Century BC.

*Aesop's Fables* (c. early 6th Century BC)
Translated by Laura Gibbs. Oxford World's Classics, 2008, 352 pages.

Collected and written down for the first time in the 3rd Century BC, Aesop's fables were considered literature for adults, not children, in the ancient world. These brief stories often featured anthropomorphic animals ("The Ant and the Grasshopper," "The Tortoise and the Hare") and served a didactic purpose. The fables typically end with a moral to make sure their point is clear. This edition includes 600 fables with an introduction and notes.

**McKirahan, Richard D.,** Translator. *A Presocratics Reader: Selected Fragments and Testimonia* (6th–5th Centuries BC)
Hackett, 1996, 126 pages.

The birth of philosophy can be traced back to the wise men of Greece who preceded Socrates, such as Thales, Anaximander, Anaximenes, Pythagoras, Xenophanes, Heraclitus, Parmenides, Anaxagoras, Empedocles, and the Sophists. These Presocratic philosophers broke with the religious myth and established reason as the new standard for knowing the world. This edition contains a significant selection of their works, which survive only in fragments.

**Aeschylus** (525–456 BC) is the founder of Greek tragedy. He introduced a second actor into the drama, creating dramatic action through dialogue. Aeschylus wrote some 90 plays, of which seven have survived. Altogether he won 14 first-place prizes at the Athenian festivals, the first in 484 BC. Indeed, all of his extant plays, except for *Prometheus Bound*, won first place at the festival of Dionysia. The inscription on Aeschylus's gravestone makes no mention of his literary renown, as he wanted to be remembered only for the valor he displayed while defending Greece at the Battle of Marathon.

*Seven Against Thebes* (467 BC)
In *The Complete Aeschylus: Volume II: Persians and Other Plays.*
Oxford University Press, 2009, 432 pages.

In this spare tragedy Aeschylus presents the fratricidal conflict between Eteocles and Polyneices over the kingship of Thebes. This tale of civic strife unfolds through conversations between the Chorus and a sequence of characters. At the end of the play, the overlapping laments of sisters Ismene and Antigone dramatize the family tragedy from a private perspective.

**Aeschylus (cont.)**

*The Oresteia* (458 BC)
In *The Oresteia: Agamemnon; The Libation Bearers; The Eumenides*.
Translated by Robert Fagles. Penguin Classics, 1984, 336 pages.

The great drama *Oresteia* shows the working out of the curse of the House of Atreus through suffering and expiation. The trilogy is unparalleled as a work of dramatic unity, exceptionally rich in action, character, and symbolism. *Agamemnon* enacts the king's murder by his wife Clytemnestra. In *The Libation Bearers*, Orestes, son of Agamemnon and Clytemnestra, kills his mother in revenge, but is driven mad by her Furies. In *The Eumenides*, Orestes flees the Furies, who agree to release him only after he is tried by an Athenian jury.

Also read: *Prometheus Bound* (c. 480s).

**Pindar** (522–443 BC). Pindar was a Greek lyric poet known for the grandeur of his verse and for the skillful weaving of myth and symbol into his victory odes. Born to a noble Spartan family, Pindar studied in Athens. Hieron I of Syracuse commissioned him to write odes celebrating victories at the Olympics and other athletic games.

*The Odes of Pindar* (c. 498–444 BC)
Translated by C. M. Bowra. Penguin Classics, 1982, 256 pages.

The complete odes of Pindar celebrate victories in the Greek athletic games as epiphanies bringing man closer to the gods. Pindar's best odes grace the winning athletes with immortal glory by associating them with key myths. Read: "Olympian I" (Tantalos), "Olympian III" (Herakles), "Pythian IV" (Jason and the Golden Fleece), and "Nemean I" (Baby Herakles).

**Sophocles** (c. 496–406 BC). The great tragedian Sophocles was an innovator who introduced the third actor into Greek tragedy. In his plays, human action plays a decisive role, while fate plays a lesser role than in Aeschylus' dramas. Born near Athens, he was twice elected to office and won 20 first-place prizes at the festivals, the most of any Greek playwright. Of his 120 plays, seven survive.

*Antigone* (c. 442 BC)
In *The Three Theban Plays: Antigone; Oedipus the King; Oedipus at Colonus*.
Translated by Robert Fagles. Penguin Classics, 2000, 430 pages.

The Greek playwright Sophocles wrote tragedies notable for their penetrating insight into the complex interplay of fate and choice in determining human action. *Antigone*, one of Sophocles' most intense and thoughtful plays, is at one level about one woman's refusal to compromise her moral integrity and sense of religious duty, even to the point of death. A deeper reading of the play suggests that Antigone's actions are also driven by a sense of despair over the misfortunes that have dogged her family line, including the tragic fate of her famous father, Oedipus.

Also read: *Oedipus at Colonus* (401 BC).

**Sophocles** (cont.)

*Oedipus the King* (429 BC)
In *The Oedipus Cycle: Oedipus Rex, Oedipus at Colonus, Antigone.*
Translated by Dudley Fitts and Robert Fitzgerald. Harvest, 2002, 272 pages.

Cited by Aristotle as the model for plot development, *Oedipus the King* is a masterpiece of Greek theater. Oedipus, the archetypal Sophoclean hero, confronts the consequences of his *hubris* (pride) at the same time that he suffers the inevitability of his tragic fate. The tension of the drama is heightened by Sophoclean irony, in which the audience already knows what the characters in the play are striving to discover.

**Herodotus** (c. 484–425 BC). Herodotus is regarded as the "Father of History" in Western culture. He systematically collected his materials in wide-ranging travels throughout Greece, Persia, and Egypt. His single narrative of the Persian Wars reports all he learned and includes some folklore and mythic elements as well.

*The Histories* (c. 431–425 BC)
Translated by Aubery de Selincourt. Penguin Classics, 2003, 784 pages.

This first work of Western history tells the story of the war between the Greeks and the Persians (490–479 BC). *The Histories* is a long, thrilling account of heroes and battles (culminating in the battles of Marathon, Thermopylae, and Salamis). Herodotus gives fascinating insights into the ancient world, often drawing on myths and legends of the gods. Book 1 on the lead-up to the Persian Wars is highly recommended.

**Euripides** (c. 480–406 BC). Euripides' dramas of psychological realism depict human nature by revealing the soul's passions and conflicts. Perhaps the most modern of Greek dramatists, he wrote 90 plays of which 19 survive. Born in Salamis, Euripides won five first-place prizes at the Athenian festivals. His innovative plays often feature prominent female characters.

*Medea* (431 BC)
In *Ten Plays by Euripides.*
Translated by Moses Hadas. Bantam Classics, 1990, 432 pages.

Euripides' tragedy dramatizes the fate of his larger-than-life heroine, Medea, who personifies the irrational in human nature. As Medea once betrayed her kin for love of Jason, so now, at the start of the drama, she plots a grandiose, horrific vengeance in response to her betrayal by Jason. This tense drama realizes Euripides' tragic vision of humankind beset by unruly passions.
Also read: *Hippolytus* (428 BC), *Helen* (412 BC), and *Iphigenia at Aulis* (408 BC).

**Thucydides** (c. 460–395 BC). The Greek historian Thucydides is considered the father of "scientific history" because of his strict standard of evidence and his analysis of events without appeal to the gods. His account of the Peloponnesian War displays an interest in human nature, as he sought to explain why humans engage in such behaviors as genocide and civil war.

*History of the Peloponnesian War* (c. 431–395 BC)
In *On Justice, Power, and Human Nature: Selections from the History of the Peloponnesian War*
Translated by Paul Woodruff. Hackett, 1993, 172 pages.

Thucydides' *History of the Peloponnesian War* tells the story of the 27-year-long conflict between Athens and Sparta up to the end of the 21st year of the war in 411 BC. He vividly recounts many episodes in which he himself took part. This accessible abridgement comes with introduction, notes, glossary, maps, and chronology.

**Aristophanes** (c. 456–386 BC). Aristophanes, the great Athenian playwright, wrote comedies known for their dialogue and outrageous humor, and won six first-place prizes at the religious festivals. He was tried for treason due to an attack on the demagogue Cleon in his play *The Babylonians*. In his political plays, Aristophanes opposed his government's war policy.

*The Clouds* (423 BC)
In *Four Plays by Aristophanes: The Birds; The Clouds; The Frogs; Lysistrata.*
Translated by William Arrowsmith. Plume, 1994, 624 pages.

Aristophanes sends up Socrates and the Sophists in this comedy pitting rustic Everyman Strepsiades against the urban lifestyle and the New Learning. When Strepsiades enrolls his son in Socrates' academy to teach him to defraud the family's creditors, the boy's success in rhetoric has unexpected consequences. Aristophanes' historically inaccurate caricature of Socrates is integral to this satire. Also read: *The Birds* (414 BC), *Lysistrata* (411 BC), and *The Frogs* (405 BC).

**Plato** (427–347 BC). The student of Socrates and founder of the Academy in Athens, Plato laid the foundations for Western philosophy and science. Along with Aristotle's works, Plato's dialogues rank as the most important philosophical works of the Western world. Their influence is reflected in the works of later philosophers and in the development of Christian theology.

*Apology*
In *Five Dialogues: Euthyphro, Apology, Crito, Meno, Phaedo.*
Translated by G. M. A. Grube. Hackett, 2nd ed., 2002, 156 pages.

Plato's early "Socratic" dialogues recount the last days of his beloved teacher Socrates, who plays the dominant role in all of his dialogues. The *Apology* recounts Socrates' defense at his trial. Here we witness the character of Socrates and the Socratic method of philosophy in action as Socrates refutes the charges against him—impiety and corrupting the youth of Athens. His defense against his accusers is unsuccessful as he is condemned to death by the jury.

**Plato** (cont.)

*Phaedo*
In *Five Dialogues: Euthyphro, Apology, Crito, Meno, Phaedo*.
Translated by G. M. A. Grube. Hackett, 2nd ed., 2002, 156 pages.

The *Phaedo* recounts the last hours of Socrates. Seeking to persuade his friends that a just man has nothing to fear from death, Socrates launches into four arguments for the immortality of the soul. The dialogue ends with his own dramatic death, which he faces in a state of utter repose as he believes death is the liberation of the soul from the mortal realm. In no other dialogue is Plato's dictum that philosophy is "the art of dying" so effectively portrayed. This dialogue also introduces us to Plato's famous doctrine of Forms, which holds that the material world of change known by the senses is only a shadow of a higher reality. The universal Forms or Ideas are the only object of study that can provide genuine knowledge.

*Republic*
Translated by C. D. C. Reeve. Hackett, 2004, 358 pages.

The *Republic* is considered Plato's most important dialogue. Socrates seeks the nature of justice to be found in both the soul and society. Following the principle that society is the soul writ large, Plato describes an ideal city where justice rules because just men, philosopher-kings, rule. Most recommended are Book 4, where Plato explains his psychology of the tripartite soul, and Book 7 on the education of the philosopher, which is illustrated in the famous parable of the cave.

*Symposium*
Translated by Alexander Nehamas & Paul Woodruff. Hackett, 1989, 80 pages.

The *Symposium* is the more famous of Plato's two dialogues on love (the other being the *Phaedrus*). It is Plato's most dramatic dialogue and the only one named after an event. The occasion is a drinking-party where six of Athens' leading men give different views on the nature of Love. Of course the greatest speech is delivered by Socrates, whose wisdom derives from a prophetess named Diotima who taught him the Ladder of Love that ascends to the True, the Good, and the Beautiful.

**Aristotle** (384–322 BC). The student of Plato and the teacher of Alexander the Great, Aristotle was one of the most important founding figures of Western philosophy. He wrote on every area of learning, including the natural sciences, logic, aesthetics, poetry, rhetoric, morality, politics, and metaphysics. Aristotle profoundly influenced medieval philosophers and theologians.

*Poetics*
Translated by Malcolm Heath. Penguin Classics, 1997, 144 pages.

This work combined with the *Rhetoric* comprise Aristotle's work in literary analysis. The *Poetics* is a short, fragmentary work, often claimed to be the greatest work of literary criticism. For Aristotle poetry treats of tragedy, comedy, and epic verse. The *Poetics* concentrates mostly on tragedy, and Aristotle often draws on the three masters of the Greek theater–Aeschylus, Sophocles, and Euripides–to illustrate his analysis.

**Aristotle (cont.)**

*Nicomachean Ethics*
Translated by Terence Irwin.  Hackett, 2nd ed., 1999, 361 pages.

Not a published work but a collection of lecture notes, Aristotle's *Ethics* explores the highest goal of man conceived as happiness that is defined as "an activity of the soul in accord with virtue." What follows is an analysis of the moral and intellectual virtues that constitute the good life.  This is a challenging work that promises many rewards.  Most recommended are Books 1, 2, 6, and 10, though readers interested in Aristotle's discussion of friendship should also read Books 8 and 9.

*Politics*
Translated by C. D. C. Reeve.  Hackett, 1998, 384 pages.

One of the most widely read books on government, the *Politics* is a continuation of Aristotle's *Ethics* in that it applies his theories on the good of the individual to the good of society.  Together these works comprise Aristotle's "philosophy of human affairs."  Based on the factors that contribute to man's happiness, the *Politics* explores the social institutions and forms of government that are most conducive to attaining those goals.  Recommended are Books 1, 4, and 6.

# D. Rome

The history of ancient Rome extends over a thousand years from its founding in 753 BC. Rising as a small city amidst the declining Etruscan civilization of west-central Italy, it gradually conquered neighboring territories over the next two centuries. In 510 BC Rome constituted itself as a republic, governed by a Senate of nobles and wealthy landowners. By the mid-2nd Century BC, the Roman Republic had emerged as the dominant military power in the Mediterranean. The Republic came to an end with the reign of Julius Caesar, who was assassinated in 44 BC.

Rome's Imperial Age began when Augustus was declared emperor in 27 BC. For four centuries the Roman Empire expanded and flourished, establishing what became known as the Pax Romana, or peace of Rome, throughout the Mediterranean world. Through a network of well-maintained roads and public services, including an advanced judicial system, Rome established a level of social order and a standard of living not seen again for more than a millennium. The division of the empire between East and West began in 330 AD, when Emperor Constantine moved the capital from Rome to Byzantium, which he renamed Constantinople (today Istanbul). The Western Roman Empire eventually succumbed to invading barbarian tribes in 476 AD, when the last Western emperor, Romulus Augustus, was deposed by Odoacer, a Germanic general.

Roman literature continued the cultural tradition of Greece. Although Rome had a more effective military and political structure that enabled it to conquer Greece, Greece's higher culture greatly influenced Roman civilization. Pragmatic by nature, more interested in the social than in the individual, and somewhat skeptical of religion, Roman writers typically used Greek myths as a means for exploring the various ways in which human beings either contribute to a society's flourishing or aid in its decline. Roman literature is also marked by an elegant, sophisticated use of language, owing to the emphasis in Roman education upon the rhetorical arts. Latin, the language of Roman literature, continued to be the *lingua franca* of Europe long after Rome's fall, and it was to the great authors listed here that students of Latin turned for their instruction.

The literature listed in this section falls into several categories. There is the compelling imaginative literature of Virgil, Ovid, Horace, and Seneca, as well as examples of Rome's great rhetorical tradition in the essays of Cicero, the reflections of Marcus Aurelius, and the pronouncements of Roman law codified by emperor Justinian. But the highest literary achievement of the Romans was in history— Polybius, Plutarch, and Livy. These writers applied Rome's practical sensibility to the realm of political and social history.

The books listed under History: Survey, History, Biography, and Literature: Reading Guide provide a substantive overview of ancient Rome. These books tell the fascinating story of a successful, dominant civilization that lasted over a thousand years and that underlies our own. They are also very helpful introductions to Roman literature, philosophy, and historical writing, as they provide a valuable context for understanding the primary texts that follow.

### History: Survey

Woolf, Greg, Editor.  *Cambridge Illustrated History of the Roman World*
Cambridge University Press, 2003, 384 pages.

In this general introduction, a group of leading international scholars provide a cogent summary of
Roman history from its mythical founding in the mid-8th Century BC to its fall in the early 5th
Century AD.  Chapters on a broad range of topics follow a rough chronological order.  The weight
is given to the imperial period.  Like all volumes in the *Cambridge Illustrated History* series, the color
illustrations throughout are a visual feast.

Zoch, Paul A.  *Ancient Rome: An Introductory History*
University of Oklahoma, 2000 (1998), 300 pages.

This is an introductory history of ancient Rome for the general reader, covering the period from
Rome's mythical origins to the reign of Marcus Aurelius.  The focus is political and military history
but is weighted toward early Rome and the Republic.  Though the imperial period is condensed, this
straightforward, informative overview brings to life the most important figures and episodes in Rome's
history, as well as their moral and political lessons.

### History

Connolly, Peter and Hazel Dodge.  *The Ancient City: Life in Classical Athens and Rome*
Oxford University Press, 2000 (1998), 256 pages.

Few books make ancient history come to life like this visual tour of classical Athens and Rome.
The full-page color drawings are stunning and full of detail.  Numerous photographs and artistic
reproductions enhance this extensive survey of the daily life, history, and architecture of Athens in the
5th Century BC and Rome during the early empire.  A wealth of information is presented in concise
sections in each of the 24 topically arranged chapters.  It's a feast for the eye and the mind.

Goldsworthy, Adrian.  *Roman Warfare*
Phoenix Press, 2007 (2000), 240 pages.

This is not a history of Rome's wars but how it made war.  The Roman army was the most
proficient fighting force in the world, vanquishing its enemies and making Rome the Master of the
Mediterranean.   The author charts the rise and progress of the Roman military system from the
early republic to the fall of the empire.  Numerous photos, maps, charts, diagrams of battles, and
informative appendices flesh out this beautiful volume.

**BIOGRAPHY**

Bradford, Ernle. *Hannibal* (248–182 BC)
Wordsworth, 2000 (1981), 224 pages.

This incisive biography of the famous Carthaginian general is weaved into a history of the Second Punic War (218–201 BC). The author covers all the major battles as he follows Hannibal's campaign into Spain, across the Alps, down the length of Italy, and finally back to North Africa. He tells how the Romans, after taking huge military losses, eventually prevailed through dogged persistence. This is a captivating story of the character of Hannibal and the long war he waged.

Everitt, Anthony. *Cicero: The Life and Times of Rome's Greatest Politician* (106–43 BC)
Random House, 2003, 400 pages.

Best known as Rome's greatest orator, philosopher, and defender of republicanism, Cicero was at the center of Roman politics in the last years of the Republic. Everitt brings to life the man and his work in this absorbing biography. He situates Cicero's life in the momentous events of his time, taking us from Cicero's early life, through the years of Rome's political turmoil and expanding empire, to his tragic ending. It's a masterful tale of the man and his legacy.

Freeman, Philip. *Julius Caesar* (100–44 BC)
Simon & Schuster, 2008, 416 pages.

In this highly readable biography, Freeman provides a fascinating look into the character and deeds of the famous Roman general and statesman who dominated the late Roman republic and shaped its destiny. Caesar was a complex man, both hero and villain, and Freeman presents him in all his dimensions and contradictions from his early years to his assassination in 44 BC. This is a captivating, action-packed story of one of the great figures of history.

**LITERATURE: READING GUIDE**

Hamilton, Edith. *The Roman Way*
W. W. Norton, 1994 (1932), 185 pages.

Following her earlier *The Greek Way*, the author illuminates the life and spirit of ancient Rome through its greatest men of letters: Plautus, Terence, Cicero, Caesar, Catullus, Horace, Virgil, Livy, Seneca, Tacitus, and Juvenal. Cicero is given the greatest length because his writings are the richest source of information for any period of Roman history. Written in 1932, this work remains a fine introduction to Roman literature.

LITERATURE

**Polybius** (c. 203–120 BC). Polybius was a Greek historian who also served as a soldier and statesman. He traveled widely and had personal knowledge of the events he narrates. He is often regarded as the successor of Thucydides because of his objective historical research. He is among the first historians to present history as a sequence of causes and effects.

*The Histories* (c. 150–120)
In *The Rise of the Roman Empire.*
Translated by Ian Scott-Kilvert. Penguin Classics, 1980, 574 pages.

Originally written in forty volumes, Polybius' *Histories* gives a pragmatic account of how Rome became a dominant world power by subjugating Carthage in the three Punic Wars covering the years 264–146 BC. Highly recommended are Book III, which covers the conflict with Hannibal in the Second Punic War, and Book 6, the long digression on the Roman constitution where Polybius explains why the Roman military and political order were superior to all others.

**Cicero** (106–43 BC). Cicero was Rome's chief political theorist, philosopher, orator, and statesman. A prolific writer, he introduced Romans to the major schools of Greek philosophy. He is remembered as the great defender of the Roman Republic, and is known mostly for his philosophical and political writings, as well as his humanism.

*The Republic* (54–51 BC) and *The Laws* (c. 51–43 BC)
Translated by Niall Rudd. Oxford World's Classics, 2008, 288 pages.

Cicero's two dialogues, loosely modeled on Plato's dialogues of the same name, were written just before the civil war that brought the Roman Republic to an end. In the *Republic* he analyzes Rome's superior constitutional order against alternatives, while the *Laws* expounds upon his theory of the Natural Law. Both works, which survive in large fragments, extol the virtues of Rome's republican order.

**Virgil** (70–19 BC). Virgil, who wrote at the apex of the Roman empire, is generally regarded as Rome's greatest poet. His best known work is the epic poem, the *Aeneid*, which tells of the founding of Roman civilization.

*The Aeneid* (29–19 BC)
Translated by Robert Fagles. Penguin Classics, 2008, 384 pages.

This epic poem written nearly 800 years after Homer wrote the *Iliad* and the *Odyssey*, continues Homer's narration of the Trojan War and its aftermath by telling the story of the founding of Roman civilization. The poem chronicles the attempts of the Trojan hero, Aeneas, to found a new city (what is to become Rome) after the destruction of Troy. Like Homer's poems, Virgil's epic is rich in character, language, and incident. It is also deeply symbolic, as Virgil intended for it to be a testament to the glory of Roman civilization.

**Horace** (65–8 BC).  Horace was a Roman lyric poet who had an important influence upon such writers as Shakespeare, Wordsworth, and T. S. Eliot.

*The Complete Odes and Epodes* (30–13 BC)
Translated by W. G. Shepard.  Penguin Classics, 1983, 256 pages.

Horace's Odes are notable for their lyrical richness, their gentle wisdom, and their depth of insight into human things.  The universality of the themes they address, such as the nature of friendship, love, and honor, continues to make them relevant for readers today.

**Livy** (59 BC–17 AD).  Livy was one of the towering figures of Roman letters.  His monumental *History of Rome* is one of the pioneering works of history writing.

*The Early History of Rome* (27–25 BC)
Translated by Aubrey de Selincourt.  Penguin Classics, 2002, 528 pages.

The books in *The Early History of Rome* cover the founding of Rome (c. 753 BC) to the time of its invasion by the Gauls in 386 BC.  Writing at a time when Rome was in decline after an unprecedented period of political and civic success, Livy hoped to remind the Roman people of the virtues that had made them great by calling attention to the excellence of its past leaders.  He was also interested in capturing the scope and drama of Roman history for future readers, like us.  Recommended: pages 33–139.

**Ovid** (43 BC–17 AD).  Ovid, one of the pillars of Roman literature, is best known for his enduringly popular and highly influential work, the *Metamorphoses*.

*The Metamorphoses* (8 AD)
In *Tales From Ovid*.
Translated by Ted Hughes.  Farrar, Straus and Giroux, 1999, 272 pages.

The *Metamorphoses* is one of the most popular and influential works of classical literature due to Ovid's highly inventive take on popular Greek myths.  His reworkings are chiefly notable for their unorthodox treatment of heroes and gods—a treatment that reflects the skeptical attitude of Roman civilization toward the Greek pantheon.  Ted Hughes, a renowned poet in his own right, brings to life some of the most compelling of these myths in this vibrant translation.

**Seneca (the Younger)** (4 BC–65 AD).  Seneca was a Roman playwright who had an important influence upon such writers as Dante and Shakespeare.  His work is chiefly notable for its intense depiction of human suffering.

*Trojan Women* (c. 54 BC)
Translated by Frederick Ahl.  Cornell University Press, 1986, 248 pages.

Seneca's dramatic depiction of extreme human experience equals anything one might find in a modern thriller.  Hecuba and Andromache, widows of the King of Troy and his son, are forced to come to terms with everything they had held sacred after their city is destroyed by the Greeks in the Trojan War.
Also read: *Phaedra* (c. 1st Century AD)

**Plutarch** (c. 46–120 AD). Plutarch was a Roman biographer and historian of Greek ancestry who wrote in Greek. His *Lives of the Noble Greeks and Romans* (commonly called *Parallel Lives*) was originally arranged in 23 pairs of biographies to illustrate the common vices and virtues of the famous men of antiquity.

*Lives of the Noble Greeks and Romans* (c. 98–120 AD)
In *Greek Lives* and *Roman Lives*, 2 Volumes.
Translated by Robin Waterfield. Oxford World's Classics, 1998 & 2000, 483 & 551 pages.

Plutarch's illuminating account of great Greek and Roman figures is a significant source for our knowledge of the classical world, and it reveals the impact of human character on political events. The biographies of Greeks Solon, Pericles, Alcibiades, and Alexander are recommended, as are the biographies of Romans Sulla, Pompey, Caesar, and Antony.

**Marcus Aurelius,** (121–180 AD). The closest Rome ever came to a philosopher-king, Marcus Aurelius was the last of Rome's "good emperors." His reign was marked by incessant wars in Iran against the Parthians and in Gaul (France) and across the Danube (Germany) against Germanic tribes. He was a noted Stoic philosopher influenced by the writings of Epictetus.

*Meditations* (170s AD)
Translated by A. S. L. Farquharson. Oxford World's Classics, 1998, 195 pages.

Emperor Marcus Aurelius kept a journal of reflections while on campaign against the Germanic barbarians in the last decade of his life. Written in Greek, largely as a guide for self-improvement, this spiritual diary is a valuable resource of Stoic philosophy. Controlling one's emotions and living soberly by reason is the path, if not to a happy life, then at least to a life well lived. Many of the emperor's sage insights are timeless and universal.

**Justinian** (483–565 AD). One of the most important figures of late antiquity, Justinian was the Byzantine Emperor (527–565 AD) who fought to regain Roman provinces from barbarian invaders. He is known for his reorganization of the imperial government, his codification of Roman law, and the building of Hagia Sophia, the great Eastern Orthodox church in Constantinople (today Istanbul).

*The Digest of Roman Law: Theft, Rapine, Damage and Insult* (529–534 AD)
Translated by C. F. Kolbert. Penguin Classics, 1979, 192 pages.

The *Body of Civil Law*, codified under Justinian's reign, was the organization of all Roman legal practices and imperial pronouncements dating back to the early 2nd Century AD. Justinian's codification revived Roman law and gave it an authoritative standing that lasts to this day. The first part, called the *Digest*, was a collection of the writings of 39 jurists. The *Digest* is a particularly interesting part of the *Body of Civil Law*, as it provides a vivid glimpse into the everyday life of Roman citizens by shedding light on legal issues they had to contend with, i.e., laws regarding theft, plunder, damage, and libel.

# E. The Judeo-Christian Period

The Judeo-Christian tradition extends over a long span of time, well over 3000 years. This section covers the first half of this long history. Early Judeo-Christian history begins with the ancient Hebrews (13th–6th Century BC), proceeds into the Second Temple Period (539 BC–70 AD), and continues in the life and teachings of Jesus and his disciples. With the rise of Christianity in the First Century AD, Judaism split into two religious traditions: rabbinic Judaism and Christianity. This period covers the entire sweep of Biblical history from Moses in the13th Century BC up through the early councils of the Church (following the Christian trajectory) in the mid-5th Century AD.

This section contains a short selection of works from this period. The history books cover the origins of the Jewish people and the emergence of Christianity and the developing Church. The two biographies listed are reconstructions of the life of King David and Saint Paul. Since the Hebrew Scriptures (the Old Testament of the Christian Bible) are listed under the Ancient Middle East, the most important literature in this section is the New Testament. The *Gospels, Acts*, and *Epistles* are essential reading because they preserve the history of Christian origins and contain the timeless principles and beliefs that underlie the Western tradition. These foundational writings have had a profound influence on the development of ethics, politics, economics, art, and science in Western history and culture.

## HISTORY

Cahill, Thomas. *The Gifts of the Jews: How a Tribe of Desert Nomads Changed the Way Everyone Thinks and Feels*
Random House, 1999 (1998), 304 pages.

In this second volume in his *Hinges of History* series, Cahill returns to the roots of Western civilization to tell the story of the ancient Hebrews and their impact on history. Beginning with their Sumerian origins, he follows the biblical journey of this migratory tribe to Canaan, to their struggles in Egypt, to their return to Canaan and the forging of a nation, to their exile in Babylon, and finally to their return to Judea. Filled with wonderful nuggets, this is a fascinating account of the "chosen people" who gave us linear history, monotheism, and the Bible.

Cahill, Thomas. *Desire of the Everlasting Hills: The World Before and After Jesus*
Random House, 2002 (1999), 368 pages.

Continuing the story of the roots of Western culture in the third volume of his *Hinges of History* series, Cahill now relates the story of Jesus in the context of the Jewish, Greek, and Roman world of the 1st Century. Drawing on the perspectives of Paul and the four gospels, he explains how Jesus and the movement that sprung from him altered the course of Western history. Cahill's own speculative interpretations enhance this engaging account of Christian origins.

Chadwick, Henry. *The Early Church*
Penguin, rev. ed., 1993 (1967), 320 pages.

The first in the *Penguin History of the Church* series, this volume by the eminent patristic scholar and historian examines the first centuries of the Christian movement from St. Paul up through the 5th Century. In chapters that arrange the material thematically, Chadwick discusses the important Church Fathers, theological debates, heresies, Church councils, and the spread of the early Church. This is a fine introduction to early Church history and Chadwick's insights are always instructive.

Stark, Rodney. *The Rise of Christianity: How the Obscure, Marginal Jesus Movement Became the Dominant Religious Force in the Western World in a Few Centuries*
HarperCollins, 1997, 288 pages.

The subtitle captures the substance of this book by a sociologist who seeks to explain how in the course of three centuries Christianity became the main religion of the Roman empire. Drawing on the methods of social science, statistics, and historical data, Stark identifies the various factors that contributed to the successful spread of the Christian movement. Stark's *Cities of God* (HarperCollins, 2006) explores further his sociological analysis of the rise of Christianity.

**BIOGRAPHY**

Pinsky, Robert. *The Life of David* (c. 1037–970 BC)
Schocken, 2007 (2005), 224 pages.

Pinsky is the former poet laureate of the United States, so one might expect here a poetic account of the shepherd boy who became the king of Israel. Indeed, with literary flourish Pinsky reconstructs and elaborates on the biblical narratives to depict the complex character of the poet-warrior-king in his full humanity, warts and all. David emerges as a great but flawed man, whose stellar achievements made him larger than life and a major hero of the Jewish people.

Stourton, Edward. *Paul of Tarsus: A Visionary Life* (died c. 64–65 AD)
Paulist Press, 2005, 224 pages.

Paul, the Apostle to the Gentiles, contributed greatly to the development of Christianity in its early years. In this sympathetic portrait, Stourton, an accomplished British journalist, fleshes out the life and teachings of this elusive but influential figure. He takes the reader on a journey to the most famous sites Paul visited while spreading the Gospel. This well-researched but highly readable introduction to Paul and his travels illuminates the origins of Christianity.

LITERATURE

### *The New Testament* (c. 50–140 AD)

The writings of the New Testament comprise the second division of the Christian Bible. Its 27 books, originally written in Greek, contain the earliest documents related to the life and death of Jesus, along with his teachings, the witness of the apostles, and the establishment of the early Church. The New Testament should be read by believers and unbelievers alike, for its moral and spiritual value is nonpareil. The Old and New Testaments together comprise the most important writings in Western civilization. A study Bible is recommended, such as *The New Oxford Annotated Bible* (NRSV) or the *New International Version* (NIV).

### **Arnold, Eberhard,** Editor. *The Early Christians: In Their Own Words*
Translated by Society of Brothers, Rifton, NY. Plough Publishing, 1997, 365 pages.

This sourcebook of early Christian writers includes excerpts from Tertullian, Hermas, Justin, Ignatius, Polycarp, Irenaeus, Origen, and Clement of Alexandria. Also included are the extra-biblical sayings of Jesus, the *Didache*, and the early creeds of the Church. Arranged topically, this valuable collection records the life, faith, and development of the early Christian movement (2nd–4th centuries). It can be read as a spiritual guide for Christians today as well as a history of the early Church.

# III. The Middle Ages and the Early Modern Period

The Middle Ages extend from the fall of the Western Roman Empire in the late 5th Century AD up to the end of the 15th Century. Historians usually mark the Early Middle Ages as 500–1000 AD, the High Middle Ages as 1000–1300 AD, and the Late Middle Ages (which includes much of the Renaissance) as 1300–1500 AD.

The Early Modern Era begins in the late 15th and early 16th Centuries with the invention of movable type, the discovery of America, and the division of Christianity into the Catholic and Protestant Churches in the Reformation. It extends to the late 17th Century with the climax of the Scientific Revolution. This era includes the late Renaissance, the Reformation, the Age of Exploration, and the Scientific Revolution.

These two periods together represent the centuries-long transition in Western history from the classical civilization of antiquity to modernity. This transition was marked by the formative impact of Christianity and the Germanic kingdoms, the economic progression from feudalism to the rise of commercial interests and early capitalism, and increasing urbanization and growing royal power.

The titles from these periods are divided into two subsections. The first of these, the Early and High Middle Ages, covers 500–1300 AD, and the second, the Late Middle Ages and Early Modern Era, 1300–1700 AD. We put the Late Middle Ages with the Early Modern period because together they mark the transition from the Middle Ages to the modern world. The books in this second subsection are generally divided by an organizing theme, like the Reformation or Scientific Revolution, except for the last subsection, the Early Modern Period—General, which lists general histories of the period.

This entire section of the booklist, covering about 1,200 years of Western history, represents an immensely fruitful time in the development of Western culture. Though long past, the events of the medieval and early modern periods are of critical importance, as they shaped the modern world we live in today. The history books listed here cover this period in some depth. The selected biographies include some of history's most important and interesting figures, who still speak powerfully to us from across the centuries. The works of literature listed here are well-known classics that include some of the greatest works ever written. In religious thought this literature ranges from Saint Augustine and Saint Aquinas to Dante, Luther, and Milton. The non-religious literature ranges from Beowulf to Chaucer to Shakespeare.

There are several ways you could use this list: You could just read individual books that interest you. If you become especially interested in a particular period, you can pursue that interest as far as you wish. Or, you could decide in advance to learn about one specific period by reading its history and/or literature, then move on to another period that interests you. If you are very interested in this era between the classical foundations of the West and its modern expansion, you could read chronologically through this entire section, reading as much history and literature in each period as you find interesting.

# A. The Early and High Middle Ages

The Early and High Middle Ages extend from 500 to 1300 AD. This was an enormously rich and fruitful period in Western history. Unfortunately, this period was labeled the "Dark Ages" by Petrarch in the 1330s, a term that eventually referred to just the Early Middle Ages (500–1000 AD). This pejorative label is no longer used by scholars, who now recognize the extraordinary civilizational accomplishments made during this period. During these centuries the civilizing power of Christianity served as the mediating force that united Germanic kingdoms, the remnants of Greco-Roman civilization, and Christendom itself to create Western civilization as we know it. During the High Middle Ages (1000–1300 AD), medieval Europe reached a high point in its cultural flowering. Socially the period was marked by a robust population increase; intellectually by the spread of learning and the rise of the university; artistically by Gothic cathedrals and medieval art; economically by the increasing prosperity of towns and villages and the birth of capitalism in the powerful Italian city-states; and politically by the rise of the modern nation-states.

The titles in medieval history listed here treat both secular and religious history. Cantor's survey covers the entire Middle Ages and both Eastern and Western Europe. The history of the Eastern Roman Empire, later termed the Byzantine Empire (which lasted until the fall of Constantinople in 1453), is nicely treated in Herrin's book on Byzantium. Most of the other books focus on Western Europe. The listed biographies include some of the most significant figures of the period, both secular and religious, such as St. Augustine, Charlemagne, and Eleanor of Aquitaine.

A number of books listed in the literature section are works of Christian philosophy, theology, and mysticism. Among them are selected writings of St. Augustine, St. Aelred of Rievaulx, and St. Thomas Aquinas. Listed under Literature: Reading Guide is a book by G. R. Evans that would be helpful for those new to medieval thought, as it explains the philosophy and theology of the period.

During this period, European civilization gave birth to four great epics written in the vernacular, and a masterwork of Norse mythology. This literature features both pre-Christian motifs and Christian themes, and depicts epic heroes whose strength and courage are tested in battles with supernatural beings, human foes, and enemy armies. *Beowulf*, written in Old English between the 8th and 11th Centuries, is the foundational epic of English literature. *The Song of the Nibelungs* (*Nibelungenlied*), written between 1180 and 1210, is drawn from pre-Christian Germanic mythology. Both of these fantastical epics depict heroes battling monsters. *The Song of Roland*, France's national epic, expresses the Christian and feudal values of the 12th Century. *The Song of the Cid*, the first literary work written in Spanish, enshrines El Cid as Spain's legendary national hero. These last two *Songs* are realistic epics recounting historical battles between Christian forces and the (Muslim) Moors. Finally, *The Prose Edda*, written around 1220, is a compilation of pre-Christian myths depicting the heroic deeds of the Norse gods. This work of Norse mythology offers a wonderful symbolism of human experience, with human beings represented as inhabiting a middle realm between the underworld of the giants and the heaven of the gods.

### HISTORY: SURVEY

Cantor, Norman F. *The Civilization of the Middle Ages*
HarperCollins, 1994, 604 pages.

Though billed as a popular history for general readers, this majestic work might intimidate the casual reader. It's a comprehensive survey of the various social, political, intellectual, and religious forces that shaped the Christian European culture of the Middle Ages. Cantor covers the years 300 to 1500 in 21 substantive chapters, piecing together the major and minor events of this era and relating them to each other. For lovers of history, this book is a grand introduction to the enthralling medieval period.

Herrin, Judith. *Byzantium: The Surprising Life of a Medieval Empire*
Princeton University Press, 2008, 440 pages.

In this accessible overview, Herrin brings the latest scholarship on the Byzantine empire to a general audience. Covering over a thousand years from its rise in 306 AD (as the Eastern Roman Empire) to its fall to the Ottomans in 1453, Herrin approaches the subject by theme rather than straight chronology. She argues that without Byzantium there would be no Europe as we know it, for Byzantium served as the eastern defender of Christendom against Muslim expansion.

### HISTORY

Baldwin, John W. *The Scholastic Culture of the Middle Ages, 1000–1300*
Waveland Press, 1997, 125 pages.

In this small book, Baldwin surveys the learning, art, and architecture of the High Middle Ages. The opening chapters cover medieval urban culture, the medieval universities, and the educational movement of scholasticism. The remaining chapters discuss the secular studies of the arts, medicine, and law, as well as theology, the queen of the sciences. A final chapter treats the art and architecture of the Gothic cathedrals. This is an excellent introduction to the topic.

Cahill, Thomas. *How the Irish Saved Civilization: The Untold Story of Ireland's Heroic Role from the Fall of Rome to the Rise of Medieval Europe*
Anchor Books, 1996 (1995), 246 pages.

Cahill's popular book on the medieval Irish is the inaugural work in a seven-volume series entitled *The Hinges of History*. This delightful history of the "Dark Ages" tells how the monks and scribes in the land of St. Patrick, untouched by the barbarian invasions, preserved the great texts of Greek and Roman antiquity. The work is a homage to the Irish character and the role these Irish scholars played in preserving our civilization.

Cahill, Thomas. *Mysteries of the Middle Ages: And the Beginning of the Modern World*
Random House, 2006, 343 pages.

Cahill is a great storyteller and popularizer of history. In this fifth volume of his *Hinges of History* series, he brings to life the iconic figures and places of medieval Europe and explores the intellectual and cultural developments that shaped the medieval worldview and foreshadowed the Renaissance. His treatment of this rich period is more impressionistic and conversational than systematic, but it is always enlightening. The text is beautifully illustrated in color.

Craughwell, Thomas J. *How the Barbarian Invasions Shaped the Modern World: The Vikings, Vandals, Huns, Mongols, Goths, and Tartars who Razed the Old World and Formed the New*
Fair Winds Press, 2008, 320 pages.

The author tells the dramatic stories of the various marauding hordes that transformed Europe and Asia during the Middle Ages. He vividly describes the terror the barbarians created in their destructive conquests, along with the forces that motivated them. These were conquests that brought about the fall of the Roman Empire, the rise of new nations, and the unification of China. Color illustrations, maps, timelines, and vignettes enhance the narrative.

Dawson, Christopher. *Religion and the Rise of Western Culture*
Doubleday, 1991 (1950), 242 pages.

Dawson was one of the great historians of the 20th Century. In this classic work, he explores the origin of Europe and the religious roots of Western culture. Dawson brings an encyclopedic knowledge to bear on his thesis (rather unpopular today) that the spiritual and intellectual qualities that derived from Christian faith transformed European culture and made the West what it is today. This is an exciting read that is definitely worth the time and effort.

Howarth, David. *1066: The Year of the Conquest*
Penguin, 1981 (1977), 207 pages.

The focus of this story is just one year—the watershed year in European history when England was conquered by the Normans. The book opens up the entire world of the early Middle Ages and describes some of its more significant characters, particularly Duke William "the Conqueror" and King Harold. Told from the point of view of a common Englishman, this engaging story explains the background to the conquest and culminates in the final battle at Hastings.

Southern, R. W. *Western Society and the Church in the Middle Ages*
Penguin, 1990 (1970), 384 pages.

This is the second volume in the *Penguin History of the Church* series. Though the subject is the medieval Church from the 8th to the 16th Century, it is also a history of European society during this period of extraordinary development. The author highlights the religious and secular forces that ordered medieval Europe, focusing mostly on the relation between church and state, the East-West schism, the papacy, bishops and archbishops, and the various religious orders.

## BIOGRAPHY

Wills, Garry. *Saint Augustine: A Life* (354–430 AD)
Penguin, 2005, 175 pages.

The biographies in the *Penguin Lives* series introduce great figures in a brief, easy-to-read style. In this selection, Wills traces the major events in the life of St. Augustine, giving a new reading to his early years. He also describes at length Augustine's mature years as bishop when he fought against the heresies of his day. Wills effectively illuminates the nature of this complex thinker and theologian, whose life was essentially the journey of a sinner who became a saint.

Freeman, Philip. *St. Patrick of Ireland: A Biography* (c. 390–460 AD)
Simon & Schuster, 2004, 256 pages.

As an expert in Irish history, Freeman brings to life the story of the real Patrick, the man behind the myths he inspired. Set during the turbulent last years of the Roman Empire, the story follows the journey of the young abducted British aristocratic who spent six years in Ireland as a slave, only to escape and return years later to minister to its people as priest and bishop. This gripping story of Ireland's patron saint is based on the two surviving letters Patrick wrote at the end of his life, which are also included in new translations.

Wilson, Derek. *Charlemagne: A Biography* (742–814 AD)
Doubleday, 2005, 226 pages.

This is a fairly short, straightforward account of the life and times of the Frankish king who in 800 AD was crowned emperor by the pope. The author's emphasis is on how Charlemagne's reign and accomplishments shaped the development of Europe. The last third of the book goes beyond the life of the emperor to discuss how his image was transformed after his death. Accordingly, Wilson relates the impact of Charlemagne's vision of a united Europe on the European Union today.

Burge, James. *Heloise and Abelard: A New Biography* (Abelard: 1079–1142; Heloise: 1101–1164)
HarperCollins, 2003, 319 pages.

One of history's great love stories is told in this updated version. Burge describes the social, political, and religious background of the passionate affair between the scholastic philosopher and his bright, young student, both of whom sought refuge in the Church (they eventually became abbot and abbess) after their clandestine relationship was discovered. Drawing on 113 newly discovered letters attributed to the lovers, Bruge makes a convincing case for their authenticity.

Weir, Alison. *Eleanor of Aquitaine* (1122–1204)
Ballantine Books, 2001, 480 pages.

One of the great heroines of the Middle Ages is given a thorough treatment in this scholarly but readable biography. Eleanor, the wife of two kings and the mother of two more, played a very prominent role in the politics of her day. Weir's detailed research separates myth from reality in her vivid, objective portrait of this exceptional woman. The Middle Ages is richly presented in this engaging romp through 12th-Century France and England.

Chesterton, G. K. *St. Thomas Aquinas* and *St. Francis of Assisi* (Thomas: 1225–1274; Francis: 1181–1226) Ignatius Press, 2003 (1923; 1932), 275 pages.

This volume brings together Chesterton's concise semi-biographies of the two very different saints who represent the rich and vast range of Christian life in the 13th Century. The spiritual kinship the author felt with his two subjects is quite palpable in these personal and illuminating portraits. In his inimitable style, Chesterton describes the essence of each man's character and impact on the world. Fans of Chesterton will be richly rewarded.

## Literature: Reading Guide

Evans, G. R. *Philosophy and Theology in the Middle Ages*
Routledge, 1993, 152 pages.

This is an introduction to the lively intellectual debates of the Middle Ages that began the transformation of the ancient world into the modern. The first part provides an overview of the great medieval scholars and schools and discusses the problems of logic, language, and rhetoric upon which medieval scholarship was based. The second part discusses the topics of God, cosmos, and man. This is a very helpful guide to the world of medieval thought.

## Literature

**St. Augustine** (354–430 AD). Among the early Fathers of the Church, St. Augustine is the most important and most influential. A scholar of rhetoric, he was deeply influenced by Neo-Platonism. After his conversion to Christianity, he was ordained and eventually made bishop of Hippo, where he defended Christianity against its heretics and detractors.

*Confessions* (397–398 AD)
Translated by Owen Chadwick. Oxford World's Classics, 1998, 311 pages.

The *Confessions* is the world's first autobiography, written not as a factual account of a man's life but as a prayer to God. Augustine tells the story of his journey from sinner to saint, identifying all the persons, events, and forces that eventually brought about his Christian conversion. His rhetorical genius is fully displayed in this spiritual classic. Chadwick's translation is masterful, and he provides a very helpful introduction. Books 1–9 on Augustine's life are highly recommended.

*City of God* (430 AD)
Translated by Henry Bettenson. Penguin Classics, 2003, 1,184 pages.

Augustine's masterpiece was written as a defense of Christianity against its detractors in the wake of the sack of Rome by the Visigoths in the year 410 AD. This large work deals with the themes of God, faith, martyrdom, the Church, and theology. Augustine often digresses in his discussion of philosophical subjects to point out the flaws of pagan religion. The primary theme is the presentation of human history as a conflict between the City of Man and the City of God. Books 1, 11, 14, 19, and 22 are recommended.

**Heaney, Seamus,** Translator. *Beowulf* (c. 8th–11th Century AD)
W. W. Norton, 2001, 215 pages.

This epic poem, written sometime between the 8th and 11th Centuries AD, is one of the lasting expressions of Anglo-Saxon culture at a time when it was being slowly transformed by Christianity. Set in Scandinavia, although written in England, the poem chronicles the magnificent actions of the great hero Beowulf as he battles a series of evil monsters, including the hellish monster Grendel and Grendel's vicious mother. This translation by Nobel Prize-winning poet Seamus Heaney is accessible and absorbing.

**Radice, Betty,** Translator. *The Letters of Abelard and Heloise* (composed c. 1132–1138; first published in Latin in 1616)
Penguin Classics, rev. ed., 2004, 384 pages.

The story of the secret love affair between the medieval scholastic philosopher, Abelard (1079–1142), and his bright young student, Heloise (1101–1164), is legendary. Bound by their shared passion for knowledge and faith, Abelard and Heloise reveal through their letters their continuing love, years after they were forced to separate (when he became a monk and she an abbess). Their letters reveal a love that is as inspiring as it was tragic. This edition includes Abelard's autobiographical *Story of His Misfortunes* and two hymns.

**Burgess, Glyn,** Translator. *The Song of Roland* (1140–1170)
Penguin Classics, 1990, 224 pages.

This epic, sung by oral poets, is the oldest masterpiece of French literature. When Roland's stepfather nominates him for a dangerous post—commander of the rearguard in Charlemagne's army—the Emperor is powerless to change Roland's fate. Once the rearguard is betrayed to the enemy, Oliver, the prudent knight, begs Roland to recall the departing army. Roland's decision reflects the martial code of this knight of Christendom.

**St. Aelred of Rievaulx** (1110–1167). A medieval humanist and Cistercian monk, Aelred became abbot at Rievaulx Abbey in Yorkshire in 1134. He wrote several influential books on spirituality along with works of history. His most famous work was *The Life of Saint Edward, King and Confessor*, about the last Anglo-Saxon king of England.

*Spiritual Friendship* (1150–1165)
Translated by Mary Eugenia Laker. Ave Maria Press, 2008, 147 pages.

Aelred explicates Cicero's theories of friendship in the form of a dialogue with friends. He explores the virtues and conditions of friendship on both the natural and supernatural levels, thus revealing genuine friendship to be a medium of divine love. For those seeking true intimacy, this spiritual classic is a fount of wisdom that resonates even today. This edition provides a brief overview of Aelred's life and teaching.

**Raffel, Burton,** Translator.  *Das Nibelungenlied: Song of the Nibelungs* (c. 1180–1210)
Yale University Press, 2008 (2006), 351 pages.

The *Nibelungenlied* was an important inspiration for Richard Wagner, who based his great *Ring* cycle of operas upon core elements of the story.  The epic poem is an intriguing hybrid of medieval chivalry and classical heroism, as Siegfried travels to a distant land to woo the beautiful Kriemhild.  The tale quickly segues into a dramatic tale of deceit, envy, betrayal, and human passions gone haywire, as Siegfried is tragically slain and Kriemhild enacts bloody revenge.

**Raffel, Burton,** Translator.  *The Song of the Cid* (c. late 12th century)
Penguin Classics, 2009, 252 pages.

*The Song of the Cid* is an anonymous poem set in 12th-Century Spain.  The poem is one of the central literary expressions of medieval Christianity and neatly reflects the conflict between Christianity and Islam.  The hero of the poem, the Cid, relentlessly pursues the conflict against the Muslims despite many setbacks.  The central action of the poem occurs when the Cid, in order to please his lord but against his own better judgment, marries off his daughters to two rivals.  The Cid secures bloody justice when the inevitable happens and his daughters are dishonored.

**Sturluson, Snorri** (1179–1241).  Snorri Sturluson was an Icelandic poet, historian, and politician.  He was author of the *The Prose Edda*, a compilation of Norse Mythology, and the *Heimskringla*, a history of Norwegian kings.  He was twice elected speaker of the Icelandic parliament and became a vassal of King Haakon IV of Norway.

*The Prose Edda: Norse Mythology* (c. 1220)
Translated by Jesse Byock.  Penguin Classics, 2006, 304 pages.

The *Prose Edda* is the most extensive source for Norse mythology.  The *Prologue*, a Christian account of Norse myths, is followed by *Gylfaginning* ("the tricking of Gylf"), tales of creation and destruction, *Skáldskaparmál* ("the language of poetry"), and *Háttatal* ("list of verse forms"), a discourse on myth and poetry.  Tales from the creation myth to the final battle of Ragnarok are included.

**Aquinas, St. Thomas** (1225–1274). St. Thomas was the most important and influential theologian of the medieval Church. Often referred to as the Angelic Doctor, Thomas was a member of the Dominican Order and became the foremost proponent of scholasticism, which sought to reconcile Greek philosophy (primarily Aristotle) with Christian theology.

*Summa Theologica* (1265–1274)
In *A Shorter Summa: The Essential Philosophical Passages of St. Thomas Aquinas' Summa Theologica*, ed. Peter Kreeft.
Translated by Fathers of the Eastern Dominican Province. Ignatius, 1993, 162 pages.

The *Summa Theologica* is the greatest work of medieval theology. It explores and synthesizes the truths of faith and reason in a systematic whole and is written in the form of a structured debate. This is the best condensation of Thomas's massive work available. Aimed at the beginning student, this edition contains the most important passages from the *Summa*. The selected articles have explanatory footnotes and are preceded by a very helpful introduction and glossary of terms.

**Egan, Harvey D.,** Editor. *An Anthology of Christian Mysticism*
Liturgical Press, 2nd ed., 1996 (1991), 700 pages.

This comprehensive collection of the writings of 57 Christian mystics spans the entire Christian tradition. Of the medieval mystics (12th–16th Centuries) included in this volume, Hildegard of Bingen, Francis of Assisi, Hadewijch, Bonaventure, Meister Eckhart, Catherine of Siena, the *Cloud of Unknowing*, Julian of Norwich, Teresa of Avila, and John of the Cross are recommended. Each selection is preceded by an interpretive overview of the author's life and writings.

# B. The Late Middle Ages and the Early Modern Period

The Late Middle Ages (1300–1500 AD) and the Early Modern Era (1500–1700 AD) constitute the transitional period between medieval Europe and the modern world.  The history and biography books of this period are arranged according to five categories that represent historic developments in Western history:

1.  The Late Middle Ages and the Renaissance: Meaning "rebirth," the Renaissance was a period of cultural renewal that began in the 14th Century in northern Italy and spread to the rest of Europe by the 16th Century.  It was marked by a recovery of classical (Greco-Roman) learning, the rise of humanism, and revolutionary developments in art and science.  The cultural and intellectual transformation that resulted represents a bridge between the Middle Ages and the Early Modern era.

2.  The Age of Exploration: Also known as the Age of Discovery, the Age of Exploration was the period in European history when the great sea voyages of discovery were made.  European powers—particularly Portugal, Holland, Spain, and England—explored the world by sea from the 15th through the 17th Centuries, searching for trade routes to the Far East.  The period was marked by advances in science, vast economic growth, and imperial expansion.

3.  The Reformation: Beginning in the early 16th Century, the Protestant Reformation was the Christian reform movement that divided Christendom between the Catholic Church led by the pope in Rome, and the Protestant Reform churches led by various figures such as Martin Luther in Germany, John Calvin in Switzerland, and King Henry VIII in England.

4.  The Scientific Revolution: The Scientific Revolution was the period in European history that laid the foundation for modern science.  Breaking with ancient and medieval doctrines about nature, it was marked by discoveries in physics, astronomy, biology, anatomy, and chemistry that were based on empirical observation and experimentation.  Beginning in the mid-16th Century with discoveries by Copernicus, it extends to the work of Isaac Newton in the late 17th Century.

5.  The Early Modern Era—General: The early modern era is the transitional period between the Late Middle Ages and Modernity.  The history books in this section cover political, economic, intellectual, and cultural developments from the late 15th through the 17th Centuries.

The biographies listed in these five sections include some of the most important figures of the period, such as Christopher Columbus, Martin Luther, Isaac Newton, and William Shakespeare.  These biographies richly illuminate the history of Europe during this transitional period.

The great work of literature at the beginning of this period is Dante's *Divine Comedy*.  This three-part epic poem represents one of the highest expressions of medieval Christianity in its unique melding of Christian symbolism, thought, and expression.  The great work of literature near the end of this period is Milton's *Paradise Lost*, an epic poem about the fall of man that represents one of the highest expressions of early modern Christianity.  Between these two extraordinary Christian epics lies the magnificent work of William Shakespeare, whose plays draw equally upon classical, medieval, and early modern thought and expression in presenting a complex and aesthetically rich vision of human experience.

The trajectory from Dante through Shakespeare to Milton suggests the profound achievement of this period, when the political and economic developments of European civilization were matched by an extraordinary flowering in its art and literature.  The richness of this period is further reflected in Chaucer's *Canterbury Tales*, one of the greatest achievements of English literature; Cervantes' *Don Quixote*, considered by some to be not just the first but the greatest novel ever written; and the remarkable thought and writing of such diverse figures as Erasmus, Machiavelli, and Montaigne.  All told, the reader will find here a wonderfully rich and diverse body of literature that combines the highest pleasures of language with some of the richest expressions of human thought.

# 1. The Late Middle Ages and the Renaissance

## HISTORY: SURVEY

Manchester, William. *A World Lit Only by Fire: The Medieval Mind and the Renaissance*
Back Bay Books, 1993, 322 pages.

This popular, entertaining history concerns the long period of transition from the Roman Empire to the Renaissance and Reformation. The first chapter briefly reviews the entire medieval period, while the rest of the book explores the prominent figures and significant events of the 16th Century. Manchester concludes with the story of Magellan, whose circumnavigation of the globe marked the end of one age and the beginning of another. This is an adept, thematic reconstruction of an enthralling period.

## BIOGRAPHY

Lewis, R. W. B. *Dante* (1265–1321)
Penguin, 2001, 224 pages.

Another in the *Penguin Lives* series, the author sketches the life and writings of the world's most revered poet and the times in which he lived. Lewis weaves together politics, history, love, religion, and literature in capturing the essential events and forces that shaped Florence's favorite son. This short biography makes a good introduction to Dante's masterpiece, *The Divine Comedy*, not least by following Dante's own journey through hell, purgatory, and paradise.

Gordon, Mary. *Joan of Arc* (1412–1431)
Penguin, 2008, 208 pages.

Another in the *Penguin Lives* series, this is the story of the peasant girl who rose from obscurity to glory when she took up arms to defend France in the Hundred Years War. The work provides a sympathetic but unsentimental account of Joan's short life in this "biographical meditation." Gordon paints a spare but vivid portrait of the young heroine determined to follow the voice of God, even though it led to her execution at age 19. Readers will be stirred by Joan's courage and faith.

Nuland, Sherwin. *Leonardo da Vinci* (1452–1519)
Penguin, 2004, 176 pages.

Nuland, a surgeon and medical writer, is well fit to write this short biography, also in the *Penguin Lives* series, about his hero, the great visionary painter, architect, inventor, engineer, anatomist, and scientist. He summarizes Leonardo's vast achievements, emphasizing his anatomical studies. One comes away with a profound appreciation of the artistic and scientific genius of the prototypical "Renaissance Man" who was so ahead of his times.

King, Ross.  *Machiavelli: Philosopher of Power* (1469–1527)
HarperCollins, 2007, 256 pages.

Known best for his controversial tract on statecraft, *The Prince*, Machiavelli may be one of the most misunderstood figures of history.  In this concise biography in the *Eminent Lives* series, King provides a compelling portrait of the famous Florentine political philosopher, writer, and diplomat.  He examines Machiavelli's life and career in its historical context: the violent political turmoil of Renaissance Italy.  This work makes a good introduction to Machiavelli's writings.

## 2. The Age of Exploration

### HISTORY: SURVEY

Fernández-Armesto, Felipe. *Pathfinders: A Global History of Exploration*
W. W. Norton, 2007, 428 pages.

This is a comprehensive account of world exploration from the last ice age to the 19th Century. The author packs a wealth of information in a narrative of adventure and daring, following the great explorers, known and unknown, on their various journeys of discovery. He explains the role that politics and economics played, as well as the technological breakthroughs that made their discoveries possible. The volume is amply supplied with maps and illustrations.

Fritze, Ronald H. *New Worlds: The Great Voyages of Discovery 1400–1600*
Praeger, 2003 (2002), 285 pages.

This beautifully illustrated book narrates the important period in Western history when the European world and worldview were transformed. Beginning with a portrait of medieval Europe, the work focuses on the great voyages of discovery by Columbus, da Gama, Cabot, Magellan, etc., which led to the huge expansion of trade and the rise of colonial empires. New research brings to life this critical period that gave birth to the modern world.

### BIOGRAPHY

Russell, Peter. *Prince Henry "the Navigator": A Life* (1394–1460)
Yale University Press, 2000, 448 pages.

Known as the precursor of Columbus, Prince Henry of Portugal was the man who spearheaded the Age of Exploration by opening a school of navigation and sending his captains to explore the west coast of Africa. This well-researched biography, the first in a hundred years, portrays Henry as a flawed man of the late Middle Ages who was driven by a crusader's fervor and commercial ambition to explore the unknown. Lavishly illustrated with maps and paintings.

Morison, Samuel Eliot. *Admiral of the Ocean Sea: A Life of Christopher Columbus* (1451–1506)
Little Brown, 1991 (1942), 680 pages.

Morison was a sailor and scholar whose classic tale of Columbus' life and journeys won the Pulitzer Prize for biography in 1943. This remains the most vivid and authoritative account of Columbus' voyages, as it is informed by the author's own 1939 voyage in a 147-foot schooner, a voyage that duplicated Columbus' route and the conditions of his journey. This splendid work is illustrated with charts and maps detailing Columbus' four voyages that changed the world.

Bergreen, Laurence. *Over the Edge of the World: Magellan's Terrifying Circumnavigation of the Globe* (1480–1521)
Harper Perennial, 2004, 512 pages.

Based on the original logs and diaries of Magellan's shipmates, Bergreen tells the dramatic tale of the first voyage around the world. Along the way we learn of the horrendous storms, mutinies, executions, hunger, disease, and battles that marked the three-year odyssey, culminating in Magellan's own tragic death in the Philippines. Bergreen richly evokes the Age of Discovery in this very readable account of a riveting, true-life adventure.


Sobel, Dava. *Longitude: The True Story of a Lone Genius Who Solved the Greatest Scientific Problem of His Time* (John Harrison, 1693–1776)
Walker and Company, 2007 (1995), 208 pages.

The most vexing problem for seafarers in the age of sail was determining east-west location at sea. John Harrison, an 18th-Century clockmaker, eventually solved the problem. Sobel tells the little-known story of Harrison's 40-year obsession with developing the marine chronometer. It's a dramatic chronicle of one man's persistence in pursuit of a practical, scientific goal. The 1998 illustrated edition includes photos of Harrison's clocks.

## 3. The Reformation

**HISTORY**

Chadwick, Owen. *The Reformation*
Penguin, 1990 (1964), 464 pages.

In this third volume in the *Penguin History of the Church* series, Chadwick analyzes the work of Erasmus, Luther, Zwingli, Calvin, Tyndale, and Wesley and the religious forces that divided Christendom in the 16th Century, which provoked the tumultuous wars of religion that devastated Europe. The second half covers the Counter-Reformation, the Eastern Orthodox Church, and the impact of the Reformation on the church and society. A good summary for someone new to the subject.

Dawson, Christopher. *The Dividing of Christendom*
Doubleday, 1967 (1965), 237 pages.

Dawson was one of the foremost historians of the 20th Century. This is his classic work on the Reformation, delivered as part of a series of lectures on the history of Christianity when he held the Stillman Chair of Catholic Thought at Harvard Divinity School. It traces the factors leading to the Reformation and then surveys the centuries of schism up to the French Revolution. This is a masterful study that is challenging but worth every effort.

**BIOGRAPHY**

Marty, Martin E. *Martin Luther: A Life* (1483–1546)
Penguin, 2008 (2004), 224 pages.

This is the best short biography of Luther available. Written by an esteemed Lutheran theologian and historian, it accurately portrays Luther as a man of contradictions. Marty presents a balanced picture, honestly detailing Luther's struggles with himself, the Roman Church, and other reformers. He also provides an excellent overview of Luther's extensive writings. This is a fine introduction to the life of one of the most important religious figures in Western history.

## 4. The Scientific Revolution

### HISTORY

Henry, John. *The Scientific Revolution and the Origins of Modern Science*
Palgrave, 3rd ed., 2008 (2001), 176 pages.

This is the best short survey of the Scientific Revolution available. Covering the 16th to the 18th Centuries, the author discusses all the major figures and many minor ones too. Skirting technical details, he emphasizes the social, intellectual, and cultural factors that shaped the development of early modern science. The third edition enhances and modifies the text based on new research, and the extensive annotated bibliography and glossary make this a great resource for students.

### BIOGRAPHY

Grayling, A. C. *Descartes: The Life and Times of a Genius* (1596–1650)
Walker and Company, 2006, 303 pages.

René Descartes is known as the father of modern philosophy. This new account of his life unfolds against the political and religious turmoil of the early 17th Century. Based on surviving correspondence, Grayling follows the frequent travels of the famous thinker who laid the foundations for modern thought. Descartes' philosophy is briefly introduced in an appendix, and a middle section of color and black-and-white plates illuminates the subject.

Sobel, Dava. *Galileo's Daughter: A Historical Memoir of Science, Faith, and Love* (b. 1600)
Penguin, 2000, 420 pages.

The author of *Longitude* also wrote this fascinating account of the famous scientist and his eldest daughter, Maria Celeste. Placed in a cloistered convent at age 13, she became her father's greatest supporter during his time of trial. Sobel skillfully interweaves the saga of the persecuted Galileo, which is the focus of the story, with the tale of his equally persecuted daughter, which is revealed in her adoring letters to him. This amply illustrated book is a gripping page-turner.

Gleick, James. *Isaac Newton* (1643–1727)
Vintage, 2004, 288 pages.

Gleick, an acclaimed science writer, has penned an excellent introduction to one of the world's undisputed geniuses. This short, elegant biography does justice to the man who revolutionized modern science. Foregoing depth for breadth, Gleick recounts Newton's ideas and discoveries in a non-technical, accessible manner. Torn by conflicting impulses, Newton's eccentric personality is also intimately portrayed. The book includes pictures of Newton's manuscripts and notebooks.

## 5. The Early Modern Period—General

### HISTORY: SURVEY

Rice, Jr., Eugene F. and Anthony Grafton. *The Foundations of Early Modern Europe, 1460–1559*
W. W. Norton, 2nd ed., 1994 (1970), 234 pages.

This first volume in the *Norton History of Modern Europe* series is a superb survey of the developments that created the modern world. The authors take a thematic approach to this very complex period that includes the high Renaissance, the Reformation and Counter-Reformation, European economic expansion, the voyages of exploration, the rise of capitalism, and the formation of the early modern state. This lucid book contains illustrations and maps throughout.

Dunn, Richard S. *The Age of Religious Wars, 1559–1715*
W. W. Norton, 2nd ed., 1979 (1970), 322 pages.

The second volume in the *Norton History of Modern Europe* series covers the century and a half from the end of the Reformation to the early 18th Century. In terse, concise style Dunn discusses the major trends and events that occurred throughout the continent. The narrative is organized around the big themes, such as Europe's devastating civil wars, its political transformation, and its intellectual and cultural achievements. Copious maps and illustrations augment the text.

### HISTORY

Kamen, Henry. *Golden Age Spain*
Palgrave, 2nd ed., 2005 (1988), 112 pages.

Spain's golden age was mostly the 16th Century when its empire controlled vast regions of the New World. In this volume in Palgrave's *Studies in European History* series, the author discusses the rise and decline of the Spanish Empire during this period. The second edition updates the research and includes new chapters on religion and culture, including speculation on why Spain never had a Reformation. An extensive bibliography is included.

MacKenney, Richard. *The City-State, 1500–1700*: *Republican Liberty in an Age of Princely Power*
Palgrave, 1996 (1989), 84 pages.

One of many volumes in Palgrave's *Studies in European History* series, this short work discusses the rise of absolutism during the period that saw the triumphant dominance of local princes in European affairs, a development that threatened the liberties which towns had won in the Middle Ages. The author provides an overview of city-state organization in this often neglected story in the history of early modern Europe.

Wilson, Peter H.  *The Holy Roman Empire, 1495–1806*
Palgrave, 1999, 112 pages.

Voltaire once quipped that the Holy Roman Empire was neither holy, Roman, nor an empire, despite covering most of central Europe for over a millennium.  Drawing on new research, the author explains the Empire's development and organization when it was a weak institutional structure.  Like all volumes in Palgrave's *Studies in European History* series, this is a brief introduction that includes an extensive bibliography for further reading.

## BIOGRAPHY

Greenblatt, Stephen.  *Will in the World: How Shakespeare Became Shakespeare* (1564–1616)
W. W. Norton, 2005, 430 pages.

Precious little is known about Shakespeare outside of his published works.  Drawing on the few available documents, Greenblatt, one of the world's preeminent Shakespeare scholars, has constructed a biography based on conjecture.  It is more an analysis of the Bard's works, the times in which he lived, and their possible connection to his life.  Readers who have some familiarity with Shakespeare's plays will gain most from this imaginative and insightful work.

# 6. Literature

## LITERATURE: READING GUIDE

Thompson, Bard. *Humanists and Reformers: A History of the Renaissance and Reformation*
William B. Eerdmans, 1996, 804 pages.

In this expansive volume, Thompson, a professor of church history, provides a comprehensive overview of these two important movements in Western history. In its two sections, he provides an in-depth look at the major figures, writing, artwork, and developments of the two periods. The ample black and white photos and full-color plates of Renaissance art make this book a virtual museum. This hefty tome is a superb introductory volume for students.

## LITERATURE

**Alighieri, Dante** (1265–1321). The Italian poet Dante Alighieri was one of the principal writers of the Middle Ages. He is best known as the author of the *Divine Comedy*, his epic rendering of the Christian spiritual vision.

*The Divine Comedy: Inferno; Purgatorio; Paradiso* (1308–1321)
Translated by Allen Mandelbaum. Knopf Doubleday, 1995, 798 pages.

In this extremely influential, three-part epic poem, Dante imagines himself as a pilgrim led by various persons through the realms of hell, purgatory, and heaven in search of spiritual enlightenment. The *Inferno*, which charts Dante's journey through the nine circles of hell, is particularly bracing. Dante brilliantly blends together satire, humor, and, yes, horror into this most cautionary part of his tale.

**Boccaccio, Giovanni** (1313–1375). One of the chief literary figures of the Italian Renaissance, Giovanni Boccaccio is best known as the author of *The Decameron*, a delightful stew of 100 stories.

*The Decameron* (1353)
Translated by Mark Musa. Signet Classics, 2002, 848 pages.

*The Decameron* is framed as a storytelling marathon that occurs among a group of persons forced to flee Florence during the Black Plague. The stories reflect the theological and philosophic preoccupations of medieval Christendom, but not with so reverent an aim as the work of Boccaccio's Italian forebear, Dante Alighieri. Rather, they are hilarious and oftentimes bawdy tales highlighting the vice, folly, and hypocrisy of the medieval world.

**Armitage, Simon,** Translator. *Sir Gawain and the Green Knight* (14th Century)
W. W. Norton, 2008, 208 pages.

This delightful, 14th-Century English poem is one of the centerpieces of medieval literature. Sir Gawain, a member of King Arthur's Round Table, was widely represented as a paragon of knightly virtue. One Christmas he loses a peculiar contest to an unusual guest in King Arthur's hall. When Gawain stands by his word to meet that same guest one year later—to receive what promises to be his death blow—he finds his virtue tested by the wife of a lord who puts Sir Gawain up for a few nights. The reader will best judge how well Sir Gawain fares.

**Chaucer, Geoffrey** (1343–1400). The English poet Geoffrey Chaucer miraculously managed to produce one of the richest bodies of poetry in all of literature while maintaining a highly involved career as a public official.

*The Canterbury Tales* (1380–1400)
Translated by Burton Raffel. Modern Library, 2008, 672 pages.

*The Canterbury Tales* is one of the great literary accomplishments of the Middle Ages. The many tales that make up this masterwork are by turns comic, serious, irreverent, and pious, and are uniformly delightful to read. The frame for the tales is provided in the Prologue, where we read about a diverse group of men and women preparing to set off on a pilgrimage who decide to relieve the tedium of the journey by holding a contest to see who can tell the best tale. Read especially "The Prologue," "The Knight's Tale," "The Man of Law's Tale," "The Nun's Priest's Tale," "The Pardoner's Tale," "The Clerk's Tale," "The Franklin's Tale," and "The Second Nun's Tale."

**Erasmus, Desiderius** (1466–1536). Erasmus of Rotterdam was a Dutch Renaissance humanist, priest, and Catholic theologian. A classical scholar, he was noted for his editions of classical authors, church Fathers, and the New Testament, as well as for his own works. His criticism of church abuses and popular Christian beliefs contributed greatly to the Protestant Reformation.

*Praise of Folly* (1511)
Translated by Betty Radice. Penguin Classics, 1993, 188 pages.

*Praise of Folly* is the best-known of Erasmus's works. Though written as a fantasy-satire, this controversial work is a serious indictment of the theologians and religious practices of his time. As such it had a profound influence on the leaders of the Protestant Reformation. It ends with praise of the Christian faith and virtues, what St. Paul called "the folly of the cross." Erasmus's wit and wisdom continue to entertain and provoke readers today.

**Machiavelli, Nicoló** (1469–1527). Machiavelli was the great Florentine political theorist and historian. He was also a reputable civil servant of the Florentine republic, serving as a clerk, diplomat, and Secretary of the Chancery (the government organization that administered domestic and foreign affairs). Machiavelli viewed human nature as venal and self-serving, and thus believed ruthless cunning was necessary for effective government.

*The Prince* (1513, published 1532)
Translated by Harvey C. Mansfield. University of Chicago Press, 2nd. ed., 1998, 151 pages.

Next to Plato's *Republic* and Aristotle's *Politics, The Prince* has become the most famous book on politics ever written. This classic study of power (written as a handbook for rulers and dedicated to Lorenzo de Medici, the ruler of Florence) overturned the traditional ideals of government and inaugurated the modern approach to "realism" in political thinking. His shocking assertions (e.g., a prince should rule by force rather than law) continue to provoke debate.

**More, St. Thomas** (1478–1535). More was an English lawyer, author, and statesman. He was a Renaissance humanist scholar and the faithful servant of King Henry VIII, serving as Lord Chancellor (1529–1532). However, he was beheaded for refusing to sign the Act of Supremacy, which declared Henry head of the Church of England. He was canonized in 1935.

*Utopia* (1516)
Translated by Paul Turner. Penguin Classics, rev. ed., 2003, 176 pages.

Nineteen years before More's execution for treason, he published this provocative book detailing the life of a fictional island society (in Greek, utopia means "no-where land"). Written against the backdrop of an uncharted New World, the work offers not so much a blueprint for a perfect society as a critique of the chaotic politics of More's own day. This is another stimulating and controversial work of the high Renaissance.

**Luther, Martin** (1483–1546). Luther was the German priest, theologian, and church reformer who spearheaded the Protestant Reformation. A prolific author and translator of the Bible into German, Luther was excommunicated by Pope Leo X and declared an outlaw by Emperor Charles V in 1521. His break with Rome led to the founding of the Lutheran Church.

*The Ninety-Five Theses* (1517)
Translated by Stephen J. Nichols. P & R Publishing, 2003, 48 pages.

Luther is best known for his 95 theses that launched the Protestant Reformation. Allegedly nailed to the doors of the castle church in Wittenburg in 1517, Luther's list of arguments against church teachings and practices fomented both theological debate and a rebellious religious movement. This edition includes a helpful introduction and commentary to most of the theses.

**Luther, Martin (cont.)**

*On Christian Liberty* (1520)
Translated by W. A. Lambert. Fortress, 2003, 92 pages.

This famous pamphlet was the third of Luther's three treatises that appeared in 1520. It sets out his teaching on justification by faith alone and the priesthood of all believers. As such it became the cornerstone of the Lutheran movement. Though more conciliatory than the first two treatises, it still captures Luther's revolutionary zeal and theological boldness. This new translation includes a helpful introduction, glossary, and notes, as well as Luther's "Letter to Pope Leo X."

**Las Casas, Bartolomé de** (1484–1566). Las Casas was a Dominican priest who, at the age of 18, left Spain for the New World where he was ordained and worked to evangelize the Indians. In 1512 he participated in the conquest of Cuba. Later he became the first to expose the oppression of the Indians and to call for the abolition of their slavery.

*A Short Account of the Destruction of the Indies* (1552)
Translated by Nigel Griffin. Penguin Classics, 1999, 143 pages.

After witnessing the brutal treatment and massacre of the natives in the New World, Las Casas wrote this work as an indictment of the genocidal colonization by the Spanish conquistadors. Anticipating the ideals of the Enlightenment, Las Casas argued that the Indians should be treated with dignity and given their basic rights as human beings. This gripping account of brutality continues to stir righteous indignation against the systematic mistreatment of the Indians.

**Rabelais, François** (1490–1553). A major writer of the Renaissance, Rabelais used parody, satire, and allegory to disguise progressive ideas linked to the social, religious, and scientific issues of his day. Condemned by the Sorbonne and banned by the church, Rabelais won the patronage of King François I, enabling him to publish his works.

*Gargantua and Pantagruel* (1532–1564)
Translated by M. A. Screech. Penguin Classics, 2006, 1,104 pages.

The rollicking, rowdy adventures of Rabelais' earthy giants, Gargantua and Pantagruel, can be read for entertainment alone. But the Renaissance thirst for knowledge, freedom, and the good life is apparent in descriptions of Gargantua's education, the utopian Abbey of Thélème, and the quest for the Divine Bottle.

**Montaigne, Michel de** (1533–1592).  Montaigne, who grew up speaking Latin, was a major humanist of the 16th Century.  An originator of the essay genre, he sought to use his natural judgment in his writing.  Influenced by the stoicism of his intimate friend Étienne de la Boétie, Montaigne wrote three books of essays on the human condition.

*The Complete Essays* (1580)
Translated by M. A. Screech.  Penguin Classics, 1993, 1,344 pages.

Famous for his oblique approach, Montaigne uses brilliant digressions, anecdotes, and commentaries as stepping stones to wisdom.  His *Essays*, steeped in Renaissance learning, broach surprisingly modern topics.  Among the best essays are: "On Friendship," "On Cannibals," "On Books," "On Some Verses of Virgil," "On Coaches," and "On Experience."

**Cervantes, Miguel de** (1547–1616).  The colorful life of the Spanish author Miguel de Cervantes rivals that of his famous hero, Don Quixote.  Legend has it that the idea for *Don Quixote* came to Cervantes while in prison.

*Don Quixote* (1605)
Translated by Burton Raffel.  W. W. Norton, 1999, 880 pages.

Cervantes' episodic masterpiece is by turns comic, farcical, philosophical, and endlessly surprising as it chronicles the exploits of the would-be knight-errant Don Quixote, a most enigmatic figure whose view of reality is strongly colored by the popular, chivalric romances of his day.  The irrepressible knight is joined by Sancho Panza, a squat fellow-townsman who not always so happily assists Quixote in his quest to rescue damsels who are not always in distress.

**Shakespeare, William** (1564–1616).  One of the most prolific and extraordinary writers in the Western canon, Shakespeare needs little introduction.  Readers who are new to Shakespeare's work can hardly do better than begin with the intriguing history play, *Henry IV, Part 1*, or perhaps with the delightful comedy, *A Midsummer Night's Dream*.  Those who like tragedy should read the timeless *Romeo and Juliet*.

*Romeo and Juliet* (1594)
Folger Shakespeare Library.  Washington Square Press, 1994, 336 pages.

Shakespeare's tale of star-crossed lovers continues to be a perennial favorite for a very good reason: it is expertly constructed, wonderfully written, and deeply moving.  The story is set against the backdrop of a long-standing feud between two families, the Montagues and the Capulets.  Complications necessarily ensue when Romeo, a Montague, falls in love with Juliet, a Capulet.  For tragedies, also read: *Julius Caesar* (1599), *Hamlet* (1600), *Othello* (1603), *King Lear* (1606), and *Macbeth* (1606).

**Shakespeare, William** (cont.)

*A Midsummer Night's Dream* (1595)
Folger Shakespeare Library. Washington Square Press, 2004, 256 pages.

This comedy serves as an excellent introduction to Shakespearean drama. The play is a delightful stew of comedy, fantasy, and romance with just the right pinch of dramatic tension thrown in for good measure. At the center of the plot is a mysterious drug that causes the person who unwittingly takes it to fall in love with the first person he sees. Needless to say, desire turns topsy-turvy while true love waits in the wings.
For comedies/romances, also read: *Comedy of Errors* (1592), *The Taming of the Shrew* (1593), *The Merchant of Venice* (1596), and *The Tempest* (1611).

*Henry IV, Part 1* (1597)
Folger Shakespeare Library. Washington Square Press, 1994, 336 pages.

For those new to Shakespeare, this history play will serve as an ideal introduction. It is among Shakespeare's most popular for a reason: it is a compelling character study filled with humor and drama and driven by Shakespeare's remarkable use of language. The play tells the story of an errant prince who wiles away his youth in the company of a colorful cast of misfits, which includes the grand comic figure of Falstaff. But when rebellion threatens to topple the English crown, Henry is given an opportunity to redeem his bad name.
For history plays, also read: *Richard II* (1595), *Henry IV, Part 2* (1598), and *Henry V* (1599).

**Marlowe, Christopher** (1564–1593). Christopher Marlowe, along with Shakespeare, was one of the leading lights of the Elizabethan stage up until his tragic death at the early age of 29.

*Dr. Faustus* (1604)
Signet Classics, 2007, 240 pages.

Marlowe's play about the brilliant Dr. Faustus who sells his soul to the devil is one of the highlights of Renaissance drama. Although the legend of Faust was well known throughout Europe, Marlowe invested it with dramatic tension, wit, insight, and macabre humor as Faust frivols away his powers on ephemeral goods. The play takes on a rich complexity, however, when Faust, despite his eventual misery and despair, resists repenting of his hellish bargain. The play's ambiguous ending makes us wonder, even so, if salvation is still his for the taking.

**Milton, John** (1608–1674). John Milton was one of the towering figures of 17th-Century English literature. His masterpiece, *Paradise Lost*, has a ubiquitous presence in the Western imagination.

*Paradise Lost* (1667)
Penguin Classics, 2003, 512 pages.

Milton's epic poem carves out its own place in the epic tradition by depicting the foundational story of Judaeo-Christianity. The poem moves from the fall of Satan through the fall of mankind and concludes with the future promise of Christian salvation. The poem does more than tell a story, however—it is also an intriguing meditation upon the nature of divine providence and free-will, and serves to comment as well upon the politics of Milton's England.

**Molière** (1622–1673).  Born to a prosperous family, Molière served his apprenticeship in the school of hard knocks, spending 16 years on the road as an actor and playwright.  On his résumé were bankruptcy and debtor's prison, and eventually the patronage of Louis XIV, who gave him the opportunity to become one of the world's great masters of comedy.

*The Misanthrope* (1666)
In *The Misanthrope, Tartuffe, and Other Plays*.
Translated by Maya Slater.  Oxford University Press, 2008, 400 pages.

*The Misanthrope* portrays Alceste, a young man who despairs of mankind and despises the high society phonies who surround him.  But when high-minded Alceste pursues the frivolous Célimène, he finds sincerity is an obstacle.  Molière's famous comedy exposes the weaknesses of society and its critics.
Also read: *Tartuffe* (1664) and *The Imaginary Invalid* (1673).

**Bunyan, John** (1628–1688).  A man of deep spiritual conviction, John Bunyan was imprisoned numerous times for preaching the doctrine of Puritanism.  He is best known for his spiritual allegory, *The Pilgrim's Progress*.

*The Pilgrim's Progress* (1678)
Penguin Classics, 2009, 384 pages.

*The Pilgrim's Progress* is one of the greatest examples of allegorical fiction in the Western literary tradition.  The work, strongly informed by Bunyan's Puritan philosophy, tells the story of Christian, an everyman who embarks upon a spiritual odyssey in search of renewal.  Following the allegorical nature of the work, every experience and encounter he has along the way is rich with meaning and significance.

**Racine, Jean** (1639–1699).  An orphan, Jean Racine received a classical education at the convent school of Port-Royal.  Run by followers of Cornelius Jansen, whose doctrines on grace ran counter to the Church, Port-Royal deeply influenced Racine.  France's preeminent tragedian wrote plays based on stories from Greek tragedy and the Hebrew Bible.

*Phèdre* (1677)
Translated by Ted Hughes.  Farrar, Straus and Giroux, 2000, 96 pages.

Racine's play, the epitome of French classical tragedy, draws its legend from the *Hippolytus* of Greek playwright Euripides.  Racine's tale of Queen Phèdre's fatal passion for stepson Hippolytus moves beyond the ineluctability of Greek tragedy to a personal encounter with guilt mediated by the hidden God of Racine's faith.  *Phèdre* dramatizes a soul's longing for grace while encumbered by the gravity of earthly passions.

# IV. The Modern Period

Modern history extends from 1700 to the present.  Historians view the modern period as beginning sometime in the 18th Century with the earliest beginnings of the industrial revolution.  What characterizes modernity are such developments as universal education and literacy, capitalism and globalization, humanism and individualism, civil liberties and democracy, science and technology, social movements and political revolutions, industrialization and urbanization, increased specialization and division of labor, and the information explosion and global communication.

The titles in the Modern Period are divided into four sections: European History,  American History, 20th Century and Early 21st Century World History, and Literature.  Since the histories of Europe and the United States became integrally connected in the 20th Century, the third section covers the entire world in the 20th and Early 21st Centuries.  The literature section is an introduction to the modern Western canon—the greatest works of literature written in the West during the modern period.

Modernity is a study in contrasts.  On the one hand, the period is marked by an outburst of disorder and violence: from the revolutions and civil wars of the 18th and 19th Centuries to the genocidal wars of the 20th Century.  The terror of the French Revolution and the bloodshed of the Napoleonic Wars and the American Civil War were only a prelude to the much greater toll wrought by the political ideologies of the last century.  Nazism, Fascism, Communism, nationalism, militarism, and ethnic cleansing left nearly 200 million human beings dead—killed in warfare or by their own governments.  On the other hand, modernity brought significant progress in economic, political, scientific, and cultural realms.  Individual freedom and democratic forms of government spread throughout the world, many hate-filled ideologies were exhausted, the industrial revolution and global capitalism brought most of the world population out of dire poverty, the benefits of medical advances and technological progress significantly enhanced the quality of life for all but the very poorest, and civil rights were expanded in the U.S. and abroad.

The contrasting developments of modernity suggest that our current state of affairs is pregnant with both threat and opportunity.  It is important to know about the horrors that materialized in modern history and how they arose.  But it is also important to recognize the positive forces and developments that the modern world produced, which give us a basis for hope in a brighter future.  Reading the history and literature of the modern era gives us a good sense of these contrasting developments and the forces that generated them.

Knowing something about modern history helps us understand the times in which we live.  American history is an important part of modern history.  It's our history, alive and vibrant.  Knowing about the past events that define our nation helps us understand our national identity.   Learning about our own heritage—the triumphs and tragedies that have made us Americans what we are today—helps us appreciate our freedoms and honor our values.  If we Americans are to understand our present, we need to know about our past and about the forces that continue to shape our world.

The books listed here tell us who we are and how we became what we are.  The history books tell the story of the modern world, while the biographies illuminate some of this period's most fascinating figures.  Such noteworthy individuals include George Washington, John and Abigail Adams, William

Wilberforce, Napoleon, Frederick Douglass, Abraham Lincoln, Marie Curie, Winston Churchill, Franklin and Eleanor Roosevelt, Martin Luther King, Jr., and Ronald Reagan.

The Literature list that comes at the end of this section includes novels, plays, short stories, and poetry written between 1700 and around 1970.  The books on this list are widely accepted as modern classics; works published since 1970 can be found in Part One: Contemporary Fiction.  This Modern Literature list reflects the novel's centrality from the birth of the English novel in the 1700s to the prominence of the novel in 19th and 20th-Century literature.  The novel, made possible by the invention of movable type around 1450 and by steady gains in literacy over the next several centuries, became a genre of fine apprehension and titanic imaginative power.  For the past three centuries the novel has been the premier literary medium for representing human experience.  The first three sections of the Literature list are organized by century and region, e.g., 19th Century British, and include novels and plays.  If you want to sample the modern sensibility in a more compressed literary form, you can turn to the last two sections of the Literature list, short stories and poetry.

There are several ways you could use this list: You could just read individual books that interest you, whether history, biography, or literature.  Or if you are especially interested in American, British, or European history, you could pursue that interest as far as you wish.  Alternatively, you could direct your reading to a particular kind of literature, like 20th-Century British or American literature.  Of course, if you are very curious and have plenty of time, you could read through this entire section, reading as much history and literature in each period and region as you find interesting.

## A. European History

The following section on European history chronicles British and continental European affairs in the modern period. This is a period when Europe underwent a vast social, political, cultural, and economic transformation, beginning with the Age of Enlightenment and the French Revolution in the 18th Century and continuing with the Napoleonic Wars and the Industrial Revolution in the 19th Century. Because the histories of Europe and the United States became integrally connected in the last century, European history since 1900 is not included in this section but rather in 20th Century and Early 21st Century World History, which follows the next section. Consequently, the titles in history and biography listed below are divided into three sections: Britain, 18th Century, and 19th Century. Most of the titles listed here relate to Western Europe. However, the three listed surveys in the *Norton History of Modern Europe* series provide a thorough coverage of Eastern Europe during this period.

The first section contains three broad surveys of British history. Schama's three-volume history of Britain is the most substantial, with volumes 2 and 3 covering modern British history. The seven biographies and autobiographies listed are of important British figures from the 18th through the 20th Centuries, including Jane Austen, John Wesley, and Winston Churchill.

The second section, 18th Century, contains five history books, most of which focus on the intellectual and cultural upheavals that transformed Europe during that century. The five biographies of political and cultural figures round out the century.

The third section, 19th Century, contains seven history titles. The two surveys provide a comprehensive introduction, and the remaining five books cover fascinating and important aspects of European history, including works on the Napoleonic Wars and colonialism. The biographies include Napoleon, Beethoven, and the only person to receive the Nobel Prize twice for two different sciences, Marie Curie.

# 1. Britain

## HISTORY: SURVEY

Black, Jeremy. *A History of the British Isles*
Palgrave, 2nd ed., 2003 (1997), 400 pages.

Most histories of Britain are histories of England. In this broad-ranging survey of British history, Black incorporates the history of Scotland, Ireland, and Wales as well. From pre-Roman Britain to the 20th Century, he covers in a single volume all aspects of British history—political, social, economic, and cultural—while illuminating the impact these islands had on the rest of Europe and the world. The second edition updates the book in light of recent scholarship.

Churchill, Winston. *Churchill's History of the English-Speaking Peoples*
Barnes and Noble, 1995 (1956–1958), 475 pages.

Churchill was not only a heroic statesman but a great historian. For his literary achievements he won the Nobel Prize in 1953. Begun in 1937, his four-volume history of the English-speaking peoples begins with Caesar's conquest of Britain (55 BC) and ends on the eve of the First World War (1914). This judicious, one-volume abridgement by Henry Steele Commager includes about 90 pages on the U.S. The narrative power of this majestic work makes it a classic.

Schama, Simon. *A History of Britain, Volume 1: At the Edge of the World?, 3500 BC–1603 AD*
Hyperion, 2000, 416 pages.

Schama's masterful, three-volume history accompanied a series of documentaries for the BBC and the History Channel. All three volumes are extensively illustrated in color and black and white photos drawn from the TV series. Gracefully written with wit and perception, no prior knowledge of British history is assumed. In this first volume, Schama covers the sweep of British history from pre-Roman times up through the Elizabethan Age.

Schama, Simon. *A History of Britain, Volume 2: The Wars of the British, 1603–1776*
Hyperion, 2001, 543 pages.

In this second volume, Schama covers the period when Britain grew into the most powerful empire in the world but was torn by internal strife and foreign conflicts. The author brilliantly evokes the glory and horror of these violent times that shattered the illusion of Britain's "united kingdom." The weight of the narrative falls on the English Civil War and Glorious Revolution in the 17th Century and the French and Indian War and American Revolution in the 18th Century.

Schama, Simon. *A History of Britain, Volume 3: The Fate of Empire, 1776–2000*
Hyperion, 2002, 576 pages.

The final installment of Schama's three-volume popular history takes the reader through Britain's last two centuries. He begins with the French Revolution, continues through the Victorian Age, then recounts the turbulent 20th Century when Britain underwent its decolonization and imperial decline. Schama is necessarily selective in this impressionistic narrative, so unfortunately much is left out. Nevertheless, this very readable history will inform and entertain the general reader.

### BIOGRAPHY

Tomkins, Stephen. *John Wesley: A Biography* (1703–1791)
William B. Eerdmans, 2003, 192 pages.

John Wesley, the founder of Methodism, was one of the great religious reformers of Western history. In this concise, informative biography, he is revealed as a flawed but fascinating individual, a holy man who sought perfection in God's eyes through suffering and strict self-discipline. The turbulent origins of the Methodist Church are also detailed in this engaging account (published on the 300th anniversary of his birth) of a troubled, devout soul.

Czisnik, Marianne. *Horatio Nelson: A Controversial Hero* (1758–1805)
Hodder Arnold, 2005, 240 pages.

In this intimate portrait of England's favorite naval hero, new light is shed on his complex character. In the first part the author examines the controversial episodes in Nelson's life and career. The second part analyses Nelson's reputation, showing how the real man became distorted and misunderstood as his image (in print and painting) evolved in the popular imagination. It's a very readable study of the great admiral who died in victory at Trafalgar.

Belmonte, Kevin. *William Wilberforce: A Hero for Humanity* (1759–1833)
Zondervan, 2007, 352 pages.

Rather unknown in the U.S., Wilberforce was the British statesman and abolitionist whose tireless efforts in pursuit of justice eventually led to the end of slavery throughout the British Empire. In this definitive biography, Belmonte captures the essence of Wilberforce, a man of deep faith, courage, and conviction who in every way deserves the accolade of the book's title. This is a well-researched, inspiring story that was dramatized in the motion picture *Amazing Grace*.

Shields, Carol. *Jane Austen* (1775–1817)
Penguin, 2005 (2001), 192 pages.

An acclaimed novelist herself, Shields offers a sympathetic interpretation of Austen's life and work in this brief *Penguin Lives* biography. Drawing on Austen's novels and private letters, and much conjecture, she reconstructs her life around the theme of an unmarried woman who explored the mores and manners of her day through her art. This engaging portrait is sure to provoke an interest in Austen's novels and please already faithful fans.

Smiley, Jane. *Charles Dickens* (1812–1870)
Penguin, 2002, 212 pages.

Following the popular and interesting *Penguin Lives* form, Smiley proves to be an astute biographer of Dickens. With psychological insight she sketches the life of this first modern "celebrity" from the perspective of his contemporaries, thereby revealing the great novelist's humanity, warts and all. Those familiar with Dickens's works will wish to reread them in the context of his life. Those unfamiliar will find here an invaluable guide to his novels.

Keegan, John. *Winston Churchill: A Life* (1874–1965)
Penguin, 2002, 208 pages.

The distinguished military historian has written an elegant overview of the life and achievements of England's greatest statesman, who shaped history like few figures of the 20th Century. Following Churchill's fascinating military and political career, Keegan duly honors the talented man who steered his country through its darkest hours with his unwavering determination and rhetorical power. This Penguin Life effectively puts blood, sweat, toil, and tears into context.

Lewis, C. S. *Surprised by Joy: The Shape of My Early Life* (1898–1963)
Harcourt, rev. ed., 1995 (1955), 240 pages.

In this autobiography, the popular fiction writer, literary critic, and Christian apologist recounts his spiritual journey during his early years. Lewis's story centers on his search for "joy" and how that led him on a meandering path from faith to devout atheism and back to faith. It's primarily an intellectual journey as Lewis's conversion was formed by the world of books and ideas. In many ways this unabashedly honest work is a modern-day Augustine's *Confessions*.

## 2. 18th Century

**HISTORY: SURVEY**

Woloch, Isser. *Eighteenth-Century Europe: Tradition and Progress, 1715–1789*
W. W. Norton, 1982, 364 pages.

In this title from the *Norton History of Modern Europe* series, Woloch chronicles the last years of
Europe's old order during the transformational 18th Century. He traces the cultural, economic,
political, intellectual, and religious developments that eventually led to the collapse of the *ancien régime*
in the French Revolution. This is a splendid work of history that illuminates the birth pangs of the
modern age.

**HISTORY**

Black, Jeremy. *Warfare in the Eighteenth Century*
HarperCollins, 2006 (1999), 240 pages.

It's a daunting task to cover a whole century of warfare on a global scale in an introductory volume.
The author admirably achieves this objective in this *Smithsonian History of Warfare* selection. Though
the focus is European, he also looks at Chinese, Indian, and African warfare, as well as the American
Revolution, explaining the diversity of tactics and weapons used in the horse and musket era.
Beautifully illustrated with maps and diagrams of battles.

Cragg, Gerald R. *The Church and the Age of Reason, 1648–1789*
Penguin, 1990 (1960), 304 pages.

In this fourth volume from the *Penguin History of the Church* series, Cragg covers the period from the
Peace of Westphalia to the French Revolution. He explains how changes in European society during
this time impacted the Christian Church, particularly in regard to evolving church-state relations and
the challenges of Enlightenment thought in the Age of Reason. This is a stimulating assessment of a
formative period in church history.

Porter, Roy. *The Enlightenment*
Palgrave, 2nd ed., 2001, 95 pages.

Another selection from Palgrave's *Studies in European History* series, this brief volume explores the
complexities of the 18th-Century Enlightenment and its leading lights: Voltaire, Diderot, Hume,
Rousseau, Kant, and others. Porter draws out the complexities of this many-faceted movement and
its diverse thinkers who contributed to the death of the old order and the birth of a new, modern age
based less on faith and tradition and more on reason, science, and social change.

Rude, George.  *The French Revolution: Its Causes, Its History, and Its Legacy After 200 Years*
Grove Press, 1991 (1988), 224 pages.

The French Revolution was one of the most cataclysmic events in modern history.  In this introductory survey Rude explains why it occurred, how it unfolded, and what its lasting impact was.  He skillfully moves through the fall of the monarchy, the Reign of Terror, and the ensuing dictatorship that inaugurated the reign of Napoleon.  Maps, a timeline, a glossary of terms, and an index of main characters make this a very useful text for studying this pivotal era.

## BIOGRAPHY

Damrosch, Leo. *Jean-Jacques Rousseau: Restless Genius* (1712–1778)
Houghton Mifflin, 2007 (2005), 566 pages.

This is the first single-volume biography of Rousseau in English.  Drawing mostly on Rousseau's autobiography, *Confessions*, Damrosch provides a briskly-moving, comprehensive portrait of the great 18th-Century French political philosopher and novelist.  He weaves together Rousseau's life and troubled personality with an examination of his major works.  This is a fascinating, insightful study of one of the key figures of the Enlightenment.

Troyat, Henri. *Catherine the Great* (1729–1796)
Translated by Joan Pinkham.  Penguin, 1994 (1980), 400 pages.

The rich tapestry of Russia's past comes to life in this character study of Catherine II, the German-born Russian empress who became one of history's most powerful women.  Drawing on the Czarina's memoirs and letters, Troyat skillfully examines Catherine's early years, her conniving ascension to power, and her autocratic rule that lasted over thirty years.  Fans of Russian history will marvel at the life and exploits of this fascinating ruler.

Fraser, Antonia. *Marie Antoinette: The Journey* (1755–1793)
Anchor Books, 2006 (2001), 544 pages.

This is a well-researched, sympathetic portrayal of Marie Antoinette, the Austrian princess who was married off to the future Louis XVI at age 14 only to be sacrificed to the French Revolution 23 years later.  In her absorbing biography, Fraser provides a fair, psychological portrait of the accidental queen as well as a captivating look into court life during the last years of the French monarchy.

Gay, Peter. *Mozart* (1756–1791)
Penguin, 2006 (1999), 192 pages.

As an eminent cultural historian of modern Europe, Gay is well equipped to compose this succinct account of the great composer's brief life and extraordinary work.  He traces Mozart's amazing development from child prodigy to the adult genius whose vast body of work left an indelible mark on modern music.  This is a well-researched, straightforward interpretation that debunks the romanticized legends.

Unger, Harlow Giles. *Lafayette* (1757–1834)
Wiley, 2003, 480 pages.

Against the romanticized versions, the author aims for an objective account of the French aristocrat who played an important role in both the American and French Revolutions. Unger explores in some depth Lafayette's public and private lives, particularly his relationships with Washington and with his beloved wife Adrienne. This is a very readable, psychological study of a complex man who lived an adventurous life on both sides of the Atlantic.

## 3. 19th Century

### HISTORY: SURVEY

Breunig, Charles and Matthew Levinger. *The Revolutionary Era, 1789–1850*
W. W. Norton, 3rd ed., 2002 (1970), 334 pages.

In this fifth volume of the *Norton History of Modern Europe* series, the authors chronicle the events and forces that shaped the early 19th Century. Major sections are devoted to the French Revolution, the Napoleonic Era, the industrial revolution, the revolution of 1830, the revolutions of 1848, and the cultural and social history of the period. Much ground is covered in the expanded treatment of the revolutionary era.

Rich, Norman. *The Age of Nationalism and Reform, 1850–1890*
W. W. Norton, 2nd ed., 1976 (1970), 288 pages.

The sixth volume of the *Norton History of Modern Europe* series covers the latter half of the 19th Century. Rich traces the spread of nationalism across the continent during a period of continuing economic and political disruption. He also discusses the social consequences of industrialization, the expansion of state power, political and social reforms, and the intellectual and cultural trends of the period.

### HISTORY

Price, Roger. *The Revolutions of 1848*
Palgrave Macmillan, 1988, 124 pages.

The year 1848 saw a sweeping wave of revolutions across Europe. In this brief volume from Palgrave's *Studies in European History* series, the author analyses the causes of the revolutions and their impact on European society. He also considers why governments in the aftermath were better able to prevent further disruptions by the revolutionary movements that shook Europe to its foundations.

Rothenberg, Gunther. *The Napoleonic Wars*
HarperCollins, 2006, 240 pages.

In this selection from the *Smithsonian History of Warfare* series, Rothenberg chronicles the rise and fall of Napoleon, the founder of modern warfare. In the first two chapters he summarizes the French Revolution and Napoleon's rise to power, then provides a broad survey of the major campaigns from Austerlitz to Waterloo, as well as the weapons systems and military tactics employed. Gorgeous maps, diagrams, and paintings illustrate the narrative.

Sturmer, Michael. *The German Empire: A Short History*
Random House (Modern Library Chronicles), 2002, 192 pages.

In this *Modern Library Chronicles* selection, Sturmer recounts the rise of Germany into a world power. He begins with the Franco-Prussian War and then traces Germany's unification, industrialization, and militarization that disrupted the European balance of power and led to the cataclysmic First World War. This is a clear, concise, and richly descriptive overview of imperial Germany (1870–1918).

Vidler, Alec R. *The Church in an Age of Revolution*
Penguin, 1990 (1961), 304 pages.

This fifth volume in the *Penguin History of the Church* series extends from the French Revolution to Vatican II, though it concerns mostly 19th-Century Europe. These are the turbulent years when the Christian churches reacted to modernity. In this concise, informative church history, Vidler, an Anglican theologian, offers a very balanced treatment of Protestant and Catholic movements and theology.

Wesseling, H. L. *The European Colonial Empires: 1815–1919*
Pearson, 2004, 304 pages.

This is a comprehensive and comparative look at European colonization in the 19th Century. With a long-term, global perspective, Wesseling examines all the European colonies in Africa, Asia, Oceania, and the Caribbean before and after 1880, the peak of European imperialism. His clear exposition gives due emphasis to the continental powers (French, Dutch, German, and Italian), alongside the usually privileged British Empire.

## BIOGRAPHY

Cronin, Vincent. *Napoleon* (1769–1821)
HarperCollins, 1995 (1971), 400 pages.

Cronin, a celebrated English historian and biographer, has written a very enjoyable, psychological portrait of the great Napoleon that covers his entire life. He objectively presents the emperor's virtues and flaws in a balanced manner. The focus is not military history so the discussion of Napoleon's campaigns is kept to a minimum. Rather Cronin concentrates on the events that shed light on Napoleon's character. This absorbing biography reads like a novel.

Morris, Edmund. *Beethoven: The Universal Composer* (1770–1827)
Harper Collins, 2005, 256 pages.

Morris, a music scholar and accomplished pianist, follows his longer presidential biographies of Reagan and Teddy Roosevelt with this brief life of Beethoven in Harper's *Eminent Lives* series. This lucid portrait is packed with insight about the tortured musical genius and his sources of inspiration, as well as some of his famous and lesser-known compositions. The book will appeal to those seeking a short introduction to the legendary composer.

Ferris, Paul.  *Dr. Freud: A Life* (1856–1939)
Counterpoint Press, 1999, 464 pages.

Ferris, a Welsh biographer and novelist, has penned a highly readable biography of one of the major thinkers of the 20th Century.  He objectively examines Freud's life and work without glamorizing or psychoanalyzing him.  Indeed, Freud's dark side is exposed along with the controversies surrounding his revolutionary theories.  Ferris concludes with an account of the struggles of the psychoanalytic movement that Freud began.

Curie, Eve.  *Madame Curie: A Biography* (1867–1934)
Translated by Vincent Sheean.  Da Capo Press, 2001 (1937), 448 pages.

Marie Curie was the first woman to win the Nobel Prize, and the only person to receive it twice in two different sciences, physics and chemistry.  This biography, written by her daughter, chronicles Curie's life from her childhood in Poland to her pioneering studies in radioactivity at the University of Paris to her tragic death from radium poisoning.  Amply illustrated with black and white photos, this reprint edition includes a new introduction by Natalie Angier.

# B. American History

Modern American history begins in the early 17th Century with the arrival of the first European settlers at Jamestown and Plymouth. A century and a half later, colonial America gave birth to the era of revolution and the founding of a sovereign, constitutional republic. The growth of the fledgling nation was not trouble-free, as a civil war fought over slavery threatened its demise. However, the United States survived the bloody trial and prospered to become the most free and powerful country in the world. American history is a fascinating story of hardship and promise, revolution and founding, civil war and reconstruction, immigration and urbanization, racial discord and civil rights, national unity and cultural diversity, and technical innovation and economic progress.

Today the United States is the third largest country in the world in both land area and population. It is one of the world's most ethnically diverse nations. Our country continues to be the leading economic, political, military, and cultural force in the world. No student of history can fail to be moved and enlightened by America's storied past.

The titles listed in American history and biography are divided into three sections: Surveys and American Intellectual History, 17th and 18th Centuries, and 19th Century. Since the histories of Europe and the United States became integrally connected in the last century, American history after 1900 is not included in this section but in 20th Century and Early 21st Century World History, which follows.

The first section, Surveys and American Intellectual History, contains mostly works in the history of ideas. Paul Johnson's survey of American history follows a standard chronological treatment, but the others all focus on intellectual and cultural trends.

The second section covers the 17th and 18th Centuries, from the first colonial settlements through the American founding. The biographies include the great advocate for religious freedom, Roger Williams, and the most significant revolutionary heroes: Franklin, Washington, Adams, and Jefferson.

The third section, 19th Century, includes books that cover the great themes and events of the era, particularly America's wars against England and Mexico, the Civil War, Reconstruction, Westward expansion, and industrialization/immigration/urbanization. Among the listed biographies, you will find two presidents (Jackson and Lincoln), two social activists (Stanton and Douglass), a military hero (Lee), a great industrialist (Carnegie), and a fabled Native American (Crazy Horse).

## 1. Surveys and American Intellectual History

Boorstin, Daniel J. *The Americans: The Colonial Experience*
Vintage, 1964 (1958), 448 pages.

This is the first in a trilogy of books on American history. In this volume, Boorstin, an esteemed American historian, discusses the political, cultural, and intellectual trends in colonial America from the first settlements to the Revolution. He focuses on four colonies: the Puritans of Massachusetts, the Quakers of Pennsylvania, the settlers of Georgia, and the gentlemen of Virginia. This enlightening work is full of rich anecdotes of early Americans known and unknown.

Boorstin, Daniel J. *The Americans: The National Experience*
Vintage, 1967 (1965), 528 pages.

In this second volume, Boorstin focuses on the period between the Revolution and the Civil War. He continues his entertaining, anecdotal style, chronicling not political events but a people's way of life. Major themes are the American Industrial Revolution, an emerging nationalism, and western expansion. Brief sketches of little-known Americans who shaped the nation's customs and character during a critical stage of its development help explain how we Americans became the people we are.

Boorstin, Daniel J. *The Americans: The Democratic Experience*
Vintage, 1974 (1973), 736 pages.

This final volume of Boorstin's trilogy won the Pulitzer Prize for history in 1974. The scope is ambitious as it covers the century after the Civil War. Like the earlier volumes, this is not the familiar litany of names, places, dates, and events, but rather a rich mosaic of mini-histories covering a variety of subjects from businessmen and inventions, to cattle drives and range wars, to the democratization of shopping. Together they unlock the key to America's greatness.

Grafton, John, Editor. *The Declaration of Independence and Other Great Documents of American History, 1775–1865*
Courier Dover, 2000, 64 pages.

This is an indispensable, handy resource for the study of American history. It contains 13 of the most important documents from our nation's first century, from Patrick Henry's "Give Me Liberty or Give Me Death" speech to the Gettysburg Address. An introductory note precedes each text. Collectively, these immortal words articulate the enduring principles and freedoms upon which America was built.

Johnson, Paul. *A History of the American People*
HarperCollins, 1999 (1997), 1,104 pages.

This is a lengthy, comprehensive history of America covering 400 years from the first settlements to the Clinton administration. Johnson, a British conservative, strikes an admiring, optimistic tone in covering every aspect of America's past: political, social, economic, cultural, and religious. The narrative is full of entertaining facts and stories interwoven with Johnson's personal interpretations. Bound to enlighten and provoke.

Kirk, Russell. *The Roots of American Order*
ISI Books, 4th ed., 2003 (1974), 534 pages.

Kirk, one of the founders of the post-war conservative movement, offers an ambitious survey of the historical origins of America's constitutional order. He traces this centuries-long heritage from Biblical origins to the Greeks and Romans, to medieval Christendom, to England, and then across the Atlantic. It's an optimistic, edifying reading of the American tradition. This cogent book is a great resource for those searching for the "permanent things" in Western history.

Madison, James, Alexander Hamilton, and John Jay. *The Federalist Papers*
Edited by Clinton Rossiter. Signet Classics, 2003 (1788), 688 pages.

These 85 seminal essays, written by three Founding Fathers under the name "Publius" to persuade voters to ratify the recently drafted Constitution, are some of the most important documents in American political history. Indeed, Jefferson considered them "the best commentary on the principles of government which ever was written." This is the most reader-friendly edition, complete with introduction, a brief summary of each essay, notes, index, and supporting documents.

McDonald, Forrest. *Novus Ordo Seclorum: The Intellectual Origins of the Constitution*
University Press of Kansas, 1985, 376 pages.

This scholarly work by one of the foremost historians of the American founding is an incisive, political history of the fledgling American republic. McDonald analyzes the intellectual background of the framers, which guided their experiment in republican self-government based on federalism, thus creating "the new order of the ages." The title, derived from Virgil, is the motto found on the reverse of the Great Seal of the United States.

Menand, Louis. *The Metaphysical Club: The Story of Ideas in America*
Farrar, Straus and Giroux, 2001, 568 pages.

In this Pulitzer Prize-winning work, Menand chronicles intellectual life in America between the Civil War and World War I, a period when pragmatism was the ruling philosophy. At the heart of this wide-ranging survey is an intellectual biography of four pragmatist philosophers: Oliver Wendell Holmes, Jr., William James, Charles Sanders Peirce, and John Dewey—the first three linked by a short-lived discussion group formed in 1872. This eloquent book makes the ideas of a past era come to life.

## 2. 17th and 18th Centuries

**HISTORY**

Anderson, Fred. *The War That Made America: A Short History of the French and Indian War*
Penguin, 2006, 320 pages.

This abridgement of the author's *Crucible of War* was written as the companion to the four-part PBS documentary series. Anderson provides a vivid retelling of the Seven Years War, history's first world war, focusing on the North American theater. He emphasizes the roles played in this long struggle by the young George Washington and the Native Americans, particularly the Iroquois. This thrilling and informative book includes 16 pages of color plates.

Bowen, Catherine Drinker. *Miracle At Philadelphia: The Story of the Constitutional Convention May–September 1787*
Back Bay Books, 1986 (1966), 346 pages.

This is the classic history of the Constitutional Convention held in Philadelphia in 1787. The author provides an in-depth account of how the 55 delegates debated, struggled, and compromised to produce a lasting system of republican government. After following their deliberations, the reader learns what life was like in late 18th-Century America. The last three chapters discuss the ratification process, and the Constitution and Bill of Rights are appended.

McCullough, David. *1776*
Simon & Schuster, 2006, 400 pages.

In this vibrant narrative, the esteemed American historian describes the first tumultuous year of the Revolutionary War. At the center of the drama stands Washington. McCullough vividly captures the victories and defeats of the ragtag Continental Army that Washington commanded from the siege of Boston to the Battle of Trenton. There is also an abridged, illustrated edition that includes maps, portraits, and 37 facsimile reproductions of primary documents.

Morgan, Edmund. *Birth of the Republic: 1763–1789*
University of Chicago Press, 3rd. ed., 1993 (1956), 224 pages.

Morgan is an eminent early American historian who penned this classic account of the American Revolution and Founding over 50 years ago. It remains one of the most authoritative and accessible overviews of the period, covering all the major developments from the Stamp Act to the Constitutional Convention. The Articles of Confederation, the Declaration of Independence, the Constitution and Bill of Rights, and a timeline of important events are all included.

Taylor, Alan. *American Colonies: The Settling of North America*
Viking/Penguin, 2002, 544 pages.

This is the first of a projected five-volumes in the *Penguin History of the United States* series. Taylor's history of early America is broader and richer than the usual fare, for he includes the pre-Columbian history of Native Americans, the French, Dutch, Spanish, and even Russian settlements, the British West Indies, as well as the major role played by black Africans. The 19 chapters are organized by geographical region in this fresh and compelling overview.

Wood, Gordon. *The American Revolution: A History*
Random House (Modern Library Chronicles), 2003 (2002), 190 pages.

This is a concise, lucid account of the events and circumstances surrounding our nation's birth. Written by a premier Pulitzer Prize-winning historian, this engaging story of the Revolution addresses the great themes of liberty, power, and rights. It's a great synthesis that doesn't argue for any new interpretation but reflects the scholarship of the last 30 years. Included are four maps and a chronology of events.

## BIOGRAPHY

Morgan, Edmund. *Roger Williams: The Church and the State* (1603–1683)
W. W. Norton, 2006 (1967), 176 pages.

Roger Williams was the founder of the Rhode Island colony and America's first advocate for the separation of church and state. In this biography Morgan examines the life and mind of this uncompromising Puritan-Separatist. He traces the evolution of Williams' thought based on his writings and correspondence, while at the same time providing an overview of religious developments in the 16th and 17th Centuries.

Franklin, Benjamin. *Autobiography* (1706–1790)
Touchtone, 2003 (1793), 160 pages.

Franklin's unfinished account of his life, written from 1771 to 1790, is one of the greatest autobiographies ever written. It began as a letter to his son William, in which he composed stories from his past to impart wisdom and moral guidance. Franklin's memoir evolved into a charming self-portrait that is an inspirational account of a self-made Renaissance man. This is an indispensible record of America's most accomplished Founding Father.

Ellis, Joseph J. *His Excellency: George Washington* (1732–1799)
Vintage, 2005, 352 pages.

In this follow-up to *Founding Brothers* (see annotation near the end of this Biography section), Ellis expands upon his essay on Washington offered there to present a fuller, majestic portrait. Drawing on Washington's personal papers and letters, Ellis touches on every important aspect of his public life. His focus is on the impact Washington's decisions had upon the course of his life and the life of the country. This elegantly written biography gives the reader a rich sense of Washington's humanity.

McCullough, David. *John Adams* (1735–1826)
Simon & Schuster, 2008 (2001), 752 pages.

The life and times of our nation's second President are given fresh voice in this epic, Pulitzer Prize-winning biography. McCullough provides fascinating insights about Adams's public life as lawyer, farmer, revolutionary, diplomat, and statesman, as well as his personal life as seen through his correspondence with his devoted wife Abigail and his long-time friend and rival Thomas Jefferson. This is a splendid life story of an underappreciated Founding Father. It was the basis of the HBO TV miniseries that aired in 2008.

Ellis, Joseph J. *American Sphinx: The Character of Thomas Jefferson* (1743–1826)
Vintage, 1998, 440 pages.

This is not a conventional biography of Jefferson that covers the familiar ground. Because that has been done in dozens of previous books, Ellis rather offers a compelling character study of the complicated, enigmatic individual who became our third president. Focusing on five periods in Jefferson's life, Ellis dissects his beliefs, personality, and actions. This well-written, illuminating perspective rounds out our understanding of one of America's most fascinating founders.

Akers, Charles W. *Abigail Adams: An American Woman* (1744–1818)
Pearson/Longman, 3rd ed., 2006 (1980), 256 pages.

A good supplement to McCullough's book on John Adams is this brief, admiring account of Abigail Adams in the *Library of American Biography* series. The first to draw upon her voluminous correspondence, Akers portrays this strong-minded, independent woman—the wife of one president and mother of another—as a revolutionary activist who so greatly contributed to the building of a nation that she deserves the title of Founding Mother.

Ellis, Joseph J. *Founding Brothers: The Revolutionary Generation*
Random House, 2002 (2000), 288 pages.

This collection of stories of seven founding fathers—Franklin, Washington, Adams, Jefferson, Hamilton, Burr, and Madison—tells how they confronted overwhelming challenges in the post-revolutionary period when the success of our nation was still in doubt. Written by a renowned Pulitzer Prize-winning historian, these six stories—from the Hamilton-Burr duel to Jefferson and Adams's famous correspondence—combine a lively and elegant style with deft interpretation.

Wood, Gordon. *Revolutionary Characters: What Made the Founders Different*
Penguin, 2007, 336 pages.

No one denies the greatness of America's Founding Fathers. The question is what made them great. In this captivating work, Wood provides thoughtful meditations on Washington, Franklin, Jefferson, Hamilton, Madison, Adams, Paine, and Burr. What ties these character studies together is Wood's focus on the combination of personal background and intellectual formation that uniquely shaped their characters and allowed them to combine Enlightenment ideals with practical politics.

# 3. 19th Century

## HISTORY

Borneman, Walter R.  *1812: The War That Forged a Nation*
HarperCollins, 2005, 392 pages.

Often neglected in history books, the War of 1812 was also a war nobody won.  Seeking to rehabilitate its significance, Borneman traces the major events of the war from the burning of Washington D.C. to the Battle of New Orleans.  Though the war ended in a stalemate, Borneman shows how it united a young nation and set it on the course of westward expansion.  This readable, well-researched history is a riveting account of critical years in American history.

Christensen, Carol and Thomas.  *The U.S.–Mexican War*
Bay Books, 1998, 246 pages.

This companion to the four-part PBS series details the long-forgotten war (1846–1848) provoked by Manifest Destiny.  With the aid of 11 American and Mexican historians, the authors provide a balanced overview of this controversial war that changed both countries' borders, relations, and standing in the world.  This richly illustrated volume includes personal accounts from diaries and letters as well as early photos (daguerreotypes) and artwork from both sides.

Duncan, Dayton and Ken Burns.  *Lewis & Clark, The Journey of the Corps of Discovery: An Illustrated History*
Knopf, 1999, 272 pages.

This companion volume to the PBS documentary by Ken Burns chronicles the entire journey of the Lewis and Clark expedition (1804–1806).  The narrative follows the group of intrepid explorers on their dangerous journey to find the Northwest Passage and explore the great West.  Many passages from the men's journals give the reader a first-hand account of the expedition.  A wealth of paintings, photographs, journal sketches, and maps illustrate this epic adventure.

Foner, Eric.  *A Short History of Reconstruction*
HarperCollins, 1990, 320 pages.

This is the abridged version of the author's *Reconstruction: America's Unfinished Revolution, 1863–1877*, the award-winning, definitive study of this turbulent period.  Foner endorses the revisionist scholarship that debunks the long-held view that the Radical Republicans were the bad guys and Andrew Johnson was a moderate acting in the spirit of Lincoln.  He offers a much more objective account that paints neither side as saintly.

Handlin, Oscar. *The Uprooted: The Epic Story of the Great Migrations That Made the American People*
University of Pennsylvania Press, 2nd ed., 2002 (1951), 333 pages.

Awarded the 1952 Pulitzer Prize for history, this seminal work chronicles the collective experience of the masses of European immigrants who came to America in the late 19th and early 20th Centuries. Written as a narrative, this is a sensitive and moving portrait of people whose lives were radically altered as they left their impoverished homelands to plant new roots in a foreign land and suffered untold hardship in the journey.

Licht, Walter. *Industrializing America: The Nineteenth Century*
John Hopkins University Press, 1995, 240 pages.

Licht offers a survey of the social and economic transformations that occurred as a result of industrialization in 19th-Century America. Licht sees industrialization as both a product and agent of change, and he approaches the important issues and debates from various viewpoints: labor, industrialists, government, etc. This is a very useful introduction to the history of the Industrial Revolution in America and its effects.

Riis, Jacob. *How the Other Half Lives: Studies Among the Tenements of New York*
Dover, 1971 (1890), 233 pages.

This is the book that gave birth to muckraking photojournalism. Riis, a Danish immigrant and pioneer photojournalist, brought to public attention the deplorable conditions of immigrant life in New York City tenements. His depiction of the impoverished, disease-ridden, crime-infested slums provoked needed social reforms. It is a dismal but eye-opening chronicle of the dark side of urban life at the end of the 19th Century. This edition contains over 100 of Riis's photos.

Ward, Geoffrey C. *The Civil War: An Illustrated History*
Knopf, 1992 (1990), 425 pages.

This complete narrative of the Civil War—the companion volume to the celebrated PBS documentary film series by Ken Burns—is a very useful introduction to America's epic tragedy. Five lengthy chapters follow the war year by year, telling in gripping fashion the stories of all the major battles, military leaders, and political conflicts. Essays by distinguished historians follow each chapter. The volume contains over 500 Civil War-era photographs, maps, and illustrations.

Ward, Geoffrey C. *The West: An Illustrated History*
Back Bay Books, 2003 (1996), 445 pages.

Ward's encore to *The Civil War* tells the colossal story of the discovery and settling of the American West. This companion to the PBS series by Stephen Ives and Ken Burns contains over 400 photos and numerous excerpts from letters, diaries, journals, and memoirs. Ward focuses on the turbulent relationship between the waves of white settlers and the Native Americans whose way of life was destroyed. Essays by notable historians follow each of the eight chapters.

Wills, Garry. *Lincoln at Gettysburg: The Words That Remade America*
Simon & Schuster, 2006 (1993), 320 pages.

This Pulitzer Prize-winning work analyzes the most famous speech in American history in its political and historical context. Wills details the heavy influence of the early Greeks (particularly Pericles) and the 19th-Century Transcendentalists on this brief literary masterpiece. Originally panned by newspaper reviewers, Lincoln's 272 immortal words have never before been submitted to such a provocative and illuminating study.

## BIOGRAPHY

Remini, Robert. *The Life of Andrew Jackson* (1767–1845)
Harper Perennial, 1999 (1966), 256 pages.

Remini is the leading historian of the Age of Jackson. He does a commendable job capturing the essence of "Old Hickory" in this concise biography. This admiring portrait covers all the high points in Jackson's personal, military, and political life without glossing over his failings. History lovers might wish to tackle Remini's definitive three-volume biography of Jackson, entitled *Andrew Jackson*, for a more in-depth treatment.

Blount, Jr., Roy. *Robert E. Lee: A Life* (1807–1870)
Penguin, 2006, 224 pages.

This is a very readable, thumbnail portrait of the famous Civil War general who was known for his uncanny military victories. Blount, a humorist and fellow Southerner, presents a light-hearted but informative survey of Lee's life and career. He examines Lee's family background, education, and the formative influences that shaped his character. Lee's heroic stature and complex nature are justly rendered in this brief, insightful study in the *Penguin Lives* series.

Gienapp, William E. *Abraham Lincoln and the Civil War: A Biography* (1809–1865)
Oxford University Press, 2002, 256 pages.

The bicentennial of Lincoln's birth saw a glut of new books on Honest Abe. This remains one of the most effective, short biographies of our 16th president. Lincoln's presidency gets most of the attention, as Gienapp focuses on the Civil War and Lincoln as shrewd politician and able war leader. This is not the definitive biography of Lincoln, but a very good choice for those looking for a short, manageable overview, particularly of his years as President.

Banner, Lois W. *Elizabeth Cady Stanton: A Radical for Woman's Rights* (1815–1902)
Longman, 1997 (1980), 189 pages.

Elizabeth Cady Stanton was the 19th-Century abolitionist and social activist who became the leading pioneer in the women's rights and suffrage movements. Banner examines Stanton's relationships with her husband and with Susan B. Anthony and other leading feminists of the period. This is a clear and concise portrayal that draws upon Stanton's 1898 autobiography entitled *Eighty Years and More*.

Douglass, Frederick. *Narrative of the Life of Frederick Douglass* (1818–1895)
Oxford World's Classics, 2000 (1845), 176 pages.

This classic autobiography contributed greatly to the abolitionist cause as it revealed to the world the horrors of slavery (long before *Uncle Tom's Cabin*). Born a slave, Douglass secretly learned to read and write. He escaped the brutal system and by force of will became an author, editor, orator, statesman, and forceful abolitionist. This is a moving testament to the power of literacy and sheer human fortitude. This edition includes valuable supplementary material.

Livesay, Harold C. *Andrew Carnegie and the Rise of Big Business* (1835–1919)
Pearson/Longman, 3rd ed., 2006 (1975), 230 pages.

Carnegie was one of the greatest industrialists and philanthropists in American history. His rags-to-riches story epitomizes the American dream. Livesay places into the context of industrialism and the rise of big business the life and career of the poor Scottish immigrant who became the world's richest steel magnate. This short, informative biography also serves as a good introduction to the Industrial Revolution in late 19th-Century America.

McMurtry, Larry. *Crazy Horse* (c. 1840–1877)
Penguin, 2005 (1999), 160 pages.

In this selection from the *Penguin Lives* series, the tragic life and death of Crazy Horse is told against the background of a dying Indian culture as Manifest Destiny swept the plains. Because of the sparse historical record, little is known about the Sioux warrior who became a mythic figure in American history. Sticking to the known facts, McMurtry describes Indian life, government politics, and various battles to augment this vivid but lean portrait.

Kennedy, John F. *Profiles in Courage*
Harper, 2006 (1956), 264 pages.

This inspiring account of eight unsung heroes from America's past became an instant classic and won the Pulitzer Prize for biography. Written when Kennedy was a freshman senator, it profiles the valiant actions of past U.S. senators who put their reputations and careers on the line when they took unpopular stands based on conscience. This 50th anniversary edition contains photographs, contemporary reviews, and other supplementary material.

# C. 20th Century and Early 21st Century World History

The 20th Century was the most tumultuous century in history. Two world wars, horrible genocides, government-created famines, and numerous proxy wars derivative of the larger Cold War contributed to the bloodiest century ever, in which more than 200 million human beings were killed in warfare or by their own governments. However, the century was also marked by a dramatic, worldwide increase in the standard of living, major advances in medicine, science, and technology, and the spread of civil rights and democracy around the world. This is the century when the world truly became a global village, with international telecommunication, world travel, and worldwide economic and cultural integration.

In order to participate most fully in life, it is valuable to understand the world in which we live. That means coming to grips with the forces of disorder that threaten our future, as well as the constructive forces that are the basis for our hopes. Ronald Reagan famously said, "It is morning in America." We would all like to believe that it is morning for the entire human race. Indeed there are solid grounds for such a hope. Reading the history of the 20th and early 21st Centuries gives us a good sense of how we got to where we are today, and it provides us with a basis of understanding that will help us deal with the issues we will face in the years ahead.

Because European and American affairs have been so integrated in the 20th and early 21st Centuries, we have combined their histories in this section. The three history surveys listed (under History: Survey) cover the 20th Century. The first title, *The End of the European Era: 1890 to the Present*, also covers European history in the first decade of the 21st Century. The history titles have been divided into two sections: 20th Century History, and Late 20th and Early 21st Century History. The 16 titles in the first section cover the major events of the 20th Century. The nine titles in the second section treat the most important events and developments of the latter period, including 9/11 and its aftermath, while looking forward into the 21st Century. The ten biographies flesh out our understanding of the period by telling the stories of a selection of key figures from Teddy Roosevelt and Albert Einstein to Martin Luther King, Jr. and Ronald Reagan.

## HISTORY: SURVEY

Gilbert, Felix and David Clay Large. *The End of the European Era, 1890 to the Present*
W. W. Norton, 6th ed., 2009 (1970), 666 pages.

In this final volume of the *Norton History of Modern Europe* series, Gilbert chronicles the major historical events of the 20th Century. He details developments within each of the major European powers (France, Britain, Germany, Russia, and the Austro-Hungarian Empire) in the context of the general European situation, so the reader doesn't lose the big picture. The new, thoroughly revised sixth edition brings the scholarship up to date and expands the coverage.

Gilbert, Martin.  *History of the Twentieth Century: The Concise Edition of the Acclaimed World History*
Harper Perennial, 2002, 832 pages.

Gilbert, an author of over 80 books, is one of the foremost historians of the 20th Century.  This is the condensation of his three-volume history of the 20th Century, which amounted to 2,700 pages of text.  It is a rich, multi-textured, year-by-year account of world events.  The emphasis is on political and military history, but developments in technology, the arts, culture, and religion are also treated.  This grand tour is about as spectacular as the century it chronicles.

Johnson, Paul.  *Modern Times: The World from the Twenties to the Nineties*
Harper Perennial, rev. ed., 2001 (1983), 880 pages.

In this comprehensive history, Johnson brings his opinionated, scholarly flare to the tumultuous 20th Century.  His sweeping analysis begins with the end of World War I and ends with the collapse of the Soviet Union.  The primary focus is on the major actors and the ideological forces that contributed to history's bloodiest century.  Johnson's sharp wit and unabashed conservative viewpoint make this a thought-provoking and entertaining work.

## HISTORY: 20TH CENTURY

Bessel, Richard.  *Nazism and War*
Random House (Modern Library Chronicles), 2006 (2004), 294 pages.

This is a lucid introduction to the Nazi ideology and its impact on Germany and the world.  The author looks at Nazism from its rise in the aftermath of World War I to the aftermath of World War II.  His basic thesis is that Nazism and war were inseparable.  Because Nazi war meant a racist war of extermination, once Nazism achieved power millions of human beings in Germany and around the globe were doomed.  It is a concise, authoritative account of a frightening epoch.

Courtois, Stéphane, et al.  *The Black Book of Communism*: *Crimes, Terrors, Repression*
Translated by Jonathan Murphy and Mark Kramer.  Harvard University Press, 1999, 912 pages.

This massive study documents the vast murders committed by Communist regimes worldwide.  Written by a team of mostly French scholars who obtained access to the Soviet archives, it provides a stark assessment of the criminal nature of Communism.  The atrocities and horrors catalogued here make this a very sobering read.

Durgan, Andy.  *The Spanish Civil War*
Palgrave Macmillan, 2007, 176 pages.

The Spanish Civil War (1936–1939) was provoked by rising nationalism and intervention by foreign powers.  In this introductory overview from Palgrave's *Studies in European History* series, the author discusses the origins, outbreak, and course of the war that devastated Spain and led to the dictatorship of the Franco regime.  Durgan also offers a critical evaluation of the ongoing debates in the academic literature about the war.

Filtzer, Donald A. *The Khrushchev Era: De-Stalinization and the Limits of Reform in the USSR, 1953–1964*
Palgrave Macmillan, 1993, 104 pages.

Nikita Khrushchev was noted for his startling repudiation of Stalin as well as his reorganization of the Communist Party, agriculture, and industry. Filtzer examines these social, economic, and political reforms, and locates the complex reasons for their failure in the Stalinist system itself. This succinct volume nicely supplements Graeme Gill's *Stalinism* in the same series (see annotation below).

Friedman, Norman. *The Fifty-Year War: Conflict and Strategy in the Cold War*
Naval Institute Press, 2007 (1999), 640 pages.

Friedman is a recognized authority on 20th-Century warfare and defense strategy. In this comprehensive retelling of the Cold War, he offers a broad and detailed overview of events from the end of World War II to the collapse of the Soviet Union in 1991. He discusses the Korean War, the Cuban missile crisis, the Vietnam War, and other conflicts as interconnected events in a long struggle that divided the world. Included are maps, photos, and an extensive bibliography.

Gaddis, John Lewis. *The Cold War: A New History*
Penguin, 2007 (2005), 333 pages.

This is a condensed history of the Cold War written for a post-Cold War generation. Gaddis, America's preeminent Cold War historian, synthesizes all the recent scholarship in this accessible and thematic overview. His focus is on the major events and portraits of the key political actors. He explains not just the *who, what, when,* and *where* of the conflict but also the *why.* This book includes maps, photos, and an extensive bibliography.

Gill, Graeme. *Stalinism*
Palgrave Macmillan, 2nd ed., 1998, 112 pages.

This brief volume in Palgrave's *Studies in European History* series examines the origins of Stalinism, the oppressive nature of the Stalinist regime and its economic system, and how Stalinism changed over time. The author explains how the fall of the Soviet Union was directly connected to Stalinism. This revised edition draws on the latest research made available by the opening of the Soviet archives. A chronology of events supplements the text.

Keegan, John. *The First World War*
Vintage, 2000, 475 pages.

This is the definitive military history of the Great War. The eminent British historian delivers a comprehensive account of the global conflict, detailing the war's causes, its nightmarish battles, the weapons used, the horrors of trench warfare, the generals' military strategy, and the motivations of the lofty leaders who directed the conflagration. A stripped-down, illustrated edition with over 500 photographs, drawings, and maps is also available.

Keegan, John. *The Second World War*
Penguin, 2005 (1989), 608 pages.

This is a superb, one-volume history of the most destructive war ever fought. Keegan marshals a massive amount of information in his chronological recounting of the causes and course of the war. He examines each theater of the war and its major battles, though greater weight is given to the European conflict. Keegan's gift for storytelling and analytical ability make the vast scope of his subject accessible to all readers. The numerous photos and maps enrich the narrative.

Lukacs, John. *A New Republic: A History of the United States in the Twentieth Century*
Yale University Press, rev. ed., 2004 (1984), 457 pages.

Lukacs analyzes the national trends in America since 1900. The short, first part is a summary narrative of 20th-Century American history that is followed by a longer, second part that analyzes the economic, political, cultural, intellectual, and moral transformations that occurred during this period. Lukacs's appraisal of these developments is insightful but generally critical. The revised edition includes a new introduction and a closing chapter that updates the author's views.

Patterson, James T. *Restless Giant: The United States from Watergate to Bush v. Gore*
Oxford University Press, 2007, 496 pages.

*The Oxford History of the United States* is an ambitious, well-respected, high quality series. In this final chronological volume in the series, Patterson covers the years 1974 to 2001, from Nixon's resignation to George W. Bush's inauguration. He blends social, political, cultural, and economic developments into an illuminating narrative. Given any historian's limited perspective on the recent past, Patterson offers an insightful analysis of a turbulent period.

Pipes, Richard. *Communism: A History*
Random House (Modern Library Chronicles), 2003, 192 pages.

A scholar of Russian history, Pipes tells the story of the rise and fall of Communism and its catastrophic impact on the modern world. The work is essentially a history of the Soviet Union from the October Revolution to its collapse seven decades later, though the spread of Communism to other countries is discussed as well. The author's concise account of Soviet ideology and atrocities is a stark and grim story.

Service, Robert. *The Russian Revolution, 1900–1927*
Palgrave Macmillan, 4th ed., 2009 (1986), 144 pages.

In this volume from Palgrave's *Studies in European History* series, Service examines the Russian Revolution, its origins and its consequences, covering the years 1900 to 1927. In three chapters he discusses Russia under the Romanovs from 1900, the February and October Revolutions of 1917, and then Russia under the Communists to 1927. The expanded and updated fourth edition of this popular, concise history includes a new introduction and maps.

Shlaes, Amity. *The Forgotten Man: A New History of the Great Depression*
HarperCollins, 2008, 512 pages.

Shlaes, a former Wall Street Journal editor and columnist, has written a revisionist history of the Great Depression from a free-market perspective. She argues that Hoover and Roosevelt actually lengthened the Depression by following bad monetary policy, raising tariffs, and instituting New Deal programs. This interpretive history, which covers all the major players, is a provocative and timely analysis, particularly in light of the economic events of 2008–2009.

Tuchman, Barbara. *The Guns of August*
Random House, 2004 (1962), 640 pages.

Tuchman narrates the events leading up to World War I and the war's first month. With stunning prose and meticulous detail, she brings to life the dreadful events of August, 1914. The main focus is on the movement and action of armies from first mobilization to stalemate. However, she also provides a rich description of the political and military leaders whose folly led to the deaths of over 16 million people. This masterful work won the Pulitzer Prize.

Wistrich, Robert S. *Hitler and the Holocaust*
Random House (Modern Library Chronicles), 2003, 295 pages.

An authority on the history of anti-Semitism and modern Jewry, Wistrich tells the frightful story of Europe's long history of violence against the Jews, which culminated in the Holocaust. He examines Germany's racist background, Hitler's ideology, the infernal workings of the Nazi death machine, the "final solution," the nature of European collaboration, and Jewish resistance. This penetrating study is a fine companion to Richard Bessel's *Nazism and War* in the same series (see annotation above).

### HISTORY: LATE 20TH AND EARLY 21ST CENTURY

Chollet, Derek and James Goldgeier. *America Between the Wars: From 11/9 to 9/11*
Public Affairs, 2008, 432 pages.

The title refers to the period between the Cold War and the War on Terror, that is, from the fall of the Berlin Wall to the fall of the Twin Towers. Experts on foreign policy, the authors examine the decade of the 1990s, a period of uncertainty when the world was in search of a stable international order. Many behind-the-scenes stories make this an engaging review and informative analysis of the events and forces that have shaped the post-Cold War world.

Diamond, Larry. *The Spirit of Democracy: The Struggle to Build Free Societies Throughout the World*
Times Books, 2008, 464 pages.

Larry Diamond is bullish on democracy. Compared to 1974, when a quarter of all nations were democracies, today three-fifths of the world's states are democratic. Diamond gives the end of the Cold War partial credit for the trend, but argues the greater significance of the commitment of citizens in establishing democracies worldwide.

Friedman, Thomas L.  *The World is Flat 3.0: A Brief History of the Twenty-first Century*
Picador, 2007 (2005), 672 pages.

Friedman's analysis of globalization in the 21st Century posits a level playing field where all can freely compete.  He lists ten "flatteners" of the global playing field, including the Web and open-sourcing.  Internet innovations, the outsourcing of the service sector, and the off-shoring of manufacturing have all created new economic opportunities.

Huntington, Samuel P.  *The Clash of Civilizations and the Remaking of World Order*
Simon & Schuster, 1998 (1996), 368 pages.

In this challenging but incisive work, the author presents a provocative analysis of the international political scene after the fall of communism.  Focusing not on states or superpowers but on a few major cultures as the primary players, he argues that post-Cold War conflicts will be driven by resurgent religious faith and cultural identity more than ideology.  Considered a prescient book after 9/11, it proclaimed the challenge of Islam to the West before it was popular.

Kagan, Robert.  *The Return of History and the End of Dreams*
Knopf, 2008, 128 pages.

This is a sobering essay on the looming international conflicts that America will face in the years ahead.  Hopes for a peaceful international order at the end of the Cold War have been dashed.  A growing China, a resurgent Russia, a restless India, a turbulent Middle East, and a competitive Europe all make for global strife in a world of limited resources.  With his vast knowledge of geopolitics, Kagan weighs in on the trouble ahead and how America should meet the challenge.

Khanna, Parag.  *The Second World: How Emerging Powers Are Redefining Global Competition in the Twenty-first Century.*
Random House, 2009 (2008), 496 pages.

An expert in geopolitics, Khanna argues that the 21st Century will be dominated by three superpowers: the United States, the European Union, and China.  Each will compete for allies in the resource-rich "second world" (the Middle East, Central Asia, Africa, and Latin America) to extend its power and influence.  Khanna, who spent two years traveling to 40 countries, offers an audacious survey of contemporary international affairs examining the emerging global order.

Lewis, Bernard.  *The Crisis of Islam*
Random House, 2004 (2003), 224 pages.

Lewis examines the historical roots of the Islamic resentments toward the West that find their expression in acts of terrorism.  He covers 13 centuries of history but focuses mostly on events of the 20th Century leading up to the recent violent confrontation between Islamic extremists and the West.  This is an insightful overview and commentary for those seeking to make sense out of the terrorist attacks of 9/11 and who wonder about the future course of the Islamic-Western conflict.

Lucas, Edward. *The New Cold War: Putin's Russia and the Threat to the West*
Macmillan, 2008, 272 pages.

As Moscow bureau chief for *The Economist*, Lucas witnessed Putin's rise to power after the fall of the Iron Curtain. Here Lucas describes the sweep of Putin's power and Russia's threat to the West in the form of energy dominance, "pipeline politics," and aggressive intentions towards its Eastern European neighbors.

Zakaria, Fareed. *The Post-American World*
W. W. Norton, 2009 (2008), 288 pages.

Zakaria, an editor at *Newsweek* and expert on international affairs, offers a realistic assessment of current international trends and a hopeful outlook on America's future role in the world. He argues the dynamic changes ahead will not result from the decline of America but from "the rise of the rest." With the increasing prosperity of other nations, America's superpower status must yield to the sharing of power. This is an insightful prescription and analysis of world affairs.

## BIOGRAPHY

Auchincloss, Louis. *Theodore Roosevelt* (1858–1919)
Henry Holt, 2002, 192 pages.

This was the first title issued in the popular *American Presidents* series that offers concise biographies for general readers. Auchincloss does an admirable job tracing TR's early years and his military and political career, but the focus is on his presidency and afterwards. The colorful war hero, trust-buster, and conservationist is given his due as the progressive bull moose that he was. This is a good study of TR's character, his many accomplishments, and his place in history.

Isaacson, Walter. *Einstein: His Life and Universe* (1879–1955)
Simon & Schuster, 2007, 704 pages.

This is the first biography based on Einstein's newly released personal letters and thus provides a compelling, fully-rounded portrait of the "preeminent poster boy" of 20th-Century science. We get more Einstein the man than Einstein the scientist, but his great, world-changing theories are explained in a non-technical fashion for the general reader. Isaacson portrays Einstein as a flawed but brilliant man whose scientific imagination derived from his rebellious personality.

Hebblethwaite, Peter. *John XXIII: Pope of the Century* (1881–1963)
Continuum, rev. ed., 2005 (1984), 284 pp.

Elected in 1958, Angelo Roncalli transformed the Church during his short papacy by calling for the Second Vatican Council. In his acclaimed biography, Hebblethwaite illuminates the personality, teachings, initiatives, and indeed, saintliness, of this much-beloved religious leader. This revised, abridged edition of Hebblethwaite's 1984 biography, entitled *John XXIII: Pope of the Council*, is more accessible and readable.

Jenkins, Roy. *Franklin Delano Roosevelt* (1882–1945)
Henry Holt, 2005, 208 pages.

This is an impressive, short biography of the president who steered the U.S. through two major crises of the 20th Century: the Great Depression and World War II. Jenkins, a leading British politician, historian, and biographer, nearly finished this biography for the *American Presidents* series before he died in 2003. With masterful prose he provides a unique British perspective that focuses more on FDR's character and relationships than his policies.

Youngs, William T. *Eleanor Roosevelt: A Personal and Public Life* (1884–1962)
Longman, 3rd ed., 2005 (1985), 320 pages.

This is an objective, engaging portrait that hits all the main points of Eleanor Roosevelt's life and accomplishments, trials and tribulations. Focusing mostly on her pre-White House years, Young examines her roles as social activist, wife, and mother. In the last third of the book he covers the dozen tumultuous years when she served as First Lady of the United States. From beginning to end, Young successfully conveys Eleanor Roosevelt's character and era.

Ambrose, Stephen. *Eisenhower: Soldier and President* (1890–1969)
Pocket Books, 2007 (1991), 635 pages.

This is a revision and abridgement of the author's two-volume biography of Eisenhower published in 1983–84. Ambrose offers a vivid and comprehensive portrait of the career soldier who became the Supreme Allied Commander in World War II, leading the Allies to victory. Then, as President, Eisenhower steered the U.S. through one of the most dangerous decades of the Cold War. Drawing on extensive research, including interviews with Ike himself, Ambrose's sympathetic portrait is both informative and inspiring.

D'Souza, Dinesh. *Ronald Reagan: How an Ordinary Man Became an Extraordinary Leader* (1911–2004)
Touchstone, 1999 (1997), 304 pages.

D'Souza, a former member of Reagan's White House staff, offers an inspiring portrait of Reagan's life and presidency. Reagan's presidency was highly successful on two fronts. In foreign policy he brought an end to the Cold War by implementing policies that led to the collapse of the Soviet Union, and in so doing greatly reduced the threat of nuclear war. On the domestic front he ended the stagflation and economic malaise of the 70s and ushered in two decades of sustained economic growth.

Burner, David. *John F. Kennedy and a New Generation* (1917–1963)
Prentice Hall, 3rd ed., 2008 (1988), 224 pages.

Burner tries to distinguish the Kennedy legend from reality. He covers the successes and failures of Kennedy's life and presidency, and lauds him for his modern presidential style. He is also fair in his assessment of the contradictory nature of the Kennedy administration that combined a liberal domestic agenda with a militant foreign policy. This is a very good overview of Kennedy, his presidency, and his legacy, which explores the controversies without digging too deep.

King, Jr., Martin Luther.  *The Autobiography of Martin Luther King, Jr.* (1929–1968)
Edited by Clayborne Carson.  Grand Central Publishing, 2001 (1998), 416 pages.

This authorized "autobiography" is not a work King himself wrote.  Rather it is a compilation of material assembled from King's previously published books and speeches as well as unpublished letters, diaries, and interviews.  The resulting portrait covers all aspects of King's life, especially his work as a minister and civil rights leader, his relationships with his wife and children, and his dealings with important political figures.  This inspirational book brings King's spirit to life.

O'Sullivan, John.  *The President, the Pope, and the Prime Minister: Three Who Changed the World*
Regnery, 2008 (2006), 360 pages.

O'Sullivan, a British journalist and former Thatcher speechwriter, interweaves the stories of President Reagan, Pope John Paul II, and British Prime Minister Margaret Thatcher, who together helped bring an end to Soviet communism.  Having conducted exclusive interviews with all three, he first sketches how each rose to power and then the roles they played in ending the Cold War.  This illuminating study provides a compelling perspective on the life, times, and historical impact of three heroic figures.

## D. Literature

Reading became an important part of life in the modern era as men and women across Europe and the United States made gains in literacy. The development of modern literature is closely connected to this rise in literacy. By the beginning of the 19th Century, literacy was widespread in England, France, and the United States.

With the birth of the novel in the 18th Century, readers in Europe were presented with a new, imaginative literary form that could be enjoyed in the privacy of their own homes and in the solitude of their own thoughts and feelings, rather than in a social setting like a theater. Yet the novel would become a powerful medium for portraying the relationship of the individual to society, as well as a vehicle for exploring the interior landscape of the soul. Early classic novels like *Gulliver's Travels* and *Tom Jones* combined popular features of adventure and romance with a rich and varied portrayal of human nature. Eighteenth-Century novels by French writers Voltaire and Rousseau reflected the ferment of ideas that led to the French Revolution.

The 19th-Century novel is one of the great achievements of world literature. The literature of the 19th Century portrayed human beings in the process of growth and transformation, often triggered by the social changes that characterized the century. During a time of increasing industrialization, Charles Dickens used realism to mirror society, while Emily Brontë employed romantic realism to represent the inner life. The 19th Century was also the golden age of the short story. Stories focusing on an array of social types were widely read in newspapers and magazines. In poetry, the Romantics' valuation of individual experience and of nature offered another literary response to the times.

One of the pleasures in reading the significant works of literature in any age is to see how they reflect the spirit of their times while addressing themes that are universal. The great works of the 20th Century reflect an age in which human beings were compelled to find new sources of meaning and purpose in their lives in the wake of worldwide disorder and change. They also remind us of the resilience and depth of the human spirit, which never ceases to hope and love even amidst turmoil and struggle. The very language and style of these works reflect the tone of the age, as writers discovered new and exciting ways of telling a story.

# 1. 18th Century

Eighteenth-Century literature has been called literature of the Age of Enlightenment, but it may be more fitting to call it literature of the Age of Morality. For while the Enlightenment's radical agenda of social change deeply influenced Continental European literature, English literature of the time was less extreme in its social critique, reflecting the relative stability of English society. Yet for all the differences between France and England, their literatures each belonged to a dynamic age of prose by writers who scourged society for its moral lapses.

In both England and France, the 18th Century witnessed a cultural development of singular importance: the birth of the novel. In England, Defoe's novel *Robinson Crusoe* met with immediate success upon its publication in 1719, followed by the widely acclaimed novels *Gulliver's Travels*, published in 1726 by Jonathan Swift, and *Tom Jones*, published in 1749 by Henry Fielding. In France, Voltaire published *Candide*, a novel of ideas, in 1759.

*Robinson Crusoe*, an adventure tale that pits man against nature, inaugurated an era of concern with civilization and social relationships. In *Gulliver's Travels*, Swift's hero Gulliver, in his encounter with the fantastical Lilliputians, sees the moral and political failings of his own society. While Swift's moralizing takes the form of biting satire, Fielding uses fictional characters to embody the virtues and vices of the time in his novel, *Tom Jones*. The great French moralist Voltaire uses an avalanche of misadventures to convey his ideas in the comic novel *Candide*. Rousseau's intensely personal *Confessions* introduces the reader to a new type of autobiography, one meant not only to hold up a mirror to society, but to engage in the ultimate morality of self-exposure.

**BRITISH**

**Defoe, Daniel** (1659–1731). Defoe is generally regarded as England's first writer of novels. He was deeply involved in the politics of his time for the better part of his career and didn't begin writing novels until he was almost 60.

*Robinson Crusoe* (1719)
Penguin Classics, 2003, 288 pages.

Defoe's most famous novel is structured as a series of journal entries written by Robinson Crusoe, an inveterate seafarer who persists in his love of the sea despite one misfortune after another. His latest misadventure finds him shipwrecked on a desert island where he must use all of his mental and physical resources to survive. He is eventually assisted by Friday, a native whom he rescues from a tribe of cannibals.

Also read: *Moll Flanders* (1722).

**Swift, Jonathan** (1667–1745). Swift, who was born in Ireland, remained active in Irish politics throughout his life. Although best known as the author of *Gulliver's Travels*, he was also an accomplished essayist. His most famous essay, *A Modest Proposal*, is a scathing satire of English rule in Ireland.

*Gulliver's Travels* (1726)
Penguin Classics, 2003, 336 pages.

Swift's satire of human nature is a delightful brew of scene and incident. The story follows the various misadventures of Lemuel Gulliver, whose love of travel is fulfilled in all sorts of unexpected ways upon being shipwrecked in four exotic lands. Perhaps the most famous of these lands is Lilliput, where he is taken captive by a race of pea-sized persons.

**Fielding, Henry** (1707–1754). Henry Fielding was, like Jonathon Swift, a skilled satirist who relentlessly poked fun at social mores, art, literature, and politics in his many essays, plays, and novels. He is most well-known as the author of the grand comic novels *Tom Jones* and *Joseph Andrews*.

*Tom Jones* (1749)
Penguin Classics, 2005, 1,024 pages.

One of the first novels in the English language, Fielding's comic novel is also one of the best. This rowdy, rambling, hilarious satire of English culture and society is presented as the story of Tom Jones, a foundling (or abandoned child) who is taken in by a wealthy landowner. The story chronicles Tom's growth into adulthood with particular emphasis upon his lusty but kind-hearted nature.

### FRENCH

**Voltaire** (1694–1778). François-Marie Arouet (pseudonym Voltaire) was an influential writer of the French Enlightenment who penned hundreds of works including poetry, drama, essays, and social reform pamphlets. Born in Paris, Voltaire was educated by the Jesuits and trained as a lawyer. His radical writings led to prison, exile, and lasting fame.

*Candide, or Optimism* (1759)
Dover, 1991, 112 pages.

Naïve Candide and his beloved Cunégonde face abduction by pirates, earthquake, plague, and other disasters in this vitriolic satire of philosophical optimism. While separated from his love, Candide is guided by his tutor, Pangloss, who claims that this is "the best of all possible worlds."

**Rousseau, Jean-Jacques** (1712–1778).  Rousseau was the preeminent French philosopher of the Enlightenment.  His essay, *The Social Contract*, influenced the French and the American Revolutions.  Born in Geneva, Rousseau worked in Paris as a writer and composer.  He fathered five infants with his common law wife, all of whom he placed in a foundling home.

*Confessions* (1782)
Translated by Angela Scholar.  Oxford World's Classics, 2008, 720 pages.

Rousseau's famous autobiography arguably achieves his goal of a complete and honest self-representation.  Rousseau tells all, revealing his pleasure in corporal punishment, his abject worship of powerful women, and the abandonment of his children to an orphanage.  Rousseau's account of his relationship with Enlightenment figures Diderot and Voltaire shows the undoubted historical importance of this flawed individual.

Also read: *Émile: or, On Education* (1762).

## 2. 19th Century

This list reflects the central place of the novel in 19th-Century literature. During this era, British and French authors continued to write great novels, while authors in the United States, Russia, and Scandinavia came to prominence. Realism dominates the period's meticulously crafted novel, as writers strove to represent human experience in all of its personal and social dimensions.

In England, two trends in the 19th-Century novel developed early on: social realism, as seen in Jane Austen's comedy-of-manners novels, and romantic realism, as seen in Emily Brontë's *Wuthering Heights*. Following Austen, social realism flourished in Victorian era novels by Eliot, Dickens, James, Stendhal, Balzac, and Tolstoy. Works of romantic realism by Hawthorne, Hugo, Dumas, and Wilde featured melodrama, adventure, and the supernatural.

Others writers combined realism with romance, symbolism, and even gothic horror in unique and sometimes unsettling ways. Dostoevsky's *Crime and Punishment* depicts human beings struggling for spiritual transcendence amidst the grim realities of Russian life. Mary Shelley (*Frankenstein*), Edgar Allen Poe, and Robert Louis Stevenson (*Dr. Jekyll and Mr. Hyde*) pioneered the horror genre as a way of grappling with the problem of evil.

The realist novel is known for the vitality of characters who often take on a life of their own. Russian author Tolstoy famously confessed that he fell in love with his heroine Anna Karenina. French author Flaubert saw himself in the character of Emma Bovary. Indeed, many great 19th-Century novels are named for the characters they bring to life: *Emma, David Copperfield, Jane Eyre, Jude the Obscure, Billy Budd, The Adventures of Huckleberry Finn, Madame Bovary*, and *Anna Karenina*.

The masters of 19th-Century fiction penetrated the secrets of the human heart. Realist writers used their understanding of psychology and society to represent human experience and reveal human nature. Pick one of these great works and read; you will surely enjoy literature from one of the most creative periods in history.

### British

**Austen, Jane** (1775–1817). One of the best loved English novelists in her day and ours, Austen grew up in a large family in the country. Though never married, Austen had a deep understanding of love and the human heart. Austen's lively, comic imagination shapes her characters and her perfectly crafted plots.

*Pride and Prejudice* (1813)
Penguin Classics, 2002, 480 pages.

Artfully constructed and masterfully written, *Pride and Prejudice* is generally regarded as Austen's greatest novel. Level-headed Elizabeth Bennett observes the follies of her four sisters with a mixture of pity and chagrin, increasingly convinced that romance is not for her. Certainly there is no chance of falling in love with the handsome but disdainful Mr. Darcy. But how well do we ever know ourselves, much less others? This engaging and ultimately quite moving novel argues, not very well!

**Austen, Jane (cont.)**

*Emma* (1816)
Modern Library Classics, 2001, 384 pages.

Emma is the queen bee of Highbury society, solicitously managing life for her widowed father and boldly interfering in the lives of those around her. Emma's complacency is undisturbed when her match-making schemes go awry, until a scolding from Mr. Knightley opens her eyes to her self-deception. Austen's comic exposure of the folly leading to Emma's self-discovery is a true delight.

Also read: *Sense and Sensibility* (1811), *Mansfield Park* (1814), and *Persuasion* (1848).

**Shelley, Mary** (1797–1851). Famous in her own time as the wife of the great English poet Percy Bysshe Shelley, Mary Shelley conceived the idea for her classic, *Frankenstein*, while vacationing with her husband and another great English poet, Lord Byron, near Geneva, Switzerland—the setting for the novel.

*Frankenstein* (1817)
Penguin Classics, 2003, 352 pages.

Mary Shelley's cautionary tale about the perils of unchecked science is as relevant today as when it was first written. Victor Frankenstein, a brilliant scientist, forms a creature from body parts that he scavenges from a graveyard. When he brings the creature to life, however, Frankenstein is horrified by the monstrosity he has created. Before he can destroy his creation, however, the creature escapes. While Frankenstein tries to forget about the creature, the creature isn't about to forget about his creator.

**Thackeray, William Makepeace** (1811–1863). Born in India and educated in England, Thackeray turned to writing after losing his inheritance through gambling and other reversals. He achieved success with *Vanity Fair*, published in installments in 1847. His satirical novels brought him fame in his lifetime and lasting recognition as a writer.

*Vanity Fair* (1847)
Penguin Classics, 2003, 912 pages.

Thackeray's great novel describes the fortunes and misfortunes of Becky Sharp and Amelia Sedley. This biting social satire exposes England's age of greed through the character of Becky: an amoral, designing social climber befriended by the naïve, virtuous Amelia. Thackeray's spectacle of a woman using beauty, charm, and sex to rise in society has made a byword of the name Becky Sharp.

**Dickens, Charles** (1812–1870). Dickens is arguably rivaled only by Shakespeare in the scope, quality, and originality of his literary output. Dickens' novels typically blend together the comic and tragic and the mysterious and familiar in a language that is full of wit and warmth.

*Oliver Twist* (1837–38)
Penguin Classics, 2003, 608 pages.

The rich stew of character and incident that is *Oliver Twist* has long made it one of Dickens' most popular novels. It is also a powerful novel of social consciousness, dramatizing as it does the many social ills of 19th-Century London. Dickens uses his endearing protagonist, the orphan Oliver Twist, to expose the desperate plight of poor children, who were oftentimes rescued from one perilous environment only to be thrust into another.

*David Copperfield* (1849–50)
Penguin Classics, 2004, 1,024 pages.

Readers new to Dickens will find *David Copperfield* to be an excellent introduction. In what is considered to be Dickens' most autobiographical novel, David Copperfield narrates the story of his life from birth into adulthood. It is a bumpy road indeed, as David confronts the flaws in the world around him and in his own character. Dickens' trademark weave of wry humor and deep pathos is fully on display here, as is his remarkable use of language.

*Great Expectations* (1860–61)
Penguin Classics, 2002, 544 pages.

Dickens' masterful tale is about the oftentimes mysterious ways in which we become authentic human beings. When Pip is given the means to transcend his working-class existence by becoming a gentlemen, he finds himself thrust into the high culture of London. However, after making a shocking discovery about the source of his good fortune, Pip is forced to reevaluate who he truly is.
Also read: *A Christmas Carol* (1843), *Bleak House* (1852–53), *Hard Times* (1854), and *A Tale of Two Cities* (1859).

**Trollope, Anthony** (1815–1882). England's great Victorian novelist grew up in genteel poverty in a family that was for a time supported by his mother's writing. Trollope began writing on train trips while a postal inspector in Ireland. He became a prolific writer, producing 47 novels of politics and intrigue set in town and country across the British Isles.

*Barchester Towers* (1857)
Bantam, 1984, 672 pages.

The second novel (after *The Warden*) in Trollope's *Barsetshire Chronicles* continues the story of cleric Mr. Harding and his daughter Eleanor. Trollope brilliantly exploits the comic potential of the power struggles that take place in the fictional cathedral town of Barchester, and the comic encounters of characters reflecting the social types of his day.
Also read: *The Warden* (1855) and *Phineas Finn* (1864).

**Brontë, Charlotte** (1816–1855).  The eldest of the Brontë sisters, Charlotte was born into a minister's family in rural England.  She lost her mother at five, and was sent away to the Clergy Daughters' School at eight.  Brontë worked as a governess and wrote novels under the pseudonym Currer Bell.  In 1847, she published her masterpiece, *Jane Eyre*.

*Jane Eyre* (1847)
Barnes & Noble Classics, 2004, 592 pages.

Declared a work of genius by Thackeray, *Jane Eyre* won the hearts of its first readers with its tale of the redemptive love of Jane Eyre for Mr. Rochester.  Today's readers are still fascinated and moved by the story of the orphan who achieves respectability, only to be faced with the hidden torments of her soul-mate.

**Brontë, Emily** (1818–1848).  Emily Brontë, British poet and novelist and younger sister of Charlotte Brontë, published her writings under the pen name Ellis Bell.  After her mother's death, she wrote stories based on imaginary lands invented by her siblings and herself.  In 1847 she published *Wuthering Heights*, a masterpiece of romantic literature.

*Wuthering Heights* (1847)
Barnes & Noble Classics, 2005, 400 pages.

Imbued with the atmosphere of the moors and the obscure psychology of its characters, *Wuthering Heights* is a novel of dark impressions and tremendous force.  Brontë's poetic novel tells of the adoption of Heathcliff by Mr. Earnshaw, of Heathcliff's disappointed love for Earnshaw's daughter Catherine, and of Heathcliff's sudden disappearance and tragic reappearance in Catherine's life.

**Eliot, George** (1819–1880).  George Eliot was the pen name of Victorian novelist Mary Ann Evans.  Described by A. S. Byatt as "a good hater," Eliot exposed human iniquity while writing with an abiding love of the English countryside and its people.  Eliot is known for the powerful moral vision reflected in her in-depth character depiction.

*The Mill on the Floss* (1860)
Penguin Classics, 2003, 704 pages.

Maggie Tulliver, bright, intense, and loyal, is the heroine of this novel of the English countryside.  Eliot's psychological insight informs her portraits of Maggie and brother Tom as they develop from two close, strong-willed children into estranged adults.  As Maggie and Tom struggle within the strictures of their tradition-bound society, their unfolding destinies acquire the shape of tragedy.

*Middlemarch* (1871)
Oxford World's Classics, 2008, 904 pages.

Set in the imaginary town of Middlemarch, Eliot's novel of self-delusion and moral dilemma draws its characters from an array of representative social groups, including tradesmen, the middle class, bohemians, and gentry.  At the heart of the story are idealists Dorothea Brooke and Dr. Thomas Lydgate, whose interwoven stories involve unhappy marriages and social and political struggles within their community.

Also read: *Adam Bede* (1859), *Silas Marner* (1861), and *Daniel Deronda* (1876).

**Hardy, Thomas** (1840–1928). Hardy's brooding, fatalistic vision of human existence is complemented in his rich body of work by a deep sense of humanity. Hardy's work tends to reflect the difficult realities of rural existence and the various ways in which the best-laid plans are thwarted by fate.

*Jude the Obscure* (1894)
Penguin Classics, 1998, 528 pages.

Hardy's best-known novel is renowned for its penetrating social critique and its fatalistic vision of human existence. The story centers around the character of Jude Fawley, a bright young man whose dream of rising above his lower class existence is shattered after entering into an ill-advised marriage. A series of similarly fateful decisions lead to the novel's shocking climax—one particularly so for its time.

Also read: *Far from the Madding Crowd* (1874), *The Return of the Native* (1878), *The Mayor of Casterbridge* (1886), and *Tess of the d'Urbervilles* (1891).

**James, Henry** (1843–1916). Born in New York, James grew up in a family of intellectuals. Living in England as an adult gave him his great theme: the contrast between Americans and Europeans. His novels' exploration of consciousness and use of point of view make them precursors to literary modernism.

*The Portrait of a Lady* (1881)
Penguin Classics, 2003, 656 pages.

"I should like to put a little wind in her sails," says Ralph Touchett, arranging a financial bequest for his cousin Isabel. In this tale of the perils of intimacy, James' heroine stumbles even as Ralph's money leaves her free to choose her husband. Written in subtle, cultivated prose, James' study of Americans and Europeans shows the innocence of American Isabel Archer transformed by her experience of Europe.

Also read: *The American* (1877), *Washington Square* (1880), and *The Turn of the Screw* (1898).

**Stevenson, Robert Louis** (1850–1894). Although Stevenson was regarded for many years as a writer of children's fiction (he penned the classic adventure tale, *Treasure Island*), his work has in more recent years been admired for the excellence of its prose and the interest of its varied subject matter.

*Dr. Jekyll and Mr. Hyde* (1886)
In *The Strange Case of Dr. Jeckyll and Mr. Hyde: And Other Tales of Terror.*
Penguin Classics, 2003, 224 pages.

Stevenson's suspenseful tale can be read as a morality tale, a horror story, and a deft psychological fable. When Mr. Hyde, a mysterious housemate of Dr. Jekyll's, commits a vicious assault, Mr. Utterson, Dr. Jekyll's close friend, is drawn into a mystery concerning the identity of Mr. Hyde and the nature of Dr. Jekyll's increasingly strange behavior.

Also read: *Kidnapped* (1886).

**Wilde, Oscar** (1856–1900). Although best known as the author of *The Picture of Dorian Gray*, Wilde was also an accomplished playwright and essayist. His work is known for its trenchant wit and its incisive critique of manners and morals.

*The Picture of Dorian Gray* (1891)
Oxford World's Classics, 2008, 272 pages.

Wilde's only published novel tells of a strikingly handsome young man who falls into a life of debauchery after selling his soul to preserve his beauty. The tradeoff is a painting of the young man that ages instead, and that in its aging reveals to the young man the errancy and shallowness of his debauched life.

Also read: *The Importance of Being Earnest* (first performed 1895).

### AMERICAN

**Hawthorne, Nathaniel** (1804–1864). Although best known as the author of *The Scarlet Letter*, Nathaniel Hawthorne also wrote a number of other highly regarded novels and was a master of the short story form. His work is known for its preoccupation with sin and guilt, its rich symbolism, and its psychological complexity.

*The Scarlet Letter* (1850)
Penguin Classics, 2002, 272 pages.

Hawthorne's masterpiece is set in the Puritan community of Boston, Massachusetts. Hester Prynne, after refusing to divulge the name of her child's father, is compelled by the community to wear a scarlet letter "A" (for adultery) on her gown. While Hester accepts the punishment with dignity, the child's father is tormented by guilt. Enter Hester's estranged husband, who toils relentlessly to discover the identity of the father.

*Short Stories* (1832–64)
Vintage, 1955, 384 pages.

Hawthorne's stories typically reflect a preoccupation with the nature of sin and guilt, and present a rather bleak picture of human nature. In short, they very much reflect the culture and mindset of Puritan society, even as Hawthorne is concerned to explore the internal dynamics of this society. They are, at the same time, rich in symbolism, have a great degree of psychological depth, and are wonderfully plotted and beautifully written.

Also read: *The House of the Seven Gables* (1851).

**Poe, Edgar Allan** (1809–1849). Poe was one of the pioneers of the short story form and gained an international reputation for his haunting, symbolically rich tales. His stories typically dramatize extreme mental states and unusual human behavior, possibly arising from Poe's own drug use, which no doubt contributed to his early death at age 40.

*The Fall of the House of Usher and Other Writings* (1839)
Penguin Classics, 2003, 544 pages.

Poe's stories explore the darker recesses of the human soul through a combination of symbolism, psychological tension, and supernatural dread. The story "The Black Cat," for example, is about an alcoholic who is tormented by a black cat, provoking him to commit a serious of increasingly violent actions culminating in the murder of his wife. Also read the delightfully macabre "The Pit and the Pendulum" and the sinister "The Tell-Tale Heart."

**Thoreau, Henry David** (1817–1862). Regarded today as the father of the environmental movement, Thoreau's writings are original meditations on the nature of man and his place in nature. He was also one of the most outspoken abolitionists of his day and relentlessly argued for individual rights over those of the state.

*Walden* (1854)
In *Walden and Civil Disobedience.*
Penguin Classics, 2002, 432 pages.

Thoreau's masterpiece continues to inspire readers today, and has gained a new relevance in the wake of our culture's current dialogue over the values of sustainability and self-sufficiency. In this nonfiction work, Thoreau writes of the years he spent in a cabin near Walden Lake, where he documented his experiences and observations, and reflected upon the value of a life lived attuned to nature and apart from civilization.

**Melville, Herman** (1819–1891). Dismissed during his lifetime as an incomprehensible mishmash, Melville's epic novel, *Moby Dick*, is now regarded as one of the masterpieces of Western literature. Melville also penned a number of other highly regarded novels, most of which are driven by a relatively bleak vision of human affairs.

*Moby-Dick, or The Whale* (1851)
Penguin Classics, 2002, 720 pages.

Melville's masterpiece is a multi-layered meditation on good and evil and the complex nature of reality. Ishmael narrates the story of his fateful experiences aboard the *Pequod*, a whale ship under the command of the enigmatic Captain Ahab. Ahab's obsessive pursuit of a rarely-seen white whale transforms the voyage into an ultimate test of commitment for the disparate crew.

**Melville, Herman (cont.)**

*Billy Budd* (1924, published posthumously)
In *Billy Budd and Other Stories.*
Penguin Classics, 2002, 416 pages.

Melville's masterful novella is a psychologically fraught tale of innocence and evil. When Billy Budd, a seaman in the Royal Navy who possesses both tremendous physical vitality and an almost ethereal innocence, is impressed aboard the HMS *Indomitable*, he unaccountably elicits the ire of John Claggart, the ship's Master-at-Arms, leading to tragic consequences for both.

**Twain, Mark** (1835–1910). One of the great humorists of Western literature, Mark Twain was immensely popular in his own day and remains so in ours. His many novels, short stories, and essays are typically concerned with the foibles of human beings and the various failings of human society.

*The Adventures of Huckleberry Finn* (1885)
Penguin Classics, 2002, 368 pages.

Twain's most famous novel is a delightful brew of satire, wit, and good old fashioned adventure. Huckleberry Finn, after being abducted by his abusive father and confined to a backwoods cabin on the banks of the Mississippi, manages to escape aboard a raft. His journey down the Mississippi in the company of an escaped slave becomes an exploration of the cultural mores of the antebellum South.

**Crane, Stephen** (1871–1900). When Stephen Crane died of tuberculosis at the age of 29, he left behind him one great novel and a handful of compelling short stories. His unsentimental vision of human nature and impressionistic writing style was an important influence upon such later writers as Ernest Hemingway.

*The Red Badge of Courage* (1895)
In *The Red Badge of Courage and Other Stories.*
Penguin Classics, 2005, 336 pages.

Crane's influential novel is famous for its psychological realism and its unsentimental depiction of war. The novel tracks over two days the experiences of Henry Fleming, an 18-year-old new recruit whose idealistic vision of war is quickly shattered upon fighting in his first battle. After nearly deserting, Henry finally earns by the end of the story his "red badge of courage."

OTHER

**Goethe, Johann Wolfgang von** (1749–1832). A giant of German literature, Goethe was born in Frankfurt, educated by tutors, and practiced law before joining the Duke's court at Weimar, where he wrote masterpieces of poetry, drama, theology, and science. His early romanticism was supplanted by Enlightenment works emphasizing human progress.

*Faust* (1790–1831)
W. W. Norton, 2000, 752 pages.

In this two-part drama, Goethe explores the limits of human desire in man's encounter with the transcendent. To gain knowledge, Faust makes a pact with the devil that puts his soul at risk. For Goethe, the devil Mephistopheles is a real presence, a force that wills evil but ultimately causes the good, putting Faust's fate in the balance.
Also read: *The Sorrows of Young Werther* (1774).

**Stendhal** (1783–1842). Stendhal (Henri Beyle's pen name) grew up in the provinces during the French Revolution and went to Paris at age 16 after Napoleon's *coup d'état*. He joined the French army at 17, fought in Italy, Germany, and Russia, and served with distinction in Napoleon's government until the fall of the empire. After Napoleon's fall, he wrote of the stagnation following the end of the Napoleonic era.

*The Red and the Black* (1830)
Translated by Roger Gard. Penguin Classics, 2002, 607 pages.

Stendhal's passionate protagonist, Julien Sorel, strives to emulate heroes from a bygone era of national pride, but finds that hypocrisy, not heroism, is now the key to success. Stendhal's warm sympathy for Julien and for Madame de Rênal and Mathilde de La Mole, the women Julien loves, is paired with a cool analysis of their predicaments. Stendhal deftly depicts the conflict of love and ambition.
Also read: *The Charterhouse of Parma* (1839).

**Balzac, Honoré de** (1799–1850). Balzac, one of the foundational figures of European realism, knew the importance of accurately portraying characters and the society in which they lived. Writing in France of the 1830s–40s, he launched his heroes into a society struggling to define itself after the tumult of the Revolution and the Napoleonic era.

*Père Goriot* (1835)
Translated by Burton Raffel. W. W. Norton, 1997, 384 pages.

In *Père Goriot*, we encounter two intertwined tales: the story of Eugene Rastignac's transformation from a naïve young man to a Paris gentleman, and the tragic tale of Goriot, a modern King Lear who sacrifices all for his daughters' advancement. Balzac places his typical hero, Rastignac, and Rastignac's larger-than-life mentor, the criminal Vautrin, amidst a resplendent gallery of secondary characters in a minutely observed setting.
Also read: *Lost Illusions* (1837–43) and *Cousin Bette* (1846).

**Hugo, Victor-Marie** (1802–1885). Victor Hugo, a giant of French literature, wrote poetry, plays, novels, and essays from his youth until his death at 83. Hugo's verse earned him a pension from Louis XVIII, allowing him to support his wife and four children as a writer. Hugo's political activities led him into exile from 1851 to 1870.

*The Hunchback of Notre Dame* (1831)
Translated by Walter J. Cobb. Signet, 2001, 512 pages.

Hugo's novel of medieval France intertwines the fates of the Gothic cathedral's hunchback, Quasimodo, his beloved gypsy, Esmeralda, and the archdeacon, Dom Frollo, who holds Quasimodo in his thrall and persecutes Esmeralda to rid himself of temptation. Hugo alternates fascinating descriptions of medieval people and architecture with tense action sequences in this tale of love's struggle amidst the forces of good and evil.

*Les Misérables* (1862)
Translated by Julie Rose. Modern Library Classcs, 2009, 1,376 pages.

Written during the author's exile, Hugo's *Les Misérables* is a historical novel spanning decades, beginning with Napoleon's defeat. The novel tells of Frenchman Jean Valjean, who serves a lengthy imprisonment for stealing bread. Free at last, Valjean seeks redemption while being hunted by police detective Javert. Hugo's vast romantic novel explores injustice and inequality in a country riven by social upheaval.

**Dumas, Alexandre** (1802–1870). A celebrated playwright and novelist, Dumas was the grandson of a French nobleman and an Afro-Caribbean former slave. The son of one of Napoleon's generals, he was raised in poverty. Dumas worked for the Duc d'Orléans during the Restoration, taking part in the 1830 coup that placed the duke on the throne.

*The Three Musketeers* (1844)
Signet Classics, 2006, 656 pages.

Dumas' swashbuckling romance features the trio Athos, Porthos, and Aramis, three musketeers joined by the young Gascon, D'Artagnon, in their fight to defend the king against Cardinal Richelieu's guards. The novel vividly portrays the power plays and intrigues at the court of Louis XIII, while providing romantic melodrama in the subplot centered on the scheming of Richelieu's agent, Lady de Winter.

*The Count of Monte Cristo* (1844–1846)
Penguin Classics, 2003, 1,312 pages.

Although readers sometimes assume that Dumas' swashbuckling adventure novel is a children's story, a dense plot, including a vast array of criminal acts and the transformation of naïve Edmund Dantès into the mysterious Count of Monte Cristo, make it a story for adults. Set in France and Italy during the Napoleonic era, the novel unwinds a masterful story that charts the elaborate revenge of the wrongly imprisoned Dantès. In the dynamic persona of the count, Dantès exploits his enemies' flaws and calmly watches them self-destruct.

Also read: *The Man in the Iron Mask* (1847–50).

**Turgenev, Ivan** (1818–1883). Turgenev, the author of realistic, often elegiac, fiction, is best known for his novel *Fathers and Sons*. Born into a wealthy landed family, Turgenev studied literature at universities in Russia and Germany. An opponent of serfdom and a champion of Enlightenment ideals, he often lived abroad.

*Fathers and Sons* (1862)
Translated by Michael R. Katz. Signet Classics, 2005, 256 pages.

The clear writing and vivid characters in *Fathers and Sons* make this one of the most engaging novels of its time. This classic exploration of generational conflict takes place on the country estate of Kirsanov, whose quiet life is disturbed by a visit from his son Arkady and his son's nihilist friend, Bazarov. Tensions between Kirsanov and his brother, and Arkady and Bazarov, drive the plot, as do the characters' romantic hopes.

Also read: *A Month in the Country* (1850).

**Dostoevsky, Fyodor** (1821–1881). Dostoevsky's novels of symbolic realism have brought him recognition as one of the greatest writers of modernity. His profound examination of the human spirit was influenced by a remarkable array of personal experiences, including epilepsy, arrest and imprisonment in Siberia, religious conversion, gambling addiction, army service, and eventual success as a writer.

*Crime and Punishment* (1866)
Translated by Richard Pevear and Larissa Volokhonsky. Vintage Books, 1993, 592 pages.

Dostoevsky's penetrating novel is one of the marvels of 19th-Century literature. Raskolnikov, a brilliant university student, is driven by poverty and philosophical idealism to commit a heinous crime. When the sly detective, Porfiry Petrovich, takes over the investigation, a psychological game of cat and mouse ensues, one that promises either destruction or redemption for Raskolnikov. Notable for its complex engagement with philosophical ideas and its deeply compassionate vision of human existence, this novel is not one to be missed.

*The Brothers Karamazov* (1880)
Translated by Richard Pevear and Larissa Volokhonsky. Farrar, Straus and Giroux, 2002, 824 pages.

Dostoevsky explores the tragic consequences of family conflict in this story of patriarch Fyodor Karamazov and his sons: intellectual Ivan, passionate Dmitri, saintly Alyosha, and illegitimate, self-hating Smerdyakov. In this well-plotted, philosophical novel, Dostoevsky delineates the murder of Fyodor as actual and symbolic patricide, implicating each of the brothers.

Also read: *Notes from Underground* (1864), *The Possessed* (1867), and *The Idiot* (1868).

**Flaubert, Gustave** (1821–1880).  Widely recognized as one of the great French Realists, Flaubert strove for precision of style while mastering a cool, ironic perspective that served him in his portrayal of the delusions and disillusionment infecting French society of the time.  Flaubert used his beautiful prose to dissect his characters' hopes, dreams, and failures.

*Madame Bovary* (1857)
Translated by Geoffrey Wall.  Penguin Classics, 2002, 384 pages.

This beautifully written novel chronicles the life of sensuous day-dreamer Emma Bovary, whose attachment to romantic literature offers a respite from her grimly ordinary life.  Despite her romantic adventures, Madame Bovary's world remains one in which fantasy and dreams carry greater weight than the actions of Flaubert's passive characters.  Nevertheless, readers often sympathize with Emma's longing for escape.

Also read: *Sentimental Education* (1869).

**Ibsen, Henrik** (1828–1906).  Regarded as the father of modern drama, Ibsen's plays were deeply controversial in his day for their innovative stagecraft and for challenging the mores and values of Victorian society.  They are appreciated in our own day for their compelling dramatizations of character and motivation.

*A Doll's House* (first performed 1879)
In *A Doll's House and Other Plays*.
Penguin Classics, 1965, 336 pages.

Considered an early expression of feminism, Ibsen's famous play challenges traditional conceptions of marriage.  When Nora's marriage to Torvald is threatened after the revelation of a secret that Nora had kept from him for many years, Nora is forced to confront the self-deceptions that she believes have prevented her from living an authentic existence.

*Hedda Gabler* (first performed 1890)
In *Hedda Gabler and Other Plays*.
Penguin Classics, 1951, 368 pages.

One of the great plays of 19th-Century drama and popularly performed today, Ibsen's tragic drama presages Freudian theory by over a decade in its representation of a woman driven by seemingly illogical desires to destructive ends.  Dissatisfied with her new marriage, Hedda Gabler is the central player in a causal chain of events that results in tragedy.

Also read: *An Enemy of the People* (first performed 1883), *The Wild Duck* (first performed 1884), and *The Master Builder* (first performed 1892).

**Tolstoy, Leo** (1828–1910). Recognized as one of the greatest Russian Realists, Tolstoy wrote novels unequalled for their historical scope, breadth of vision, and dynamic portrayal of Russian life. Born into a family of landed gentry, Tolstoy studied at university and traveled abroad, but subsequently repudiated Western values. He later founded a peasant school, became a religious seeker, and was sought after as a sage.

*War and Peace* (1865–69)
Translated by Richard Pevear and Larissa Volokhonsky. Vintage, 2008, 1,296 pages.

Tolstoy's novel is both a vast epic and a meditation on history. A family saga, it interweaves tales of the Rostovs, the Bezhuhovs, and the Bolkonskys with events surrounding Napoleon's invasion of Russia. Paradoxically for a novel of dramatic acts and important historical characters, the wisdom of Russian General Kutuzov is reflected in the lives of Tolstoy's fictional characters, for whom a kind of passive activity bears fruit more readily than displays of will, passion, and action.

*Anna Karenina* (1875–77)
Translated by Richard Pevear and Larissa Volokhonsky. Penguin Classics, 2004, 864 pages.

In this novel of family happiness and unhappiness, Tolstoy tells the story of Anna Karenina and her passionate love affair with Count Vronsky alongside the tale of Konstantin Levin's less turbulent but equally compelling quest for meaning in love and in life. The vitality of Tolstoy's characters and the poignancy of their struggles shape our concern about their fates.
Also read: *The Death of Ivan Ilyich* (1884).

**Chekhov, Anton** (1840–1904). Chekhov was a renowned short story writer, a dramatist who produced four classic plays, and a physician. Born the grandson of a serf, Chekhov became the family breadwinner as a young man, and wrote his first stories for money. His experience as a physician contributed to his deep knowledge of human nature.

*Uncle Vanya* (1899)
In *Five Plays*: *Ivanov*, *The Seagull*, *Uncle Vanya*, *Three Sisters*, and *The Cherry Orchard*.
Translated by Ronald Hingley. Oxford World's Classics, 2008, 336 pages.

An atmosphere of spiritual discouragement permeates *Uncle Vanya*, Chekhov's play about romantic complications and misspent lives. Originally performed as *The Wood Demon*, the play baffled audiences used to more superficial dramas. Chekhov's realistic characters vividly convey Russian ambivalence towards the countryside: Astrov's desire to save the trees versus Vanya's discontent with country life.
Also read: *The Seagull* (1896), *Three Sisters* (1901), and *The Cherry Orchard* (1904).

# 3. 20th Century

Writers in the 20th Century challenged themselves to find new ways of representing human experience and society. They wanted their work to reflect the extraordinary transformations that were taking place in the modern world—changes that they believed had significant implications for how we view ourselves, the world around us, and the meaning of human existence. The result is an extraordinarily diverse and wonderfully rich body of literature. The books on this list—all published by the early 1970s—are widely accepted as modern classics. Works published since the early 1970s can be found in Part One: Contemporary Fiction.

Movements like modernism, existentialism, and post-modernism shaped 20th-Century literature. Modernism was an international literary movement featuring experimentation and the search for a style. In the first two decades of the century, British writers Woolf and Joyce wrote stream-of-consciousness fiction that appeared alongside the finely-crafted, realistic fiction of their compatriots Conrad and Forster. By the 1920s, disillusionment with World War I had inspired a ferment of literary experimentation by European modernists Lawrence, Brecht, Proust, and Kafka, whose challenging narratives influenced writers worldwide.

American literature came fully into its own in the 20th Century. While early in the century Wharton and Dreiser wrote darkly realistic, eloquent novels, writers between the two World Wars found striking ways to represent the unique struggles facing American society. The success of such writers as Hemingway, Hurston, Fitzgerald, Faulkner, and Steinbeck gave to American literature an unprecedented prominence on the world scene. Ranging from the richly colloquial novels of Steinbeck and Hurston to the stripped-down, unsentimental novels of Hemingway to the epic grandeur of Faulkner's vision of the South, the many extraordinary works written during this period make it one of the defining eras of American literature.

Post-World War II literature was heralded by existentialism in France, where Sartre, Camus, and Beckett explored existential themes in their fiction. Postwar American writers gave unique expression to existential themes: Salinger depicted adolescent angst, Ellison portrayed African-American alienation, and novelists Malamud and Bellow wrote tragicomic fiction exploring the human condition.

In the 1950s and beyond, writers continued to produce vibrant, challenging works. Americans Updike and Baldwin and Russians Pasternak and Solzhenitsyn wrote fiction exploring the response of the individual to the radically different societies in which they lived. In the 1960s, postmodern authors wrote diverse works. Vonnegut wrote darkly humorous satire, Fowles blended psychologically complex narrative with traditional genres, and García Márquez artfully blended realism and fantasy in his novels of magical realism.

BRITISH

**Shaw, George Bernard** (1856–1950).  Shaw was an Irish writer renowned for his plays combining comedy, witty argumentation, and social criticism.  Born in Dublin, Shaw moved to London as a young man.  He was awarded the Nobel Prize for Literature in 1923, and won an Oscar in 1938 for his work on the film adaptation of *Pygmalion.*

*Pygmalion* (1913)
Penguin Classics, 2003, 176 pages.

In one of the most acclaimed plays written in English, Professor Higgins' plan to use instruction in elocution and manners to turn a Cockney flower girl into a duchess reaches comic heights and emotional depths, evoking a characteristic sense of irony when the professor's pupil declares her independence.  A proponent of Ibsen's new theater, Shaw excoriates middle-class morality and class differences in this witty comedy of ideas, while creating timeless characters in Henry Higgins and Eliza Doolittle.

Also read: *Arms and the Man* (1894) and *Saint Joan* (1923).

**Conrad, Joseph** (1857–1924).  Joseph Conrad is regarded as one of the greatest novelists in Western literature.  Conrad's varied experiences as a seaman strongly inform much of his work, which typically takes place on the sea or in exotic locales.  It is also notable for its rich probing of human psychology.

*Lord Jim* (1900)
Oxford World's Classics, 2008, 400 pages.

Among Conrad's many novels, *Lord Jim* is perhaps second only to *Heart of Darkness* in its psychological depth and lyrical richness.  When Jim, a youthful British sailor (whose surname is never disclosed), abandons his ship during an accident, he is stripped of his office by a naval court and branded as a coward.  Jim redeems himself, however, upon accepting a minor position in a remote settlement on the island of Sumatra.

*Heart of Darkness* (1902)
In *Heart of Darkness and The Secret Sharer.*
Signet Classics, 2007, 192 pages.

Told by the same narrator who relates a good part of *Lord Jim*, Marlow's story here has to do with a mission he undertook to find and return to civilization a brilliant but enigmatic westerner named Kurtz who has gone missing among the natives of Africa.  Marlow relates his trip up the Congo River in search of Kurtz and his unraveling of Kurtz's mysterious existence and identity.

Also read: *The Secret Agent* (1907) and *Victory* (1915).

**Chesterton, G. K.** (1874–1936). G. K. Chesterton's extensive body of work all grapples in one way or another with the place of faith in the modern world. His work is marked by a distinctive blend of paradox, wit, and charm, and remains influential for its inexorable confidence in the spiritual destiny of humankind.

*The Man Who Was Thursday* (1908)
Modern Library Classics, 2001, 224 pages.

Chesterton's metaphysical mystery concerns a secret anarchist group whose ambitions are spiritual rather than political in nature. When Gabriel Syme, a poet, is recruited to infiltrate the anarchist group, he discovers that he and five other members—each with a day of the week as a code name—are pawns in a scheme masterminded by the leader of the group, Sunday.

**Forster, E. M.** (1879–1970). Forster was an English writer best known for his realistic novels and for *Aspects of the Novel*, a work of criticism. Raised by his widowed mother, Forster attended Kings College, Cambridge, where he joined the Apostles, a precursor to the literary Bloomsbury Group. Forster was also a broadcaster for BBC Radio.

*A Room with a View* (1908)
Bantam Classics, 1988, 240 pages.

This comedy of manners examines the heart of proper young lady Lucy Honeychurch. In Italy, Lucy falls in with diverse social types and falls in love with the unconventional George Emerson. Back in England, Lucy's family pressures her to marry a supercilious, emotionally detached man of her class. Lucy's room with a view in Italy grants her a broad and open vision of life that is threatened by the narrow class-consciousness of her native land.

*A Passage to India* (1924)
Harvest Books, 1965, 368 pages.

Published at the height of the Indian independence movement, Forster's *A Passage to India* portrays the consequences of an ambiguous incident involving Adela, a British teacher, and Aziz, an Indian doctor, on an outing to India's Malabar Caves. Adela's accusation of attempted rape and the trial of Aziz expose the cultural gap between the Indians and the British. Though Adela makes partial atonement, Aziz must struggle with a residue of bitterness.

Also read: *Where Angels Fear to Tread* (1905) and *Howard's End* (1910).

**Woolf, Virginia** (1882–1941). Virginia Woolf was an English writer of stream-of-consciousness novels. The daughter of author Sir Leslie Stephen and artists' model Julia Stephen, she was tutored by her parents and attended Kings College, London, where she joined the Bloomsbury Group. She and husband Leonard Woolf founded Hogarth Press.

*Mrs. Dalloway* (1925)
Harvest Books, 1990, 216 pages.

Called "the first novel to split the atom" by author Michael Cunningham, *Mrs. Dalloway* is notable for its lyricism, experimental style, and vision of the infinite variety contained within each moment of mundane existence. As society woman Clarissa Dalloway prepares for a party, her thoughts ripple out from a center of consciousness, as do those of her double, veteran Septimus Warren Smith. Coincidences of time and insight unite these two disparate characters.

*To the Lighthouse* (1927)
Harvest Books, 1999, 228 pages.

Woolf's masterpiece organizes the interior monologues of her complex characters according to three sections of the novel depicting the Ramsay family's holiday retreat on the Isle of Skye. In Part I, the lively but fractious Ramsays play host; in Part II, the family is diminished and their holiday house abandoned; in Part III, the survivors carry out a long-delayed trip to the lighthouse. Woolf masterfully conveys consciousness and the passage of time.

Also read: *Orlando* (1928) and *A Room of One's Own* (1929).

**Joyce, James** (1882–1941). The work of James Joyce, who is considered one of the towering figures of modernist literature and one of the greatest Irish writers of all time, is famous for its shimmering, experimental prose. The Dublin of Joyce's youth provides the backdrop for his one collection of short stories and three novels.

*Dubliners* (1916)
Oxford World's Classics, 2008, 352 pages.

Joyce's first publication—a collection of short stories—is an intriguing read, not only for the stories in their own right but for how these stories foreshadow the concerns of Joyce's later work. The most well-known story in the collection, "The Dead," is about a man who confronts the hollowness of his existence after behaving badly at a dinner party.

*A Portrait of the Artist as a Young Man* (1916)
Penguin Classics, 2003, 384 pages.

Joyce's semi-autobiographical first novel is one of the foundational texts of literary modernism as a result of the manner in which it attempts to impressionistically represent the shifting landscape of consciousness. The story depicts some of the defining moments in Stephen Daedalus' life, from his somewhat tumultuous childhood in Dublin to his eventual rebellion against his Catholic upbringing.

Also read: *Ulysses* (1922).

**Lawrence, D. H.** (1885–1930).  Lawrence is known for his novels depicting the dehumanizing impact of modernity on individuals struggling to reclaim their wholeness.  The son of a coal miner and a teacher, Lawrence earned a teaching certificate from Nottingham University.  His novels, some of them banned in his time, won lasting fame.

*Sons and Lovers* (1913)
Signet Classics, 1995, 416 pages.

Lawrence's autobiographical novel reflects the tensions of his upbringing in this story of Paul Morel's efforts to break free of his mother's influence.  The son of a coal miner and an educated woman, Morel struggles for autonomy as his mother tries to thwart any relationship with a woman who has the potential to replace her.  Lawrence's modern Oedipal drama created controversy due to its relatively frank treatment of sexuality.

*Women in Love* (1920)
Penguin Classics, 1995, 592 pages.

This sequel to Lawrence's *The Rainbow* (1915) continues the story of Ursula and Gudrun Brangwen in the coal-mining town of Beldover.  The happier relationship of teacher Ursula and intellectual Rupert Birkin is contrasted with the stormy relationship of artist Gudrun and industrialist Gerard Critch.  The novel is notable for its exploration of human relationships and for its rendering of the English countryside and the dramatic landscape of the Alps.
Also read: *The Prussian Officer* (1914).

**Huxley, Aldous** (1894–1963).  Huxley's iconoclastic, relentlessly inquisitive spirit and his advocacy of nontraditional forms of experience and spirituality made him a hero of the counterculture in the 1960s.  He was a prolific writer, penning numerous novels, essays, articles, short stories, and plays.

*Brave New World* (1932)
Harper Perennial Modern Classics, 2005, 288 pages.

This dystopian novel parodies early 20th-Century society, driven as it was, in Huxley's view, by mass production, rampant consumerism, and moral libertinism.  The novel, set in the "year of our Ford 632," envisions a society in which children are not born but are created in hatcheries, where their development is manipulated according to the ideals of a perfectly regulated society.

**Lewis, C. S.** (1898–1963).  Although best known as the author of the fantasy series, *The Chronicles of Narnia*, C. S. Lewis also wrote several highly original novels, a number of influential works of Christian apologetics, and various other books that uniquely explore the nature of the spiritual life.

*The Screwtape Letters* (1942)
HarperOne, 2001, 224 pages.

This brilliant satire of the spiritual life is structured as a series of letters from Screwtape, a senior devil, to Wormwood, his nephew, on how to secure the damnation of a man designated in the story simply as "The Patient."  The letters of instruction ironically serve to reveal to the reader the subtle ways in which the well-meaning Christian falls into patterns of sin.
Also read: *Till We Have Faces* (1956).

**Orwell, George** (1903–1950). George Orwell is best known as the author of *Animal Farm* and *Nineteen Eighty-Four*. Both novels reflect Orwell's battle against totalitarianism and his exploration of the ways in which language can be used for deceit and manipulation.

*Animal Farm* (1945)
Signet Classics, 2004, 176 pages.

This masterpiece of political satire, published in the wake of World War II, was one of the first works to expose the true nature of Stalin's Russia to the Western world. When the animals on Mr. Jones' farm revolt and chase him off the property, they set up what promises to be a classless society. The utopian ideal is progressively compromised, however, through the repressive actions of a brutish boar.

*Nineteen Eighty-Four* (1949)
Plume, 2003, 368 pages.

Orwell's masterpiece of dystopian literature imagines a world in which the government controls every facet of social and political life, from its language and history to the behavior and thoughts of its citizens. Enter Winston Smith, an ordinary citizen whose work rewriting historical documents for the ruling party leads him to question its authority. When an intense, prohibited relationship with a beautiful co-worker seals his disenchantment with the party, Winston attempts to discover whether there is any hope of finally avoiding the lethal gaze of Big Brother.

**Waugh, Evelyn** (1903–1966). Evelyn Waugh was an English writer well known for the biting satire of novels *A Handful of Dust* and *The Loved One*, and for the complex moral vision of his masterpiece, *Brideshead Revisited*. Oxford-educated Waugh worked as a journalist and served in the army. His 1930 conversion to Catholicism defined his work.

*Brideshead Revisited* (1945)
Back Bay Books, 2008, 368 pages.

Waugh views British society before World War II with nostalgic ambivalence in this story of love's transformative power. Waugh's satire is tempered in *Brideshead*, in which the dysfunctional family of Lord Marchmain is valued for its *joi de vivre* and Catholic severity. Narrator Charles Ryder is transformed by his love for Lord Marchmain's sybaritic son and, later, for Marchmain's daughter, but ultimately by the spirituality of this aristocratic family.

Also read: *The Loved One* (1952).

**Greene, Graham** (1904–1991).  Graham Greene wrote a number of well-regarded novels that dramatize with subtle power the very human struggles experienced by the would-be person of faith. For all of its subtlety, however, Greene's work is also admired for its unvarnished but effective prose.

*The Heart of the Matter* (1949)
Penguin Classics, 2004, 288 pages.

Typical of much of Greene's work, *The Heart of the Matter* is a drama of the human soul, the principal soul in this case being Major Scobie, a British police inspector stationed in a small town on the coast of Africa.  A series of intrigues and an intense affair with a young shipwreck survivor compel Scobie to confront his conflicted relationships with his wife, his job, and God.
Also read: *The Power and the Glory* (1940) and *The Quiet American* (1956).

**Beckett, Samuel** (1906–1989).  Samuel Beckett was an Irish playwright, novelist, and poet who won the Nobel Prize in 1969.  Stylistically a minimalist, Beckett was an exponent of existentialism and of the theater of the absurd.  Born in Dublin, Beckett attended Trinity College, joined the French Resistance, taught, and directed plays.

*Waiting for Godot* (first performed 1952)
Faber and Faber, 2009, 128 pages.

*Waiting for Godot* has been described as a play in which nothing happens.  Yet audiences are riveted by Beckett's staging of two days in the lives of two men awaiting someone called Godot, perhaps because the dialogue of Vladimir and Estragon, with its Biblical allusions, dramatizes the meaning of human life.  The absent Godot, perhaps God, whose image is obscured by the limits of human understanding, stimulates an awareness of the human condition.
Also read: *Endgame* (first performed 1957).

**Fowles, John** (1926–2005).  John Fowles was an English novelist whose diverse works make use of modernist literary techniques to examine the nature of love, art, and reality.  Essex-born Fowles attended Oxford and taught on the Greek island of Spetsai.  His post-World War II novels reflect the influence of philosophy, Celtic romance, and existentialism.

*The Magus* (1965, revised 1977)
Back Bay Books, 2001, 656 pages.

On the Greek island of Phraxos a magus awaits Nicholas Urfe, a young Englishman as readily bewildered by magician Conchis' ploys as the reader is by Fowles' literary feints.  Nicholas' friendship with Conchis, the owner of an island estate, plunges him into a surreal labyrinth of torments in which he is forced to face his true nature.  Nicholas' efforts to undo the deceptions of the magus bring him up against the archetypal power of the island, and of his own psyche.
Also read: *The French Lieutenant's Woman* (1969).

AMERICAN

**Wharton, Edith** (1862–1937). The novels of Edith Wharton contrast personal aspiration with the heavy machinery of rigid social convention. Born into upper class society, Wharton was educated by tutors and prepared for marriage. When her 1895 marriage proved disastrous, Wharton turned to writing, achieving success in her lifetime.

*House of Mirth* (1905)
Signet Classics, 2000, 350 pages.

Edith Wharton's portrayal of the ineffectual rebellion of her heroine, Lily Bart, is as much a critique of the society of the Gilded Age as it is an examination of Lily's character and fate. In the manner of a tragedian, Wharton places sympathetic and despicable characters alike in situations replete with dramatic irony. Lily's fall from the upper stratum of society into genteel poverty is equal parts self-deception, persecution, folly, and bad luck.
Also read: *The Age of Innocence* (1920).

**Dreiser, Theodore** (1871–1945). Dreiser's influential novels depict determined, ambitious protagonists whose efforts are rendered insignificant by the implacable laws of society. Born into a large Indiana family, Dreiser became a journalist after flunking out of college. A committed socialist, Dreiser wrote several books on political issues.

*An American Tragedy* (1925)
Signet Classics, 2000, 880 pages.

As a newspaperman, Dreiser gathered accounts of crimes committed in the United States from 1892 to 1935. Based on the actual 1906 murder of Grace Brown by Chester Gillette, *An American Tragedy* thrusts Dreiser's protagonist, the naïve Clyde Griffiths, into the heady, amoral world of upward mobility. Clyde's fall from grace implicates American materialism as well as his own bankrupt values.
Also read: *Sister Carrie* (1900).

**London, Jack** (1876–1916). London's many novels and short stories reflect a Darwinist, survival-of-the-fittest vision of life. This vision strongly informs his most highly regarded novels, *Call of the Wild* and *White Fang*. London's work also typically reflects his colorful life as an adventurer.

*The Call of the Wild* (1903)
In *The Call of the Wild, White Fang, and Other Stories.*
Oxford World's Classics, 1998, 400 pages.

The hero of this classic tale is Buck, a St. Bernard whose comfortable, early life is disrupted when he is abducted and sold to a sled dog trainer. Buck progressively learns to depend upon his instincts after being subjected to harsh treatment by a string of vicious owners, and is eventually rescued from near starvation by a kind-hearted man. The novel's famous conclusion has been justly praised.
Also read: *The Sea Wolf* (1904) and *White Fang* (1906).

**Anderson, Sherwood** (1876–1941). Sherwood Anderson was an American short story writer described by Malcolm Cowley as "a writer's writer, the only storyteller of his generation who left his mark." Ohio-born Anderson did not graduate from high school, and worked at odd jobs and in advertising. *Winesburg, Ohio* won him lasting fame.

*Winesburg, Ohio* (1919)
Bantam, 1995, 256 pages.

*Winesburg, Ohio* is a collection of 22 short stories related by character and theme, and can be read as a novel. Protagonist George Willard, a reporter in whom the townspeople confide, is at the center of the stories. These stories reveal the lives of Winesburg's inhabitants, or "grotesques," as Anderson called them, in ways that broke the literary conventions of Anderson's time. The stories tell of loneliness, alienation, love, and inequality in an American small town.

**Cather, Willa** (1873–1947). Willa Cather's work richly evokes the pioneering life of the immigrants who first settled the Nebraska prairies. Her novels are notable for their warm humanity, for their lovely descriptions of the natural world, and for their strong female characters.

*My Antonia* (1918)
Penguin Classics, 1994, 320 pages.

Cather's most famous novel wonderfully evokes the culture of the immigrant families that first began to settle on the Nebraska prairie in the early 20th Century. It is also an unusual and moving story of friendship and love as Jim Burden narrates his lasting attachment to Antonia Shimerda, a Bohemian immigrant who arrived on the prairie at the same time as himself.
Also read: *O Pioneers!* (1913) and *Death Comes to the Archbishop* (1927).

**Lewis, Sinclair** (1885–1951). Sinclair Lewis was an American novelist known for his depiction of American society. Born in Minnesota, Lewis graduated from Yale in 1908. The enormous success of *Main Street* (1920) was a sensation in American publishing. Lewis was the first American to be awarded the Nobel Prize in Literature (1930).

*Babbitt* (1922)
Bantam, 1998, 464 pages.

When Lewis's biting social satire of middle-class America was published in 1922, critic H. L. Mencken said, "I know of no American novel that more accurately portrays the real America." Lewis excoriates George F. Babbitt for his vices: hypocrisy, complacency, and materialism. The ultimate hollow man, Babbitt turns to self-questioning and a search for meaning when his complacency is shaken by the imprisonment of his best friend.
Also read: *Main Street* (1920).

**Hemingway, Ernest** (1889–1961) (Nobel Prize, 1954).  Ernest Hemingway's work is famous for its spare prose style and unsentimental depiction of human nature.  Much of Hemingway's work is informed by his relentless pursuit of adventure and of novel experiences in his personal life, including African safaris and bullfighting in Spain.

*For Whom the Bell Tolls* (1940)
Scribner, 1995, 480 pages.

Hemingway, in typically spare prose, writes unsentimentally about the eternal themes of love and war in this cornerstone of 20th-Century literature.  Robert Jordan, an American munitions expert, is assigned the task of blowing up a bridge during the Spanish Civil War.  He is aided by a group of guerillas, including a beautiful but scarred woman with whom Jordan falls in love.

*The Old Man and the Sea* (1952)
Scribner, 1995, 128 pages.

Hemingway's masterful novella was the last major work he wrote and led to his being awarded the Nobel Prize in 1954.  The story, about an aging fisherman's epic efforts to reel in a great blue marlin, is on one level simple enough.  But told in parable-like fashion, the story accrues great depth and power in its depiction of the resilience of the human spirit.

Also read: *In Our Time* (1925), *The Sun Also Rises* (1926), and *A Farewell to Arms* (1929).


**Hurston, Zora Neale** (1891–1960).  Zora Neale Hurston was an American novelist, essayist, and theatrical producer during the Harlem Renaissance.  Born in Alabama, Hurston attended Howard University and graduated from Barnard in 1927.  She conducted anthropological research in the Caribbean and in the American South.

*Their Eyes Were Watching God* (1937)
Harper Perennial, 1998, 240 pages.

Zora Neale Hurston dramatizes an African-American woman's search for love and a sense of self in this story of Janie, an inhabitant of the all-black town of Eaton, Florida.  The narrative focuses on Janie's marriages to a farmer, a landowner, and a musician named Tea Cake, culminating in a love match that is tragically overtaken by misfortune.  Hurston's novel is renowned for its use of African-American dialect.

**Fitzgerald, F. Scott** (1896–1940). Fitzgerald, who coined the term "The Jazz Age," gave eloquent expression to the rollicking, free-spirited sensibility of the 1920s in his four novels and many short stories. Fitzgerald's early death at age 44 parallels another significant theme in his work—the defeated promise of youth.

*The Great Gatsby* (1925)
Scribner, 1999, 180 pages.

Fitzgerald's classic tale is a rich meditation on the slippery nature of love, identity, and the American dream. Nick Carraway tells the story of the unusual friendship that developed between himself and Jay Gatsby, an enigmatic playboy, during a summer spent on Long Island. Nick's discovery of the truth of Gatsby's identity coincides with his realization of the superficiality of class privilege.
Also read: *This Side of Paradise* (1920) and *Tender is the Night* (1934).

**Wilder, Thornton** (1897–1975). Wilder is chiefly known for his play, *Our Town*, and his novel, *The Bridge of San Luis Rey*, both of which won the Pulitzer Prize. They each probe in a unique way questions of meaning, existence, and human morality.

*Our Town* (first performed 1938)
HarperCollins, 2003, 208 pages.

This three-act play is one of the hallmarks of 20th-Century drama for its deceptively simple dramatization of ordinary small town American life in the first half of the 20th Century. The title of the play's three acts—"Daily Life," "Love and Marriage," and "Death and Eternity"—signal its greater ambitions, however, where the play ultimately becomes a moving meditation on the inevitability of death.
Also read: *The Bridge of San Luis Rey* (1927).

**Faulkner, William** (1897–1962) (Nobel Prize, 1949). Faulkner's body of work constitutes one of the most original and substantive contributions to American literature. His many novels are all set in fictional Yonapatawpha County, Mississippi, and dramatize the varied histories of a handful of the county's families.

*As I Lay Dying* (1930)
Vintage, 2000, 288 pages.

Perhaps Faulkner's most experimental novel but also one of his most successful, the story concerns a family's attempts to make good on their grandmother's request to be buried in Jefferson, a distant town in Mississippi. The novel is told from the perspective of 15 narrators (including Addie Bundren, the deceased grandmother) in a stream-of-consciousness fashion.

**Faulkner, William (cont.)**

*The Unvanquished* (1938)
Vintage, 1991, 262 pages.

Consisting of seven thematically-linked short stories that are all told in a relatively accessible style, *The Unvanquished* may serve as an ideal introduction to Faulkner. Set against the backdrop of the Civil War, the story concerns the various experiences of two young boys, Bayard and Ringo, whose idealization of the war comes in for tragic correction by the story's end.
Also read: *The Sound and the Fury* (1927), *Light in August* (1932), *Absalom, Absalom!* (1936), and *Go Down Moses* (1942).

**Steinbeck, John** (1902–1966) (Nobel Prize, 1962). Steinbeck's remarkable body of work is renowned for its scope, depth, and compassionate view of the human condition. Much of his work is set in California's Salinas Valley, an important agricultural center, and focuses upon the hard-scrabble lives of the laborers who worked the land.

*The Grapes of Wrath* (1939)
Penguin Classics, 2006, 464 pages.

Steinbeck's masterpiece is at once a provocative social novel and a rich meditation on the dignity and resilience of the human spirit. The story famously features the exodus of a family of sharecroppers from their home in Oklahoma to California in search of a better life, as the harsh economic realities of the Great Depression and a severe drought leave them homeless.
Also read: *Of Mice and Men* (1937), *The Pearl* (1947), and *East of Eden* (1952).

**Warren, Robert Penn** (1905–1989). Robert Penn Warren was an American poet, critic, and novelist. The first Poet Laureate of the United States, he is known for his Pulitzer Prize-winning novel, *All the King's Men*, and as a founder of the New Criticism. Kentucky-born Warren attended Yale and held several academic positions.

*All the King's Men* (1946)
Harvest, 1996, 672 pages.

Warren's 1947 Pulitzer Prize-winning novel portrays the meteoric career of Southern demagogue Willie Stark through the eyes of his handler, narrator Jack Burden. As with historical prototype Huey Long, Stark's lust for power overrides his early idealism. Burden's perspective reveals the attractions of Stark's charisma as well as the depth of his corruption. The interplay of Jack Burden's personal story with Stark's public story provides a complex storyline.

**Saroyan, William** (1908–1981). Saroyan's work is chiefly notable for its warmth, humor, and optimistic view of human nature. Saroyan's novels, plays, and memoirs are typically concerned with the Armenian-American community that settled in California's Central Valley in the first half of the 20th Century.

*The Human Comedy* (1943)
Harcourt, 1989, 256 pages.

Set in the small town of Ithaca, California, against the backdrop of World War II, this short novel exemplifies Saroyan's masterful ability to get at the depth and richness of life with the lightest of touches. At the center of the story is Homer Macauley, a 14-year-old boy who confronts the reality of sorrow and loss in his job as a telegraph boy.
Also read: *My Name Is Aram* (1940).

**Wright, Richard** (1908–1960). Richard Wright, an American writer known for his novel *Native Son*, was one of the first African-American writers to win fame in his lifetime. Wright, the grandson of slaves, was born on a Mississippi plantation and was largely self-educated. He worked as a postal clerk and as an editor while launching his career.

*Native Son* (1940)
Chelsea House, 2008, 213 pages.

Richard Wright, who lived and worked in Depression-Era Chicago, was intimately familiar with the cross currents of race, poverty, and social violence which beset Bigger, the protagonist of *Native Son*. Wright balances empathy for Bigger with an unflinching account of his crimes. The novel thus gives imaginative form to the question of whether past centuries of racial injustice constitute mitigating circumstances for criminal behavior.

**Stegner, Wallace** (1909–1993). Wallace Stegner was an American novelist, historian, and environmentalist whose work celebrated the American West. Stegner grew up in Utah and Montana and founded the Stanford Creative Writing Program, where he mentored writers. He wrote novels, historical works, and collections of stories and essays.

*Angle of Repose* (1971)
Penguin Classics, 2000, 592 pages.

The angle of repose, or the maximum angle at which loose soil settles, is an apt image for this story of California engineer Oliver Ward, who seeks repose in his marriage to Susan, an artist from the East. The narrator of the story of the Wards' pilgrimage through a series of Western mining camps is their grandson Lyman, a wheelchair-bound historian in Grass Valley, California. In "prying around" into his grandparents' lives, Lyman learns unexpected lessons from the past.

**Agee, James** (1909–1955). Agee was best known during his own lifetime for his film criticism and as the writer of the screenplay for the 1951 film, *The African Queen*. His most enduring legacy, however, is the rich, haunting novel, *A Death in the Family*, which was published two years after Agee's death.

*A Death in the Family* (1957)
Penguin Classics, 2009, 320 pages.

Agee's Pulitzer Prize-winning, autobiographical novel is an evocative meditation on grief, loss, and the complex weave of family. When Jay Follet dies in a tragic car accident at age 36, the remaining members of the family struggle to come to terms with his loss. The story is told from the various perspectives of these characters, including Jay's six-year-old son, Rufus, Agee's fictional persona.

**Williams, Tennessee** (1911–1983). One of the great innovators of American theater, Tennessee Williams wrote plays that are also among the most controversial for their stark depiction of tumultuous human desire. That they continue to be widely staged today is a testament to their ongoing relevance and power.

*A Streetcar Named Desire* (first performed 1947)
New Directions, 2004, 224 pages.

Williams won the Pulitzer Prize in 1947 for this important play, famous for its dark and unsettling dramatization of sexuality. When Blanche DuBois—whose pretensions to Southern gentility are belied by a drinking problem and a dark past—arrives in New Orleans to stay with her sister, Stella, conflict arises between Blanche and Stella's brutish husband, Stanley.

Also read: *The Glass Menagerie* (first performed 1945), and *Cat on a Hot Tin Roof* (first performed 1955).

**Malamud, Bernard** (1914–1986). Although Bernard Malamud is best known for his baseball novel, *The Natural*, his many novels are more typically about the Jewish-American experience. He also tends to write of the redemptive power of friendship and love, particularly between unlikely persons.

*The Assistant* (1957)
Farrar, Straus and Giroux, 2003, 264 pages.

As this thoughtful and challenging novel opens, Morris Bober, a Jewish immigrant and small store owner, is down on his luck. Salvation comes in the unlikely form of Frank Alpine, an enigmatic drifter who helps to revive Morris' struggling business. Complications ensue, however, when Frank becomes infatuated with Morris' beautiful daughter, Helen. A novel of tremendous spiritual depth and human insight, *The Assistant* is one of the masterpieces of 20th-Century American literature.

**Malamud, Bernard (cont.)**

*The Fixer* (1967)
Farrar, Straus and Giroux, 2004, 352 pages.

Malamud based this novel upon a 1913 case in Russia that generated international outrage. The story is about a Jewish handyman, or "fixer," who is arrested on charges of killing a Christian boy. Upon being imprisoned, he is subjected to harsh treatment and merciless interrogation, and is led to ruminate upon the tragic features of his own life and of human existence more generally.
Also read: *The Natural* (1967).

**Ellison, Ralph** (1914–1994). Ellison's renown as a writer is chiefly based upon the only novel he published during his lifetime, the masterful *The Invisible Man*. Ellison also wrote two influential collections of essays that explore with grace and subtlety various aspects of the black experience in America.

*Invisible Man* (1952)
Vintage, 1995, 608 pages.

This thought-provoking novel dramatizes the complexities of the black experience in the United States. The narrator, who goes unnamed throughout the story, relates in a somewhat sardonic tone his search for identity from youth into adulthood. The novel opens with a shocking episode of racism and culminates years later in the narrator's disillusionment with Black politics in New York City.

**Bellow, Saul** (1915–2005) (Nobel Prize, 1976). Bellow's novels tend to be comic exposes of American culture in which quirky characters bumble their way through life with a mixture of moxie, grace, and luck, both good and ill.

*The Adventures of Augie March* (1954)
Penguin Classics, 2006, 608 pages.

Set in Chicago during the middle of the 20th Century, this lively novel traces the life of its eponymous hero from childhood into adulthood. Resplendent with scene, incident, and character, the novel exemplifies Bellow's grandly comic vision of human existence, as Augie March experiences his share of hard knocks and failed relationships on his way to becoming a relatively stable adult.

*Humboldt's Gift* (1975)
Penguin Classics, 2008, 494 pages.

This Pulitzer Prize-winning novel is about a friendship between two writers: Von Humboldt Fleisher, who believes in the power of art to transform society, and Charlie Citrine, a successful writer. Written in Bellow's typical effervescent manner and shot through with wit, charm, and gently philosophic rumination, the story is a rich meditation on art, business, culture, and the American Dream.
Also read: *Henderson the Rain King* (1959) and *Herzog* (1964).

**Miller, Arthur** (1915–2005).  Considered one of America's greatest playwrights, Miller wrote some of the most enduring plays of our age, including *The Crucible* and *Death of a Salesman*.  Both plays are powerful dramatizations of the tension between social conformity and individual identity.

*Death of a Salesman* (first performed 1949)
Penguin, 1998, 144 pages.

Miller's classic play is a heartbreaking depiction of the failed hopes and broken relationships that finally overwhelm a middle-class man.  Willy Loman struggles not only with the despair of losing his once-lucrative job as a salesman, but also with the disdain of his eldest son, Biff, whose youthful idolization of his father was crushed by the discovery of an affair.

Also read: *The Crucible* (first performed 1953).

**Percy, Walker** (1916–1990).  Percy's six novels uniquely explore questions of modern existence, oftentimes through use of irony and sly humor.  Percy, who earned a medical degree, also calls into question the modern faith in science, reflecting a skeptical perspective that likewise informs his many works of nonfiction.

*The Moviegoer* (1961)
Vintage, 1998, 256 pages.

Binx Bolling, the narrator of this wry, gently philosophic novel, faces up to his alienated existence over the course of a several-day odyssey spent chasing down a suicidal cousin.  Binx, whose sense of reality is mediated largely by movies, combines the search for his cousin with a more comprehensive search for authentic selfhood, with somewhat mixed results.

Also read: *The Thanatos Syndrome* (1987).

**McCullers, Carson** (1917–1967).  Closely associated with the literature of the South—an exceedingly rich corpus that includes such authors as William Faulkner, Tennessee Williams, and Flannery O'Connor—McCullers' few novels evoke in a rich and poetic language the lives of outcasts and loners.

*The Heart Is a Lonely Hunter* (1940)
Mariner Books, 2004, 368 pages.

This warm and affecting novel, set in a small Southern town, centers around a deaf-mute, John Singer, who becomes a sounding board for four characters—a precocious young girl, a restaurant owner, a black doctor, and an alcoholic drifter.  McCullers masterfully captures the loneliness and sorrow experienced by her characters and compassionately dramatizes their desire for meaning and connection.

Also read: *The Member of the Wedding* (1946).

**Salinger, J. D.** (1919–  ).  J. D. Salinger, best known for his 1951 novel of adolescent angst, *The Catcher in the Rye*, is an American novelist and short story writer.  Born and raised in New York City, Salinger served in the army in World War II.  He wrote stories from an early age, and won recognition with his 1948 story, "A Perfect Day for Bananafish."

*The Catcher in the Rye* (1951)
Back Bay Books, 2001, 288 pages.

Holden Caulfield, a typical American adolescent hero, is in conflict with his parents, his teachers, and adult society.  His virtues are his humor, his capacity for observation, and his longing for authenticity.  About to be expelled from prep school, Holden drifts around New York City and has meaningful encounters with taxi drivers, nuns, an elevator man, tourists, a prostitute, a teacher—and finally, reassuringly, with his sister Phoebe.

Also read: *Nine Stories* (1953) and *Franny and Zooey* (1961).

**Vonnegut, Kurt** (1922–2007).  Vonnegut's darkly funny novels satirize virtually every aspect of human society, oftentimes through the medium of science fiction.  While his anti-authoritarianism made him a favorite of the 1960s counterculture, the underlying humanism of his work gives it lasting appeal.

*Slaughterhouse-Five* (1969)
Dial Press, 2005, 288 pages.

Vonnegut's zany, jumbled, anti-war novel features the aptly named Billy Pilgrim, an American soldier stationed in Dresden during the infamous firebombing of the city in World War II.  Shifting back and forth in time and between reality and fantasy, the shape and content of the narrative mirrors Billy's experience of being "unstuck in time" due to his traumatic wartime experiences.

Also read: *Cat's Cradle* (1963).

**Heller, Joseph** (1923–1999).  Although Heller wrote a number of novels, plays, and screenplays, nothing rivaled, commercially or critically, the success of his brilliant satire of war, *Catch-22*, his first published work.

*Catch 22* (1961)
Simon & Schuster, 1996, 464 pages.

This inventive, bleak but hilarious novel, set on the Mediterranean coast during the waning years of World War II, satirizes the bureaucratic nature of modern war, where soldiers' lives become merely expedient to the goal of winning.  The novel is told from multiple perspectives, the most memorable of which is that of John Yossarian, a wise-cracking soldier determined to come out of the war alive.

**Baldwin, James** (1924–1987). One of the great figures of African-American literature, James Baldwin wrote novels, essays, plays, and short-stories that are eloquent, challenging examinations of African-American experience. His most highly regarded novel, *Go Tell It on the Mountain*, is based upon his own early life.

*Go Tell It on the Mountain* (1953)
Dell, 1981, 240 pages.

This semi-autobiographical novel presents a tableau of African-American experience by dramatizing one Harlem family's struggle to come to terms with both past and present. Although framed by the character of John Grimes, who celebrates his 14th birthday during the course of the novel, the novel weaves together the life-stories of John's father, aunt, and mother.

Also read: *Another Country* (1962).

**O'Connor, Flannery** (1925–1964). Flannery O'Connor's voice is one of the most original in American literature. The great theme of her work is the tension between modern rationalism and religious faith. Her stories are typically about a deeply flawed character who experiences spiritual transcendence, often through an act of violence.

*The Complete Stories* (1946–65)
Farrar, Straus and Giroux, 1971, 555 pages.

All 31 of O'Connor's short stories collected here demonstrate her extraordinary use of language in crafting characters who are shocked out of their everyday existence into a profound engagement with meaning and truth. Read: "A Good Man Is Hard To Find," "The Displaced Person," "Everything That Rises Must Converge," and "Revelation."

Also read: *The Violent Bear It Away* (1960).

**Lee, Harper** (1926– ). If you had to write only one novel in your life, as is the case with Harper Lee, you could hardly do better than to write *To Kill A Mockingbird*. It remains one of the most widely read and best loved novels in the American canon.

*To Kill a Mockingbird* (1960)
Harper Perennial Modern Classics, 2002, 336 pages.

Harper Lee's Pulitzer Prize-winning novel radiates warmth and humanity, even as it treats of such heavy themes as racial prejudice and the loss of innocence. By turns a coming-of-age story, a legal drama, and a sketch of small-town life, the story is narrated by Scout Finch, whose father, Atticus Finch, is assigned to defend a black man, Tom Robinson, in a racially-charged rape case.

**Potok, Chaim** (1929–2002). Chaim Potok is one of the foremost Jewish-American writers of our age. While his many novels are typically set against the backdrop of Jewish culture and religion, they have a broad appeal by virtue of their wisdom, compassion, and engaging storytelling.

*The Chosen* (1967)
Ballantine Books, 1996, 304 pages.

This thoughtful novel, set in the years immediately following World War II, is about an unlikely friendship that develops between two 15-year-old boys in Brooklyn, New York. Reuven Malter, an Orthodox Jew, is befriended by a brilliant Hasidic Jew after an accident at a baseball game. The two both come to realize important truths about themselves and life through their friendship.
Also read: *My Name is Asher Lev* (1972).

**Updike, John** (1932–2009). John Updike was an American novelist, short story writer, and poet best known for his quartet of *Rabbit* novels. Born in Pennsylvania, Updike graduated from Harvard in 1954 and studied art before becoming a writer. His novels and stories describe the small-town American middle class of the second half of the century.

*Rabbit Run* (1960)
Ballantine Books, 1996, 272 pages.

This first novel in Updike's *Rabbit* tetralogy introduces Harry "Rabbit" Angstrom, a former high school basketball star whose early promise is belied by the stagnation of his adult life. Updike's lyrical prose portrays an impulsive 26-year-old stymied by a dull job and unhappy marriage, who takes to the road, visits his high school coach, and takes up with a part-time prostitute. Updike depicts a deadly dull suburbia as the backdrop for Rabbit's missteps.

**OTHER**

**Brecht, Bertolt** (1848–1956). Considered one of the most influential playwrights of the 20th Century, Brecht was a German dramaturge, director, and theatrical innovator whose epic plays challenged the conventions of theatrical illusion. Born in Bavaria, Brecht worked in Berlin until 1933, when he immigrated to the United States.

*The Threepenny Opera* (first performed 1928)
Translated by John Willett and Ralph Manheim. Penguin Classics, 2007, 176 pages.

Brecht's epic drama brings to life the underworld of London's beggars and petty crooks in this tale of the love of Polly Peachum for the amoral Mack the Knife. Brecht uses traditional elements of social satire—such as the amity of Mack the Knife and London's Chief of Police—as well as the techniques of epic theater, in which the dramatic illusion is broken by projected captions, to illustrate his critique of social hypocrisy.
Also read: *Galileo* (first performed 1938), *Mother Courage and Her Children* (first performed 1941), and *The Caucasian Chalk Circle* (first performed 1948).

**Proust, Marcel** (1871–1922). Proust was a French novelist best known for his seven-volume masterpiece, *In Search of Lost Time* (originally translated *Remembrance of Things Past*). He developed the themes of childhood, love, memory, and time over thousands of pages, exhibiting modernist narrative techniques, social satire, and rich and extended character development and metaphor.

*Swann's Way: In Search of Lost Time: Volume I* (1913)
Translated by Lydia Davis. Penguin Classics, 2004, 496 pages.

The first volume of *In Search of Lost Time* is divided into *Combray* and the third-person novella, *Swann's Love*. In the semi-autobiographical *Combray*, the narrator revisits two episodes from childhood: the drama of going to bed without his mother's kiss, and the taste of tea and *madeleine* (cake) that triggers his lost memories. In *Swann's Love*, the author recounts Swann's obsession with Odette de Crécy, recapitulating the themes of love and memory introduced in *Combray*.
Also read: *In Search of Lost Time* (1913–1927).

**Mann, Thomas** (1875–1955) (Nobel Prize, 1929). Thomas Mann is one of the great figures of 20th-Century European literature. Mann's epic novels are philosophically rich narratives that typically explore the nature of artistic creation and the tension between creation and destruction in the artistic life.

*Death in Venice* (1912)
Penguin Classics, 1999, 384 pages.

Mann's shortest work, a moving meditation on love and mortality, also happens to be one of his greatest. Gustave von Aschenback, a retired painter who has sacrificed his life to the demands of his art, decides to vacation in Venice. While there he encounters a strikingly beautiful boy who kindles in him a renewed passion for life, even as he finds himself trapped in the cholera-ridden city.
Also read: *Buddenbrooks* (1901), *The Magic Mountain* (1924), *Joseph and His Brothers* (1933–43), and *Doctor Faustus* (1947).

**Hesse, Hermann** (1877–1962) (Nobel Prize, 1946). The German writer Herman Hesse was prized by the counterculture in the 1960s for his novelistic explorations of spirituality, meaning, and authenticity. The capstone of his career is the magisterial *Glass Bead Game*, a highly original parable of the spiritual and intellectual life.

*Steppenwolf* (1927)
Picador, 2002, 224 pages.

Hesse's most beloved and most controversial novel features the character of Harry Haller, a suicidal intellectual who struggles with a powerful sense of isolation driven by his disdain of middle-class existence. Haller experiences a transformation, however, upon meeting a young woman who teaches him to value the pleasures of the sensual life alongside those of the intellectual life.
Also read: *Demian* (1919), *Siddhartha* (1922), and *The Glass Bead Game* (*Magister Ludi*) (1943).

**Kazantzakis, Nikos** (1883–1957). Nikos Kazantzakis was a preeminent Greek writer of the 20th Century. His novels resonate with existential themes, Christian spirituality, and the re-creation of classical Greek antiquity. Born on the island of Crete, Kazantzakis studied law in Athens and philosophy in Paris before becoming a successful writer.

*Zorba the Greek* (1943)
Translated by Carl Wildman. Touchstone, 1996, 320 pages.

Kazantzakis' unnamed narrator, a cerebral, ascetic writer and director of a mining operation on Crete, meets up with the passionate, sybaritic Zorba, who mentors him in living life to the fullest. Imbued with Zorba's wisdom and lust for life, the narrator gradually learns to integrate body, mind, and soul, discovering within himself a life force powerful enough to surmount personal tragedy.
Also read: *The Last Temptation of Christ* (1935).

**Kafka, Franz** (1883–1924). Kafka, one of the major writers of the 20th Century, wrote novels and stories depicting existential dilemmas and the dehumanizing effect of bureaucratization gone mad. Born in Prague, Kafka graduated from the German Charles-Ferdinand University in Prague in 1906 and worked in insurance. Most of his writing was published after his death.

*The Metamorphosis* (1914)
In *The Metamorphosis, In the Penal Colony, and Other Stories.*
Translated by Willa and Edwin Muir. Schocken, 2nd ed., 1995, 328 pages.

Kafka's extraordinary gift for depicting the human spirit through fantasy is seen in this tale of comic absurdity, angst, and moral imagination. Beginning with one of the most famous first sentences in literature ("As Gregor Samsa awoke one morning from uneasy dreams he found himself transformed in his bed into a gigantic insect."), Kafka tells the story of Samsa's metamorphosis and of his family's complicity in his suffering.

*The Trial* (1925)
Translated by Breon Mitchell. Schocken, 1995, 312 pages.

Kafka instructed his literary executor to destroy the manuscript of *The Trial,* one of the most important novels of the century. The dreamlike sequences and eerie realism of Kafka's masterpiece communicate the tale of Joseph K., a functionary who struggles to understand the nature of the unnamed crime of which he is accused. This novel has been read as a parable of the human condition, and as prefiguring 20th-Century totalitarianism.
Also read: *In the Penal Colony* (1919) and *The Castle* (1926).

**Pasternak, Boris** (1890–1960). Boris Pasternak was a Russian poet and the author of the novel *Doctor Zhivago*, for which he won the Nobel Prize in Literature. Born in Moscow, Pasternak studied music at the Moscow Conservatory and philosophy at the University of Marburg. His *Doctor Zhivago* was smuggled out of the USSR and published in the West.

*Doctor Zhivago* (1957)
Translated by Max Hayward and Manya Harari. Pantheon, 1997, 592 pages.

Boris Pasternak's life as a poet informs the dense lyricism and nature symbolism of this novel of the Russian Revolution, whose main character, Yuri Zhivago, is both doctor and poet, and author of the poems at the end of the book. Zhivago, who serves as the reader's moral compass amidst political turmoil, co-exists with ruthless revolutionaries and opportunists, yet finds meaning in love, in work, and in history.

**Sartre, Jean-Paul** (1905–1980). Jean-Paul Sartre was a French existentialist playwright, novelist, and philosopher. Born in Paris, he earned a doctorate in philosophy, served in the French army in World War II, and spent nine months in German POW camps. Incompatibility between his political beliefs and those of the judges led him to reject the Nobel Prize in 1964.

*The Flies* (first performed 1943)
In *No Exit and Three Other Plays*.
Vintage, 1989, 275 pages.

First performed in 1943, Sartre's *The Flies* reshaped the Greek myth of Orestes as an allegory for the Nazi occupation of Paris. Returning to his native Argos after the murder of his father, Agamemnon, Orestes finds a pestilence of flies and a craven populace beset by fear of King Aegisthus, who has committed the murder. Unlike his sister Electra, Orestes is able to break free from the myths of his past and find the courage to avenge his father's murder, becoming the redeemer of his city.
Also read: *Nausea* (1943) and *No Exit* (first performed 1944).

**Camus, Albert** (1913–1960). Albert Camus was a French novelist, playwright, and journalist and the recipient of the Nobel Prize for Literature in 1957. Born in Algeria, Camus studied philosophy at the University of Algiers and immigrated to France in 1938. Camus joined the French Resistance and worked as a journalist and writer in Paris.

*The Stranger* (1946)
Translated by Matthew Ward. Everyman's Library, 1993, 160 pages.

The simple prose of Camus' novel, set in Algeria, powerfully portrays the amoral Meursault, a stranger to the world and to himself. In Part One, Meursault attends his mother's funeral and commits a gratuitous murder. In Part Two, he finds an inner freedom that allows him to detach himself from the momentum of his trial. Moving beyond a merely sensory connection to life, Meursault opens himself to the world's benign indifference. Part One is as notable for its plot tension as Part Two is for its introspection.
Also read: *The Plague* (1948) and *The Fall* (1957).

**Solzhenitsyn, Aleksandr** (1918–2008). Aleksandr Solzhenitsyn was a Russian novelist and historian who won the Nobel Prize for Literature in 1970. In his writings he exposed and denounced the excesses of Soviet communism, including the vast network of prison camps known as the Gulag. Expelled from the USSR, Solzhenitsyn lived in America for several years before returning to Moscow after the fall of Soviet communism.

*One Day in the Life of Ivan Denisovich* (1962)
Translated by Ralph Parker. Signet, 2008, 176 pages.

The grim simplicity of Solzhenitsyn's prose conveys the harrowing details of one day in the life of a Soviet work camp prisoner. Solzhenitsyn's book is remarkable for its exposure of the dehumanization of the camps and for its portrait of an ordinary man who has the courage to hope against hope, and to count his blessings at the end of one day out of the three thousand six hundred and 53 days of his sentence.

*The Gulag Archipelago* (1973)
Translated by Thomas P. Whitney and Harry Willetts. Perennial Classics, 2002, 472 pages.

Subtitled "An Experiment in Literary Investigation," Solzhenitsyn's *Gulag Archipelago* is the author's chronicle of the network of Soviet forced labor camps that existed from 1918 to 1956. Solzhenitsyn describes every aspect of life in this Soviet netherworld, from intake to daily routines, blending testimony from inmates with his personal story. This record of state terror is an unparalleled historical document and literary masterpiece.

Also read: *The First Circle* (1968) and *Cancer Ward* (1968).

**Levi, Primo** (1919–1987). Levi, who was deported to the Auschwitz concentration camp in 1943, survived to become one of the most penetrating chroniclers of the Holocaust. His many memoirs are remarkable for their complex engagement with this most horrific episode in modern history.

*Survival in Auschwitz* (1947)
Classic House Books, 2008, 170 pages.

Although Levi drew on his experiences as a prisoner of Auschwitz in writing this book, it is not an autobiography so much as it is a philosophical-literary reflection on what Levi saw and experienced in the camp. Rather than play upon a preconditioned set of responses in writing about his experiences, Levi documents instead the complex system of the camps, including the various responses of the prisoners who were thrust into a dehumanized and profoundly disorienting world.

**García Márquez, Gabriel** (1927– ) (Nobel Prize, 1982). One of the greatest authors of the 20th Century, Garcia Márquez's rich body of work is remarkable for its ambition, originality, and depth. His work is typically concerned with the history and culture of Latin America, oftentimes combining realism, humor, and the fantastic.

*One Hundred Years of Solitude* (1967)
Translated by Gregory Rabassa. Harper Perennial, 2006, 448 pages.

The influential novel *One Hundred Years of Solitude* created a self-defining fable for the Colombian people—and for Latin Americans—around the fictive genealogy of the Buendí family and the imagined village of Macondo. This family chronicle is told through myths, history, and prefigured, fantastic events. Buendí patriarch José and matriarch Ursula are at the same time family prototypes and compellingly realistic characters.

Also read: *The Autumn of the Patriarch* (1975) and *Love in the Time of Cholera* (1985).

## 4. Short Stories

The modern short story collections on this list include stories written in the 19th and 20th Centuries. Stories written in the 18th Century tended to be anecdotes or philosophical tales. It was in the 19th Century that the short story came of age. With literacy in England, Europe, and the U.S. on the rise, the presses printed numerous widely-read short stories in newspapers and magazines. In Europe, it was the golden age of the short story, as seen in the work of Guy de Maupassant, Gustave Flaubert, and Anton Chekhov. These masters of the genre became models for writers of the next century.

In late 19th and early 20th-Century Britain, authors like D. H. Lawrence and W. Somerset Maugham wrote short fiction as well as novels. In America, the new century saw the emergence of writers for whom the short story was the genre of choice. American writers O. Henry, Ring Lardner, Katherine Mansfield, and Katherine Anne Porter specialized in the short story, each setting a standard for later writers.

The modern short story exhibits a number of consistent features. Most of the stories on this list are tight narratives that reach their climax at the end. There is often a surprise ending, or at least a final twist. The teller of the tale is often an integral part of the story, either in establishing point of view or as a character. Finally, with the exception of stories by Jorge Luis Borges and Ray Bradbury, most of the stories listed here are realistic. The tight frame within which the short story writer works is not conducive to experimentation.

Many stories on the Short Story list are not really short. Longer stories are to be found in the collections by Flaubert, Chekhov, Kafka, Lawrence, Mansfield, and Borges. However, even these longer stories allow for a unitary reading experience. You can read most of these stories in a single sitting, enjoying the full impact of the story as it opens, unfolds, and reaches its conclusion.

❖     ❖     ❖

**Bradbury, Ray.** *Bradbury Stories: 100 of His Most Celebrated Tales* (2003)
Harper Perennial, 2005, 912 pages.

Ray Bradbury, dubbed the "latter-day O. Henry," and one of America's most widely read writers of fiction, has chosen 100 of his stories for this eclectic collection. Reflecting the themes of his novels *Fahrenheit 451* and *Dandelion Wine*, Bradbury's tales range from conjurings of a dystopian future to nostalgic evocations of first love. Yet even Bradbury's scariest stories evoke more awe than fear. This collection includes an introduction by Bradbury in which the author explains the sources of his inspiration.

**Borges, Jorge Luis.** *Labyrinths: Selected Stories and Other Writings* (1962)
New Directions, 2007, 240 pages.

In this collection of fiction, essays, and parables, the three designated genres merge. Borges conjures up metaphysical conundrums through labyrinthine archives, a fictitious encyclopedia article, and an existential detective story. Today, writing that blends fiction and fact, creating a multi-layered puzzle, is called Borgesian. Styled as pop fiction, Borges' fables prefigure the Internet with their infinite archives and virtual worlds.

**Chekhov, Anton.** *Stories of Anton Chekhov* (2000)
Translated by Richard Pevear and Larissa Volokhonsky. Bantam, 2000, 496 pages.

Known as one of the greatest short story writers, Chekhov has been a model for young writers for more than 100 years. This collection includes an introduction to 30 tales spanning Chekhov's major creative periods, from his early sketches to later tales characterized by caustic wit and dark irony. The translators ably convey the texture of Chekhov's style and the idiosyncrasies of the Russian setting. Masterpieces "The Black Monk," "Ward No. 6," and "The Lady with the Little Dog" are included.

**Fallaize, Elizabeth,** Editor. *The Oxford Book of French Short Stories* (2002)
Oxford University Press, 2002, 376 pages.

This anthology includes French tales from the 18th Century, 19th-Century "golden age" masterpieces by Maupassant, Balzac, and Flaubert, and 20th-Century tales by celebrated writers Camus, Sartre, and Beauvoir and by innovative contemporary writers. These 28 works comprise a history of the French story, which ultimately opens up to writing by women, non-metropolitan, and Francophone authors. Yet all of these stories achieve impact through economy of style, distinctive voice, and unexpected endings.

**Flaubert, Gustave.** *Three Tales* (1991)
Translated by A. J. Krailsheimer. Oxford University Press, 1999, 144 pages.

Flaubert's three tales, first published in 1877, explore love, doubt, and religious experience. In "The Legend of Saint Julian the Hospitaller," Flaubert retells the medieval legend of an ill-fated hunter who obtains a state of grace. In "Herodias," he updates the Biblical story of Salome, emphasizing its political and historical background. In "A Simple Heart," Flaubert's stated intention of writing a compassionate portrait of humble servant Félicité is perhaps trumped by the author's characteristic detachment and irony.

**Fitzgerald, F. Scott.** *The Short Stories of F. Scott Fitzgerald* (1998)
Scribner, 1995, 800 pages.

In his lifetime, novelist F. Scott Fitzgerald was best known for short stories characterized by a deft analysis of human psychology and a keen perception of milieu. Fitzgerald's stories, most of which were originally published in magazines, range from early flapper tales and classic novellas of the Jazz Age ("The Curious Case of Benjamin Button" and "The Diamond as Big as the Ritz") to the later, darker tales that followed the author's personal struggle with alcohol and despair. Editor Mathew Bruccoli includes a brief preface to each of the 43 stories.

**Henry, O.** *The Best Short Stories of O. Henry* (1994)
Modern Library, 1994, 368 pages.

O. Henry stories, famous for their twist-in-the-tail endings, are also known for their characteristic humor, sharp observations, depiction of American social types, and optimism in the face of misfortune. While serving a prison sentence for embezzlement, one William Sydney Porter published 14 stories under various pseudonyms, but became best known as O. Henry. Among the more than 600 stories written by O. Henry, 38 chosen here include famous works "The Gift of the Magi" and "A Municipal Report."

**Kafka, Franz.** *The Complete Stories* (1971)
Schocken, 1995, 512 pages.

Franz Kafka, one of the 20th Century's most influential authors, wrote a wide range of shorter fiction, from sketches of daily life to well-known parables like "Before the Law," (from the novel *The Trial*), to longer stories probing the human condition such as "The Metamorphosis" and "The Hunger Artist." This collection includes two parables, 18 longer stories, 48 shorter stories, and an introduction by John Updike.

**Lardner, Ring.** *Ring Lardner: Selected Stories* (1997)
Penguin Classics, 1997, 410 pages.

Ring Lardner never intended to be a writer, and several stories in this collection of 21 of Lardner's best derive from his experience as a sports reporter. The humor and keen ear for American speech that catapulted Lardner from newspaperman to story-writer can be seen in the six-story ensemble, "You Know Me Al," about a semi-literate baseball player, and in "Champion," about an amoral heavyweight boxer. Non sports-related stories like "Gullible's Travels" deal ironically with human foibles.

**Lawrence, D. H.** *Selected Stories* (2007)
Penguin Classics, 2008, 400 pages.

This collection of 16 stories traces Lawrence's development from early stories that draw on his personal experience to works illustrating Lawrence's ideas about the split between human instinct and the forces of modernity. Lawrence's complex characters are found in early stories like "England, My England," which reflects the horror of World War I, and in later stories like "The Woman Who Rode Away" and "The Rocking Horse Winner," which illustrate Lawrence's take on civilization and its discontents.

**Maugham, W. Somerset.** *Collected Short Stories: Volume 1* (1951)
Penguin Classics, 1992, 448 pages.

Somerset Maugham, perhaps best known for his novel *Of Human Bondage* (1915), was a master craftsman of the 20th-Century short story. This first volume of Maugham's collected stories includes 30 tales set in Europe and the Pacific Islands. Englishman Maugham imbued his stories with a mordant wit, exposing human foibles with sympathy towards the perpetrators. This volume includes the celebrated story "Rain," which traces the moral decline of a missionary who tries to convert a Pacific Island prostitute.

**Maupassant, Guy de.** *The Necklace and Other Tales* (2003)
Translated by Joachim Neugroschel. Modern Library, 2003, 234 pages.

French writer Guy de Maupassant wrote hundreds of short stories for his 19th-Century audience and is considered one of the great masters of the short story. This volume of 12 classic stories, with an introduction by Adam Gopnik, demonstrates Maupassant's gifts as an artist and as a sharp observer of society. A brilliant creator of social types, Maupassant used his credible characters to explore the injustices of life and the randomness of fate. His stories are celebrated for their formal perfection.

**O'Sullivan, Vincent,** Editor. *Katherine Mansfield's Short Stories* (2005)
W. W. Norton, 2005, 430 pages.

Katherine Mansfield was a major short story writer during the first quarter of the 20th Century. Her depiction of the consciousness of sensitive characters vis-à-vis a harsh society can be seen in "Miss Brill," "Prelude," and "The Garden Party," three of her most frequently anthologized stories. The Norton Critical Edition includes 35 of Mansfield's stories with explanatory notes, excerpts on the craft of writing from Mansfield's correspondence, and 18 critical essays.

**Porter, Katherine Anne.** *The Collected Stories of Katherine Anne Porter* (1965)
Harvest Books, 1979, 504 pages.
When Katherine Anne Porter published fiction in the 1920s and '30s, she was acclaimed as a master craftsman of the short story. The 26 stories collected here, including 19 that won her the Pulitzer Prize, display her precise, miniaturist style and compressed imagery, as well as her subtle observations of human nature. The stories, set in Texas, Berlin, Mexico, and the Old South, include the classics "Flowering Judas" and "Pale Horse, Pale Rider."

**Twain, Mark.** *The Complete Short Stories of Mark Twain* (1865–1906)
Bantam Classics, 1984, 848 pages.

This comprehensive collection of 60 of Twain's shorter works puts Twain's comic genius on full display. These stories range from the folksy humor of Twain's early "The Celebrated Jumping Frog of Caleveras County," to Twain's examination of racism in "A True Story," to the bitter skepticism of later stories like "Some Learned Fables, for Good Old Boys and Girls." As literary craftsman and visionary, Twain is peerless.

**Welty, Eudora.** *The Collected Stories of Eudora Welty* (1955)
Harvest Books, 1982, 648 pages.

Eudora Welty is known for stories written in a wide range of styles; yet each story—whether farce, satire, or mystery—focuses on the complexity of human relationships. The publication of Welty's first short story collection in 1941 established her as a master of the genre. *The Collected Stories* includes all 41 of Welty's published stories and a preface by the author, in which Welty admits to loving all of her characters.

## 5. Poetry

Poetry is the most ancient literary form. Earlier civilizations counted upon their poets, or "singers," to memorialize the most important aspects of their history and culture. The earliest poems known to us, such as the *Psalms* of ancient Israel and the *Iliad* and the *Odyssey* of ancient Greece, served this purpose. Eventually, in classical Greece, poetry took on the additional form of drama. We think of drama as reaching its apotheosis in the plays of Shakespeare, which contain some of the most beautiful poetry in the English language.

In classical Greece, poetry took on the form of the ode, a short poem set to a lyre (a guitar-like instrument) that was sung in praise of a person or to celebrate an occasion. The ode is the earliest example of what we call today the lyric poem. In the most general terms, a lyric poem is a short poem that expresses thought and feeling. Lyric poetry came into its own in the 17th Century with the Metaphysical poetry of John Donne, George Herbert, and Andrew Marvell. With these poets, the language of poetry became a way of exploring and representing intense and deeply personal experiences.

We list below a number of the finest lyric poets of the last five hundred years, along with recommendations for specific poems to read. These poems exemplify the range, power, and beauty of lyric poetry. From John Donne's impassioned address to his lover in "The Canonization" ("We can die by it / if not live by love, / And if unfit for tomb or hearse / Our legend be, it will be fit for verse"), to the lovely vision of the great Irish poet W. B. Yeats in "The Lake Isle of Innisfree" ("And I shall have some peace there, for peace comes dropping slow, / dropping from the veils of the morning to where the cricket sings"), to Gary Snyder's clear-eyed, cosmic vision of the relationship between human beings and nature in "Above Pate Valley" ("Ate a cold trout in the / Trembling shadows. I spied / A glitter, and found a flake / Black volcanic glass—obsidian— / by a flower"), these poems invite us to see, feel, and experience our lives and the world in a new and exciting way.

The poems listed here can all be found in *The Norton Anthology of Poetry*. There are many different ways you can use this anthology. If you are new to poetry, we recommend that you read the introduction first and then read through the list of recommended poets and poems. You may also wish to sample randomly the poems included here, letting your interests and instincts guide you. We also encourage you to take a look at the poetry anthologies listed in Part One of this booklist. These anthologies focus upon the wide range of voice to be found in contemporary poetry, with an emphasis upon poems that are accessible and engaging.

*The Norton Anthology of Poetry*, eds. Margaret Ferguson, Jon Stallworthy, and Mary Jo Salter (1970) W. W. Norton, 5th ed., 2005, 1,424 pages.

### 1550–1700—Metaphysical Poets

**Donne, John** (1572–1631): "The Sun Rising," "The Canonization," "A Valediction Forbidding Mourning"

**Herbert, George** (1593–1633): "The Altar," "Redemption," "Easter Wings"

**Marvell, Andrew** (1621–1678): "The Coronet," "To His Coy Mistress," "The Garden"

### 1750–1830—Romantic Era Poets

**Blake, William** (1757–1827): "The Lamb," "The Sick Rose," "The Tyger"

**Wordsworth, William** (1770–1850): "Lines Composed A Few Miles Above Tintern Abbey," "The World Is Too Much with Us," "I Wandered Lonely As a Cloud"

**Coleridge, Samuel Taylor** (1772–1834): "The Rime of the Ancient Mariner," "Dejection: An Ode"

**Shelley, Percy Bysshe** (1792–1822): "Ozymandias," "Ode to the West Wind," "To a Skylark"

**Keats, John** (1795–1821): "Ode to a Nightingale," "Ode on a Grecian Urn," "To Autumn"

### 1830–1900—Victorian and pre-Modern American Poets

**Tennyson, Alfred Lord** (1809–1892): "Break, Break, Break," "The Eagle," "Crossing the Bar"

**Browning, Robert** (1812–1889): "My Last Duchess," "Fra Lippo Lippi"

**Arnold, Matthew** (1822–1888): "Shakespeare," "Dover Beach"

**Whitman, Walt** (1819–1892): "Crossing Brooklyn Ferry," "When Lilacs Last in the Dooryard Bloom'd"

**Dickinson, Emily** (1830–1886): "There's a certain Slant of light (58)," "I felt a Funeral in my Brain (280)," "I heard a Fly buzz—when I died (465)"

**Hopkins, Gerard Manley** (1844–1889): "God's Grandeur," "The Windhover," "Pied Beauty"

1900–1970—Modern Poets

**Yeats, William Butler** (1865–1939): "The Lake Isle of Innisfree," "The Wild Swans at Coole," "Among School Children"

**Frost, Robert** (1874–1963): "Home Burial," "After Apple Picking," "Birches"

**Stevens, Wallace** (1879–1955): "The Snow Man," "Thirteen Ways of Looking at a Blackbird," "Of Mere Being"

**Williams, William Carlos** (1883–1963): "The Red Wheelbarrow," "This Is Just To Say," "The Yachts"

**Eliot, T. S.** (1888–1965): "The Love Song of J. Alfred Prufrock," "Preludes"

**Owen, Wilfred** (1893–1918): "*Dulce et Decorum Est*," "Strange Meeting," "Futility"

**Hughes, Langston** (1902–1967): "The Weary Blues," "The Negro Speaks of Rivers," "Theme for English B"

**Roethke, Theodore** (1908–1963): "My Papa's Waltz," "The Waking," "In a Dark Time"

**Bishop, Elizabeth** (1911–1979): "The Fish" "Filling Station," "One Art"

**Thomas, Dylan** (1914–1953): "Do Not Go Gentle into That Good Night," "A Refusal to Mourn the Death, by Fire, of a Child in London"

**Brooks, Gwendolyn** (1917–2000): "The Bean Eaters," "We Real Cool," "Boy Breaking Glass"

**Levertov, Denise** (1923–1997): "Triple Feature," "O Taste and See," "Tenebrae"

**Rich, Adrienne** (1929– ): "Aunt Jennifer's Tigers," "Diving into the Wreck"

**Snyder, Gary** (1930– ): "Above Pate Valley," "Four Poems for Robin," "Instructions"

**Plath, Sylvia** (1932–1963): "Morning Song," "Lady Lazarus"

# V. Specialized Histories

The titles collected here under Specialized Histories do not fit into any one era or region, as they treat a particular subject (such as art or science) that crosses different historical periods and regions. The titles in this category are divided into seven sections: Art History, Military History, Science and Technology, Religious History, Intellectual History, Historical Atlases and Almanacs, and a final section listing a number of series in history and biography. The works in each category are as follows:

A. Art History includes four titles on the history of art and the human imagination.

B. Military History includes four titles on the history of warfare.

C. Science and Technology includes five titles that cover the development of science from antiquity to the present, as well as modern technological innovations.

D. Religious History includes five titles on the history of religions and Church history.

E. Intellectual History includes seven titles in the history of ideas and historiography (i.e., the philosophy of history, or how history is written). These are some of the most challenging books in the entire booklist.

F. Atlases and Almanacs are reference works that can be useful when you read history. It is easier to learn history if you understand geography, so having access to a good historical atlas could be helpful.

G. Additional Series in History and Biography lists ten series of books that would be a good place to find additional works of interest not included in this booklist.

## A. Art History

Bolton, Roy.  *A Brief History of Painting: 2000 BC to AD 2000*
Carroll & Graf, 2006, 300 pages.

Bolton, an art expert at Christie's in London, guides the reader through the history of painting from antiquity to the present.  He has chosen 150 landmark paintings that represent every important period.  An incisive commentary on each work is accompanied by a thumbnail sketch of the artist.  This work contains high-quality illustrations, a helpful introduction by art historian Matthew Collings, a timeline of artists and art movements, and a glossary.

Boorstin, Daniel J.  *The Creators: A History of Heroes of the Imagination*
Vintage, 1993 (1992), 811 pages.

Few historians can match Boorstin's encyclopedic scholarship or engaging writing ability.  In this follow-up to *The Discoverers*, Boorstin chronicles 3,000 years of man's artistic endeavors.  Along the way he discusses the writers, poets, musicians, painters, architects, and other artists who contributed to (mostly Western) civilization.  This panoramic history of the arts is a homage to the creative human spirit.

Janson, H. W.  *Janson's History of Art: The Western Tradition*
Prentice Hall, 7th ed., 2007 (1962), 1,200 pages.

Since its first publication in 1962, this fabulous text has inspired millions of students and art lovers around the world.  Simply known as "Janson" (he died in 1982), the eloquent narrative combined with the matchless selection of illustrations make this the art history text of choice.  This latest edition has been revised and expanded by six specialists in the field.  This is a majestic tour through the entire history of Western art.

Ramage, Nancy H. and Andrew Ramage, Editors.  *Cambridge Illustrated History of Roman Art: Romulus to Constantine*
Cambridge University Press, 1991, 304 pages.

A team of specialists has written this introductory survey of Roman art that covers 1,300 years from the Etruscans to the reign of Constantine.  The art forms covered are mostly architecture, wall painting, and sculpture, but also included are mosaics, stucco, pottery, coins, luxury arts, and even town planning.  Each historical period is treated in turn, with the art works discussed in their political and cultural context.  This is a very handsome volume that is lavishly illustrated.

# B. Military History

Keegan, John.  *A History of Warfare*
Vintage, 1994, 496 pages.

This is a comprehensive analysis of the culture of war and war-making from primitive societies to the present.  Keegan explains how warfare has evolved and how it has shaped the development of society.  In so doing he broadly compares Eastern and Western military cultures.  On a larger level Keegan examines why war occurs at all.  His intention is to debunk Clausewitz's dictum that "war is politics by other means."  The reader will have to judge how successful he is.

Parker, Geoffrey, Editor.  *Cambridge Illustrated History of Warfare*
Cambridge University Press, rev. ed., 2008 (1995), 416 pages.

This is a valuable survey of western warfare from antiquity to the present.  It covers the major personalities, weapons, strategies, tactics, and technologies used.  Parker, a leading military historian at Yale, and six other American and British experts contribute their expertise to this detailed study.  This is a well-written, handsome volume supplemented by diagrams of key battles, maps, a chronology of warfare, a glossary, and an annotated bibliography.

Porch, Douglas.  *Wars of Empire*
HarperCollins, 2006 (2000), 240 pages.

In this volume from the *Smithsonian History of Warfare* series, Porch describes the rise and fall of the great imperial powers.  Though the work discusses the 18th through the 20th Centuries, the main focus is on the 19th Century.  Instead of a straight, chronological narrative, Porch structures his material according to the strategies used by imperial powers and their enemies.  Thus he is able to focus on common military dilemmas, tactics employed, and strategic lessons learned.  This makes the maps and index a vital reference point.

Tuchman, Barbara.  *The March of Folly: From Troy to Vietnam*
Ballantine Books, 1990 (1984), 447 pages.

Tuchman analyzes an historical puzzle: why governments pursue irrational policies against their own best interests.  After discussing the fall of Troy as an introductory prototype, she explores three episodes that illustrate her thesis: the actions of the Renaissance popes that resulted in the Reformation, Britain's loss of her colonies in North America, and the Vietnam War.  Whether one agrees with her analysis or not, this is an enlightening assessment of foolhardy rulers.

## C. Science and Technology

Boorstin, Daniel J. *The Discoverers: A History of Man's Search to Know His World and Himself*
Vintage, 1985 (1983), 745 pages.

In this first of a trilogy of books, Boorstin takes the reader on a rich journey of discovery from ancient to modern times, a journey that celebrates the march of human progress. He tells the story of how the great pioneers, explorers, scientists, and inventors contributed to the growth of knowledge. The romp through the centuries is organized topically in four sections: time, geography, nature, and society. This encyclopedic history of man's quest to know is a fascinating treasure trove of information.

Gonzalez-Crussi, Frank. *A Short History of Medicine*
Random House (Modern Library Chronicles), 2007, 250 pages.

This survey explores mainly Western medicine over the past five centuries. The author covers such topics as developments in our understanding of anatomy, reproduction, and disease, advances in surgery, obstetrics, and anesthesia, the evolution of the diagnostic process, and modern psychiatric therapies. He also discusses the men and women who made or implemented the important breakthroughs and unlocked the mysteries of the human body.

Hughes, Thomas P. *American Genesis: a Century of Invention and Technological Enthusiasm, 1870–1970*
University of Chicago Press, 2004, 529 pages.

Here is the remarkable story of America's technological revolution. Hughes weaves together scientific and technological advances with other cultural trends, showing how they are linked. He begins with independent inventors such as Edison, Bell, and the Wright Brothers, and then analyzes the more complex systems of technological production that made America great, like electrical power grids, Ford's assembly plants, the Manhattan Project, and the space program.

Ronan, Colin A., Editor. *Cambridge Illustrated History of the World's Science*
Cambridge University Press, 1984, 543 pages.

This is a wide-ranging, well-illustrated survey of man's unremitting efforts to understand the natural world. From the origins of science in Egypt and Mesopotamia, successive chapters discuss the development of science in Greece, China, India, Arabia, Rome and Medieval Europe, and the Renaissance and Scientific Revolution. It then treats the development of science globally from the 17th through the 20th Centuries, covering the principal scientific disciplines in each period.

Swedin, Eric G. and David L. Ferro. *Computers: The Life Story of a Technology*
John Hopkins University Press, 2007 (2005), 192 pages.

This is an enjoyable book for those interested in the history of computers from ancient times to the present. The authors first look at early mechanical devices from the abacus to Babbage's Difference Engine. Then they explore the fascinating innovations of the electronic age from vacuum tubes to transistors to today's microprocessors. Finally they explain the key ideas in today's networking computers. This marvelous book includes photos, a timeline, and a glossary.

# D. Religious History

Bowker, John, Editor. *Cambridge Illustrated History of Religions*
Cambridge University Press, 2002, 336 pages.

This is a comprehensive survey of world religions from pre-history to the present. Every major religion is covered in depth by an expert in the field and is supported by lavish illustrations. Even aboriginal religions, as well as the religions of ancient Greece, Rome, Egypt, Persia, and Mesopotamia are included. New religious movements are briefly discussed. The text includes both a graphic and a detailed chronology for each religion and an extensive bibliography.

Shelley, Bruce L. *Church History in Plain Language*
Thomas Nelson, 3rd ed., 2008 (1982), 544 pages.

This is a very readable introduction to church history, covering mostly the Western church from a Protestant perspective. Two thousand years of Christian history are divided into eight ages and 48 short, digestible chapters. Shelley focuses on the most significant people, ideas, and movements to create a dramatic story that is clear and memorable. The third edition updates the text to include the latest developments. Summary timelines are dispersed throughout.

Stark, Rodney. *For the Glory of God: How Monotheism Led to Reformation, Science, Witch-Hunts, and the End of Slavery*
Princeton University Press, 2004, 488 pages.

In this follow-up to his ambitious study of monotheism entitled *One True God*, Stark, a sociologist of religion, explores four historical consequences of monotheistic faith in western culture. For example, he debunks the popular view of science as antagonistic to religion, arguing that science could only have evolved in a monotheistic culture that saw nature as the handiwork of a rational God. This is a very provocative and enlightening assessment of religion and culture.

Stark, Rodney. *The Victory of Reason: How Christianity Led to Freedom, Capitalism, and Western Success*
Random House, 2006, 281 pages.

In this third in a series of books studying the influence of Christianity on Western culture, Stark argues that it was faith in reason that made the great successes of the West possible, a faith that was rooted in a rational Christian theology. Prosperity and freedom—the products of capitalism and the liberal rights tradition—are in fact the natural outgrowths of Christian principles. Stark's thesis is compelling and worth serious consideration.

Ware, Timothy. *The Orthodox Church*
Penguin, 2nd ed., 1993 (1963), 359 pages.

This is the standard introduction to the history, beliefs, and practices of Eastern Orthodox Christianity. In the first part, the author, an Orthodox bishop and former Oxford scholar, traces the entire history of the Orthodox Church. The second part covers faith and worship, including important theological issues. Ware ends with a hopeful reflection on the possible reunion of East and West.

# E. Intellectual History

Boorstin, Daniel J. *The Seekers: The Story of Man's Continuing Quest to Understand His World*
Vintage, 1999, 298 pages.

In this volume, which completes his trilogy on humanity's quest for understanding, Boorstin turns to Western religion and philosophy. He studies the great seekers whose search for truth and meaning left an indelible mark on civilization. This grand narrative traces man's unquenchable desire to know, from the ancient prophets and philosophers to modern theorists and skeptics. The book's 41 short chapters consist mostly of short biographies of select figures.

Collingwood, R. G. *The Idea of History*
Oxford University Press, rev. ed., 1994 (1946), 576 pages.

This is a classic work in historiography, or the philosophy of history. Collingwood examines how the understanding of history has evolved from Herodotus to the 20th Century. His basic thesis is that history is not a bland retelling of the past but an historian's ever-evolving recreation of the past in the present. The revised edition includes three additional lectures that Collingwood delivered in 1926–1928. This is a rewarding work, though it may be too academic for casual readers.

Dawson, Christopher. *Dynamics of World History*
ISI Books, 2002 (1958), 512 pages.

This is a collection of 31 essays on the philosophy of history selected from the author's previously published works. Dawson, a committed Catholic scholar, believed religion was the great creative force in any culture and that the loss of a society's historic religion would lead to social dissolution. This is a work of great wisdom and learning, and is remarkably accessible. It's an essential source for understanding civilization and the role religion plays in preserving it.

Elton, Geoffrey. *The Practice of History*
Blackwell, 2nd ed., 2002 (1969), 224 pages.

This work was written as a manifesto to explain the author's practice as an historian. It was also written to rebut E. H. Carr's classic text *What Is History?* (Palgrave, 1961), which adopted a relativist view. Elton, whose prestige and influence among historians still lingers, presented a more orthodox, objective position toward the writing of history. This is an engaging introduction to the field of historiography that sheds much light on the debates over what history is and how it is "practiced."

Tarnas, Richard. *The Passion of the Western Mind: Understanding the Ideas That Have Shaped Our World View*
Ballantine Books, 1993 (1991), 544 pages.

In this large but lucid volume, Tarnas offers a comprehensive intellectual history of Western civilization. He summarizes and comments on the pivotal ideas of the great thinkers from the ancient Greeks to postmodernism, yet he doesn't attempt to be encyclopedic. His focus is the main trajectory of Western thought viewed as a complex interplay of spiritual, philosophical, and scientific forces. This guide through the history of ideas includes a useful, 21-page chronology.

Van Doren, Charles. *A History of Knowledge: Past, Present, and Future*
Ballantine Books, 1992, 422 pages.

As former editor of the Encyclopedia Britannica, Van Doren embarked on the Herculean task of chronicling the long advance of human knowledge from antiquity to the present. The result is a sweeping but completely accessible tour of human progress that brings together in one volume all the great theories and discoveries of Western civilization. The final chapter, "The Next Hundred Years," speculates on future advances. This is intellectual history on a grand scale.


Voegelin, Eric. *Order and History, Volume 1: Israel and Revelation* (*The Collected Works of Eric Voegelin, Volume 14*)
University of Missouri Press, 2001 (1956), 656 pages.

Eric Voegelin (1901–1985) was a masterful philosopher whose life-long search for the sources of order in history and society culminated in his five-volume *magnum opus*, entitled *Order and History*. In this first volume he examines the ancient Near Eastern civilizations, especially Israel, and their experience of cosmic-divine order. What emerges is a sophisticated account of biblical revelation and what it established: human existence in its historical form. This difficult but profound work of scholarship is an essential companion to the study of the Old Testament.

# F. Historical Atlases and Almanacs

Daniels, Patricia and Steve Hyslop. *National Geographic Almanac of World History*
National Geographic Society, 2006, 384 pages.

Designed as an authoritative reference, this comprehensive almanac offers a blend of narrative, analysis, detailed facts, timelines, sidebars, and more than 220 maps, photographs, and illustrations. It covers all of world history from the first civilizations to the 21st Century. The easy-access entries, essays, and summaries in each chapter make this a very useful, accessible tool for students. *The National Geographic Almanac of American History* is also available.

Haywood, John. *The Penguin Historical Atlas of Ancient Civilizations*
Penguin, 3rd ed., 2005, 144 pages.

The study of history requires knowledge of geography, and the Penguin series of historical atlases readily fits the bill. Each volume includes over 70 full-color maps, as well as timelines, photographs, and artwork reconstructions. This volume covers the world's ancient cultures around the globe. Other titles in the series include: *Ancient Egypt, Ancient Greece, Ancient Rome, The Medieval World, The British Empire, Russia, The Vikings,* and *The Third Reich.*

O'Brien, Patrick K., Editor. *Atlas of World History*
Oxford University Press, 1999, 368 pages.

This is the most comprehensive one-volume historical atlas available. Organized into five parts, it illuminates the major events and themes of world history over all the continents from the origins of humanity to the start of the 21st Century. This great reference work includes 450 color maps and 160 illustrations, diagrams, and photographs. A concise edition without the 24 pages of time charts and 600 encyclopedic entries on events, people, and places is also available.

# G.  Additional Series in History and Biography

Listed below are some of the most distinguished series in history and biography available.  In Part Two of this booklist we have annotated a number of books that are part of these series.  If you are interested in an historical event, topic, or person not covered in this booklist, you may find what you are looking for in one of these series.

### HISTORY

*Cambridge Illustrated History* (Cambridge University Press, 1984–present)

These lavishly illustrated books are accessible and authoritative histories that offer a comprehensive treatment of their subject (e.g., Ancient Greece, Ancient Rome, China, Islam, the British Empire, France, Germany, and the Middle Ages).  Each volume is written by a team of specialists and features copious full-color photographs, maps, and timelines.

*Modern Library Chronicles* (Modern Library, 2000–present)

This series features the world's great historians on a wide range of subjects.  Lively, accessible, and brief (170–200 pages), these authoritative histories are designed to appeal to students and general readers.

*Oxford History of the United States* (Oxford, 1982–present)

This acclaimed series provides a comprehensive summary of the political, social, and cultural history of our nation.  Written for a general audience, this multi-volume history is authored by stellar historians.  Several of the books in this series have been awarded the Pulitzer Prize for history.

*Smithsonian History of Warfare* (Collins, 2004–present)

Originally published in Great Britain as *The Cassell History of Warfare* (1999–2001), this is a multi-volume history of war from ancient to modern times.  This lavishly illustrated series is edited by John Keegan, one of the foremost military historians of our time.

*Studies in European History* (Palgrave, 1986–present)

This series contains concise, elegant accounts by distinguished historians of significant periods and events in European history.  These introductory works of 100–200 pages include extensive bibliographies that guide readers to additional resources.

*The Peoples of Europe* (Blackwell, 1990–present)

This series covers the European tribes and peoples from their origins in prehistory to the present day.  Each volume presents a fresh account of a group's culture, society, and turbulent history.  Together these accessible but scholarly volumes provide a comprehensive and vivid picture of European society and the peoples who formed it.

**BIOGRAPHY**

*American Presidents* (Times Books, 2002–present)

This series presents the panorama of our chief executives in compact, lucid volumes. Each volume is an incisive, biographical essay (about 150 pages) that focuses on the subject's presidency, but also offers a distillation of his life, character, and career.

*Eminent Lives* (HarperCollins, 2004–present)

This is a series of brief biographies of important historical figures written by distinguished authors. Several volumes have been published to date, including Muhammad, Machiavelli, Shakespeare, Beethoven, Freud, de Tocqueville, Francis Crick, and Presidents Washington, Jefferson, and Grant.

*Library of American Biography* (Pearson/Longman, 1988–present)

Originally published by Little, Brown (1954–1980), this revised and updated series is a great resource for students of American history. These concise biographies are designed to be interesting, accessible overviews of famous figures in American history from John Smith to Betty Friedan. Each reissued volume includes a study guide and discussion questions.

*Penguin Lives* (Penguin, 1996–2004)

This is a popular series of short, fresh biographies of famous individuals, written with a personal tone by celebrated authorsa. These concise, informative portraits (150–200 pages each) are eminently readable, yet scholarly.

# World History and Literature

World History and Literature is divided into six major sections according to region: India and Southeast Asia, China, Japan, the Middle East, Africa, and Latin America. The list of books in each of these sections is organized by genre: history, biography, ancient literature (China and India only), medieval literature (all but Africa and Latin America), and modern literature.

In all of these sections, the history books include at least one broad survey of the region or civilization. The biographies include some significant political, religious, and literary figures. The literature from the ancient and medieval periods includes myths, stories, scripture, poetry, and philosophical and religious texts from the canon of world literature—the most important works in each tradition. In most cases, the modern literature was written in the native language and translated into English. This is the case with China, Japan, the Middle East, and Latin America. In the regions colonized by the British, such as India and Africa, most of the literature was written in English.

The works that appear here include the classics of these civilizations—the greatest works of literature they have to offer. Reading these texts can not only add to our knowledge of the world but also enhance our intellectual, moral, and spiritual development. For example, the ancient religious traditions of India, particularly Hinduism and Buddhism, offer a deep reservoir of wisdom. Confucianism in China, which to this day reinforces strong Chinese family traditions, has long been a significant cultural resource. The great literature of Latin America has enormous depth and meaning, making it a valuable resource for all people. Other regions represented in this booklist have their own unique values and stories to tell.

There are a number of ways you could use this list. You could find individual works that interest you. If this gets you excited about a particular civilization, you could then read as much of its history and literature as you find interesting. Alternatively, you could decide in advance to educate yourself in a particular region or civilization. You might choose, say, Latin America or China, and read a selection of books from that section. If you enjoy that approach, you could do the same for another region or civilization, or a few. This is your list; you decide how you want to use it.

# I. India and Southeast Asia

India has a very long history. The Indus Valley Civilization, dating back to 3300 BC, was followed by the Vedic period, which laid the foundations of Hinduism. Around 500 BC, when Buddhism appeared, India saw the rise of numerous kingdoms across the country, which were united by the 3rd Century BC. Following invasions from Central Asia between the 10th and 12th Centuries AD, most of northern India was ruled from Delhi by a series of Muslim dynasties. Starting in the early 16th Century, several European powers established trading posts in India, eventually establishing colonies in the country. By 1857 most of India was under the control of Great Britain. The 20th Century saw a nation-wide struggle for independence, which was eventually achieved under the leadership of Mohatma Gandhi in 1947. At that time, large, Muslim-dominated areas in the northwest and east were partitioned to form the independent state of Pakistan, which later split into Pakistan in the west and Bangladesh in the east.

Today India is the seventh-largest and second-most populous country in the world, with a population of roughly 1.2 billion people. It is by far the most populous democracy and boasts one of the world's fastest growing economies. Four major religions originated in India: Hinduism, Buddhism, Jainism, and Sikhism. India is an immensely diverse culture: multilingual, multiethnic, and multireligious.

The three history books listed below are surveys of the region, Wolpert's history of India being the most comprehensive. All three biographies are of spiritual leaders from the Indian subcontinent: the Buddha, Gandhi, and the Dalai Lama.

Ancient and medieval Indian literature, written mostly in Sanskrit, is primarily religious in nature, combining elements of folk poetry, myth, and religious doctrine and speculation. In the 8th Century BC, the earliest religious verse, the *Vedas*, were recorded in scriptures known as the *Upanishads*. Like the *Upanishads*, the *Mahabharata* and the *Ramayana*, India's great epics, greatly influenced later Indian literature. The *Mahabharata*, in particular, is a foundational text comparable in its impact on Indian literature to the impact of the Bible on Western literature. India's premier devotional poem, the *Bhagavad-Gita*, is part of the *Mahabharata*.

Modern Indian literature arose in 19th-Century Bengal, stimulated by the English-language education system. This literature breaks with the past in two ways: it is written primarily in English, and it focuses on secular concerns. Modern Indian writers have used fiction to explore social themes such as the caste system, the legacy of British colonialism, and the relation between East and West. Selections from India's modern literature include works by Nobel Prize winner Rabindranath Tagore, and a number of fascinating novels by authors including Anita Desai, Vikram Seth, Arundhati Roy, and Kiran Desai.

## HISTORY

Brown, Colin. *A Short History of Indonesia: The Unlikely Nation?*
Allen & Unwin, 2004, 288 pages.

The archipelago nation of Indonesia, the largest country in Southeast Asia, has the largest Muslim population in the world. In this readable, comprehensive history, the author charts the growth of Indonesia and its multi-ethnic peoples from its earliest recorded history through its classical empires, to the era of colonialism and Japanese occupation, to the regimes of Sukarno and Suharto. This fine overview explains how Indonesia came to be and what its future might hold.

Heidhues, Mary Somers. *Southeast Asia: A Concise History*
Thames & Hudson, 2001, 192 pages.

The region of Southeast Asia includes Indochina, Indonesia, Malaysia, Singapore, and the Philippines. Heidhues covers the history of this vast region from the earliest prehistoric peoples to the most recent developments. She also examines the culture, politics, economics, and religion of these countries. This concise, richly illustrated history will appeal to historians, students, and travelers alike. Eleven maps and a glossary are also included.

Wolpert, Stanley. *A New History of India*
Oxford, 8th ed., 2008 (1977), 560 pages.

This is the best introductory survey of the history and culture of India. India is a complex, pluralistic civilization comprising different races, religions, languages, and cultures. Wolpert has condensed over 4,000 years of Indian history in a thorough, authoritative guide that is also readable and engaging. The whole Indian subcontinent is covered, including India, Pakistan, Bangladesh, and Sri Lanka. The latest edition brings the story right up to the present.

## BIOGRAPHY

Armstrong, Karen. *Buddha* (c. 563–483 BC)
Penguin, 2004 (2001), 205 pages.

In this *Penguin Life* Armstrong examines the life and times of Siddhartha Gotama, whose quest for enlightenment led to his spiritual awakening and his becoming the founder of one of the world's great religions. It's an unconventional biography, as few details of Buddha's life and personality survive. Thus Armstrong fleshes out her sympathetic portrait by drawing on legends, mythology, philosophy, and the history of the time. A helpful glossary is included.

Gandhi, Mohandas K. *An Autobiography: The Story of My Experiments with Truth* (1869–1948)
Translated by Mahadev Desai. Beacon Press, 1993 (1957), 528 pages.

One of the great figures of the 20th Century, Gandhi recounts the significant episodes in his life and explains how he developed his principle of nonviolent resistance, which propelled the struggle for Indian independence. Unfortunately the story ends in 1921 when Gandhi was in his early 50s. One would have to read a biography (such as Yogesh Chadha's *Gandhi: A Life*) to get his complete life story. Nevertheless, this is an inspiring read.

Dalai Lama.  *My Land and My People: The Original Autobiography of His Holiness the Dalai Lama of Tibet* (1935– )
Grand Central Publishing, 1997 (1962), 256 pages.

This is the very moving memoir of Tenzin Gyatso, the 14th Dalai Lama, who is the head of the Tibetan government in exile, the spiritual leader of Tibetan Buddhists, and the winner of the 1989 Nobel Peace Prize.  Written when he was a young monk in exile, this personal narrative tells the story of his humble beginnings, his selection as the reincarnated leader of his people, his experience of the Chinese conquest of Tibet, his flight to India, and his passionate struggle to save his people.

### Ancient Literature

**Easwaran, Eknath,** Translator.  *The Upanishads* (8th Century BC and later)
Nilgiri Press, 2nd ed., 2007, 368 pages.

These Hindu scriptures comprise a series of mystical and philosophical works that date from the 8th Century BC to the early modern period.  These Sanskrit texts constitute the core teaching of Vedanta, the spiritual tradition concerned with self-realization by which one follows the path to union with Brahman, the ultimate reality.  Easwaran's translation of the 11 principal and four minor Upanishads are easy to read, and each is given an introduction.  He also provides endnotes, a general introduction, and a glossary.

**Narayan, R. K.,** Translator.  *The Mahabharata: A Shortened Modern Prose Version of the Indian Epic* (c. 8th Century BC and later)
University of Chicago Press, 2000, 182 pages.

A major text of Hinduism, this is one of the two great Sanskrit epics of ancient India.  Traditionally ascribed to Vyasa, ancient India's Homer, its 74,000 verses and long prose passages make this the longest composition in the world.  It tells the story of the great war between two ruling families, the Kauravas and the Pandavas.  Narayan's abbreviated prose version makes a very accessible introduction to the complicated tale that captures the heart of Indian mythology and folklore.

**Easwaran, Eknath,** Translator.  *The Bhagavad-Gita* (c. 5th–2nd Century BC)
Nilgiri Press, 2nd ed., 2007, 296 pages.

The most famous section of the *Mahabharata*, the *Gita* has become the great devotional classic of Hindusim.  It consists of a 700-verse dialogue between Arjuna, the hero of the epic, and his charioteer Krishna, an avatar of Vishnu, on the eve of the decisive battle.  Their dialogue captures the essence of Hindu philosophy.  Easwaran provides a synopsis of each of the 18 chapters, a general introduction, endnotes, and glossary.

**Narayan, R. K.,** Translator. *The Ramayana: A Shortened Modern Prose Version of the Indian Epic* (c. 4th Century BC)
Penguin, 2006, 159 pages.

This is the second great Sanskrit epic of ancient India, traditionally ascribed to Valmiki, the father of Indian poetry. The poem tells the story of Lord Rama, the unjustly exiled prince of the Ayodhya kingdom. The poem's 24,000 verses are judiciously condensed in this very readable retelling of the story, which is based on the Tamil version by the medieval poet Kamban. The epic can be enjoyed for its spiritual wisdom as well as its thrilling story of abduction, battle, and romance.

**Easwaran, Eknath,** Translator. *The Dhammapada* (c. 3rd Century BC)
Nilgiri Press, 2nd ed., 2007, 256 pages.

The Buddhist scriptures date from the 3rd Century BC, though they are traditionally ascribed to the Buddha (563–483 BC) himself. These teachings (*dharma*), written in Pali, derive from Theravada, the oldest tradition of Buddhism. The essential subject matter concerns training the mind in order to liberate oneself from suffering. Easwaran's clear, contemporary translation brings the Buddhist philosophy to life. He also summarizes the life of the Buddha and the main tenets of his teaching in a lengthy introduction.

**Adigal, Prince Ilango** (c. 1st Century AD). Adigal was a Tamil poet and Hindu monk. According to legend, he was the older brother of the 1st-Century Chera king Senguttuvan (modern day Kerala, in South India), but renounced the throne to become a saint.

*Shilappadikaram* (*The Ankle Bracelet*) (c. 1st Century AD)
Translated by Alain Daneliou. New Directions, 1965, 224 pages.

One of the classics of Indian literature, this is the first known epic poem in Tamil. It is ascribed to the poet prince Ilango Adigal. The story involves the three ancient Tamil kingdoms and centers on Kannagi, a faithful wife wronged by her husband. After losing him to a miscarriage of justice at the court of the Pandya king, she wreaks her revenge on the kingdom. A work of history and myth, this lovely old romance paints a vivid picture of early Indian life and religion.

**Kālidāsa** (c. 370–450 AD). Kālidāsa was a renowned classical Sanskrit writer. His poems and plays are based on Hindu mythology and philosophy. Though little is known of his life, he is considered the Shakespeare of Sanskrit literature.

*The Recognition of Śakuntalā* (c. 4th Century AD)
Translated by W. J. Johnson. Oxford World's Classics, 2001, 192 pages.

This play concerns King Dusyanta's love for the country girl Śakuntalā, their separation by a curse, and their eventual reunion. The erotic love story is based upon an episode in the *Mahabharata*, which is included in this edition. The introduction puts the play in the aesthetic and cultural context of ancient India. One might also wish to read Kālidāsa's exquisite lyric poem *The Cloud Messenger*.

## MEDIEVAL LITERATURE

**Kabir** (1398–1448).  Kabir is the most beloved saint of medieval India.  A weaver by profession, he wrote mystical poems that greatly influenced the *Bhakti* tradition of India, a spiritual practice that emphasizes loving devotion to God.  Raised by Muslim parents, Kabir turned to Hinduism and sought the inner truth of both faiths.  His devotional poetry has a strong iconoclastic strain.

*The Bijak of Kabir* (early 15th Century)
Translated by Linda Hess and Shukdev Singh.  Oxford University Press, 2002, 216 pages.

The *Bijak* is the most important collection of Kabir's poetry.  In these brief poems, Kabir fearlessly invites one to experience the divine mystery that refuses to be confined within a religious system.  These poems beautifully express Kabir's universal view of spirituality and reveal a strong Sufi influence.  The translators provide a very helpful introduction to Kabir's life and work.

**Mirabai** (1498–1550).  Mirabai (also spelled Meera) is a celebrated, Hindu mystical poet.  Born a Rajput princess in northwest India, she fought tradition to pursue an independent life.  A woman of immense talent and devotion, Mirabai wrote in the *Bhaki* tradition and composed as many as 1,300 prayerful songs that focus on the love of Lord Krishna.

*Ecstatic Poems* (early 16th Century)
Translated by Robert Bly and Jane Hirshfield.  Beacon Press, 2004, 103 pages.

This recent collection of Mirabai's poems will appeal to anyone interested in spiritual poetry.  The translators render her wisdom and passion in a modern, interpretive rephrasing, which makes clear that Mirabai's poetry transcends her time and culture.  An afterword by John Stratton Hawley provides what is known of Mirabai's life and reputation.

## MODERN LITERATURE

**Tagore, Rabindranath** (1861–1941).  Nobel Prize winner Rabindranath Tagore is the acclaimed author of novels, stories, songs, dramas, and essays in the Bengali language.  A Brahmin from Kolkata (Calcutta), Tagore managed family estates in Bengal, founded an ashram, and set up the Institute for Rural Reconstruction.

*The Home and the World* (1916)
Translated by William Radice.  Penguin Classics, 2005, 240 pages.

Tagore's prophetic novel, written in 1916, focuses on three characters whose struggles foretell the conflicts brought about by Partition in 1947.  Sandip, a passionate advocate of "Swadeshi," or the appreciation of all things Indian, pursues a romantic relationship with Bimala, whom he sees as "Mother India," while Bimala's husband, Nikhil, maintains a mature, detached perspective.

**Tagore (cont.)**

*Selected Poems* (1985)
Translated by William Radice. Penguin Classics, 2005, 209 pages.

Tagore's poems, among the most evocative in literature, express man's yearning for God, the gulf between the transitory and the eternal, and the poet's love of nature and joy in living. This edition has an introduction describing Tagore's Bengali background.

Also read: *Farewell Song* (1929) and *Selected Short Stories* (1991).

**Anand, Mulk Raj** (1905–2004). Born in Peshawar, India, Anand studied in England, earning his Ph.D. from Cambridge in 1929. Anand wrote *Untouchable* in response to the excommunication of an aunt from his family for eating with a Muslim. Returning to India in 1936, Anand became a prolific writer of poetry, plays, and novels in English.

*Untouchable* (1935)
Penguin Classics, 1990, 160 pages.

In his 1935 novel, Anand recounts one day in the life of Bakha, a member of India's untouchable caste. Championed by E. M. Forster as a story that "has gone straight to the heart of its subject and purified it," this tale shows Bakha working at his lowly job and seeking an answer to his fate in dialogues with a missionary and a follower of Ghandi, only to conclude that it is technological progress that will finally liberate his caste.

**Narayan, R. K.** (1906–2001). Born in Madras, the son of a schoolmaster, R. K. Narayan did not excel in school. However, he wrote 14 novels, several volumes of short stories and nonfiction, and translated Indian epics. An Indian writer in English who spent most of his life in India, he was a prolific author and an avid reader.

*The Guide* (1958)
Penguin Classics, 2006, 224 pages.

Just out of prison, Raju finds a new career when local peasants mistake him for a priest. Though at first he impersonates a holy man to get food and shelter, Raju gradually grows into the role of spiritual advisor. Narayan's deft narrative interweaves Raju's adventures as a holy man with flashbacks to his childhood and career as a tour guide.

Also read: *Swami and Friends* (1935).

**Desai, Anita** (1937– ).  Among the first successful Indian writers in English, Desai has described her stories and novels as "private attempts to seize the raw material of life."  Born to a Bengali father and a German mother, Desai was educated in Delhi.  Desai is the mother of four children, including author Kiran Desai.

*Fire on the Mountain* (1977)
Penguin, 1977, 146 pages.

Nanda Kaul's plan to spend her last years cultivating tranquility is dramatically disrupted when Raka, her great-granddaughter, comes to live with her.  Described by Desai as the first novel in which she controlled her own style, *Fire on the Mountain* vividly portrays the inner worlds of Nanda and interloper Raka, who gradually draws Nanda back to life.
Also read: *Clear Light of Day* (1980) and *Fasting, Feasting* (1999).

**Seth, Vikram** (1952– ).  Born in Kolkata (Calcutta), India, Vikram Seth studied economics at Oxford and at Stanford, where he was Wallace Stegner Creative Writing Fellow in 1977.  Now residing in England, Seth writes poetry, novels, biography, and memoir.

*A Suitable Boy* (1991)
Harper Perennial, 1993, 1,474 pages.

This richly imagined novel of national and domestic drama interweaves the tale of a Hindu family's search for a husband for their daughter with the sprawling saga of four families set against the background of post-colonial India of the 1950s.  Seth brings the tale of the Mehras, Kapoors, Chatterjis, and Khans vividly to life while accurately relating the conflicts between Hindus and Muslims in Nehru's India.
Also read: *Mappings* (1980), *An Equal Music* (1999), and *Two Lives* (2005).

**Mistry, Rohinton** (1952– ).  Born in Mumbai (Bombay), Rohinton Mistry earned a degree in mathematics and economics from Bombay University in 1973.  In 1975 he immigrated to Canada and attended the University of Toronto, where he won prizes for his short stories.

*A Fine Balance* (1995)
Vintage, 2001, 624 pages.

Set in Mumbai during India's State of Emergency in 1975–77, Mistry's novel traces the fates of four characters whose improbable interdependence enables their survival.  Forced by a housing shortage to share an apartment, seamstress Dina lives with two tailors and a displaced student.  The narrative cuts back and forth between past and present, relating India's troubled history from the Partition of 1947 on.
Also read: *Such a Long Journey* (1991).

**Ghosh, Amitav** (1956– ). Born in Kolkata (Calcutta), India, Ghosh was educated in Delhi and England, where he received a Ph.D. in social anthropology from Oxford. Ghosh, a professor of literature at the City University of New York, is the author of historical fiction highlighting issues of post-colonialism.

*Sea of Poppies* (2008)
Farrar, Straus and Giroux, 2008, 528 pages.

*Sea of Poppies*, planned as the first book in a trilogy, is set in India of 1838, just prior to the Opium Wars. Ghosh gathers his teeming cast of characters together on the Ibis, a former slave-ship now plying the opium trade in the Indian Ocean. The author mounts a scathing critique of the British opium trade in this tale of pirates, villainy, mutiny, secret love affairs, heroism, and transformation aboard the ultimate ship of fools.

Also read: *The Circle of Reason* (1986) and *The Shadow Lines* (1990).

**Divakaruni, Chitra Banerjee** (1956– ). Born in Kolkata (Calcutta), India, Divakaruni studied in the United States, earning her Ph.D. from the University of California, Berkeley, in 1985. A poet, novelist, and professor of creative writing at the University of Houston, her novels include works for children and a recasting of the *Mahabharata*.

*Sister of My Heart* (1999)
Anchor Books, 1999, 322 pages.

Set in Calcutta, India, and in California, Divakaruni's tale of two cousins born on the same day and raised together cuts back and forth between the story of gentle Sudha, whose arranged marriage keeps her in India, and rebellious Anju, who follows her husband to San Francisco. Diverging paths and dissimilar natures separate but cannot alienate the cousins, bound as they are by their commonality as South Asian women.

Also read: *Mistress of Spices* (1987) and *The Palace of Illusions* (2008).

**Roy, Arundhati** (1961– ). Born to a Syrian Christian mother who advocated for women's rights and a Bengali tea planter, Arundhati Roy grew up in Kerala, studied architecture in Delhi, and has worked as a writer and a human rights activist. Her novel, *The God of Small Things*, won the Booker Prize in 1997.

*The God of Small Things* (1997)
Random House, 2008, 352 pages.

Set in Kerala, India, during the social upheavals of the 1960s, Roy's novel interweaves the story of fraternal twins Estha and Rahel with that of their mother Ammu and untouchable family friend Velutha. Roy's characters are irreparably affected by the clash between communism and the caste system. Her theme of conflicted love is tinged with sadness, but her vibrant characters and enchanting descriptions infuse the novel with zest.

**Desai, Kiran** (1971–  ).  Indian-born Kiran Desai has lived in India, England, and the United States, where she studied creative writing at Bennington College and Columbia University.  Her second novel, *The Inheritance of Loss*, won the 2006 Man Booker Prize and the National Book Critics Circle Award.

*The Inheritance of Loss* (2006)
Grove Press, 2006, 357 pages.

Set in the Himalayas on the eve of the Nepalese insurgency, Desai's extraordinary novel relates India's social unrest of the 1980s and its impact upon the small world of retired Judge Jemubhai Patel, his orphaned granddaughter Sai, and his cook.  As the narrative cuts from India to New York, where the cook's son Biju struggles to make his way, social unrest is seen to threaten Patel's view of his past and Sai's prospects for the future.

Also read: *Hullabaloo in the Guava Orchard* (1998).

# II. China

Ancient China is one of the oldest centers of human civilization. By 5000 BC late Stone-Age cultures with agriculture, pottery, and textiles emerged in China's Yellow River Valley in the north and Yangzi River Valley in the center. Around 2000 BC a more complex civilization marked by writing and metal-working emerged in the north-central plains. This period is associated with the legendary Xia Dynasty, the first described in ancient historical records. Other dynasties followed until the more stable Han Dynasty appeared and ruled a unified Chinese state from 206 BC to 220 AD. The Han greatly expanded China's territory, but their collapse brought disintegration. In 580 AD China was reunited under the Sui, who were followed by other Chinese dynasties until China was conquered by the Mongols in the late 13th Century. After conquering much of the Eurasian continent, including parts of Eastern Europe, Russia, and the Middle East, the Mongols were overthrown in China in 1368 when the Ming Dynasty was founded. In 1644 the Ming fell to the Qing Dynasty, which lasted until 1912 when China's last emperor abdicated.

In 1912 Sun Yat-sen established the unstable Republic of China, but the country remained fragmented until Chiang Kai-shek was able to reunify it in the late 1920s. China's war with Japan led to an alliance between Chiang's Nationalists and the Communists under Mao Zedong, but after World War II Mao prevailed in a civil war that brought his Communist regime to power. The People's Republic of China was founded in 1949, but communist rule under Mao was a disaster. Thirty-six million people died in the Great Famine of 1958–1961 caused by Mao's Great Leap Forward. Mao's Cultural Revolution (1966–1976) left China's economy and education system in shambles. Political and economic reforms since Mao have turned the country around. In the last 20 years, China, the most populous country in the world with a population of roughly 1.3 billion people, has seen rapid economic growth. Still, China's authoritarian government maintains strict restraints on personal freedom.

The two history books listed below are comprehensive surveys of China. Four biographies highlight the lives of two fascinating, medieval figures and two modern figures that depict China under communist rule.

Ancient Chinese literature is renowned for its wisdom. The 6th and 5th Centuries BC saw the emergence of two influential philosophical traditions: Taoism, based on Lao-Tzu's *Tao Te Ching*, and Confucianism, based on the moral and philosophical writings of Confucius, chiefly the *Analects*. The 4th and 3rd Centuries BC brought a continuation of philosophical speculation by Mencius and Han Fei Tzu, successors of Confucius, and Zhuangzi, a successor of Lao-Tzu.

Medieval China saw a growth of popular literature written in colloquial Chinese, such as the 14th-Century classic novels, *The Romance of the Three Kingdoms* and *Outlaws of the Marsh*. Early modern Chinese fiction saw its greatest expression in two classic works, *Journey to the West* and *The Dream of the Red Chamber*, which is considered China's greatest novel.

Modern Chinese literature was drastically impacted by the tumultuous events of the 20th Century. It all but disappeared during the upheaval of civil war and the founding of Mao's Communist China. It also languished during the Cultural Revolution when writers were severely persecuted. Beginning in the 1980s, Chinese literature reawakened from its suppression and many novelists wrote critiques of modern Chinese history and satires of Communist China. Others wrote about formerly taboo topics like spirituality and the private life of feeling.

### HISTORY

Ebrey, Patricia Buckley, Editor. *Cambridge Illustrated History of China*
Cambridge University Press, 1999 (1996), 352 pages.

This is a splendid synthesis of China's long history from its Neolithic origins to the end of the 20th Century. Ebrey's focus is political and social history following China's many dynasties, but technological and economic advances and major military conquests are also covered. The text is wonderfully illustrated throughout with detailed maps, photographs, and artwork. This comprehensive introduction is an authoritative guide to Chinese civilization past and present.

Spence, Jonathan. *The Search for Modern China*
W. W. Norton, 2nd ed., 1999 (1990), 728 pages.

This is a comprehensive, well-researched history of modern China from the fall of the Ming Dynasty in the 17th Century to the aftermath of Tiananmen Square. Spence offers insight and information on Chinese politics, religion, culture, land use, wealth and poverty, literature and the arts, interactions with the West, efforts at population control and modernization, and China's prevailing Confucian ideals. Very readable and heavily illustrated with over 200 photos.

### BIOGRAPHY

Clements, Jonathan. *Wu: The Chinese Empress Who Schemed, Seduced and Murdered Her Way to Become a Living God* (625–705 AD)
The History Press, 2007, 239 pages.

Here is the dramatic tale of the ruthless Chinese Empress Wu Zetian, the only woman ever to rule China in her own name. Her beauty led her at age 13 to be chosen concubine to Emperor Taizong of the Tang Dynasty. After a series of cunning lies and murders, she eventually became supreme ruler herself, reigning under the new Zhou Dynasty until she was deposed in old age. This is an exciting, true story of court intrigue, seduction, and lust for power.

Dreyer, Edward L. *Zheng He: China and the Oceans in the Early Ming Dynasty, 1405–1433* (1371–1433)
Longman, 2006, 256 pages.

Chinese scholar Dreyer outlines what is known about the life of the Chinese admiral Zheng He, a eunuch in the royal court and adviser to the emperor. Dreyer examines his seven voyages to Southeast Asia and the Indian Ocean, their political purpose, and their impact on Chinese society during the early Ming period. Working from the primary sources, Dreyer sheds new light on why China did not follow the same path of development as the European powers.

Spence, Jonathan. *Mao Zedong: A Life* (1893–1976)
Penguin, 1999, 208 pages.

In this *Penguin Life*, eminent Chinese historian Spence offers a concise biography of Chairman Mao that condenses the major events of Mao's life into a very readable portrait. Spence traces Mao's developing character and ascension to power from young naive idealist to ruthless, personality cult leader whose megalomania and devastating rule resulted in the deaths of tens of millions of human beings.

Zhengguo, Kang. *Confessions: An Innocent Life in Communist China* (1944– )
Translated by Susan Wilf. W. W. Norton, 2007, 455 pages.

Yale University professor Kang gives a harrowing account of the oppressive conditions in China from the beginning of communist rule in 1949 to Tiananmen Square and afterwards. Coming of age during Mao's Cultural Revolution, he was a defiant, 20-year-old literature student when he was sent to prison for three years for requesting a library copy of Pasternak's *Doctor Zhivago*. This memoir is a moving testament to human resilience in the face of totalitarian conformity.

### ANCIENT LITERATURE

**Lao Tzu** (c. 6th Century BC). Lao Tzu was an ancient Chinese sage who is traditionally regarded as the author of the *Tao Te Ching*, and is thus the founder of Taoism.

*Tao Te Ching* (c. 6th Century BC)
Translated by Jonathan Star. Tarcher, 2008, 105 pages.

Next to the Bible, the *Tao Te Ching* is the most widely translated book in the world. The classic manual in the art of living, the "Book of the Way" is the foundation of Taoism, one of world's great wisdom traditions. Composed 2,500 years ago, its 81 verses are given a fresh, literary translation that clearly renders the meaning of the *Tao* (the basic principle of the universe) for modern ears. Dozens of English translations exist, but this is one of the best.

**Sun Tzu** (c. 6th Century BC). Sun Tzu is traditionally believed to be the author of *The Art of War*, an ancient book of military strategy. Traditional accounts claim he was a general of the King of Wu who lived c. 544–496, but historians have questioned whether he was an historical figure.

*The Art of War* (c. 6th Century BC)
Translated by Samuel Griffith. Forgotten Books, 2007, 52 pages.

This classic treatise on military strategy and tactics continues to influence not just generals and war planners, but also leaders in business and management. Though there are many English translations (with scholarly annotations and commentary) of this brief work in print, this edition contains only Sun Tzu's words, which is all that is necessary to appreciate the value of his advice (such as that in a competitive environment fixed plans are useless when one must respond to changing conditions).

**Confucius** (551–479 BC).  Confucius, whose name means "Master Kong," was an ancient Chinese thinker and social philosopher.  His teachings developed into a philosophy known as Confucianism, which has had a profound impact on Chinese thought and life.  Though it lacks the formal elements of a religion, many Chinese follow Confucianism in a religious manner.

*The Analects* (c. 5th Century BC)
Translated by Raymond Dawson.  Oxford World's Classics, 2008 (1993), 160 pages.

The *Analects* is regarded as the record of the words and acts of the great Chinese philosopher Confucius and his disciples.  This translation of the aphoristic fragments, by a foremost scholar of classical Chinese, comes with an Introduction and explanatory notes.  Along with *The Great Learning*, *The Analects* contains the heart of Confucianism.

**Walker, Brian Browne,** Translator.  *I Ching*, or *Book of Changes*: *A Guide to Life's Turning Points* (c. 5th–3rd Century BC)
St. Martin's Griffin, 1992, 144 pages.

One of the oldest classical Chinese texts, the *I Ching* describes an ancient system of philosophy and cosmology.  It is based on discerning the order behind random events through such principles as the inevitability of change and the dynamic balance of opposites Yin and Yang.  Its popularity lies in what it teaches about attaining prosperity, perspective, and peace of mind.

**Mencius** (c. 372–289 BC).  Mencius was the most famous Confucian philosopher after Confucius himself.  According to legend, he was an itinerant philosopher, traveling throughout China for 40 years offering advice to rulers.

*Mencius* (late 4th Century BC)
Translated by D. C. Lau.  Penguin Classics, rev. ed., 2004, 304 pages.

The *Mencius*, easier to read than the *Analects*, consists of the sage's long conversations with rulers, disciples, and rival philosophers of his time.  His essential teaching focuses on the inherent goodness of the individual, but also the corrupting influence of society.  This updated translation includes a helpful introduction, appendices, glossary, and notes.

**Zhuangzi (Chuang Tzu)** (369–285 BC).  The intellectual and spiritual successor of Lao Tzu, Zhuangzi was a Taoist philosopher whose style was less poetic and more conversational than Lao Tzu.  His philosophy was very influential in the development of Zen Buddhism in China and Japan.

*Basic Writings* (late 4th Century BC)
Translated by Burton Watson.  Columbia University Press, 2003 (1964), 168 pages.

This collection contains the central writings of the Taoist sage.  The central tenet of Zhuangzi's teaching is that happiness and freedom come only with understanding the Tao (the Way of Nature).  Some regard his teaching as a precursor to skepticism, relativism, and even anarchism.  Watson's lucid translation is supplemented by a helpful introduction and an outline of early Chinese history.

**Han Fei Tzu** (c. 280–233 BC).  A Confucian philosopher, Han Fei was a prince in the small state of Han.  He was the founder of Legalism, which focuses on the ruler who governs the state through power, action, and law.

*Basic Writings* (3rd Century BC)
Translated by Burton Watson.  Columbia University Press, 1996 (1964), 134 pages.

Unlike Confucius, who stressed virtue and morality, Han Fei emphasized the more pragmatic force of law, which steers people through a combination of coercion and self-interest.  Watson's selection of writings from the *Han Feizi* is accompanied by a helpful introduction that places Han Fei in his intellectual and historical context, and includes an outline of early Chinese history.

## MEDIEVAL LITERATURE

**Wang Shifu** (c. 1250–1337).  Little is known of Wang Shifu other than that he was born in Dadu (Beijing) and was a successful dramatic playwright of the Yuan Dynasty, which saw the flowering of Chinese drama.  Fourteen plays are attributed to Wang, though only three are extant.

*The Romance of the Western Bower* (early 14th Century)
Translated by Zhang Xuejing.  New World Press, 2000, 224 pages.

This play, also known as *Romance of the West Chamber*, is considered China's greatest love comedy and the best of the surviving works of Wang Shifu.  Based on a short story by Yuan Chen (779–831), the play follows the secret love affair of a young scholar and the daughter of the late prime minister of the Tang court.  Illustrating the many obstacles they must overcome to find happiness, the play shows the conflict between love and family honor.

**Shi Nai'an** (c. 1296–1392).  Not much is known about Shi Nai'an.  Some scholars doubt that he actually existed, and suggest that he may simply have been a pseudonym for Luo Guanzhong (see below).

*Outlaws of the Marsh* (14th Century)
Translated by Sidney Shapiro.  Foreign Language Press, 2001, four-volume set, 2,149 pages.

This 14th-Century Chinese epic is set in the 12th-Century Song Dynasty.  Also known as *Water Margin*, this is the second of the Four Great Classical Novels of Chinese literature.  In 100 chapters, the story follows a roaming band of the emperor's warriors who fight for loyalty and honor.  It has it all: adventure, intrigue, murder, corruption, warfare, good and evil, and romance.

**Luo Guanzhong** (c. 1330–1400). Almost nothing is known about the life of Luo. He is traditionally credited as the author of the classic novel *Romance of the Three Kingdoms* and the last 30 chapters of *Outlaws of the Marsh (Water Margin)*. Luo may have been a disciple of Shi Nai'an, but many scholars now believe that Luo and Shi were actually the same person.

*The Romance of the Three Kingdoms* (14th Century)
In *Three Kingdoms: Chinese Classics*.
Translated by Moss Roberts. Foreign Language Press, 2005, four-volume set, 2,340 pages.

*The Romance of the Three Kingdoms* is a 14th-Century national epic that tells the story of the turbulent years at the end of the Han dynasty (169–280 AD) when ancient China was divided into three empires. It is the first of the Four Great Classical Novels of Chinese literature, commonly regarded by scholars as the greatest works of classical Chinese fiction. Unfortunately, no abridged version is in print, so this novel, like the other three, is for the ambitious reader who has time for long sagas.

**Wu Cheng-En** (c. 1500–1580). Wu was a Chinese novelist and poet of the Ming Dynasty who is the probable author of *Journey to the West*. He sought to be become a mandarin in his early life but did not pass the examinations. He later served briefly as an official in Beijing but did not enjoy the work. He resigned and spent the rest of his life as a hermit and writer.

*Journey to the West* (1590s)
Translated by W. J. F. Jenner. Foreign Languages Press, 2003, four-volume set, 2,346 pages.

This is the third of the Four Great Classical Novels of Chinese literature. Published during the Ming Dynasty, the novel is a fictionalized account of the Buddhist monk Xuanzang's pilgrimage to India with his three disciples during the Tang Dynasty (618–907 AD). It is an adventure story as well as a fount of spiritual insight. Arthur Waley's 1943 abridged translation of the story, entitled *Monkey: Folk Novel of China*, is also available.

**Lanling Xiaoxiao Sheng** (c. late 16th–17th Century). Lanling Xiaoxiao Sheng is the pseudonym of the anonymous author of the famous *Chin P'ing Mei (The Plum in the Golden Vase)*.

*The Plum in the Golden Vase, or Chin P'ing Mei*, Volume One: *The Gathering* (first published: 1618)
Translated by David Tod Roy. Princeton University Press, 1993, 610 pages.

Written in the late 16th Century, this novel is sometimes called the Chinese *Decameron* and is considered to be the fifth great classical Chinese novel. It describes the downfall of the Ximen household in the early 12th Century, and is known for its explicit depiction of sexuality. Though not yet complete, this is the best English translation. The first three of the projected five volumes had been published by 2009. See Volume Two: *The Rivals* (2001), and Volume Three: *The Aphrodisiac* (2006).

**Cao Xueqin** (c. 1715–1763). A poet, painter, and novelist, Cao Xueqin was a highly talented man who spent a decade writing *The Dream of the Red Chamber*, which was mostly completed by his death. In his later years he lived in the Western suburbs of Beijing in poverty, selling off his paintings.

*The Dream of the Red Chamber* (mid-18th Century)
In *The Story of the Stone*.
Translated by David Hawkes. Penguin, five volumes, 1973–1980, 2,564 pages.

The last of the Four Great Classical Novels, entitled *The Dream of the Red Chamber* (also known by its original title, *The Story of the Stone*), is considered the greatest. It is a Romeo-and-Juliet story of two warring households of the same family in Beijing. The epic sheds vivid light on Chinese aristocratic life and is known for its revolutionary portrayal of women. An abridged version, translated by Chi-Chen Wang in 1929 and revised in 1958, is also available.

## MODERN LITERATURE

**Hsun (Xun), Lu** (1881–1936). Lu Hsun, one of the founders of modern Chinese literature, wrote stories in classical Chinese and in the vernacular. Born Zhou Shuren, he wrote using the pen name Lu Hsun. Though his simple style and sympathetic portrayal of Chinese workers won the communists' praise, Lu Hsun never joined the party.

*Selected Stories of Lu Hsun* (1919–35)
Translated by Yang Hsien-yi and Gladys Yang. W. W. Norton, 2003, 288 pages.

The style and content of these stories made them groundbreaking when they were first published. Lu Hsun's story "A Madman's Diary" was written in the Chinese vernacular, and his "The True Story of Ah Q" offered a scathing critique of privilege in feudal China. Ha Jin's introduction to the book discusses Lu Hsun's place in Chinese literature.

**She, Lao** (1899–1966). Lao She is a renowned novelist and playwright. Born in Beijing, he worked his way through teaching college after his father was killed in battle. From 1924 to 1929 he taught Chinese in London, and from 1946 to 1949 he lived and wrote in America. He returned to China in 1949 and served on several government cultural committees.

*Rickshaw* (1936–7)
Translated by Jean M. Janes. University of Hawaii Press, 1979, 264 pages.

While teaching Chinese at London's School of Oriental and African Studies, Lao She read the novels of Charles Dickens. Dickens' novels of the individual and society influenced Lao She's portrait of rickshaw man Hsiang Tzu. Hsiang Tzu's destiny is shaped by luck and fate as well as by his wit and initiative.

**Cha, Louis (pen name Jin Yong)** (1924–  ).  A native of Zhejiang province in China, Cha is the author of fiction in *Wuxia*, or the martial arts and chivalry genre.  Popular throughout the Chinese-speaking world, Cha's fiction has been translated into several languages and has been adapted for television, comics, and video.

*The Book and the Sword* (1955)
Translated by John Minford.  Oxford University Press, 2005, 536 pages.

Set in 18th-Century China, Cha's novel uses the changeling motif to explore the origins of Emperor Quianlong.  Amidst multiple story elements including knights, kung fu masters, a lost city, and the Red Flower Society's quest to overthrow the government, is the tale of Quianlong, who claims to be Han, not Manchu, by virtue of a baby exchange.

**Xingjian, Gao** (1940–  ).  Born in Ganzhou, China, Xingjian won the Nobel Prize for his stories, novels, and dramas.  Today a French citizen, Xianjian earned his degree in French from Beijing's Department of Foreign Languages in 1962.  He was sent to a reeducation camp during the Cultural Revolution.

*Soul Mountain* (1990)
Translated by Mabel Lee.  HarperCollins, 2000, 510 pages.

Gao Xingjian's autobiographical novel features a protagonist who wins a reprieve from death when his diagnosis of lung cancer proves false.  Freed from the past, he begins a long journey to the Sichuan mountains.  Populated with Daoist and Buddhist characters, *Soul Mountain* is an existential meditation on the soul's journey through life.

Also read: *One Man's Bible* (2002) and *Buying a Fishing Rod for My Grandfather* (2005).

**Sijie, Dai** (1954–  ).  Acclaimed author and director Dai Sijie was born in China.  He was sent to a reeducation camp in Sichuan province from 1971 to 1974.  In France on scholarship in 1984, Sijie became a filmmaker and novelist.  His novels about China were written in French.  His documentary film, *China, My Sorrow* (1989), is available in English.

*Balzac and the Little Chinese Seamstress* (2002)
Translated from the French by Ina Rilke.  Anchor Books, 2001, 184 pages.

Living rough in a remote reeducation camp, two city boys form ties with a local beauty known as the Little Seamstress.  Sijie's narrator describes the growing attraction between the girl and his friend Luo as the two pygmalions read to her from the forbidden Balzac.  Surprises abound as love and the best laid plans for improving a peasant girl go awry.

**Yan, Mo** (1955– ). Mo Yan is the author of social commentary novels in the tradition of Lu Hsun. Born in Shandong, China, to a family of farmers, Yan is a prolific writer whose novels have often been adapted as films.

*Red Sorghum* (1987)
Translated by Howard Goldblatt. Penguin, 1994, 368 pages.

Set in rural China, Mo Yan's four-part novel describes the impact of Chinese history on the countryside from the time of the Japanese invasion in 1937 to the present. Yan's panoramic tale of family history and political conflict, adapted as the 1987 Oscar Award-winning film of the same name, is legendary throughout China.

Also read: *The Republic of Wine* (1992) and *Life and Death are Wearing Me Out* (2008).

**Jin, Ha** (1956– ). Born in Liaoning, China, the son of a military officer, Jin joined the People's Liberation Army in 1969 during the Cultural Revolution. In 1981 he earned a degree in English Studies from Heilongjiang University. In 1985 he immigrated to America. Jin's works about China are written in English.

*Waiting* (1999)
Vintage, 2000, 320 pages.

This 1999 National Book Award winner is the story of the divided world of doctor Lin Kong, who shuttles between the urban scene of his sophisticated mistress, Manna Wu, and the traditional village of his wife Shuya, to whom he is bound by an arranged marriage. Since army regulations forbid Lin Kong to divorce his wife until 18 years have passed, the doctor must wait. His divided self reflects China's political tensions.

Also read: *Ocean of Words: Stories* (1996) and *A Free Life* (2007).

**Lianke, Yan** (1958– ). Born in Henan Province, China, and based in Beijing, Yan Lianke graduated from the People's Liberation Army Art Institute in 1991. The recipient of China's Lu Hsun and Lao She literary awards, Lianke has nevertheless been subjected to censorship by the Chinese government for his satires.

*Serve the People!* (2007)
Translated by Julia Lovell. Grove Press, 2008, 240 pages.

*Serve the People!* is a pointed satire of the robotic, slogan-chanting followers of Mao Zedong. Peasant soldier Wu Dawang faces a conundrum when he must interpret the dictum to "Serve the People!" in light of the demands of his division commander's wife. Lianke depicts simple characters in an absurd world, and lets the reader connect the dots.

**Shuo, Wang** (1958– ). Wang Shuo is the author of novels written in the hooligan style. Born in Beijing, he turned to hooliganism as a teen when his parents were sent to the countryside during the Cultural Revolution and he and his brother lived alone in Beijing. Adolescent rebellion led to jail, followed by a stint in the navy.

*Playing for Thrills* (1989)
Translated by Howard Goldblatt. Penguin, 1998, 336 pages.

Decadent former soldier Fang Yan, the narrator of this quirky thriller, worries that jail is in his future when a police investigation exposes his apparent guilt for the murder of his army buddy. A pioneer of the hooligan style, Shuo has created a world of Chinese noir.

Also read: *The Vanished Woman* (1993) and *A Sigh* (2000).

**Chen, Ran** (1962– ). Born in Beijing, Ran Chen is a Chinese avant-garde writer whose works appeared throughout the 1990s. In addition to her novel *A Private Life* (1996), Chen has published numerous short stories and won several Chinese literary prizes, including the first "Contemporary China Female Creative Writer's Award."

*A Private Life* (1996)
Translated by Howard Gibbon. Columbia University Press, 2004, 256 pages.

Set against the background of the Cultural Revolution and the Tiananmen Square demonstrations, Chen's coming-of-age novel portrays Ni Niumiu, overlooked at home and quietly rebellious at school. Haunted by the past, she disengages from politics and cultivates the world of her imagination. The translation conveys Chen's lucid style.

# III. Japan

Early settlements in Japan go back many thousands of years. In fact the oldest pottery in the world is Japanese, dating from 10,000 BC. But a bronze-age, agricultural civilization did not appear until the Yayoi culture in the 3rd Century BC. In the mid-6th Century AD, Buddhism was introduced from Korea, and it became widely accepted during the Asuka period (7th Century). The Nara period (8th Century) marked the rise of a strong central Japanese state as well as the appearance of the earliest Japanese written literature. The subsequent Heian period (9th–12th Centuries) saw a distinctly native Japanese culture develop. Feudal Japan (12th–19th Centuries) was marked by a ruling class of warriors, the samurai, who engaged in seven centuries of clan warfare. Though Japan had an emperor with nominal authority during this period, the warring shoguns held the real power. The 16th Century saw Japan engage in modest commercial and cultural exchanges with the West, but in 1603 the Tokugawa shogunate came to power, inaugurating more than two centuries of general national unity and international isolationism.

In 1854 U.S. Commodore Matthew Perry forced the opening of Japan to the outside world, which caused Japan's ruling elite to rethink the country's relations with the West. In the latter part of the 19th Century, Japan adopted Western institutions and became an industrialized world power. Beginning in the late 19th Century, Japan engaged in a series of military conflicts against China and Russia in order to expand its wealth, power, and influence. The early 20th Century saw the rapid rise of Japanese militarism and expansionism. In 1931 Japan conquered Manchuria and the following year invaded other parts of China, which precipitated another Chinese war. On December 7, 1941 Japan attacked Pearl Harbor, forcing the U.S. into the Second World War. The atomic bombings of Hiroshima and Nagasaki in 1945 brought the war against Japan to an end. Since the 1960s Japan has achieved tremendous economic growth. Today Japan is the world's second largest economy and boasts the world's longest life expectancy, but its low birthrate and aging population portend potentially significant challenges in the future.

The one history book listed below surveys Japan's development over the last 1500 years, and the three biographies illuminate the lives of three important 20th-Century Japanese figures.

Japan's early literature blossomed during the Heian period, an era of peace, prosperity, and cultural achievement by the court nobility at Kyoto. Japanese noblewomen authored two of the great works of the Heian era: *The Pillow Book* and *The Tale of Genji*. Japanese literature reached another high-water mark during the Edo period (1603–1868), which is known for the revival of scholarship and the birth of the haiku.

Modern Japanese literature blends reflections on Japanese character and society with Western ideas and motifs. When the feudal Tokugawa society collapsed in 1868, Japanese scholars turned to the study of humanism, and Japanese writers began translating European literature. Novelist Ogai Mori returned from studying in Germany and introduced Western ideas into Japanese society. Modern Japanese literature includes fiction by Nobel Prize winners Yasunari Kawabata and Kenzaburo Öe, and by acclaimed writers Kazuo Ishiguro and Haruki Murakami. While Kawabata is notable for his depiction of Japanese sensibility, many other modern Japanese writers feature contemporary themes familiar to Western readers. Less well-known in the West are authors Junichiro Tanizaki, whose novels focus on changes in Japanese society, and Yasushi Inoue, whose historical novels reflect his interest in Asia.

## HISTORY

Beasley, W. G. *The Japanese Experience: A Short History of Japan*
University of California Press, 2000 (1999), 317 pages.

Beasley examines 1,500 years of Japanese history in this very digestible survey. He begins with Japan's mythic origins and the arrival of Buddhism in the 6th Century AD, and then sketches Japan's development through its long feudal period up to the 20th Century when Japan emerged as an imperial power. A final chapter discusses the "economic miracle" of postwar Japan. The text is supplemented with black and white photos, a glossary, maps, and an annotated bibliography.

## BIOGRAPHY

Bix, Herbert P. *Hirohito and the Making of Modern Japan* (1901–1989)
Harper Perennial, 2001, 832 pages.

This is the first complete biography of the emperor who ushered Japan into the modern world during his 63-year reign. Bix focuses on the vital part Hirohito played in Japan's imperial expansion and military policy leading to the China War of 1937 and World War II. Against the conventional portrayal of Hirohito as a helpless figurehead overshadowed by Japanese militarists, Bix emphasizes his decisive role in war-making and wartime operations.

Chadwick, David. *Crooked Cucumber: The Life and Zen Teaching of Shunryu Suzuki* (1904–1971)
Broadway, 2000, 464 pages.

Shunryu Suzuki was the patriarch of American Zen Buddhism, having founded the San Francisco Zen Center in 1961. Chadwick, a Buddhist priest and Suzuki's student, follows his master's life from his childhood in Japan to the turbulent 60s in San Francisco. This is a touching account of Suzuki's life and teachings, drawing on memories of his students, friends, and family. The book includes excerpts from Suzuki's unpublished lectures.

Nathan, John. *Mishima: A Biography* (1925–1970)
Da Capo Press, 2000, 348 pages.

This is a personal and compelling portrait of the legendary Japanese writer Yukio Mishima. Japanese scholar Nathan, who was Mishima's friend and translator, draws heavily upon interviews with Mishima's family and friends. He traces the life of this tortured genius from his oppressed childhood, through his years during and after the war, to his infamous death by ritual suicide (*seppuku*) in public following the samurai honor code.

## MEDIEVAL LITERATURE

**Ō no, Yasumaro** (d. 723 AD).  Yasumaro was a Japanese nobleman, bureaucrat, and chronicler. He is most famous for compiling the *Kojiki*, the oldest extant work of Japanese history.  He was commissioned to write it by Empress Genmei (reigned: 707–721 AD), no doubt to add legitimacy to the imperial throne.

*The Kojiki: Records of Ancient Matters* (712 AD)
Translated by Basil Hall Chamberlain.  Tuttle Publishing, 2005, 592 pages.

The *Kojiki* is the oldest surviving Japanese book.  Completed in 712 AD, the *Kojiki* preserved for later generations the record of ancient Japan.  It is a collection of early Japanese mythology, legendary history, genealogy, and poetry that provides a view of Japan during its formation.  This is also the fundamental scripture of Shinto.  The text comes with extensive explanatory notes, introduction, and appendices.

**Shonagon, Sei** (c. 966–1017).  Sei Shonagon was a Japanese writer who served as court lady to the young Empress Teishi, who died in childbirth in the year 1000.  Little is known about Shonagon's life apart from what is found in *The Pillow Book*, which brought her fame.  She is known for her rivalry with Murasaki Shikibu, another court lady and writer (see below).

*The Pillow Book* (1002)
Translated by Meredith McKinney.  Penguin Classics, 2007, 364 pages.

*The Pillow Book* is the collection of observations and musings by the court lady Sei Shonagon during her service to Empress Teishi in Kyoto.  Written for her own amusement, this record of reflection, recollection, gossip, poetry, and tales offers a fascinating glimpse into the confined court life in classical Japan.  This edition includes an introduction, appendices, maps, glossary, chronology, and notes.

**Shikibu, Murasaki** (c. 973–1014).  Shikibu was a Japanese novelist, poet, and noblewoman who served as lady-in-waiting for Princess Shoshi in the imperial court.  Three works are attributed to her: *The Murasaki Shikibu Diary*, *The Murasaki Shikibu Collection*, which were both published posthumously, and *The Tale of Genji*, her most important work.

*The Tale of Genji* (early 11th Century)
Translated by Royall Tyler.  Penguin Classics, 2002, 1,216 pages.

*The Tale of Genji* is often considered the world's first novel, due to its internal unity, psychological depiction, and vivid characterization.  The story follows the life, career, and loves of Genji, the Shining Prince, who was the son of a 9th-Century emperor.  It offers a fascinating look into aristocratic life at the time.  This edition is reader friendly with generous footnotes, character lists, and illustrations.  Penguin also has an abridged version of Tyler's translation.

**Kakuichi, Akashi** (d. 1371). Kakuichi was a blind monk who compiled *The Tale of the Heike*. The epic has no single author but rather developed over many years in a series of oral stories recited by traveling monks. Kakuichi's compilation, completed in 1371, became the most highly regarded version.

*The Tale of the Heike* (1371)
Translated by Helen McCullough. Stanford University Press, 1988, 504 pages.

This is the second great Japanese epic. This episodic tale is about the 12th-Century civil war between the rival Taira and Minamoto clans, which ended in the Taira victory in 1185. Primarily a samurai epic focusing on warrior culture, the central theme of the story is the Buddhist teaching on the impermanence of all things. This authoritative translation comes with extensive glossary, chronology, and helpful appendices that provide an overview of the story for Western readers.

**Bashō, Matsuo** (1644–1694). Japan's most revered poet, Bashō was the master of haiku. He made his living as a teacher, but renounced the urban life of literary circles. He was known to travel throughout the Japanese countryside to gain inspiration for his poetry and writings.

*Bashō: The Complete Haiku* (late 17th Century)
Translated by Jane Reichhold. Kodansha International, 2008, 432 pages.

This is the first compilation of all of Bashō's poems in English. In addition to her own artistic translations, Reichhold includes all of the poems in their original Japanese along with literal translations and notes so the reader can appreciate more deeply their literary quality. In addition she includes a biography of Bashō, a glossary, notes on each poem, a chronology, and an index to flesh out this beautiful volume.

*The Narrow Road to the Deep North and Other Travel Sketches* (later 17th Century)
Translated by Nobuyuki Yuasa. Penguin Classics, 1966, 167 pages.

Late in life, when he turned to Zen Buddhism, Bashō undertook a thousand-mile pilgrimage through Japan, traveling by horse and foot. In his travel sketches, which are filled with haiku, Bashō reflected on the awesomeness and beauty of nature. In reading these poetic travelogues, the reader is reminded that in life it is not the destination but the journey itself that matters. This edition includes five of his travelogues and comes with introduction and notes.

## MODERN LITERATURE

**Mori, Ogai** (1862–1922). Mori was Surgeon-General of the Japanese Army and a writer of the Meiji and Taisho eras. He studied the Confucian classics and European Literature. While serving in the army, he published his own literary journal (1889–94). The romantic realism of his novels is characterized by a strong humanist element.

*The Wild Geese* (1911–13)
Translated by Kingo Ochiai and Sanford Goldstein. Tuttle Publishing, 1989, 128 pages.

The lucid style of Ogai Mori's novella vividly recreates the exciting time of transition between the end of Japan's Meiji era and Japan's entry into the modern world. Mori deftly paints the characters of Otama, who has become a mistress to support her father, of Suezo the moneylender, and of the student Okada. As the narrator of this story of unfulfilled love gradually emerges as a character, the tale takes a surprising turn.

**Tanizaki, Junichiro** (1886–1965). Junichiro Tanizaki was a writer of novels, plays, and essays. His writing portrays love and family life in the context of the dramatic changes occurring in Japanese society in the 20th Century. Born in Tokyo, Tanizaki moved to Kyoto after the 1923 earthquake. He translated *The Tale of Genji* into modern Japanese.

*The Makioka Sisters* (1943–48)
Translated by Edward G. Seidensticker. Vintage, 1995, 544 pages.

Tanizaki's *A Light Snowfall*, published in English as *The Makioka Sisters*, is a detailed chronicle of the lives of four sisters from a wealthy Osaka family whose way of life erodes in the 1930s. In a decade marked by flood and war, Tsuruko clings to the past, Sachiko sacrifices herself for her younger sisters, Yukiko is bound by the vicissitudes of match-making, and Taeko openly rebels, each contributing to family cohesion or strife.

**Kawabata, Yasunari** (1899–1972). Novelist Yasunari Kawabata is celebrated for his simple prose style and for the psychological insight of his character depiction. Born in Osaka, Kawabata was raised by his grandparents after the early death of his parents. He graduated from Tokyo Imperial University in 1924 and won the Nobel Prize in 1968.

*Snow Country* (1933–7)
Translated by Edward G. Seidensticker. Vintage, 1996, 192 pages.

The author shows the changing relationship of geisha Komako and Tokyo dilettante Shimamura as reflected in the changing seasons at a mountain resort in western Japan. Through nuanced descriptions of a love that is doomed from the start, *Snow Country* depicts Shimamura's visits to the resort and the couple's search for love during spring, fall, and winter in the snowiest region on earth.

**Inoue, Yasushi** (1907–1991). Yasushi Inoue was a Japanese writer known for his historical novels depicting life in Ancient Japan and China. Born on Hokkaido Island, Inoue graduated from Kyoto Imperial University in 1936. He became a reporter, making his debut as a novelist in 1949. Inoue traveled to China on several occasions.

*The Samurai Banner of Furin Kazan* (1959)
Translated by Yokio Riley. Tuttle Publishing, 2005, 224 pages.

Yasushi Inoue's historical novel, written from the point of view of the samurai Kansuke, recounts the conflicts of Japan's Warring Era (1467–1573) when three warlords ruled Japan. As chief strategist and adviser to warlord Takeda Shingen, Kansuke is at the center of history as it unfolds. In his fateful role, Kansuke advises Takeda on his marriage as well as planning the final battle between Takeda and rival warlord Uesugi Kenshin.

Also read: *Shirobamba* (1962) and *Wind and Waves* (1963).

**Endo, Shusaku** (1923–1996). Shusaku Endo was a renowned Japanese writer whose work was deeply influenced by his Catholicism. Born in Tokyo, Endo grew up in Japanese-occupied Manchuria and in Kobe, Japan. Raised a Catholic, Endo studied French literature at the University of Lyon from 1950 to 1953 before returning to Japan.

*Silence* (1966)
Translated by William Johnston. Taplinger Publishing, 1980, 201 pages.

The silence of Japan's "Hidden Christians" and the silence of God are at the heart of Endo's compelling novel. In a letter by Father Rodriguez, the novel's main character, the Jesuit priest describes his arrival in Japan, his witnessing of the persecution of Japanese Christians, and his journey toward martyrdom. Endo's historical novel weaves together the fictional tale of Father Rodriguez with the historical apostasy of Father Ferreira.

**Abe, Kobo** (1924–1993). Kobo Abe is a Japanese writer whose works are often compared to those of Franz Kafka for their surreal settings, dark allegories, and theme of alienation. Born in Tokyo, Abe grew up in Manchuria, China. He earned a medical degree from Tokyo Imperial University in 1943, but turned to writing plays and novels.

*The Woman in the Dunes* (1962)
Translated by E. Dale Saunders. Vintage, 1991, 256 pages.

In this dark allegory, entomologist Niki Jumpei is kidnapped by the inhabitants of a remote seaside village and forced to join a captive woman in the Sisyphean task of digging sand. Removed from his familiar cultural environment and imprisoned in a hole in the sand dunes, Jumpei comes to know his basic self. Abe's strangely haunting novel combines psychological symbolism with suspense and sheer terror.

**Mishima, Yukio** (1925–1970). Yukio Mishima wrote novels, short stories, essays, and plays. Born into a samurai family, he was imbued with the samurai code of honor. He organized a private "army" of unarmed young men, and practiced body-building, karate, and kendo, becoming a kendo master. He committed *seppuku* (ritual suicide) in 1970.

*Spring Snow* (1968)
Translated by Michael Gallagher. Vintage, 1990, 400 pages.

The first novel in Mishima's tetralogy, *Spring Snow*, set in 1912 Tokyo, describes the social transformations of the Meiji Restoration, when the decline of the old aristocracy gave rise to a newly powerful social class. Enmeshed in these social changes and in their ambivalence towards the West, Mishima's characters act from conflicted motives. When Kiyoaki's indecision threatens his love for Satoku, a tragic outcome looms.

Also read: *The Sailor Who Fell from Grace with the Sea* (1963).

**Öe, Kenzaburo** (1935– ). Novelist and short story writer Kenzaburo Öe is one of Japan's most important post-World War II writers and the winner of the 1994 Nobel Prize in Literature. His work explores issues of social import, such as nuclear weapons, as well as his personal experience as the father of a mentally handicapped son.

*Teach Us to Outgrow Our Madness* (1977)
Translated by John Nathan. Grove Press, 1994, 261 pages.

Confronted by an upheaval in values in postwar Japan, the heroes of the four novellas in this collection seek equilibrium. "Teach Us to Outgrow Our Madness" describes the exclusive bond between a father and son. Öe mythologizes the past in "Prize Stock," and uses the supernatural to depict alienation in "Aghwee the Sky Monster." In "He Himself Shall Wipe My Tears Away," Öe breaches the boundary between physical illness and psychosis.

Also read: *Nip the Buds, Shoot the Kids* (1958) and *A Personal Matter* (1969).

**Murakami, Haruki** (1949– ). Haruki Murakami is the writer of accessible works of fiction that explore complex themes of identity from an existential perspective. Born in Kyoto, Murakami graduated from Waseda University in 1975, and lived abroad in Europe and the United States from 1986 to 1995 before returning to Japan.

*Kafka on the Shore* (2005)
Translated by Philip Gabriel. Vintage, 2005, 480 pages.

Haruki Murakami's warmth and affection for his characters is apparent even as he propels them into the terror of the unknown. In *Kafka on the Shore*, Murakami's narrative alternates between the story of Kafka Tamura, a 15-year-old runaway, and that of the mysteriously demented Nakata, who lives on a government "sub city" (subsidy) and talks to cats. Metaphysical questions and dim memories prefigure the resolution of the two storylines.

Also read: *Norwegian Wood* (1987) and *The Wind-up Bird Chronicle* (1997).

**Ishiguro, Kazuo** (1954– ). Kazuo Ishiguro is a British writer whose novels, set in both East and West, feature lucid first-person narratives that develop a deep exploration of character. Born in Nagasaki, Ishiguro moved to England in 1960. He graduated from the University of Kent in 1978. He won the 1989 Booker Prize for *The Remains of the Day*.

*When We Were Orphans* (2000)
Vintage, 2001, 362 pages.

Christopher Banks is a celebrated detective and the toast of London society, but his childhood in Shanghai, where his parents mysteriously disappeared, remains cloaked in obscurity. Returning to Shanghai during the Japanese occupation, Banks tries to solve the riddle of his loss amidst the dark labyrinths of a war-torn city and the twisted paths of his memory. Ishiguro's suspenseful novel delineates the journey toward self-acceptance.

Also read: *An Artist of the Floating World* (1986) and *The Remains of the Day* (1989).

# IV. The Middle East

The Middle East is a region that encompasses southwestern Asia and northeastern Africa. It includes Turkey to the north, Iran to the east, Egypt to the west, and the Arabian peninsula to the south. The Middle East has long been an area of conflict and war. Since the discovery of the region's vast reserves of crude oil, it has become an area of great strategic and economic importance. Most recently, the volatility of the Middle East has been fueled by the two Iraq Wars, the Israeli-Palestinian conflict, and the threat of Iran as a nuclear power.

The oldest civilizations in the world emerged in the Middle East, particularly in the Fertile Crescent in Mesopotamia and the Nile Valley in Egypt. In this booklist you can find the history and literature of this ancient period in the Antiquity section of Western History and Literature. The section you are reading focuses on the history of the Middle East since the rise of Islam in the 7th Century AD. The history books listed below thoroughly cover the history of the Middle East and its incessant struggles. The biographies include Muhammad, the founder of Islam, and two important political leaders of the late 20th Century, representing Israel and Egypt.

Middle Eastern literature has been composed primarily in Arabic and Persian. On the Arabian peninsula, a rich body of oral poetry was recorded in the 8th and 9th Centuries. The Muslims' holy book, the Qur'an, dominated written culture, resulting in the growth of disciplines used to interpret the Qur'an: grammar, law, history, and theology. After Muslim Arabic armies conquered Persia in 640 AD, Persian literature blended with Arabic writing and culture. The Persian Renaissance from 850 to 1258 AD gave rise to a Persian verse form, the *rubaiyat* (or quatrain), to humanistic philosophy, and to mystical poetry. In the 10th Century, the Persian philosopher Alfarabi wrote on Plato and Aristotle, and Omar Khayyam, a Persian scientist, composed *The Rubaiyat*. In the 11th Century, Persian philosopher Al-Ghazali encouraged the growth of Sufism, a mystical branch of Islam that permeates Persian poetry. In the 12th and 13th Centuries, Persian poets Attar and Rumi wrote in the Sufi tradition. After the sack of Baghdad by the Mongols in 1258 AD, Arabic literature declined. However, a classic of Arabic literature, *One Thousand and One Nights* was composed during the Mongol era.

The modern literature of the Middle East emerged in response to the events of modern history. From Napoleon's Egyptian campaign of 1798 to colonization by the British Empire, the Middle East felt the power of the West. Yet the 20th Century was a period of cultural renewal. In 1923, Syrian Khalil Gibran published the international bestseller *The Prophet*, a book of Christian wisdom. In Egypt, Nobel Prize winner Naguib Mahfouz emerged as the foremost novelist in the Arabic language. Egyptian Edwar Al-Kharrat, a Coptic Christian, wrote novellas about his heritage. Yusuf Idris (Egypt) and Zakaria Tamer (Syria) crafted fiction reflecting the social changes of the times.

After the biblical era, Hebrew literature all but vanished, but with the establishment of Israel as a Jewish state in 1947, Hebrew literature was reborn. Amos Oz, perhaps the foremost Israeli author, has written numerous works of fiction and non-fiction in Hebrew. Contemporary Israeli and Arabic writers have also turned to fiction to understand Israel's ongoing political strife. Israeli novelists David Grossman and A. B. Yehoshua inquire into Israeli politics and identity, while writers Ghassan Kanafani and Elias Khoury explore the Palestinian experience.

## HISTORY

Hopkins, T. C. F. *Empires, Wars, and Battles: The Middle East from Antiquity to the Rise of the New World*
Forge Books, 2008, 256 pages.

This is a short but detailed history of the Middle East from the ancient Mesopotamian world to the late 17th Century when the Ottoman Empire began its decline. Hopkins offers a fast-paced chronicle of the rise and fall of civilizations in the region, culminating in the 500-year conflict between the Christian Byzantines and Ottoman Turks. This book goes a long way to explain the very old rivalries and hostilities that have plagued the region for millennia.

Lewis, Bernard. *The Middle East: A Brief History of the Last 2,000 Years*
Simon & Schuster, 1997, 448 pages.

Lewis, the erudite emeritus professor at Princeton, is the dean of Middle East historians. In this well-crafted history, he explains the myriad forces that shaped the region over the centuries, following its political, social, economic, and cultural developments. The first third of the book surveys 2000 years of history while the rest examines significant topics related to Islamic culture, the challenges of modernity, and the various struggles between Islam and the West.

Robinson, Francis, Editor. *Cambridge Illustrated History of the Islamic World*
Cambridge University Press, 1999 (1996), 352 pages.

This is a beautifully illustrated history of Islamic civilization written by a team of scholars. The first half covers the history of Islam from its origins in the 7th Century up through the 20th Century. The second half discusses the social and economic order of expanding Islamic societies and their intellectual and cultural traditions. Throughout the emphasis is placed on the relation between Islam and the West. Includes a timeline of rulers, glossary, and annotated bibliography.

Viorst, Milton. *Storm from the East: The Struggle Between the Arab World and the Christian West*
Random House (Modern Library Chronicles), 2007, 224 pages.

A journalist and scholar, Viorst is the *New Yorker's* Middle East correspondent. In this lucid, compact book he explores the historical roots of the age-old conflict between the Islamic Middle East and the Christian West. Over five chronologically ordered chapters, he explains the sources of Arab nationalism and its resistance to Western hegemony that he believes is at the heart of the current unrest throughout the region. This is essential reading for anyone seeking to understand the conflict.

## BIOGRAPHY

Lings, Martin. *Muhammad: His Life Based on the Earliest Sources* (570–632 AD)
Inner Traditions International, rev. ed., 2006 (1987), 384 pages.

A British scholar of Arabic and convert to Islam, Lings presents the life of Muhammad from the perspective of reverence based on traditional Muslim sources. He covers Muhammad's life and teachings in an absorbing narrative that makes a good introduction to Islam as well. Those seeking a historical-critical treatment of the prophet might turn to other scholars like Robert Spencer or Paul Fregosi, whose works look at the dark side of Muhammad and Islam.

Finklestone, Jos. *Anwar Sadat: Visionary Who Dared* (1918–1981)
Routledge, 1996, 298 pages.

One of the great statesmen of the modern era, Anwar Sadat gave his life in the cause of peace in the Middle East. In this very readable study, Finklestone, a foreign affairs journalist, traces Sadat's political career from fanatical nationalist to Nasser's successor as the president of Egypt, serving from 1970 to his assassination in 1981. This is a sympathetic portrait of Sadat's life and achievements, which included the 1978 Nobel Peace Prize.

Bar-Zohar, Michael. *Shimon Peres: The Biography* (1923– )
Random House, 2007, 576 pages.

Shimon Peres has been at the center of Israeli politics for 60 years, having twice been elected prime minister and currently serving as Israel's president. The author, a former Knesset member, provides a richly textured portrait of this enigmatic and controversial statesman and Nobel Peace Prize winner, from his birth in Poland in 1923 to his second term as prime minister that ended in 1996. This is required reading for anyone interested in the history of modern Israel.

## MEDIEVAL LITERATURE

**Abdel Haleem, M. A. S.,** Translator. *The Qur'an* (610–632 AD)
Oxford World's Classics, 2008, 502 pages.

The Qur'an is believed by Muslims to be the word of God revealed to the prophet Muhammad. As the supreme authority of Islam, the Qur'an establishes its creed, rituals, ethics, and law. This new modern translation is easy to read yet remains faithful to the original Arabic. It comes with sufficient footnotes and commentary to help the reader understand the structure and meaning of the text. Haleem also provides an introduction that traces the history of the Qur'an and examines its stylistic features and problems of interpretation.

**Alfārābī** (c. 872–950 AD).  Abū Naṣr al-Fārābī, known in the West as Alfarabi (al-Fārābī), was a Muslim scientist and philosopher from Persia.  Little is known of his early life, but in 901 AD he moved to Baghdad to pursue higher studies.  He remained there for over 40 years, acquiring a mastery of many languages and fields of knowledge.  In his time, the Arabs called Alfarabi "the Second Master," because they regarded him as the greatest philosopher after Aristotle.

*Philosophy of Plato and Aristotle* (early 10th Century)
Translated by Muhsin Mahdi.  Cornell University Press, rev. ed., 2002, 158 pages.

Alfarabi was the first philosopher to attempt to harmonize Greek philosophy with Islam.  Known primarily for his political philosophy, he was the first to introduce Plato and Aristotle to the Muslim world.  This updated edition of Alfarabi's commentaries on Plato and Aristotle also includes *The Attainment of Happiness*.  Together they provide a philosophical foundation for understanding his political works.  The translator's introduction explicates his life and thought.

*The Political Writings* (early 10th Century)
Translated by Charles E. Butterworth.  Cornell University Press, 2004, 296 pages.

This collection includes four of Alfarabi's most important texts: *Selected Aphorisms*, *Enumeration of the Sciences*, *Book of Religion*, and *The Harmonization of the Two Opinions of the Two Sages: Plato the Divine and Aristotle*.  Butterworth's preface puts the essays in their historical, literary, and philosophical context.  A glossary and an index are also provided.

**Khayyam, Omar** (1048–1122).  The Persian philosopher, mathematician, and astronomer, Omar Khayyam, is known mostly for his poetry.  He wrote about 1,000 four-line verses or quatrains (*rubaiyaas*).  The 19th-Century British poet Edward Fitzgerald made Khayyam the most famous poet in the East by issuing five editions of his quatrains in free-wheeling English translation.

*The Rubaiyat* (earliest manuscript: 1460)
In *The Quatrains of Omar Khayyam: Three Translations of the Rubaiyat*
Translated by Edward Fitzgerald, Justin McCarthy, and Richard Le Gallienne.  Bardic Press, 2005, 212 pages.
This edition of Omar Khayyam's quatrains contains three different translations of the poems by three 19th-Century translators, which allows the reader to appreciate the range of interpretation.  Fitzgerald's classic, creative translation is accompanied by a literal prose translation by Justin McCarthy and a more poetic version by Richard LeGallienne.

**Al-Ghazālī** (1058–1111). Regarded as Islam's St. Augustine, Al-Ghazali was the Persian philosopher, theologian, and mystic who contributed greatly to the development of Sufism and its integration into mainstream Islam. He is considered one of the greatest scholars in the history of Islamic thought.

*The Alchemy of Happiness* (1097)
Dodo Press, 2008, 82 pages.

*The Alchemy of Happiness* is a brief version, written in Persian, of Al-Ghazali's much longer *The Revival of Religious Sciences*, and is considered a great work of mystical literature. See also his autobiography, entitled *The Deliverance from Error*, and another major (though rather abstruse) work, *The Incoherence of the Philosophers*, where he attempts to demonstrate the feebleness and vanity of philosophy and its unsuitability as a replacement for revelation.

**Averroes (Ibn Rushd)** (1126–1198). Born in Cordova, Spain, Averroes was the Islamic philosopher and polymath whose commentaries on Aristotle had a profound impact on Christian thinkers. Averroism, a reconciliation of Aristotelianism with Islamic faith, has been regarded as a precursor to modern secularism. His most important philosophical work was *The Incoherence of the Incoherence*, which attacked Al-Ghazali's claims in *The Incoherence of the Philosophers*.

*Decisive Treatise and Epistle Dedicatory* (1180)
Translated by Charles E. Butterworth. Brigham Young University Press, 2002, 170 pages.

The *Decisive Treatise*, written sometime before 1,180, is the major text where Averroes attempts to reconcile faith with reason and science against the attack of Al-Ghazali, who believed any such attempt was a violation of Islamic faith. Averroes claimed that philosophy is not forbidden by the Qur'an, but is in fact commanded.

**Attār (Farīd ud-Dīn)** (c. 1142–1220). Attar was a Persian Sufi master known for his masterpiece *The Conference of Birds*. He was a pharmacist by profession, which he eventually abandoned to travel widely, meeting Sufis and promoting Sufi ideas. He took the pen-name Attar, which means "druggist."

*The Conference of Birds* (1177)
Translated by Afkham Darbandi and Dick Davis. Penguin Classics, 1984, 234 pages.

This 4,500-line mystical poem—an epic allegory of the seeker's journey to God—is considered a classic of Islamic spirituality and Persian literature. The essential theme of the poem is that the road of life is hard and long, and that ultimate happiness can be achieved only through divine love. As a collection of tales detailing a spiritual pilgrimage, the poem captures the heart of Sufism much as Dante and Milton did for Christianity.

**Rūmī, Jalāl al-Dīn Muhammad** (1207–1273). Greatly influenced by Attar, Rumi is the most famous Sufi poet of all. Besides being a Persian poet, he was also an Islamic jurist, theologian, and mystic. Rumi is a descriptive name meaning "the Roman," since he lived most of his life in the area of Anatolia called Rūm because it was once ruled by the Byzantine Empire.

*Essential Rumi*
Translated by Coleman Barks. HarperCollins, 1997, 310 pages.

*The Soul of Rumi: A New Collection of Ecstatic Poems*
Translated by Coleman Barks. HarperOne, 2002, 448 pages.

Rumi has become the best-selling poet in America today, thanks largely to the work of Coleman Barks who has translated Rumi in numerous volumes. These two collections are excellent introductions to Rumi's inspirational love poetry. Like all Sufi poetry, Rumi focuses on the ecstatic experience where human and divine love meet.

**Haddawy, Husain,** Translator. *The Arabian Nights* and *The Arabian Nights II* (2 Volumes)
W. W. Norton, 1995 & 1996, 464 & 266 pages.

*One Thousand and One Nights* is a collection of medieval stories, many with ancient roots, which are all framed by the initial story of the Persian ruler, Shahrayar, and one of his wives, Shahrazad, who prevents her execution—the fate of all the king's previous wives—by keeping him entertained with endless stories. Some of the best known are "Aladdin's Wonderful Lamp," "Ali Baba and the Forty Thieves," and "The Seven Voyages of Sinbad the Sailor." These three are contained in the second collection of these wondrous stories that delight young and old alike.

## Modern Literature

**Gibran, Khalil** (1883–1931). Best-selling poet Khalil Gibran is known for his writings on spiritual love and other Christian themes. Born into a Christian Marionite family in modern day Lebanon, Gibran emigrated to the United States in 1894. He received formal schooling in the U.S. and later studied in Syria. Gibran was an artist as well as a poet.

*The Prophet* (1923)
Knopf, 1973, 107 pages.

As the prophet Al-mustafa prepares to depart from a foreign city, the people gather to ask him questions. Gibran relates the prophet's aphorisms in 26 poetic essays covering such topics as beauty, children, giving, self-knowledge, and work. Gibran's *The Prophet*, which draws on wellsprings of wisdom from all faiths, has sold over six million copies worldwide since the book was first published in 1923.

Also read: *Love Letters in the Sand: the Love Poems of Khalil Gibran* (1926).

**Mahfouz, Naguib** (1911–2006). Egyptian novelist Naguib Mahfouz was among the first writers of modern Arabic literature, and was the first Arab writer to win the Nobel Prize for Literature. Born to a Muslim family in Cairo, Mahfouz graduated from the University of Cairo in 1934 and worked in journalism and government before becoming a writer.

*Palace Walk* (1956)
Translated by William Hutchins and Olivia Kenny. Anchor, 1990, 512 pages.

The first volume of Mahfouz's *Cairo Trilogy* introduces the Muslim family of al-Sayyid Ahmad, a middle class merchant, describing their lives in Cairo during Egypt's occupation by the British in the early 1900s. This absorbing saga focuses on Egyptian middle-class morality and culture, and develops the themes of authoritarianism and authority in private and public life. Mahfouz's distinctive characters are expertly drawn.

Also read: *Palace of Desire* (1957) and *Sugar Street* (1957).

**Al-Kharrat, Edwar** (1926– ). Edwar al-Kharrat is an Egyptian novelist who has developed the themes of identity formation and ethnic conflict in novels suffused with lyricism. Born to a Coptic Christian family in Alexandria, he became his family's sole breadwinner at 17 and graduated in law from Alexandria University in 1946.

*City of Saffron* (1986)
Translated by Frances Liardet. Quartet Books, 1998, 174 pages.

Edwar al-Kharrat admonishes readers that his writings are not autobiography, but "clouds of memories which should have taken place." This story of a Coptic Christian boy growing up in Alexandria of the 1930s and 40s interweaves the author's heritage with that of Arabic culture in Egypt and Western literary influences. Al-Kharrat tells an absorbing coming-of-age story in a language rich in symbol and metaphor.

Also read: *Girls of Alexandria* (1993) and *Stones of Bobello* (2005).

**Idris, Yusuf** (1927–1991). Yusuf Idris is widely recognized as the master of the Arabic short story. Born in a village in Egypt's Delta, he became a doctor and a public-health inspector. Idris was impelled to write by his belief that the Egyptian stories of his day did not reflect his experience. In addition to leaving a legacy for Arabic writers, he has been translated into several languages.

*The Sinners* (1959)
Translated by Kristen Peterson-Ishaq. L. Rienner Publishers, 1995, 118 pages.

*The Sinners*, set on a cotton estate in the Egyptian Delta before the 1952 revolution, relates the tale of Aziza, a seasonal worker and the mother of an illegitimate child. Idris addresses the plight of Aziza, who lives a marginal existence due to her economic and social status, in a story rich in local color and distinctive Egyptian characters.

Also read: *The Cheapest Nights* (1954) and *The City of Love and Ashes* (1956).

**Tamer, Zakaria** (1931– ). Tamer is a renowned master of the Arabic short story. Born in Damascus, Tamer left school at 13 and worked as a locksmith to support his family. His first collection of colorful, allegorical stories won him fame in 1957. Fired from his editing job in 1980 for writing against tyranny, Tamer immigrated to Britain.

*The Hedgehog* (2005)
Translated by Denys Johnson-Davies. American University in Cairo Press, 2009, 208 pages.

This collection of stories (by Zakaria Tamer) includes the novella "Hedgehog" and 24 very short stories previously published in *Tigers on the Tenth Day*. In his tightly controlled novella, "The Hedgehog," Tamer presents the world from the child's-eye-view of his five-year-old narrator. Tamer's simply told short stories are fables and parables by a renowned children's author here writing for adults.

Also read: *Breaking Knees* (2002).

**Kanafani, Ghassan** (1932–1978). Kanafani, one of Palestine's leading prose writers, published five novels, five short story collections, and several studies of Palestinian literature. Born in Palestine, he worked as a journalist and teacher in Damascus. A political activist, Kanafani was killed by a car-bomb in Beirut.

*Men in the Sun and Other Palestinian Stories* (1956)
Translated by Hilary Kilpatrick. L. Rienner Publishers, 1998, 117 pages.

This collection, widely acknowledged as Kanafani's masterpiece, includes the novella "Men in the Sun" and five additional stories set in Palestine. Kanafani's depiction of the complex social and political reality of the Palestinians is animated by his mastery of modernist literary techniques, subtle shifts in point of view, and deft characterization.

**Oz, Amos** (1939– ). Amos Oz is an Israeli writer of fiction and nonfiction and a professor of literature at Ben-Gurion University. Born and raised in Jerusalem, the author joined a kibbutz at age 15 and changed his surname to "Oz," Hebrew for strength. He studied at Hebrew University in Jerusalem and published his first stories in the 1960s.

Oz, Amos. *A Perfect Peace* (1982)
Translated by Hillel Halkin. Harvest Books, 1993, 384 pages.

A perfect peace eludes a diverse array of characters in Amos Oz's richly lyrical novel of Israeli life. Set on a kibbutz in 1965, Oz's novel insightfully portrays Jewish settlers and their children. Conflict between generations comes to a head when the disaffected Yonatan, 26, leaves the kibbutz where his father is secretary. Oz shows the clash between the idealistic founders and the practical second generation in Israeli society.

Also read: *My Michael* (1968), *Black Box* (1987), and *To Know a Woman* (1989).

**Khoury, Elias** (1948– ). Elias Khoury, a Lebanese novelist and playwright, is acknowledged as one of the leading contemporary Arabic writers. Born in Beirut, Khoury studied sociology at the Lebanese University and in Paris. A youthful supporter of the PLO, Khoury left militant politics to become a writer, newspaper publisher, and editor.

*Gate of the Sun* (1998)
Translated by Humphrey Davies. Picador, 2007, 544 pages.

Just as Shahrazad tells stories to save her life in *One Thousand and One Nights*, so Dr. Khalil, narrator of *Gate of the Sun*, tells stories to save the life of a comatose patient, veteran soldier Yunes. Khalil's stories—comic tales, tales of love, and tales of tragedy—comprise an epic of the Palestinian people. Presenting storytelling as an ambiguous exercise, Khoury evokes memory: "the process of organizing what to forget."

Also read: *The Little Mountain* (1977) and *The Kingdom of Strangers* (1993).

**Pamuk, Orhan** (1952– ). Orhan Pamuk is a Turkish writer and winner of the 2006 Nobel Prize in Literature for his novels exploring the encounter between Islamic and Western culture in Turkey. Born in Istanbul, Pamuk studied architecture and journalism, graduating from the University of Istanbul in 1977. He teaches at Columbia University.

*Snow* (2002)
Translated by Maureen Freely. Vintage, 2005, 480 pages.

When a snowstorm seals off the Turkish city Kars, visiting poet Ka finds himself swept up in a maelstrom of personal emotions and political turmoil as he investigates a wave of suicides among Turkish girls forbidden to wear headscarves to school. Ka's encounter with Islamic radicals and with fomenters of a military coup proves disruptive; at the same time, his search for God and his creative breakthrough introduce him to universal order.

Also read: *The Black Book* (1990) and *My Name is Red* (1998).

**Grossman, David** (1954– ). David Grossman is an Israeli author of novels, stories, nonfiction, and children's books. Born in Jerusalem, Grossman graduated from Hebrew University in 1979 and worked as a correspondent and radio actor before publishing his first book of stories. His *The Yellow Wind* is a study of the West Bank and the Gaza Strip.

*The Smile of the Lamb* (1983)
Translated by Betsy Rosenberg. Picador, 1990, 325 pages.

*The Smile of the Lamb* explores the blurring of truth and falsehood in a land beset by conflict. Though Grossman's narrative shifts back and forth between the four main characters, the story centers upon Uri, an Israeli soldier stationed in a small Palestinian village, and his friendship with Palestinian storyteller Khilmi. As Khilmi's stories become allegories for the violence of occupation, Uri seeks to understand the ambiguities of citizenship, marriage, and friendship.

Also read: *The Yellow Wind* (1988) and *See Under: Love* (1989).

**Yehoshua, A. B.** (1956– ). A. B. Yehoshua is a leading Israeli writer. A representative of Israel's "new wave" generation, he uses an array of narrative methods to examine Israeli identity and politics. Born in Haifa, Yehoshua studied at Hebrew University and taught in Paris from 1963 to 1967. He is a professor of literature at Haifa University.

*A Woman in Jerusalem* (2004)
Translated by Hillel Halkin. Harvest Books, 2007, 256 pages.

Assigned to identify the victim of a suicide bomb, a human resources manager ponders the woman's computer image, unable to recall an employee others considered beautiful. Impelled to affirm the victim's humanity, the manager fights red tape and media hacks, embarking on a pilgrimage to return the woman's body to her birthplace in a former Soviet republic. This artfully told tale traces a man's spiritual journey from apathy to moral engagement.

Also read: *The Lover* (1997) and *A Journey to the End of the Millennium* (1998).

# V. Africa

Africa is widely regarded by scientists to be where human beings originated. Fossil remains of homo sapiens dated to roughly 200,000 years ago have been found in Ethiopia. Throughout its pre-history Africa was inhabited by tribes of hunter-gatherers. By 5000 BC populations trekked out of the desert regions into the Nile Valley, where permanent settlements were established. Africa's historical record begins around 3300 BC in ancient Egypt, where the pharaohs ruled for almost three millennia. Over a period of a few hundred years, Egypt was conquered by the Persians, the Greeks, and finally the Romans (in 30 BC), whose empire included all of North Africa until its collapse in the 5th Century AD. By the 4th Century AD Christianity had pervaded the Roman Empire, but Christianity was supplanted by Islam in North Africa in the 7th Century.

Africa south of the Sahara was comprised of thousands of local kingdoms and tribes through the 8th Century AD. By the 9th Century a string of dynastic states began to appear in central Africa. In the 15th Century the vastness of the continent was discovered by Portuguese voyagers. The Atlantic slave trade that followed competed with the longer-lasting Arab slave trade. In the early 19th Century the decline of the slave trade caused West African states to adopt new economies, bringing about the rise of legitimate commerce but also paving the way for European colonization. By the late 19th Century, Europe had colonized most of the continent in a competitive effort to secure natural resources. Since the end of World War II, all colonial states have obtained independence. Today Africa consists of 53 independent nations, many rich in natural resources but also hampered by political and economic instability, poverty, and violence.

The two history books listed below are excellent surveys of the continent's storied past. The biographies include two heroes from South Africa, Nelson Mandela and Desmond Tutu, Nigeria's favorite son, Chinua Achebe, and the Leakey family, who discovered the evidence for human origins in Africa.

Because Africa is such a vast and diverse region, it is more accurate to refer to the literatures of Africa than to African literature. This section of the booklist lists books from south of the Sahara. North African literature is culturally Arabic and can be found in the previous section, The Middle East. Africa has a rich tradition of modern literature written in African languages and also written in English, French, and Portuguese, due to the long-term impact of colonization by those countries. Because literature in African languages and French and Portuguese is largely unavailable in English, most of the literature listed here comes from English-speaking former British colonies, notably Nigeria and South Africa.

Amos Tutuola's *The Palm-Wine Drinkard* (1952) was one of the first works of African literature in English to gain international recognition, inspiring the work of other African writers. As most African nations gained independence in the 1950s and 60s, African literature developed rich traditions in poetry, drama, and the novel. Chinua Achebe's *Things Fall Apart* (1958), describing the clash between tribal and modern ways, introduced Achebe to an international audience. In 1986, Nigerian writer Wole Soyinka won the Nobel Prize in literature.

Modern African writers have focused on political issues such as the legacy of colonialism, apartheid in South Africa, and class and gender in African society. White African Nadine Gordimer and Afrikaner J. M. Coetzee used fiction to attack apartheid, detailing the human costs of racial segregation. Sembène Ousmane's *God's Bits of Wood* describes a railroad workers' strike in Sénégal. Nigerian novelists Buchi Emecheta and Ben Okri treat social themes such as inequality and the changing role of women in modern Africa.

## HISTORY

Collins, Robert O. *Africa: A Short History*
Markus Wiener Publishers, 2006, 250 pages.

This is a straightforward history of Africa that does not get bogged down in details. Collins's concise and elegant narrative takes the reader from the dawn of humankind to the present. He covers the evolution of African societies into kingdoms, the entrance of Christianity and Islam, migrations, the slave trade, European colonization, and the nationalist movements for independence. Collins ends with an account of the struggles of Africans in recent years.

Oliver, Roland and J. D. Fage. *A Short History of Africa*
Penguin, 6th ed., 1990 (1962), 336 pages.

Here is a full survey of African history that covers all the regions of this vast continent. The authors recite the political, economic, and religious developments from pre-history to the 1970s. Much attention is given to the period of European colonization and subsequent independence movements. Though it needs to be updated to cover the last three decades, this is an excellent primer for those seeking a comprehensive but accessible overview.

## BIOGRAPHY

Morell, Virginia. *Ancestral Passions: The Leakey Family and the Quest for Humankind's Beginnings* (Louis Leakey: 1903–1972; Mary Leakey: 1913–1996; Richard Leakey: 1944– )
Touchstone, 1996, 640 pages.

The legendary Leakey family contributed more than anyone else to our understanding of human origins. Louis Leakey, a native of Kenya, his wife Mary, and their son Richard were the pioneer paleoanthropologists whose painstaking fossil discoveries and theories brought to light human evolutionary development in Africa. Morell, a science writer, documents their many scientific achievements while candidly exposing their personal travails as well.

Mandela, Nelson. *Long Walk to Freedom: The Autobiography of Nelson Mandela* (1918– )
Holt McDougal, 2000 (1994), 507 pages.

The celebrated anti-apartheid activist and recipient of the 1993 Nobel Peace Prize wrote much of his memoir secretly during his 27 years in prison. It is a heart-wrenching story that details his childhood, his practice as a lawyer, his struggles as a freedom fighter, and his time in prison. It ends with his election as president of South Africa in 1994. This is an inspiring story about the power of the human spirit to overcome adversity.

Ezenwa-Ohaeto. *Chinua Achebe* (1930– )
Indiana University Press, 1997, 352 pages.

The renowned Nigerian writer is best known for his celebrated novel *Things Fall Apart* (1958), the most widely read work of modern African literature. The author, a former student of Achebe's, respectfully chronicles all aspects of his life from his birth in 1930 up to 1993. He describes Achebe's support for human rights, his role in Nigeria's tangled political history, his vast literary contributions, and his work as a professor of African literature.

Allen, John. *Desmond Tutu: Rabble-Rouser for Peace, The Authorized Biography* (1931– )
Lawrence Hill Books, 2008, 496 pages.

Desmond Tutu is the Anglican archbishop and activist whose fight against apartheid in his native South Africa in the 1980s led to his world-wide fame and his receiving the Nobel Peace Prize in 1984. This engaging, well-researched biography by a longtime associate captures Tutu's spiritual worldview, passion, courage, and towering moral stature. It's also a behind-the-scenes look at South Africa's long struggle for human rights as it underwent the transition to democracy.

## MODERN LITERATURE

**Lessing, Doris** (1919– ). Nobel Prize winner Doris Lessing is a British writer who spent her childhood in Rhodesia (Zimbabwe), but whose opposition to apartheid caused her to be banned from Rhodesia and South Africa for several years. She studied at the Dominican Convent High School in Salisbury, but left at age 14 and became self-educated.

*The Grass is Singing* (1950)
Harper Perennial, 2008, 272 pages.

Doris Lessing's darkly drawn portrait of white farmers in British Rhodesia examines the interdependence of a solitary farming couple and their black laborers. The conflicted relationship of farm wife, Mary Turner, and enigmatic black house servant, Moses, embodies the arrogant intolerance, on the one hand, and the explosive frustration, on the other, of the colonists and the colonized in 1940s southern Africa.

**Tutuola, Amos** (1920–1997). Tutuola was a Nigerian writer known for his stories and novels based on West African folklore. Born in Abeokuta, Tutuola left school after sixth grade and worked as a blacksmith. He was a metalworker for the Royal Air Force during World War II. His first novel, *The Palm-Wine Drinkard*, created an international sensation.

*The Palm-Wine Drinkard* (1952)
Grove Press, 1993, 256 pages.

This novel, featuring stories from West African folklore written in a naïve, simple style, was the first novel to be published by a Nigerian writer. Warmly praised by American and English reviewers, the novel was controversial in Nigeria due to its reliance on oral tradition. Tutuola describes the spiritual odyssey of a practiced palm-wine drinker through what Dylan Thomas has called "a nightmare of indescribable adventures."
Also read: *My Life in the Bush of Ghosts* (1954).

**Ousmane, Sembène** (1923–2007). Sembène Ousmane was a Sénégalese writer of Francophone literature. Educated in Arabic and French, Ousmane worked as a plumber and bricklayer in Dakar. Ousmane fought for the Free French Forces in World War II, and worked as a docker in Marseilles. His novels of African society are written in French.

*God's Bits of Wood* (1960)
Translated by Francis Price. Heinemann, 1996, 256 pages.

This novel depicts the 1947–48 railroad strike in Sénégal, a nationwide event that transformed the French colony. Ousmane's story takes place in three locations—Bamako, Thiès, and Dakar—and pits French manager Dejean against Bakayoko, the strike leader. The women's four-day march from Thiès to Dakar is the climactic event of the novel, showing the transformation of the indigenous people from resignation to assertion.
Also read: *Xala* (1973).

**Gordimer, Nadine** (1923– ). Nadine Gordimer is a South African writer and political activist whose novels explore ethical and racial issues from apartheid to immigration. Born in Spring Guateng, Gordimer was educated at a Catholic convent school and studied at Witwatersrand University. She won the Nobel Prize for Literature in 1991.

*Burger's Daughter* (1979)
Penguin, 1980, 368 pages.

Haunted by her father's legacy of political engagement, Rosa wavers between emulating his devotion to social justice and finding her identity. Gordimer's evocative prose captures the sensory pleasures of the South of France to which Rosa escapes, brilliantly contrasting Provence and urban Europe with Rosa's conflict-ridden home in South Africa. This novel reveals both the need for political involvement and its human cost.
Also read: *The Conservationist* (1974) and *July's People* (1981).

**Achebe, Chinua** (1930– ). Chinua Achebe is a Nigerian writer whose novels chronicle changes in Nigeria from the tribal traditions of the Igbo to colonial and post-colonial Nigeria. Born in southeastern Nigeria, Achebe worked for the Nigerian Broadcasting Service in Lagos. In 1967, Achebe served as ambassador of newly independent Biafra.

*Things Fall Apart* (1958)
Anchor, 1994, 224 pages.

Achebe's masterpiece, written in a simple prose reflecting Igbo oral tradition, tells the story of Okonkwo, strongman of his native village, Umuofia. The self-made Okonkwo, driven by the fear that he will turn out like his easygoing, feckless father, suffers a rude awakening when tribal values clash with British colonialism. In this novel with a plot reminiscent of Greek tragedy, Okonkwo's fall results from his character as well as from outside forces.

Also read: *No Longer at Ease* (1960) and *A Man of the People* (1966).

**Fugard, Athol** (1932– ). Athol Fugard is a South African dramatist, director, and actor whose plays address the political and philosophical questions posed by apartheid. Born in Middelburg to Afrikaner and English parents, Fugard worked on a steamer in Asia and as a courtroom clerk in Johannesburg. He currently teaches playwriting at UC San Diego.

*Master Harold. . . and the Boys* (1982)
Penguin, 1984, 64 pages.

Black waiters Willie and Sam are Master Harold's second family: employed by his father, they offer Harold the companionship and support he is missing due to his father's alcoholism. This powerful three-person play explores the relationship of 17-year-old Harold to the two men, allowing the audience to draw conclusions about the political implications of a world in which the boy is "master" and the men are "the boys."

Also read: *The Blood Knot* (1961) and *A Lesson from Aloes* (1978).

**Soyinka, Wole** (1934– ). Soyinka is a Nigerian playwright, poet, and essayist. Born to a Yoruba family in Abeokuta, he graduated from the University of Leeds in 1957 and taught in Nigeria. During the Nigerian Civil War he was imprisoned for trying to broker peace. A critic of political tyranny, Soyinka won the Nobel Prize for Literature in 1986.

*The Lion and the Jewel* (first performed 1959)
Oxford University Press, 1966, 72 pages.

*The Lion and the Jewel* portrays traditional African courtship in collision with European etiquette and mores. Wole Soyinka's comedy dramatizes the plight of tribesman Baroka, called "the Lion," who spars with modern man Lakunle over the right to marry Sidi, the jewel of the village. Lakunle, who struggles to modernize his community and change its conventions, is up against the manly charms and tribal street smarts of Baroka.

Also read: *The Bacchae of Euripides: A Communion Rite* (first performed 1972) and *Death and the King's Horseman* (first performed 1987).

**Coetzee, J. M.** (1940– ). J. M. Coetzee, winner of the 2003 Nobel Prize, is a writer whose densely metaphorical, character-driven novels describe the impact of apartheid on South Africa. Born in Cape Town, Coetzee graduated from the University of Cape Town with degrees in English and math. In 2006 he became an Australian citizen.

*Age of Iron* (1990)
Penguin, 1998, 208 pages.

Late in life, a former Cape Town professor, Mrs. Curren, bears witness to the evils of apartheid by recording her insights in a series of letters to her daughter. Mrs. Curren, who has always opposed apartheid, relinquishes her protected status by chronicling the murder of her housekeeper's son, the burning of a black township, and the rise of black militancy. The novel prophesizes a reign of justice in South Africa out of the crucible of racial turmoil.

Also read: *Waiting for the Barbarians* (1980) and *Foe* (1986).

**Emecheta, Buchi** (1944– ). Buchi Emecheta is a Nigerian writer whose novels describe women's changing roles in urban Nigeria. Born in Lagos, Emecheta was married at 16 and moved to London with her husband, bearing him five children. Emecheta earned a B.S. in sociology from University of London in 1972, and a Ph.D. in 1991.

*The Joys of Motherhood* (1979)
George Braziller, 1980, 224 pages.

The title of Buchi Emecheta's book is ironic: Nnu Ego's devotion to her children follows a first marriage that fails because of her supposed barrenness. Set in Lagos, Nigeria, Nnu Ego's story is that of a young Igbo woman sent to the primarily Yoruba capital to marry a man she has never seen. Emecheta's account of a young woman's struggles in 1950s Lagos treats the themes of polygamy, motherhood, and female independence in Nigeria.

Also read: *Second Class Citizen* (1974) and *The Bride Price* (1976).

**Okri, Ben** (1959– ). Ben Okri is a Nigerian writer whose realistic and postmodern novels reflect the social concerns of the "first generation" of Nigerian writers. Born in Nigeria, Okri spent his childhood in London and studied at the University of Essex. He won the 1991 Booker Prize for his tale of Nigeria in transition, *The Famished Road.*

*The Famished Road* (1991)
Anchor, 1993, 512 pages.

Azaro, the narrator of Ben Okri's novel of magic realism, is a spirit child who travels between the world of the living and the world of the dead. While Azaro's father tries to escape the limitations and injustices of life in a small, Third World village by adopting different vocations, Azaro feels the pull of the spirit world and its release from suffering and toil. Okri blends detailed realism with Yoruba lore in this tale of life and death.

Also read: *Songs of Enchantment* (1993).

# VI. Latin America

Latin America includes South America, Central America, Mexico, and the Caribbean. This region is called Latin America because Spanish, Portuguese, and French—the romance languages derived from Latin—are the primary languages spoken there.

It is believed the Americas were first inhabited by people who migrated from Asia over the Bering Land Bridge that formed during the last Ice Age. Over millennia they spread throughout the Western Hemisphere and became the Native American peoples. The most advanced civilizations that developed were the Aztecs of Mexico, the Maya of southern Mexico and Central America, and the Inca of Peru. Mayan civilization had already collapsed by the time the Aztecs and Incas were conquered in the 16th Century by Spanish conquistadors, whose weapons and diseases decimated the native populations. Portugal ruled Brazil and Spain ruled most of the rest of Latin America from the 16th through the early 19th Century, when England and France attempted to supplant Spain in the New World. American President Monroe articulated the Monroe Doctrine at that time and prevented any further European interference in the Western Hemisphere.

In the early 19th Century various independence movements sprang up throughout the region, and by 1825 all of Spanish Latin America had gained its independence except Cuba and Puerto Rico. The war for Mexican independence ended in 1821 and a republic was formed in 1824. The northern half of Mexico was ceded to the United States as a result of the Mexican-American War of 1846–48. In the 20th Century the region saw tremendous population growth and economic expansion. However, in the 30 countries of Latin America today, poverty and economic policy continue to be major challenges.

The history titles listed below include three books on Pre-Columbian America and one survey of Latin American history. Three of the listed biographies flesh out the history of Latin America. Cortez's biography fleshes out the history of the Conquest, Bolivar's the history of the independence movements, and Zapata's the history of the Mexican revolution. There is also a biography of Pablo Neruda, probably Latin America's most renowned poet.

Latin American literature began with the arrival of the Europeans, as Native Americans had no writing system (except for Mayan hieroglyphs). In the late 19th Century, Latin American literature began to emerge as a unified body of writing. In the early 20th Century, Gabriela Mistral's lyrics formed the basis of a poetic tradition that would be developed by her student Pablo Neruda. Catalyzed by European modernism, authors from different countries developed common themes, experimented with literary forms, and criticized society. In the 1940s Jorge Luis Borges published *Fictions*, a groundbreaking collection of short fiction, and novelist Miguel Asturias published *Men of Maize*, a modernist epic of Guatemala. In the 1950s, Alejo Carpentier of Cuba and Carlos Fuentes of Mexico wrote modernist works on national themes.

In the 1960s, Latin America dazzled the world with an outpouring of pioneering fiction, including novels that redefined the genre. The Latin American novel of the 60s, a major event in 20th-Century literature, emerged in response to the stimulus of European modernism, but surpassed modernism in energy and innovation. In this decade, Latin America produced more than ten masterworks in the novel alone, including Julio Cortázar's *Hopscotch*, Mario Vargas Llosa's *The Time of the Hero*, and

Gabriel García Márquez's *One Hundred Years of Solitude*. García Márquez in particular redefined the modern novel by creating the genre of magical realism.

Following the 1960s, Latin American writers continued to be at the forefront of world literature, producing popular works of realism and experimentation. Brazilian Pablo Coelho's fable *The Alchemist* is one of the best-selling novels of all time. Chilean Roberto Bolaño's novel *The Savage Detectives* blends detective fiction with avant-garde style. Junot Díaz's *The Brief and Wondrous Life of Oscar Wao* tells the story of a Dominican family afflicted by dictatorship.

## PRE-COLUMBIAN HISTORY

Adams, Richard E. W. *Ancient Civilizations of the New World*
Westview Press, 1997, 176 pages.

In this concise but comprehensive survey, the author explores the ancient cultures of Mesoamerica and the Andes, including the Olmec, Toltec, Maya, Aztec, and Inca peoples. He examines their origins and development from simple agricultural societies to fairly advanced, urban civilizations. He also explores the causes of their rapid collapse after the European conquest. This is a laudable introduction to these fascinating civilizations.

Longhena, Maria. *Ancient Mexico: The History and Culture of the Maya, Aztecs, and Other Pre-Columbian Peoples*
Stewart, Tabori & Chang, 1998, 292 pages.

This beautifully illustrated, coffee-table size book traces the development of the pre-Columbian cultures of Mesoamerica (the Olmecs, Zapotecs, Toltecs, Mayas, and Aztecs). The author, an historian and archeologist, examines the history, religion, customs, art, and architecture of these peoples. This splendid volume contains nearly 450 full-color, glossy photos of Mesoamerican artifacts and ruins, along with a fold-out timeline and detailed maps of archeological sites.

Mann, Charles C. *1491: New Revelations of the Americas Before Columbus*
Vintage, 2006, 541 pages.

1491 refers not to a specific year but rather to the time before Europeans arrived in the New World. Based on the research of archaeologists and anthropologists, Mann, a science journalist, offers the latest theories about pre-Columbian America and its inhabitants. Much of this history is necessarily speculative, but Mann's eye-opening, accessible survey of America's past will certainly revise one's view of its native inhabitants and their various cultures.

## MODERN HISTORY

Eakin, Marshall C. *The History of Latin America: Collision of Cultures*
Palgrave Macmillan, 2007, 448 pages.

Eakin surveys five centuries of Latin American history in four parts. Beginning with a review of the Americas before Columbus, Part I recounts the European conquest. Parts II and III discuss the wars of liberation in the early 19th Century and the new nations and peoples that arose in their aftermath. Part IV covers the transforming social, political, and economic developments of the 20th Century. The central theme is the collision of cultures—Native American, European, and African—that defines Latin America.

## BIOGRAPHY

Levy, Buddy. *Conquistador: Hernan Cortes, King Montezuma, and the Last Stand of the Aztecs* (Cortes: 1485–1547; Montezuma II: 1466–1520)
Bantam, 2008, 448 pages.

Drawing on Spanish and Aztec sources, Levy tells the story of the Spanish conquest of Mexico (1519–1521). Focusing on the two leaders and their radically different cultures (without glamorizing or demonizing either), Mann recounts the last days of the Aztec empire when the worlds of Montezuma and Cortes collided. This is an unforgettable tale of conquest and the demise of a civilization as the result of the pursuit of "God, gold, and glory."

Lynch, John. *Simon Bolivar: A Life* (1783–1830)
Yale University Press, 2007, 349 pages.
The revolutionary hero Simon Bolivar, known as "The Liberator," was one of the most important leaders in Spanish America's struggle for independence. The intellectual Venezuelan aristocrat turned military general and ruler contributed decisively to the liberation of Venezuela, Colombia, Ecuador, Peru, Panama, and Bolivia. In this definitive biography, Lynch vividly narrates Bolivar's passions, battles, and leadership in their historical context.

Newell, Peter E. *Zapata of Mexico* (1879–1919)
Black Rose Books, 1997, 180 pages.

This is a short but original biography of Emiliano Zapata, one of the leading figures in the Mexican Revolution that began in 1910. Zapata commanded the most important revolutionary force, the Liberation Army of the South, and fought for agrarian rights among the poor. Newell treats with honor and respect the man who has become a revered national hero to many Mexicans. The book includes a number of historical black and white photographs.

Feinstein, Adam. *Pablo Neruda: A Passion for Life* (1904–1973)
Bloomsbury, 2005, 512 pages.

The Chilean Nobel laureate Pablo Neruda was one of the great poets of the 20th Century. Feinstein's ambitious biography covers Neruda's life in depth, including his bohemian years in the 1920s, his role in the Spanish Civil War, his years as a wandering diplomat, his many loves and betrayals, his activism in Chile's Communist party and forced exile, as well as his extensive literary output. This riveting portrait includes many beautiful photos.

## MODERN LITERATURE

**Mistral, Gabriela** (1889–1957). Mistral, born Lucila Godoy Alcayaga in Chile, was the first Latin American to win the Nobel Prize in Literature. Mistral's lyric poetry on the diverse themes of love, loss, recovery, and Latin American identity is known for its crystalline beauty. Mistral was a schoolteacher, diplomat, and mentor of Pablo Neruda.

*Selected Poems of Gabriela Mistral* (1914–1957)
Translated by Ursula K. Le Guin. University of New Mexico Press, 2003, 431 pages.

This bilingual edition provides a collection of poems from all of Mistral's major creative cycles. The translations by Ursula K. Le Guin, done in conjunction with experts familiar with Spanish and English, reflect the mood and the lyricism of the Spanish. This volume includes narrative poems and songs as well as political and visionary poetry.

**Borges, Jorge Luis** (1899–1986). Borges was an Argentine writer of postmodern stories that defy the limitations of genre. Raised bilingual in Spanish and English and schooled in Switzerland, Borges worked as a librarian. He won international acclaim as a writer in spite of being persecuted by the Perón government and afflicted with blindness.

*Labyrinths: Selected Stories and Other Writings* (1962)
New Directions, 2007, 240 pages.

In this collection of fiction, essays, and parables, the three designated genres merge. Borges conjures up metaphysical conundrums through labyrinthine archives, a fictitious encyclopedia article, and an existential detective story. Today, writing that blends fiction and fact, creating a multi-layered puzzle, is called Borgesian. Styled as pop fiction, Borges' fables prefigure the Internet with their infinite archives and virtual worlds.

Also read: *The Aleph* (1949), *A Personal Anthology* (1961), and *Fictions* (1962).

**Asturias, Miguel Ángel** (1899–1974). Asturias was a Guatemalan poet, novelist, and diplomat, and winner of the Nobel Prize for Literature in 1967. His writings inquire into political realities such as dictatorship in Latin America and the plight of the continent's indigenous peoples. He studied anthropology in Paris and spent decades living abroad.

*Men of Maize* (1949)
Translated by Gerald Martin. University of Pittsburgh Press, 1995, 466 pages.

Miguel Asturias explores the mysticism of the Maya in his modernist epic of the Guatemalan Indians. Asturias' mythic history of the white man's impact on South America's Indians is structured according to three phases of production aligned with the tripartite Mayan cosmic design. A curse bedevils the descendants of an apothecary who poisons a Mayan chief, spreading misfortune to those who abuse the sacred grain.

Also read: *The President* (1946).

**Neruda, Pablo** (1904–1973). Chilean poet Pablo Neruda was awarded the Nobel Prize in Literature in 1971. He began writing poetry at age ten. At 12, he was encouraged by Chilean poet Gabriela Mistral. Neruda held diplomatic posts in Southeast Asia and Europe. García Márquez called him "the greatest poet of the 20th Century in any language."

*Residence on Earth* (1925–33)
Translated by Donald Devenish Walsh. New Directions, 2004, 352 pages.

The poems contained in this volume were written while Neruda served as Honorary Consul in Burma and held other diplomatic posts in Asia. Surrounded by Asian languages and culture, Neruda experienced a heightened sense of himself as a Latin American and of his identity as bound up with the Spanish language. These poems, rendered in simple verse, interweave the diverse themes of nostalgia, solitude, mortality, and identity.

Also read: *Twenty Love Songs and a Song of Despair* (1923) and *Canto General* (1950).

**Carpentier, Alejo** (1904–1980). Carpentier was a Cuban novelist and musicologist. His novels explore power imbalances in Latin America through a literature of the absurd, reflecting the influence of the surrealists he met during his political exile in Paris from 1928 to 1939. Carpentier was the first to use the term "magical realism" to describe Latin American literature.

*The Lost Steps* (1953)
Translated by Harriet de Onís. University of Minnesota Press, 2001, 296 pages.

The author drew on his 1948 expedition to the upper Orinoco in Guyana in this story of Victor, a composer who travels to South America in pursuit of primitive musical instruments and authenticity. Searching for meaning in his life as well as for his Latin American identity, Victor comes to see himself and his bohemian circle against the backdrop of nature, and questions whether he has lost access to authentic existence.

Also read: *The Kingdom of this World* (1949) and *Explosion in a Cathedral* (1962).

**Paz, Octavio** (1914–1998).  Perhaps the greatest Mexican writer of his generation, Octavio Paz won the Nobel Prize for Literature in 1990.  Paz published his first volume of poetry in 1933, and worked as an editor and journalist.  He became a diplomat in 1945, and was Mexico's Ambassador to India from 1962 to 1968.

*The Labyrinth of Solitude* (1959)
Translated by Lysander Kemp.  Grove Press, 1996, 398 pages.

Octavio Paz is best known in the non-Spanish speaking world for his collection of essays on Mexican traditions, character, and history.  The collection includes Paz's essay, "The Labyrinth of Solitude," in which Paz lifts the Mexican "mask," revealing the many complex strands of Mexican identity.  Other essays describe the Mexican intelligentsia, the Mexican attitude towards death, and Mexico's place in Latin America and the world.

Also read: *The Collected Poems of Octavio Paz* (1957–87).

**Cortázar, Julio** (1914–1984).  Cortázar was an Argentine writer of fiction known for his modernist use of interior monologue and for the surrealist composition of his writing.  Born in Belgium and raised in Buenos Aires, Cortázar left Argentina in 1951 in opposition to ruler Juan Perón.  He lived and worked in France for the rest of his life.

*Hopscotch* (1963)
Translated by Gregory Rabassa.  Pantheon, 1987, 576 pages.

*Hopscotch* is a book consisting of many books, and its episodic chapters can be read in sequence or according to a "table of instructions."  In either case, the tantalizingly absurd storyline stays intact, unfolding the tale of Horacio Oliveira, a writer who leaves his bohemian circle in Paris following a death and a baffling disappearance.  Back in Argentina, Oliveira's adventures include work as a cat trainer and as an asylum attendant.

Also read: *Final Exam* (1950), *All Fires the Fire* (1966), and *A Model Kit* (1968).

**Garro, Elena** (1920–1998).  Garro was a Mexican writer.  Her *Recollections of Things to Come*, called "one of the most important Mexican novels of the 20th Century," is a precursor of magical realism.  She married Octavio Paz in 1927, broke with him and other Mexican intellectuals in the 1960s, and lived abroad.  Garro returned to Mexico in 1991.

*First Love* and *Look for My Obituary* (1996)
Translated by David Unger.  Curbstone Press, 1997, 102 pages.

Elena Garro's clarity of style and dramatic plotting are as apparent in her realistic novella, "First Love," as in the dream-like sequences of "Look for My Obituary."  In "First Love," the friendship between two tourists and a German POW in France is fatefully affected by the community's disapproval of fraternization.  In "Look for My Obituary," a man enters into a surreal, perhaps unreal, romantic entanglement.

Also read: *Recollections of Things to Come* (1963).

**García Márquez, Gabriel** (1927–  ).  García Márquez, one of the most significant authors of the 20th Century, is a Colombian writer of novels and stories.  Raised by his grandfather, he attended a Jesuit college, studied law, and worked as a journalist.  He was awarded the 1982 Nobel Prize in Literature for novels pioneering the genre of magical realism.

*One Hundred Years of Solitude* (1967)
Translated by Gregory Rabassa.  Perennial, 1998, 464 pages.

The influential novel *One Hundred Years of Solitude* created a self-defining fable for the Colombian people—and for Latin Americans—around the fictive genealogy of the Buendí family and the imagined village of Macondo.  This family chronicle is told through myths, history, and prefigured, fantastic events.  Buendí patriarch José and matriarch Ursula are at the same time family prototypes and compellingly realistic characters.

Also read: *The Autumn of the Patriarch* (1975) and *Love in the Time of Cholera* (1985).

**Fuentes, Carlos** (1928–  ).  Carlos Fuentes is a Mexican writer of fiction and essays.  Born in Panama City to Mexican parents, Fuentes lived in several Latin American capitals as the son of a diplomat.  From 1965 to 1978 he served as a diplomat in London, Paris, and other capitals.  He has taught at several universities, and currently teaches at Brown.

*The Death of Artemio Cruz* (1962)
Translated by Alfred MacAdam.  Farrar, Straus and Giroux, 2009, 320 pages.

Fuentes' novel of modern Mexico follows protagonist Artemio Cruz from the Mexican Revolution, experienced in all its idealistic fervor, to the postwar period of opportunism and greed.  The novel, which shifts back and forth in time, begins with Cruz on his deathbed, and ranges from Cruz's recollections of his past to authorial commentary on Mexican history and society.

Also read: *A Change of Skin* (1967) and *Terra Nostra* (1975).

**Llosa, Mario Vargas** (1936–  ).  Llosa is a Peruvian writer of novels, mysteries, political thrillers, and historical fiction.  Politically active on the left in his youth, Llosa ran for the Peruvian presidency in 1990 as a center-right candidate.  His recent novel, *The Feast of the Goat* (2000), describes the Dominican Republic under the Trujillo dictatorship.

*The Time of the Hero* (1963)
Translated by Lysander Kemp.  Faber and Faber, 2004, 416 pages.

This autobiographical novel offers an insider's view of the military ethos by Llosa, who attended the Leoncio Prado Military Academy in Lima.  Llosa's story of the murder of a cadet is told from multiple perspectives, alternating between first and third person and moving back and forth in time.  Llosa, known as the conscience of Peru, explores the theme of the individual in conflict with the system in this tale of institutional mayhem.

Also read: *The Green House* (1955) and *The War of the End of the World* (1981).

**Arenas, Reinaldo** (1943–1990). Cuban-born Arenas wrote nine novels, three books of stories, poetry, essays, plays, and a memoir. He won international recognition when his novel *Hallucinations* was smuggled out of Cuba and published in France. A political prisoner from 1973 to 1976, Arenas escaped to America in 1980 as part of the Mariel Boatlift.

*Mona and Other Tales* (2001)
Translated by Dolores Koch. Vintage, 2001, 208 pages.

This collection of 14 short stories covers Reinaldo Arenas's career, from his recently rediscovered early stories written in a Cuban prison to his last stories written in New York. Arenas's range is as wide as his insight is deep in these tales of country poverty, revolutionary fervor and disillusionment, creative struggle, love, and literary legacy. The title story, "Mona," is a bold amalgam of surrealism, humor, and melodrama.
Also read: *Hallucinations* (1988) and *Singing from the Well* (1982).

**Coelho, Paulo** (1947– ). Brazilian Coelho's fable *The Alchemist* is one of the best-selling novels of all time. Placed in a mental institution by his parents as a teen, Coelho briefly attended law school after his release, then immersed himself in 1960s hippie culture. His spiritual awakening, following a 1986 pilgrimage to Santiago de Compostela, led to a creative breakthrough.

*The Alchemist* (1988)
Translated by Alan R. Clarke. HarperCollins, 1988, 167 pages.

Santiago, a Spanish shepherd, dreams of a trip to Egypt in search of treasure. On the advice of a wise man, he sells his sheep and travels to Africa, only to be robbed in the streets of Tangier. Realizing his dream, Santiago eventually journeys to Egypt and meets an alchemist who provides a key to his destiny. In this fable Coelho offers insights on life's journey.
Also read: *By the River Piedra I Sat Down and Wept* (1990).

**Bolaño, Roberto** (1953–2003). Roberto Bolaño was a Chilean novelist and poet. Bolaño moved to Mexico City when Chile's military government came to power in the 1960s. He dropped out of school as a teenager and educated himself by reading. In Mexico, he founded the infrarealist movement. Bolaño moved to Spain in 1977.

*The Savage Detectives* (1998)
Translated by Natasha Wimmer. Picador, 2008, 672 pages.

Bolaño's polyphonic detective novel is written from the perspective of some 50 characters. The tale centers upon two friends, writers Arturo and Ulise, who crisscross the globe in search of a missing poet. Bolaño's novel, which he called a "love letter" to his generation, pivots around a violent encounter in the Sonoran desert that has Arturo and Ulise on the run for 20 years of incomparable adventure.
Also read: *By Night in Chile* (2000) and *2666* (2004).

**Díaz, Junot** (1968– ). Junot Díaz is a Dominican-American writer. Díaz's writing is sociological and political, rich in character and incident, and linguistically innovative. Born in the Dominican Republic, he moved with his family to New Jersey in 1974. Díaz's novel *The Brief Wondrous Life of Oscar Wao* won the Pulitzer Prize in 2007.

*The Brief Wondrous Life of Oscar Wao* (2007)
Riverhead Trade, 2008, 252 pages.

This narrative's ironic premise is that of the tale of "loser" Oscar Wao as told by his hip womanizer buddy, Yunior. Oscar de León is a ghetto nerd whose passionate longing for love is thwarted by bookish reticence and a family curse. Foreshadowed in several family narratives, Oscar's fate is tragically bound up with the rule of Dominican dictator Trujillo. Díaz's playful style includes factual footnotes on Dominican history.

Also read: *Drown* (1996).

# A Guide to Reading the Annotations

## I. How Information is Presented within an Annotation

### Dates

The year in parentheses is the work's original date of publication. For example, the entry below indicates that *The House of the Spirits* was first published in 1982, and the most recent edition of the book was published in 2005.

> Allende, Isabel. *The House of the Spirits*
> Dial Press, 2005 (1982), 448 pages.

In entries for modern plays, we have included the year in which the play was first performed. For example, the entry below indicates that *A Doll's House* was first performed in 1879. The most recent edition of the book containing this play was published in 1965.

> *A Doll's House* (first performed 1879)
> In *A Doll's House and Other Plays*.
> Penguin Classics, 1965, 336 pages

Dates following the title of a biography indicate the lifespan of the subject:

> Akers, Charles W. *Abigail Adams: An American Woman* (1744-1818)
> Pearson/Longman, 3rd ed., 2006 (1980), 256 pages.

### Titles

If the title of a primary text is different from the title of the book it is found in, then the title of the book follows on the second line. The entry below indicates that *The Metamorphoses* is found within the book *Tales From Ovid*. As above, the date in parentheses, 8 AD, is the work's original publication date. The date following the publisher, 1999, is the publication date of *Tales From Ovid*.

> *The Metamorphoses* (8 AD)
> In *Tales From Ovid*.
> Translated by Ted Hughes. Farrar, Straus and Giroux, 1999, 272 pages.

### Authors and Translators

When an entry for a classic text lists a translator, but not an author, this means that the author is unknown. For example, the author of *Beowulf* is unknown. The entry only lists the name of the translator, Seamus Heaney.

> **Heaney, Seamus,** Translator. *Beowulf* (c. 8th-11th Century AD)
> W.W. Norton, 2001, 215 pages.

In Part Two, Western History and Literature, we have included biographical information for authors of classic literature. If the author is unknown and only a translator or editor is listed, or if it is not a primary text, biographical information is not included. In Part Two, World History and Literature, biographical information is provided for all authors of ancient, medieval, and modern literature, if such information is known.

## II. How Books are Organized within a Section

### Part One

**Contemporary Fiction:**

Books are listed alphabetically by the author's last name, except in the Introduction to the Classics section, where the books are listed chronologically by the birth date of the author.

**Contemporary Nonfiction:**

Books are listed alphabetically by the author's last name, except in the Journals and Magazines section, where the titles are listed alphabetically in each subsection.

### Part Two

**Western History and Literature:**

In the first major section, Surveys of Western History, the books are listed alphabetically by the author's last name.

The three middle sections, Antiquity, The Middle Ages and the Early Modern Period, and The Modern Period, are each divided into subsections. The subsections are arranged chronologically by sub-period or by region. Each of these subsections in turn is organized by genre: history first, biography second, and literature third. Books listed under History are organized alphabetically by author's last name. Books listed under Biography are organized chronologically by the birth date of the subject. Books listed under Literature are organized chronologically by the birth date of the author. When there are two or more works listed for a single author, they are presented chronologically according to publication date.

In the final section, Specialized Histories, books are listed alphabetically by the author's last name.

**World History and Literature:**

World History and Literature is divided into six major sections according to region. The list of books in each of these sections is organized by genre: history, biography, ancient literature (China and India only), medieval literature (all but Africa and Latin America), and modern literature. Books listed under History are organized alphabetically by author's last name. Books listed under Biography are organized chronologically by the birth date of the subject. Books listed under Ancient, Medieval, or Modern Literature are organized chronologically by the birth date of the author.

# INDEX

# About the Authors

**Linda Colman**

Linda Colman was introduced to the joy of reading by her mother, who taught English Literature at Drake University. Linda earned an A.B. from Stanford University and an M.A. in Comparative Literature from the University of California at Berkeley, where she studied French, Russian, German, and Ancient Greek, and taught undergraduates for four years. Linda taught for the Institute of Reading Development for several years before becoming a curriculum developer in 2002. She developed the Institute's booklists for elementary school, middle school, and high school students, and helped develop the Institute's reading assessment program for elementary school students.

**Michael Morrissey**

Michael Morrissey began working with the Institute of Reading Development as a curriculum developer in 1996. He is formerly an Assistant Professor of theology at the University of St. Thomas in St. Paul, MN, and is Adjunct Professor of philosophy and religion at Dominican University in San Rafael, CA. He received a M.Ed. from Boston College and Ph.D. from the Graduate Theological Union in Berkeley, CA. Mike is the author of *Consciousness and Transcendence: The Theology of Eric Voegelin* (University of Notre Dame Press, 1994), and has published a number of articles in philosophy and religion.

**Luke Schlueter**

Luke Schlueter joined the Institute of Reading Development in 1999, working first as a teacher and then as a curriculum developer. Since 2001 he has been deeply involved in developing the literature components of the Institute's programs for late elementary, middle school, high school, and adult students, and is the author and creative director of the Institute's video companion series for late elementary school students. Luke earned his Master's degree in English from the University of Dallas and his Ph.D. in English from Kent State University, where he continues to teach literature and writing courses.

# About the Editor

**Paul Copperman**

Paul Copperman founded the Institute of Reading Development in 1971 and has served as its president ever since. He graduated Phi Beta Kappa in Mathematics from the University of California at Berkeley, and received a M.Ed. from Lone Mountain College in San Francisco. Paul is the author of *The Literacy Hoax: The Decline of Reading, Writing, and Learning in the Public Schools and What We Can Do About It* (William Morrow and Co., 1978) and *Taking Books to Heart: How to Develop a Love of Reading in Your Child* (Addison Wesley Publishing Co., 1986). He was appointed by President Reagan and confirmed by the United States Senate to serve as a Member of the National Council on Educational Research.